LIVE LETTERS

ARCHBISHOP DANIEL E. PILARCZYK

LIVE LETTERS

*Reflections on
the Second Readings
of the Sunday Lectionary*

ST. ANTHONY MESSENGER PRESS

Cincinnati, Ohio

Scripture quotations are from the *New Revised Standard Version Bible*, copyright © 1989 by the Division of Christian Education of the National Council of the Churches of Christ in the U.S.A. Used by permission. All rights reserved.

Cover design by Constance Wolfer
Book design and page layout by Sandy L. Digman
Clip art reprinted from *Clip Art for Year A* by Steve Erspamer, copyright ©1992, Archdiocese of Chicago: Liturgy Training Publications, 1800 North Hermitage Ave. Chicago IL 60622.
1-800-933-1800. All rights reserved. Used with permission.

ISBN 0-86716-399-2

Library of Congress Cataloging-in-Publication Data

Pilarczyk, Daniel E.
  Live letters : reflections on the second readings of the Sunday lectionary / Daniel E. Pilarczyk.
      p. cm.
  ISBN 0-86716-399-2
  1. Bible. N.T. Epistles—Meditations. 2. Catholic Church. Lectionary for Mass (U.S.) I. Title.
  BS2635.54 .P55 2002
  264'.02034—dc211

                                    2001005137

CONTENTS

PART THREE — *Lent*

PART FOUR — *Easter*

PART FIVE — *Ordinary Time*

PART SIX — *Solemnities*

Introduction

This book consists of short commentaries on the second readings
that we hear at Mass on Sundays. These readings are almost all
from the writings of the apostles in the New Testament, most of
which are in letter form. They are important for the nourishment
of our faith life, but they are often overlooked or disregarded.

The Second Vatican Council called for a reform of the
Sunday readings. Before the Council, there were only two readings
at each Mass, an epistle reading and a Gospel reading, and there
was only one set of readings, which was unvaried from year to
year. The Council fathers, in the decree on the liturgy, determined
that there should be "more reading from holy Scripture," and that
it was to be "more varied and suitable" (*Sacrosanctum Concilium*
35 [*S.C.*]). They wanted the treasures of the Bible "to be opened
up more lavishly, so that richer fare may be provided for the
faithful at the table of God's word" (*S.C.* 51). A more representative
portion of the holy Scriptures was to be read to the people over a
set cycle of years (*S.C.* 51)."

The result of the Council's mandate was the lectionary, whose
first Latin edition was published in 1969. A revised Latin edition
appeared in 1981. The purpose of the lectionary was "to draw up
and edit a single, rich, and full Order of Readings that would be
in complete accord with the intent and prescriptions of the
Council" (Introduction to Second Edition, no. 59). The lectionary
offers "an arrangement of biblical readings that provides the
faithful with a knowledge of the whole of God's word" (*S.C.* 60).
There was now a three-year cycle with three readings for each
Sunday. The first reading is generally from the Old Testament, the

second from the writings of the apostles (usually letters), the third from the Gospels.

The lectionary with its three-year Sunday cycle has been one of the great successes of the post-conciliar Church. The faithful are exposed to a much wider selection of Scripture and those who preach have a much richer source with which to work. Everybody has reason to be grateful for it.

Yet the lectionary has not yet been fully exploited. Most preachers seem to prefer to concentrate on the Gospel readings, bringing in allusions to the first and second readings as they see fit. It seems to be unusual for a preacher to give major attention to the second reading. This is unfortunate because the writings of the apostles have much to teach us, much to say about the circumstances and needs of our contemporary Church. They are not just relics of the past, but offer life-giving wisdom for the present.

The selection and arrangement of the apostolic writings in the lectionary is not uniform. Sometimes (for example, during Advent and on solemnities) the second reading is chosen for its connection with the theme of the day. But more often these readings are in a cycle of their own and are arranged in a more or less continuous reading of the various apostolic letters, with the result that, over a period of a few weeks, we hear the highlights of one single epistle. These series of "semi-continuous" readings are independent of the other two readings.

My intent in this series of reflections is to focus on the second readings in the hope of clarifying their relationship with the other readings, where this is applicable, and of communicating the significance of the letters as a whole when they are read semi-continuously and without reference to the other readings. It is my hope that these reflections may be helpful to Scripture study groups and prayer groups as well as to those who exercise the responsibility of preaching. Ultimately, I hope that they may prove helpful to all those to whom these apostolic letters are addressed, that is, to all and each of us. Maybe we will get to know the apostles better, learn more about what they have to communicate to us, and be more deeply enriched on Sunday when we hear their words proclaimed in the liturgy.

Each reflection offers something about the *context of* each reading—how each fits into the liturgy and/or to the letter of which it forms a part. Then comes something about the *content*—what the selection says and means—and then something about its *consequences*—how it applies to us. Finally there are questions for discussion—subjects for *conversation* with God or with other readers of the live letters.

I believe that the best way for the reader to engage these reflections is to read the reading in your Bible or worship aid first, then to read and consider what is offered here (perhaps with the text open alongside) and then to pay special attention to the reading at the Sunday liturgy. (Note that the translation of the New Testament used in the second edition of the lectionary is a modified version of the *Revised New American Bible*.)

I have chosen to entitle the series *Live Letters* to contrast the readings that form their subject from *dead letters*. Dead letters are letters that the post office cannot deliver because their addressees are not known and there is no indication of where they come from. We know to whom these "live" letters are addressed: to us. And we know where they come from: from the Holy Spirit through the instrumentality of the apostles of the Lord. They are not dead letters!

But there is another reason for the title. We speak of a "dead letter" as something that is still officially on the books, but really doesn't have any force any more. By contrast, the letters that Scripture offers us are still very much alive and offer nourishment and challenge to all who receive them.

These reflections could also be called *Life Letters*, because, in the final analysis, they deal with Christ's life in us. The Christian tradition sometimes calls this life salvation, sometimes justification or sanctification or grace or holiness or new creation. It is a life that involves faith and hope and love. It involves God's plan for creation expressed in and through the community that is the Church, a plan that is directed toward the final fulfillment of salvation when Christ comes again at the end of time. It is Christ's life in us that forms our basic Christian identity, an identity that forms us into unity with one another and with God the Father and the Holy Spirit.

These "life themes" are among the most basic matters that the earliest proclaimers of the good news declared to their hearers and readers. We hear these themes in the lectionary's second readings for Sundays. These readings do not form a carefully articulated exposition of the whole Christian faith (as, for example, the *Catechism of the Catholic Church* does). Rather, they express the intense and, at times, passionate response of their writers to the needs of the earliest generations of believers.

I pray that these reflections on the apostolic writings will serve to enliven the faith and commitment of those who read them even as the original live letters in the New Testament enlivened the faith and commitment of their original readers.

PART ONE

Advent

First Sunday of Advent (A)

Romans 13:11-14

Advent has to do with futures. The Gospel readings for each week are concerned with looking forward. This Sunday's is about looking forward to the final coming of Christ at the end of time. On the Second and Third Sundays of Advent the Gospels speak of John the Baptist and how he directed the attention of the people of his time to the Messiah whose ministry was to begin shortly. The Gospel of the Fourth Sunday has to do with the events that provided the immediate preparation for the birth of Jesus. Throughout these four weeks, the Gospel readings are concerned with futures, remote or immediate.

The Old Testament readings for these weeks are about the future, too. They all consist of prophetic passages about the future Messiah and the Messianic age.

The Advent apostolic readings, our live letters, are commentaries on various aspects of what we hear in the Gospels and the readings from the Hebrew Scriptures.

For this first Sunday our live letter is from Paul's letter to the Romans. (We'll be hearing quite a bit from Romans during this first year of the lectionary cycle.)

This Sunday's reading comes from the last main part of Romans, the section dealing with behavior. Paul has been telling the Romans how they ought to relate to one another and to the demands of civil society. He tells them that they have to keep loving those around them.

Our reading explains *why*. (In the full text of Romans, our first verse begins: "And do this because ....") We are to love and reverence those around us because we know what time it is. It's time to wake up. It may seem that we are in a time of darkness, but full daylight is almost here. The universal fulfillment of salvation is nearly upon us. Paul goes on to describe what this awakening involves. It involves getting rid of the attitudes and practices that constitute moral darkness: selfish things like overindulgence in food and drink and sexual misbehavior; contentiousness that undermines our relationships with other people. All this has to be repudiated, taken off like dirty clothes. In their place we are to "put on the Lord Jesus Christ," who serves as armor fit to be worn in the realms of light. If we do that, we won't need to worry about satisfying the needs of our weak human nature, vulnerable to sin ("the desires of the flesh").

This passage is filled with contrasts: wakefulness and sleep, night and day, darkness and light, taking off and putting on. Paul is telling the Romans—and us—that we are living in pivotal times, that where and what we are at this moment is not where and what we are going to be in the near future. A different kind of life lies ahead of us. A basic element of Christian life on this earth is the expectation of change.

The change that we are invited to look forward to is the advent of the final stage of salvation, when the risen Christ will take into his glorified life all of creation, once and for all, finally. There will be a new heaven and a new earth in which sin and selfishness will be definitively rejected, in which only that which is clean and bright and holy will have a place. Our incorporation into Christ by faith and baptism has given us an initial association with the glory of the end. But more, much more, is still to come.

And in all this we each have a part to play. While our sharing in the life of Christ is pure gift which we can never earn or deserve, we are expected to exert ongoing moral effort to assimilate that life ever more deeply, ever more intensely. We have to divest ourselves of "the works of darkness," the desires and sins like those Paul mentions, and "put on the Lord Jesus Christ," that is, allow ourselves to be clothed in Christ so that we take on his likeness ever more clearly.

Taking off sinfulness and putting on Christ is the basic, ongoing task of our Christian existence. It's a task that was made possible by the life and ministry of Jesus, by his death and resurrection. These are events of the past that determine our present. But these realities also direct us toward the future. Each day offers us the opportunity to move closer to the final and eternal brilliant daylight of heaven. Moreover, the unfolding of our life offers us the chance to help bring all creation a little closer to final life in Christ through our action in the world, through our love and care for those around us. We each have a part to play in the history of salvation, not just a part in our own individual history, but a part in the history of it all, the history that begins with the very beginning of the past in creation and stretches to the ultimate future in the final coming of the Son of Man.

As this new Church year begins, God's word says to us, "Get up! Get dressed! Get busy! It's almost light and you've got an important day ahead of you!"

FOR DISCUSSION AND REFLECTION

How is my life directed by the past?

How is my life oriented toward the future?

First Sunday of Advent (B)

I Corinthians 1:3-9

The First Sunday of Advent is the beginning of the Church's liturgical year. The purpose of the "liturgical year" is to keep us aware that the mission of Jesus—his life, death and resurrection—are not just events of the past, but a life-giving undertaking that continues throughout the whole framework of time. As the Church walks us through the story of Jesus each year, it teaches us that the action of Jesus is still going on. Jesus is still teaching, healing, saving in our time just as he did during the brief years of his earthly life. Week by week the Lord is with us. Week by week the Lord is active in our lives.

As the word "advent" suggests, this season of the Church's year has to do with "coming." During these four weeks the Church's liturgy invites us to prepare to celebrate Christ's first coming into the world at Christmas, but it also directs our attention toward the second coming of Christ at the end of time. In fact, the theme of Christ's second coming is more prominent in Advent than is the Christmas theme.

There is a kind of overlap here in that the Church's liturgical year also ends with the Gospel readings that have to do with Christ's second coming. Thus, the end of the Church year and its beginning both deal with the final victory of Christ. The implication seems to be that the basic fabric of Christian life—its end and its beginning—is hope in the final fullness of Christ's presence which constitutes the completion of God's plan of love for his human creatures.

Each of the four Sundays of Advent has its own specific subject, enunciated by the Gospel, to which the other two readings refer. The First Sunday deals directly with the second coming. The Second and Third Sundays show us John the Baptist calling for repentance in view of the One still to come. The Fourth Sunday deals with the events that provided proximate preparation for Our Lord's birth.

This Sunday's apostolic letter is from the beginning of Paul's first letter to the Corinthians. Paul begins most of his letters with a thanksgiving section in which he expresses his gratitude to God for the gifts that the letter's addressees have received. Today he offers God thanks for the abundance of what has been given to the Corinthians. "You were enriched in every way. ...You are not lacking in any spiritual gift." But he is quick to suggest that they are not therefore permitted to sit back and relax. They are still waiting for "the revelation of Our Lord Jesus Christ." They would need to keep "firm to the end," so as to be "irreproachable on the day of Our Lord Jesus Christ." Their time of waiting, however, was not to be a period of anxiety and worry. They could rely on the ongoing generosity of Christ and the unswerving care of his heavenly Father. "God is faithful."

What Saint Paul wrote to the Corinthians applies to us, too. We have been gifted by God in more ways than we can count, in more ways than we are even aware of. Life, faith, the Church, the sacraments, an assurance of worth and meaning for our lives, our families and friends, personal security, a standard of living that most people in the world's history could not even imagine—all are gifts of God that come to us without any merit or deserving on our part. We are enriched in every way.

But that doesn't mean that we can now sit back and relax. We have to be alert, aware of what uses we can make of the gifts that God has given us, awake to the fact that Christ will demand an accounting of us when he comes again in glory.

It's easy to take everything for granted. We get so used to God's blessings that we are sometimes not even conscious of them. Or we begin to think that they are ours by right, that we can do with them as we please. But that's not the way it is. God's gifts are given to be shared, not at some future time but now, today. Our faith and all that goes with it constitute a vocation to carry on the mission of Jesus and the way we have carried on that mission will constitute the agenda for determining the final worth of our earthly existence "on the day of Our Lord Jesus Christ."

Perhaps we could spend some time this week counting our blessings. We won't be able to count them all, because they are too numerous, too diverse, too subtle. But when we have established some idea of the riches God has given us, we must then ask ourselves how we are spending them. On ourselves? On our own comfort? Are we doing anything with what we have received, anything of significance that will stand to our credit when the Master comes to settle accounts?

As Paul told the Corinthians, the Lord wants to "keep" us "firm to the end." How firm are we now? He also told them, "God is faithful." How faithful are we?

FOR DISCUSSION AND REFLECTION

What gifts of God am I most conscious of in my life?

How does my use of God's gifts reflect my faith?

First Sunday of Advent (C)

I Thessalonians 3:12-4:2

Every well-considered beginning looks toward a well-planned conclusion. That's why, as we begin another liturgical year, the Church directs our attention to the conclusion toward which we are headed, the ending that God had in mind when he began to implement the plan of our salvation.

One of the purposes of the Church's liturgical year is to keep us aware that God works in time, that God is involved with the passage of one year into another. Every year involves beginning again and repeating the same events and seasons. Each year constitutes a cycle. But God's more basic involvement in time is linear, that is, it moves in one direction only, forward to the final stage of his plans for us and our world. God is not forever beginning over, starting new projects, rejecting what he had been involved in before. No, there is one plan for salvation, an unchanging one that starts at a definite beginning and is directed toward a definite end. That's part of what we recall when we come to the end of one year and launch into another. Well-considered beginnings always have to be seen in the context of the end toward which they are directed.

The readings for the First Sunday of Advent in each of the three yearly cycles are about the conclusion, the fulfillment of our salvation. They deal with the second coming of Christ at the end of time. This, of course, is the same theme that was dealt with last Sunday when we celebrated the ending of the Church's year with the feast of Christ the King. The final reign of Christ is both the final goal and original purpose of God's whole plan for salvation.

Our live letter for this first Sunday of Year C is from Paul's first letter to the Thessalonians, the earliest book of the New Testament. It was probably chosen for this Sunday because it mentions the final coming of the Lord, a theme in which the Thessalonians seem to have been particularly interested. Our passage straddles the two parts of the letter, the first of which is concerned with encouraging the new Christians to remain faithful, the second with providing practical directives for Christian living.

Paul tells his readers that, if they want to be holy and without reproach when Jesus comes at the end of time, they have to be strong in their love for one another. Paul prays that their love may be strengthened so they can love each other as he loves them. He then proceeds to encourage them to be observant of the directions he had given them for their day to day living. He is sure that they are behaving as God desires, but he urges them to be even more careful about pleasing God. (In the part of First Thessalonians that follows our reading, Paul gives instructions about sexual conduct, mutual charity, hope for those who have died, and vigilance in faith.)

The context of what Paul teaches the Thessalonians in this reading is the second coming of Christ. That's the ending they have to keep their eye on, the conclusion toward which their Christian life and faith is to be directed.

But their attention to the final fulfillment of creation and salvation is not to be mere passive waiting. They are not like people standing on a street corner waiting for something to happen. No, they have a role to play in this interim time between the beginning and the end of salvation. That role is to extend the life and love of Christ to each other and to the world around them. By their observance of the moral norms that Paul had outlined for them their participation in the life and holiness of Christ would grow so they would be ready to fit in with all the holy ones of Christ when he finally comes.

What Paul says to the Thessalonians applies to us, too. We have to be attentive to what God has in store for us in the final fulfillment of the world and its history in the coming of Christ. But this attention is not just speculative. We have an agenda to deal with as we wait, and the agenda is the agenda of the Lord Jesus. We are called to help get ourselves ready to meet the Lord. We are called to help others get ready to meet the Lord through the love of Christ that we extend to them. We are called to help the world become ever more attuned to the final state to which Christ will finally bring it. We may not think that our individual human existence has spiritually cosmic potential, but it does, not because of what we bring to our life, but because of what Christ has brought to it. We are all part of his plan, his process, his initiative, his final purpose.

Often people make new year's resolutions at the beginning of a civil year. The beginning of a new liturgical year is a good time for resolutions, too. We each have elements in our life that could use improvement. But maybe we all need to try to be a little more aware of where we are headed as this new year begins and how each of us shares responsibility for helping all of us get to where God wants us to be.

FOR DISCUSSION AND REFLECTION

What can I do to "increase and abound in love?"

Is there a sense of direction in my life? How is it expressed?

Second Sunday of Advent (A)

Romans 15:4-9

Like last Sunday's second reading, this week's is taken from the final section of Paul's letter to the Romans. This section offers

Paul's readers a series of moral exhortations that provide direction for their daily life. The part that we read from on this second Sunday of Advent is concerned with the ever-sensitive question of the relationship between Jewish Christians and gentile Christians. Paul has just told the Romans that they need to defer to one another's wishes and offers the example of Christ whose life was spent not in doing what he wanted, but in carrying out the will of his Father. To strengthen his example, Paul cites Psalm 69:10.

As our reading begins, Paul goes off on a couple of digressions, the first of which is to explain why he cites Scripture. Scripture (that is, the Hebrew Scripture that we call the Old Testament) is written for our instruction, in order to give us hope through the perseverance it nurtures in us. Paul prays that this perseverance will lead Christians to live in harmony with one another, giving glory to the Father by their unanimity in Christ Jesus.

He now returns to the main theme he had been treating and encourages the Jewish and gentile Christians to "welcome" one another, that is, to be open to one another, to reach out to one another even as Christ was accepting of all of them. Both groups have been the recipients of God's attentions: the Jews exemplifying God's faithfulness to the promises made to their patriarchs; the gentiles being the recipients of God's mercy. Finally comes a closing Scripture quotation (Psalm 18:50) that alludes to God being glorified among the gentiles. (In the full text of Romans, this quotation is followed by three more, all speaking of the place of the gentiles in God's plans.)

This reading is composed of three small paragraphs dealing, in order, with hope, harmony and hospitality. Our loving outreach to one another should result in peace and unanimity which, in turn, will serve to strengthen our hope, our expectation of future blessings still to come from God. It is fitting that Jewish and gentile Christians love and care for and defer to one another in view of the care that has already been addressed to each group by God.

This little passage is held together by groups of words that lead from one part to the next. Endurance and encouragement in Scripture are connected with the God of endurance and encouragement granting Christ's people harmony. This harmony involves glorifying God with one accord and one voice. As Paul returns to the main subject of this section of Romans in the last sentences of our reading, we find God's "truthfulness" (that is, faithfulness) to "the circumcised" and "the prophets" set forth in reflection to God's "mercy" to "the gentiles." It's a carefully balanced passage in which we seem to see one idea leading to another in an overall context dealing with the relationships between the two groups of Christians.

But what does all this have to do with Advent and with us? It may be that this passage from Romans was chosen for this Sunday as a commentary on the first reading, which concludes with Isaiah prophesying the gentiles' search for the future Messiah of the Jews. It may also be intended to shed light on the Gospel reading in which we hear John the Baptist warning the Pharisees and Sadducees that they shouldn't put their hope for salvation in their being descendants of Abraham.

The lesson for us, as we move into the third millennium of Christ's Church, is that the final state of Christ's kingdom, the future toward which we are all moving together, will not be characterized by exclusion but by inclusion. The salvation that Jesus accomplished is not meant to be for a few people, carefully selected from restricted groups. It is to be a universal salvation, open to everyone, extended to everyone, appropriate for everyone. The reason why salvation will be for everyone is simply because God loves everyone and salvation is a matter of being loved by God.

It's important for us to remind ourselves occasionally that salvation is directed toward everyone, because we are inclined to think sometimes that salvation will be limited to a few, to an elite group that carefully keeps the rules and diligently learns the required lessons, a group that deserves to be with God because of who and what they are, a group that, obviously, includes only people like ourselves. Deep in our hearts, thanks to the inheritance of original sin, we want to believe that, if we just try hard enough, we can make God love us and make God give us a happiness from which others will be excluded.

God's treatment of both Jews and gentiles over the centuries teaches us that it isn't like that. God's love is freely given to us all. God's salvation is freely granted to us all. Our task is to respond to God's loving and God's giving by the loving and giving we offer to one another.

FOR DISCUSSION AND REFLECTION

To whom do I find it difficult to reach out in welcome?

How do I respond to the universality of God's call to salvation?

Second Sunday of Advent (B)

II Peter 3:8-14

This Sunday we meet John the Baptist in the Gospel. He's a strange figure, strangely clad and strangely fed, but a man with a message. And the message is: Change your way of life and get rid of your sins because somebody very important is on his way here. John's message found fulfillment in the beginning of the public life of Jesus, but it also applies to the second coming of Christ to which we give our attention during the season of Advent. It is this second coming that our live letter for today addresses.

This is the only time in the Church's three-year cycle of Sunday readings that we hear from the Second Letter of Peter. This book of the New Testament does not seem to be the personal work of the apostle Peter but is attributed to him by its author because the author appeals to the authority of Peter and presents a message that he is convinced Peter would have conveyed if he were still alive. It is not addressed to a specific community, as are Paul's letters to the Romans or the Corinthians, but is a kind of general exhortation in letter form. Hence it is classed among the "general" or "catholic" epistles. Scholars think that it is among the last books of the New Testament to have been written.

In the section of the letter that we hear today, the author seems to be addressing some sceptics who held that God is a distant God who is not involved in the world. "Nothing has ever changed and nothing is going to change. There's not going to be any 'Second Coming' of Jesus!"

In response, the author offers what has been called "a theology of delay." Delay of the second coming does not mean that it's not going to occur. God's idea of time is not our idea of time, and if God seems to be taking too long to fulfill his promises, it's in order to give us time to get ready. But "the day of the Lord" will come, not when we expect it but when God has planned it. And will there be change? Everything will be changed! The sordid world that we know will be purified and transformed into "new heavens and a new earth in which righteousness dwells." In the meantime, we are to conduct ourselves "in holiness and devotion, waiting for and hastening the coming day of God."

The author's exhortation is addressed to us. First of all, we are to wait. The waiting is not to be the passive waiting of someone in an airline terminal, but the alert waiting of someone with an eye on the clock, busy accomplishing a mission. This is the kind of waiting that Saint Paul spoke to the Corinthians about last week.

As we wait, we are to conduct ourselves "in holiness and devotion." It's important for the Christian believer to have correct ideas about holiness and devotion.

Most people associate holiness with very special people and very special activities. We look on Mother Teresa and the pope as holy because of their extraordinary dedication to God and to

God's people. That's quite correct, but that's only one part of holiness. Most basically, holiness means being like God, and all those who are like God are holy, and we are all like God because we have been made over into the image of Christ in baptism. Holiness is not something that a few people acquire by extraordinary efforts. Holiness is something that we are all given through the generosity of God. We are holy because Christ lives in us and because we live in Christ.

Similarly, "devotion" is not just a matter of saying certain prayers or engaging in certain practices like saying the rosary or visiting the Blessed Sacrament. In the Christian tradition of spirituality, devotion means dedication and loyalty to the Lord. It's another name for religious consistency.

Consequently, when the author of Second Peter calls us to conduct ourselves "in holiness and devotion," he is calling us to be aware of who and what we really are and to behave accordingly. He's calling us to be alert to Christ's life in us and to carry out with consistency the implications of that life in the circumstances of our own particular situation. This requires some attentiveness and some determination, to be sure, because we are so easily distracted from the really important things in our lives. But it doesn't require extraordinary efforts to make ourselves holy to start with. God has already taken care of that.

Finally, the author speaks of "hastening the coming day of God." The author seems to suggest that our living out of the holiness that God has given us, our consistent response to what God has made us to be will somehow speed up the coming of the day of the Lord, perhaps because our holiness and devotion will make the world a little more ready for its final righteousness.

The Lord will surely come. It doesn't really matter if he delays, because there's plenty for us to do in the meantime—starting today.

How do I express holiness and devotion in my life?

How does my life hasten the coming of the Lord?

Second Sunday of Advent (C)

Philippians 1:4-6, 8-11

The Second and Third Sundays of Advent show us John the Baptist at work. He is proclaiming to the people of his time the advent of the teaching, healing and saving public mission of Christ. But what he proclaims is offered in the context of the final triumph of God's love when "every valley shall be filled and every mountain and hill shall be made low."

The second reading for this second Sunday of Advent in Year C is from the beginning of Paul's letter to the Philippians. Almost all of Paul's letters begin with a paragraph or so of thanksgiving to God for his gifts to the addressees and a prayer for the continuance of those gifts. The letter to the Philippians (for whom Paul had a special affection) is no exception.

This Sunday's reading offers us excerpts from the petitionary part of the letter's opening. Paul expresses his affection for the Philippians and prays for them with joy in view of their faithfulness to the gospel. He is confident that God will continue his work in them and bring it to fulfillment in "the day of Christ Jesus." He prays that they will grow in love, in knowledge and in the ability to discern where goodness lies. The result of such growth will be that they will be appropriately prepared for "the day of Christ," filled with the holiness ("righteousness") of Jesus that will enable them to offer glory and praise to God.

There are at least three important teachings for us in these verses, three items of instruction to guide our Christian life during these weeks of Advent—and beyond.

The basic truth on which Paul is basing his prayer for the Philippians is that Christian believers have been gifted with holiness, with "righteousness that comes through Jesus Christ." This is the holiness or righteousness that Christian reflection has called "grace," and which consists in our sharing the life of the Lord Jesus, both human and divine. The good work that God has begun in us is this participation in the life of the risen Jesus. That's the foundation on which all of Christian life and virtue is based. That's the basic reality that makes us Christians. That's what gives meaning to everything else.

The second truth that is involved in Paul's prayer is that the life of Christ in us involves growth and development. It is not an object but a relationship, a relationship of love, of God's love for us and of our love in return for God in and through Christ, a relationship in which our love can grow. This is why Paul can pray that God will continue to work on what he has begun in us and that our love may "increase more and more."

This love (the sharing of ourselves in response to the goodness of God and of our neighbor) is the basic Christian virtue. It is the goal toward which our faith is directed. Christian love, however, is not a matter of feeling or emotions, like the romantic love of the movies. It is a matter of the will: willing to respond to God's love for us, wanting and willing what is beneficial to our neighbor. It involves knowledge (grateful and obedient recognition of God's demands) as well as discernment (a practical understanding of how moral principles are to be applied). This love and knowledge and discernment will help us understand and appreciate what is important in the project that God has undertaken in us and assist us in our participation in its development.

Finally, this Sunday's reading reminds us that God's association with us is directed toward a final purpose, toward the one event of salvation that is still to come: the day of Christ when all God's plans for us human creatures will come to definitive fulfillment, when all creation will be finally united to Father and

Holy Spirit through the life of the risen Son.

God's initial gift of faith and life, our response and growth in love, ultimate fulfillment in Christ "for the praise and glory of God": That's the pattern of Christian life that Paul outlines in his thanksgiving and prayer for the Philippians. That's the pattern of life that God sets out for each one of us.

The initiative of Christian life is God's, not ours. We cannot produce our own salvation. We cannot provide definitive worth for ourselves. Yet we do have a part to play in our life in Christ. We are called to love, to love God in return for the generosity that has been shown to us, to love ourselves insofar as we are God's redeemed creatures and to love our neighbor in the context of his or her relationship with God. By the love we express for our neighbor, for ourselves, for God we contribute to the work that God has undertaken in us. We become collaborators with God in his plan for each and all of us. We help God make us "pure and blameless for the day of Christ, filled with the fruits of righteousness."

Advent keeps us conscious of where we are supposed to be headed. It reminds us that Christ will come again to take us and our world definitively to himself in love. But it also teaches us that, although the final act of salvation is the day of the Lord, it is our day, too.

FOR DISCUSSION AND REFLECTION

How am I conscious of the righteousness or holiness of Christ in me?

How do my personal goals and ambitions harmonize with the day of the Lord?

Third Sunday of Advent (A)

James 5:7-10

The three readings for this Sunday form a series. Isaiah looks forward to the saving advent of the Messiah when the eyes of the blind will be opened and the ears of the deaf will be cleared. In the Gospel reading we see Jesus calling John's disciples to notice that now, through his ministry, the blind are regaining their sight and the deaf hear. The implication is that the prophecy of Isaiah has been fulfilled. Then, in our second reading, the author of James invites his readers to be patient because the Lord is going to come still again. God's word invites us to keep looking forward.

The letter of James seems to be addressed to a group of young churches which have experienced a strong Jewish influence, perhaps because they were evangelized by Christians from Jerusalem. The section that the lectionary gives us for this Sunday follows immediately on an extended rebuke to the rich for the injustice they inflict on the poor. Now the text addresses itself to the poor. It is divided into three sections.

The first section is the longest. The author calls on his readers to wait with patience for the coming of the Lord. (He uses the term *Parousia*, which would become a technical theological term to signify the final advent of Jesus at the end of time, when he would judge the living and the dead and establish the final stage of his kingdom.) They have to wait as a farmer waits for the harvest that would only come after the two rainy seasons that were included in the growing season. There's no point in trying to hurry things like that! They should find strength in the assurance that the Lord is on his way and will arrive soon. Their suffering at the hands of their oppressors would then reach a conclusion.

The second section of our reading tells the readers that they have to be patient with one another, too. Interpersonal tensions and judgments about one another are not appropriate. It is not their task to judge. God is the judge and he is already on the way to bring justice to his people.

Finally, the author gives another example of patience for his readers to imitate, that is, the example of the prophets who patiently endured hardship in their mission for the Lord. (It is not clear which prophets the author has in mind here. Perhaps he is offering a general observation as Jesus did in Matthew 5:12.)

Our live letter's message to us for this Advent Sunday is relatively simple. The Lord is coming again and we have to wait for his coming with patience. It is the Lord who controls the timetable, not we.

Our faith conviction about the coming of the Lord, about Jesus' Parousia has at least two implications for us. The first is that there is a direction and purpose in all of human history. What goes on in this world of ours is not without interest to the Lord, not without meaning for the implementation of God's plans for human salvation. We are not able to interpret the ultimate significance of the events of human history, but they are not for that reason meaningless. Our faith teaches us that all human activity has a moral dimension, an aspect that connects it with God's plans for humanity. These plans lead creation to a final fulfillment in which all of created reality will be assumed into the final glory of the risen Christ. All history is somehow salvation history.

Secondly, if this is true in universal history, it is also true in the history of each individual. We are all called to life in Christ. We each have a definitive destiny that involves final consummation in the company of the blessed. That final consummation will come with the final coming of the Lord.

The interim period, the time between now and then, is not necessarily a time of effortless euphoria. In fact, for most of us, this interim time involves struggle and effort and pain. That's why God's word calls us to patience. Patience means bearing pain and trial calmly and without complaint.

But Christian patience is not the same thing as resignation. Resignation can be a response to a situation of futility, to a set of circumstances in which there is no meaning, no outcome, no relief. We suffer with resignation because there is nothing else to do, because any other response would constitute a waste of energy. But that's not the situation of the Christian in the world. No matter how painful our situation may be, we know that the power and love of Christ are strong enough to overcome it. Christ is going to come again, and that's a source of hope, a reason for looking forward with confidence and gladness to what the Lord has promised. Christian patience, therefore, always includes hope.

Often our attitude toward God, individually and corporately, has a degree of immaturity to it. Are we there yet? How much longer is it going to be? How come it's taking so long? Why can't we stop now? On this Sunday God's word quietly invites us to grow up. Be patient! The Lord knows what he is doing and where he is taking us and he'll get us there at the right time.

FOR DISCUSSION AND REFLECTION

What aspects of my life require patience?
To what do I look forward from the Lord?

Third Sunday of Advent (B)

I Thessalonians 5:16-24

Once more we hear the preaching of John the Baptist, this time as recorded in the Gospel of John. The questioners want to know about the Baptist—who are you and what are you up to—and he insists on telling them who he is not. He says, in effect, "I'm not the Christ, not Elijah, not the Prophet that Moses spoke of. I'm just the advance man for somebody that's already here in your midst and who is to come after me."

The apostolic reading tells us what John the Baptist's response to his questioners means for us. Jesus is in our midst, too, and is still to come.

The First Letter to the Thessalonians is the first of the letters that Paul wrote to his converts and is the oldest book of the New Testament. It's a short letter, filled with encouragement. Like most of Paul's letters, it has a section at the end devoted to practical matters, generally matters having to do with Christian moral life. Our reading is from this exhortatory section in the First Letter to the Thessalonians.

Paul invites the Thessalonians to live in joy, prayer and thanksgiving. That's what God wants from them. They are to use and appreciate the gifts that they have been given. Paul prays that they may be made "perfectly holy" and preserved from sin in view of the coming of Christ. He invites them to be confident, since "the one who calls you is faithful, and he will also accomplish" what has been promised.

This reading is a call to hope, and it constitutes the agenda for Christian believers of every age.

The "coming of our Lord Jesus Christ" is something that we are all invited to look forward to, not as some secondary feature of God's plan for salvation, but as a central feature of it. The coming of Jesus at the end of time is the final fulfillment of what God had in mind for us from the beginning. In one of his sermons (9.4) Saint Augustine says, "Anyone who doesn't think about the age to come, and is not a Christian precisely in order to receive what God promises at the end, is not yet a Christian."

In the meantime, however, Christ and his Holy Spirit are not absent, as if waiting offstage for their entry cue. No, they are present and active in the Christian community now. Their presence and action is expressed primarily in the holiness that we have been given, the life of Christ to live in our lives, a life that is not some sort of inert image imprinted on our souls, but a living life that calls for development and growth. Responding to and expressing the life of Christ in our individual existence is one of our primary responsibilities as believers. We are called to make the Lord present and active in our families and our homes, in our jobs and in our leisure, in outreach and care for those in need. In our personal spirituality, we are called to grow, through prayer and reflection, in awareness of the Lord's presence and action in who we are and in what we do. We are already holy, but Jesus calls us forward to becoming "perfectly holy" by cultivating the basic gift we have received. "Do not quench the Spirit."

But holiness is not the only gift we have received. There are more specific gifts, too, that we are called to treasure and use, gifts of personal talents and abilities, gifts of love and friendship that are extended to us through those whose lives touch ours, gifts that come to us through the community of the Church. We have all sorts of personal equipment to help us grow in our own holiness and to help others grow in theirs.

True, we are called to look forward and to wait, but the waiting has a purpose. The waiting is to be productive. And the God who calls us to the future can be relied on to be busy with us here and now as well.

This is where joy and thanksgiving come in. Our life as believers is not a list of do's and don'ts and rules to keep. It's not a matter of sitting in some sort of life-long dentist's chair waiting for God to be finished with us. Our life as believers is a matter of working with the Lord to bring his world to fulfillment, of doing our part to bring about ultimate happiness for all those who will accept it. And the Lord promises to work with us, just because he loves us, just because he is faithful.

Real Christian believers are people of hope. They know that they have wonderful things to look forward to in the ultimate future, but they also know that today and tomorrow are the context for God's blessings, too. They know that what is to come is God's gift, but they also know that they have been enlisted as God's collaborators in the giving. They know that their life has never-ending significance because of what God has done for them and because of what God has enabled them to do for him. That's why they "give thanks in all circumstances." That's why they "rejoice always."

FOR DISCUSSION AND REFLECTION

How do I cultivate the Spirit in my life?

How is my life an ongoing act of thanksgiving?

Third Sunday of Advent (C)

Philippians 4:4-7

This Sunday's readings continue to call our attention to the advent of Christ, but they emphasize a particular aspect of it. Christ is most emphatically still to come in final glory at the end of time, but he is not for that reason distant from us in the meantime. In the Gospel, John the Baptist offers his own moral directives to his hearers, but also speaks of the one who "is coming." The reading from Zephaniah tells us how we are to interpret this "coming" when it proclaims that "the Lord, your God, is in your midst, a mighty savior." The apostolic live letter also speaks of the nearness of the Lord. Christ is still to come, but he is here.

The second reading is again from the letter to the Philippians, one of Paul's warmest and friendliest epistles. Our portion is from its final chapter in which Paul is giving practical instructions to the community.

The basic idea on which Paul hangs his teaching for the Philippians is at the very center of our reading: "The Lord is near." In view of that nearness, the Philippians should be cheerful. In fact, cheerfulness should be an ongoing feature of their ecclesial personalities. ("Rejoicing" is one of the recurrent themes of Philippians. This is the tenth time in this epistle that Paul invites his readers to rejoice.) They should be conspicuous for their gentleness and forbearance and thoughtfulness for one another. There is no need for them to worry. They should be lovingly familiar with God in prayer, asking for what they need with trust and thanksgiving. If the nearness of Christ leads them to respond in the ways that Paul suggests, they will enjoy the peace of God, that harmonious fullness of life and action that comes into our hearts with Christ and that can be operative even in the most unexpected circumstances.

One of the foundation stones of Catholic Christian spirituality is that the Lord is near. True, he first came among us at a specific time in the past and is no longer with us in the same way he was then. True, he is still to come in a new way in the fullness of his glory at the end of time, as we have been hearing from God's word over the last two Sundays. But he is also with us now, and that presence of his in our midst is what makes life different and distinctive for us believers.

Jesus is near us in lots of ways. Most basically, he lives in our hearts through the sharing of his life that we call grace. He is present to us in sacred Scripture through which he continues to teach us as he taught his first followers. He is present in the sacraments through which he touches and directs our lives. In a unique way, Jesus is near us and with us in the Holy Eucharist through which he not only offers us his presence for our adoration, but, more importantly, nourishes and directs us by means of the life and energy that he shares with us when we are fed with the eucharistic bread and wine. Jesus is also in touch with us through other believers, women and men who extend the life and love of Jesus to the world in which they find themselves. The living Lord Jesus is all over the place, with us in all kinds of ways at every turn! One of the fundamentals of our Christian lives is that the Lord is near.

The presence and nearness of the Lord call for some responses. One is rejoicing. The Lord wants us to be glad that he is with us, to take joy in his contact with us. The Lord of the universe is alive in our hearts because he knows us and loves us. He guides us and nourishes us and teaches us. Nothing that can happen to us can outweigh the gift of himself that Jesus makes to us. All the questions and problems and uncertainties that can occur in human existence have their answer and solution in him. Every life that is filled with Christ is a life that has eternal meaning and purpose and coherence. It is a life of peace.

Rejoicing in the nearness of Christ also involves reaching out to others with the warmth and kindness and forbearance of Christ. Christ is not in us like a biology specimen in a jar, kept there to be looked at and admired. Christ is in us as the source of energy and direction for our whole life. He lives and works through our life and work. He loves through our love for one another.

The presence of Christ in us also calls for prayer, for deliberate attention to the presence and action of Christ in us. It is prayer that is founded on thanksgiving, on an awareness of what God has given us already, on a conviction that God wants to continue to look out for us and take care of us.

The nearness of the Lord makes it possible for us to be consistently optimistic, patient, grateful, free from fear, attentive to the Lord, rejoicing in the Lord always.

We Christians are able to be secure, happy, contented people because of our awareness and acceptance of what the Lord has already done for us in the past, because of the glory that is still to come in the future and because of the peace and joyfulness that arises from the present nearness of the Lord.

FOR DISCUSSION AND REFLECTION

How is the nearness of Christ a source of joy for me?

In what circumstances do I perceive "the peace of God that surpasses all understanding" in my heart?

Fourth Sunday of Advent (A)

Romans 1:1-7

All three readings for this Fourth Sunday of Advent share a common element: they are all concerned with the house of David. In the first reading (Isaiah 7:10-14), Isaiah proclaims the future birth of a special child who would be a sign of God's care for the Davidic dynasty of the skeptical King Ahaz. In the Gospel reading (Matthew 1:18-24), the angel tells Joseph what arrangements he must make to guarantee that Mary's child would be counted as a member of Joseph's family, the house of David. In our second reading, Paul makes quite clear that Christ was fully human, "descended from David according to the flesh." Jesus' humanity was not an appearance or a pose. He was completely one of us, born into a specific human family as each of us is.

Paul's allusion to Jesus' full humanity comes in the opening of his letter to the Romans. Usually the greeting in a letter would be brief. "Cicero sends greetings to Atticus." Paul's introductions tend to be longer than this, but in Romans he outdoes even himself. Perhaps because he was not personally acquainted with the church of Rome he felt the need to be as clear as possible about himself, his teaching and his attitude toward his addressees. We can almost imagine Paul's stenographer struggling to keep up as Paul added one clarifying clause after another. The result is a single sentence that is seven verses long and almost incomprehensible. One wonders what the Romans made of it.

If this opening sentence were to be rewritten according to more contemporary stylistic tastes, it would be broken down into several sentences and might go something like this:

Dear Romans, my name is Paul. I am an apostle, totally dedicated to Christ. God called me to proclaim his gospel.

This gospel has its foundation in the prophets of old and is concerned with God's Son. In terms of his humanity, this Son was a descendant of David. Because of his death and resurrection and his sharing in the holiness of God, however, this Son has been identified as nothing less than the Son of God.

Through this Son I have been called to invite the gentiles into an association of faith with him. That includes you. You are beloved of Christ, called to belong to him, gifted with a sharing in his holiness. May God the Father and our Lord Jesus Christ continue to bless you!

In these seven grandiose and complicated verses, Paul offers three characteristics of himself (slave [that is, total devotee] of Christ, called to be an apostle, set aside for the gospel of God). He assures the Romans that he recognizes their standing as Christian community (three more characteristics: beloved of Christ, belonging to him, called to share in his holiness). He gives an overview of salvation history and explains his own part in that history (to bring the gentiles to faith). In the course of all this, Paul alludes to the major ideas that he will develop in the course of the rest of the letter: gospel, grace, apostolate, the commitment of faith, the importance of faith, the Scriptures, the role of Christ Jesus. It's almost as if Paul were trying to put all sixteen chapters of the letter into the very first sentence!

Yet these opening verses of Romans have a single theme, a theme that is of fundamental importance for us. These verses are concerned with identity, the identity of Christ, of Paul, of the Romans—and of us Christian believers reading this live letter two thousand years after its delivery.

Who are we? We are sharers in the life of Christ, partakers of the divine life of the God-man who entered fully into human history on the first Christmas. Humanly speaking, he was an offshoot of the family to which David had belonged. The other side of him, however, is nothing less than the life of God, a life that he translated into humanity and spent among us in order to bring us into lasting communication with his own godliness. We are "saints," not because of our spiritual achievements, but because of Christ's generosity. That's what Paul was. That's what the first recipients of the letter to the Romans were. That's what every Christian believer has been from the very beginning of the unfolding of God's project of salvation.

The implications of that identity stretch from the first moment of creation to the last instant of time. They form the outline of the whole of human history. They color every aspect of our individual human existence. They determine the worth with which we begin our lives and the final fruitfulness with which we end them. Who are we? What are we? Nothing less than the extension of the life of the Son of God, all of us together forming one life in him.

In these closely written and solemn verses with which Paul begins his letter to the Romans, he is sketching the meaning of salvation and also sketching us: called, set apart, obedient in faith, belonging to Jesus Christ, beloved of God, saints, all thanks to our incorporation into the son of David who was also Son of God.

FOR DISCUSSION AND REFLECTION

In practice, how does my faith contribute to my identity?
How does the identity of Christ shape my life?

Fourth Sunday of Advent (B)

Romans 16:25-27

"Glory be to God!" That's the bottom line of our live letter for this fourth Sunday of Advent. It represents the response of the Church, expressed in the words of Saint Paul, to the announcement that is made to Mary in the Gospel reading. She would become a mother through a unique intervention of the Holy Spirit and her child would be the Son of the Most High who would rule over a kingdom that would have no end.

This apostolic reading is closely packed and difficult to grasp, like much of Saint Paul's writing, especially his letter to the Romans. One gets the impression sometimes that Paul wanted to say more than ordinary modes of human communication could bear. The result is a kind of writing that requires careful effort to be understood, line by line and word by word analysis. We have to go through it slowly and reflectively if we are going to be able to see what it means for us.

To begin, we need to say something about "mystery." "Mystery" is an important word for Saint Paul. It occurs more than twenty times in the Pauline letters.

In our ordinary usage, "mystery" is a secret or a riddle to which no answer has yet been found, something whose significance is hidden. "I don't know. It's a mystery to me."

In Saint Paul's usage, "mystery" means God's plan for the world that is in the process of being executed, and, in the process of being brought to fulfillment, is also being revealed. It is the disclosure of God's intentions for the world, hidden up to a certain point but now becoming a kind of open secret. It is what God had in mind from the beginning and what becomes known through the life and death and resurrection of Jesus. It is the plan that will unfold in the ministry of Jesus, but which will continue to be implemented until the world's final reunion with God at the end of time. It is the manifestation of the secret of the world, of the world that is now and of the world that is to be.

Now let's paraphrase our text. It comes at the very end of the Letter to the Romans and constitutes a kind of summary and final prayer of praise. "I have preached the gospel to you," Paul says, "the gospel that Jesus preached, the gospel that is about Jesus. What I have taught you constitutes the mystery, the plan of God that is now becoming known. It's a plan that began to be revealed through the prophets, but which is now being fully manifested in God's own time. The plan calls for all of humankind, Jews and gentiles, Greeks and Romans, and everybody else to be made one through their acceptance of Christ in faith. This plan of God's offers strength and fullness to your lives. It's a plan that only the wisdom of God could conceive. Glory be to God!"

Over the past weeks the Church's liturgical readings have been teaching us about the second coming of Christ in glory, the final stage of God's plan for his world. At Christmas, the Church celebrates the initiation of that final stage, the birth of Christ who would unite everything in himself and present it to his heavenly Father at the appointed time. From that moment on the final fulfillment begins to take shape. The birth of Christ is the beginning of the end.

The mystery of Christ, God's plan to save a sinful world and give it everlasting significance, includes us. All too often we tend to cast our lives in dimensions that are too small. We are busy with our responsibilities to our family and our work. We are concerned about our health or our economic situation. We try to be faithful to God in our behavior by avoiding sin. Obviously there's nothing wrong with any of that, but it doesn't do God's plan full justice.

Sometimes we are able to look a little bit beyond ourselves by using our time and our resources for the benefit of others. We may even become active in the life of our parish. That's a step in the right direction.

But most of the time we find that we and our own interests, personal or local, occupy center stage. We forget that we are participants in a larger drama. Our life is not just an individual, private occurrence in the thousands of years of the world's history. Our life is part of the mystery of Christ. It's a carefully crafted episode in God's plan to extend the life and work of Jesus through all places and all times. When God became a human being at that moment of the Annunciation to Mary, he gave a whole new dimension to the life of each one of us. We have a different significance than we would otherwise have had. Each of us is precious, each of us is important because we share the life of Christ, because we share Christ's mission to bring the world back to God. Christmas isn't just about Jesus. It's about us, too. It's about us now and it's about us in the final kingdom of God.

Glory be to God, indeed.

FOR DISCUSSION AND REFLECTION

How does my life contribute to fulfilling the mystery of Christ?

Who is the central character in the drama of my life?

Fourth Sunday of Advent (C)

Hebrews 10:5-10

The Gospel readings for the Fourth Sunday of Advent deal with
the events that prepared immediately for the Lord's birth. In Year
C we have the narrative of Mary's visit to Elizabeth. The Old
Testament readings throughout Advent are prophecies about the
Messiah and the Messianic age. The second readings provide
commentary on the various themes of Advent, not necessarily
connected with the other readings. This Sunday's live letter, a
passage from the Letter to the Hebrews, offers us a brief yet
immensely rich explanation of the nature and purpose of the
salvation that Jesus came to offer us.

This book of the New Testament is intended to offer
encouragement to a group of Jewish Christians. Our passage is
from the section in which the author is describing how the
priesthood and sacrifice of Jesus surpass the priesthood and
sacrifices of the Jewish ritual law. As happens frequently in
Hebrews, the author bases his teaching on a quotation from the
Hebrew Scriptures.

The quotation that lies at the foundation of our reading is
from Psalm 140. This is a prayer of someone who has been
delivered from illness. The psalmist realizes that ritual sacrifices
of thanksgiving are not an adequate response to God's gift, and
that what is called for is obedience to God's will, an obedience to
which we are called by the basic import and intent of God's law
("in the written scroll it is prescribed for me").

The author of Hebrews puts these verses of Psalm 140 into

the mouth of Christ as he was entering the world. They constitute, as it were, his motto, his mission statement. This is what he is all about. Then the text offers some more detailed, though rather repetitious commentary. The psalm text (both in its original context and as taken up by Christ) makes it clear that the various kinds of ritual sacrifices prescribed by the Jewish law were, in the final analysis, not pleasing to God. (This is a point that Hebrews makes over and over again.) What is pleasing to God is that his will be carried out by his human servants. God's will takes the place of the old ritual sacrifices. The Son's taking on human nature, his human life, his faithful offering of himself even to the point of death have made us holy because all this was done in response to God's will.

There are three important elements here. The first is God's will, the ultimate reality that gives direction and meaning to everything else. The will of God in our regard, what God wants from us, is that we respond to his love for us by loving in return, that we acknowledge God's sovereignty by our willingness to carry out his plans for creation. Therein lies our purpose. Therein lies our happiness. The original sin consisted precisely in turning away from God's will, in setting ourselves up as the center of our human existence, in making our will the driving force of our lives. Reversing this original sin would necessarily entail reversing the self-serving and self-centered direction that humanity had taken on. This reversal would need to be undertaken by somebody who could represent and act for all of us, even as our first parents acted for all of us at the beginning.

The second important element in our reading is obedience. What Adam and Eve refused to give to God was obedience. They were unwilling to be God's servants. What Jesus, the divine Son of the eternal Father, came to offer was precisely obedience. In his human nature he intended to live a human life of service and dedication to the Father, a life that would proclaim the lordship of God and the essential subordination of humanity. The meaning and worth of Jesus' life begins at his birth and lasts all the way through until the last moment of his life on the cross. It was a total life of total obedience, and, because it was lived by one who embraced and represented all humanity, it was a life that had an effect on us all.

Finally, the text speaks of "the offering of the body of Jesus Christ once and for all." This offering consists of Jesus' acceptance of the human condition, of his determination to live out the human condition in faithfulness to his heavenly Father no matter where that determination led him. In fact, it led him to public rejection and the death of a criminal. The suffering and death of Jesus were not redemptive because they were painful, but because they were a continued expression of Jesus' dedication and obedience. They were indeed a sacrifice, but their sacrificial worth did not consist in blood and suffering, but in the faithfulness to the Father that led him to the cross. All of Jesus' life was redemptive, not just his death.

In Jesus, God became human in order to be obedient, to give himself to the Father even to the extent of dying as a result of his obedience. Jesus restored the relationship between humans and God and gave us all a new start. The Redemption is a single story, a single undertaking that begins at Bethlehem and ends at Calvary—but that still continues as we make his story our own.

FOR DISCUSSION AND REFLECTION

How do I practice obedience in my life?

In what way is my life an offering to God?

PART TWO

Christmas

Christmas, Mass at Midnight (ABC)

Titus 2:11-14

When the liturgy celebrates the events of Christ's life, ministry, death and resurrection, its purpose is not merely to remember, to think back over what happened to Jesus in the course of his human existence. That's part of it, of course, but more important in our liturgical celebration is the deepening of our awareness of the meaning of what Jesus experienced and of its significance for our salvation. In addition to increased understanding, these liturgical observances alert us to the continued presence and action of Christ in our world today.

Today's live letter is intended to remind us of the practical consequences for us of God's coming into our world as a human participant.

The reading is from the letter to Titus. This book of the New Testament is addressed to a young bishop in the name of Paul. It is devoted mostly to moral direction, practical guidelines for virtuous living that the young bishop is to preach to his people. Immediately prior to this Sunday's reading there is a long section in which the author tells Titus what to tell to older men and older women, younger women and men, slaves and masters. Now, in our reading, the author gives the theological underpinning for what he has been saying.

He speaks of the two comings of Christ. The kindness of God (that is, Christ) has already appeared in the world for our salvation. (The tense of the Greek verb used here suggests not only a past action or event but also results of that action continuing into the present.) This appearance of Christ with its perduring results serves as a source of moral training for us, as a kind of school to help us learn how to live. Christ's life and ministry teach us to offer to God the service that belongs to him and to turn away from giving any priority to earthly values. We are to practice self-control and gladly offer to our neighbor and to God what is owing to them. Our Christian life should be a life of peaceful equilibrium with ourselves, with our neighbor, with God. That's where Christ's birth leads us.

If we learn from what the earthly life and ministry of Christ teach us, we will be able to look forward in hope to the next coming of Christ, when he will appear again in the full and final glory of his divinity. By then we will have been freed from the demands of sinfulness and will be constituted as a people of holiness, capable for all eternity of being and doing what God desires.

The use of this piece of the New Testament for Christmas makes it clear to us that the birth of Christ was more than a quaint happening in picturesque circumstances long ago. The birth of Christ changed everything for all of us. Because God was now living a human life, all human life has a different dimension. Jesus unites us to himself through the gift of his life, but he also directs us by his action and his teaching in the ways of human behavior, in God's own idea of how people should conduct themselves.

God's initiative of salvation that manifests its final stage in the birth of Jesus is a gift to us, something that we do not deserve but can only receive. But salvation is not an inert thing that God gives us to hold onto. It is a relationship between persons and such relationships call for a response, for an exchange of attentiveness. The response that God's gift of himself to us calls for is consistency, living in a way that is in harmony with the life of God that Christ has shared with us. This involves rejecting "godless ways and worldly desires." It means living "temperately and justly and devoutly." Those are all things that go with trying to express the life of Christ through our individual human existence. If we learn these lessons that the life of Christ wants to teach us, we will become God's people, practiced enough in goodness to fit into eternal life with him.

The appearance of Christ at the beginning of his earthly life and his final appearance at the end of time call for response and consistency on our part. But they also call for gratitude. God's appearances, past and present, are God's gift to us. The loving kindness that lies behind God's appearances are a unique source of instruction for us. God does not prepare us for goodness by threats and punishments, but by becoming one of us and by calling us to live a life that is his. We are not slaves or employees. We are God's children whom he schools to live as members of his family. And that calls for gratitude.

The infant Jesus lying in the manger is a dear image in the Christian imagination. During any Christmas season we will see it expressed in hundreds of ways in crib scenes and Christmas cards, in school plays and in carols. But the infant Jesus lying in the manger is also a challenge to response, to consistency and to gratitude. "Here I am," Jesus says. "What are you going to do about that?"

FOR DISCUSSION AND REFLECTION

How does Christ appear in my life?

Why do I try to behave according to God's law?

Christmas, Mass at Dawn (ABC)

Titus 3:4-7

The Christmas Mass at dawn is called the Shepherds' Mass. At the midnight Mass the Gospel (Luke 2:1-14) described the circumstances of the birth of Jesus and told us how the angel appeared to the shepherds. The angel announced to them that a savior had been born for them, and that the infant wrapped in swaddling clothes and lying in a manger would be a sign for them. Now, at the dawn Mass, we see the shepherds hurrying to Bethlehem and finding exactly what the angel had foretold. This child, then, must be the savior!

Our apostolic reading is taken from the letter to Titus. This brief letter may have been written late in Paul's career, or even by one of his followers. It is addressed to Titus, who had been one of Paul's traveling companions earlier on. The letter to Titus is read in the Sunday liturgy only during Christmas time, that is, at the midnight Mass and the dawn Mass for Christmas day, and on the feast of the Baptism of the Lord (in Year C) at the very end of the liturgical Christmas season.

These readings from Titus seem to have been chosen because they have to do with salvation and help us understand what it means to say that Jesus is our savior.

In ordinary language, "saving" has two main meanings. It means to rescue from danger or harm. "Saved by the bell!" It also means to put something aside, to preserve it. It's the opposite of throwing away. "Don't throw that away. It's worth saving." The criterion for saving or throwing away is value. We save what is worth something to us. We throw away what is not.

When we say that Jesus has saved us, therefore, we mean two related things. We mean that Jesus has rescued us from danger, from the danger of the human sinfulness that is so pervasive and that could lead us to a wasted life that is little better than death. We also mean that Jesus gives our lives a special worth or value, that he makes us worth bothering about, worth preserving, that he makes us precious to God in a way that we would not be if he had not brought us salvation.

Our salvation consists in the fact that we are made over by Jesus into participants in his life. We are no longer mere human creatures, members of an historically sinful race, a race hostile to God. We are now extensions of the life of the God-man Jesus who modeled what human existence was meant to be and who thus lifted human existence to a whole new level of meaning and worth. We are precious to our heavenly Father because we are part of the life of his only Son. Salvation makes us sharers in the innermost life of God.

This is what our live letter for today is about. Paul reminds Titus that, out of his own love and kindness, God decided to save us, to deliver us from ultimate harm and to make us precious enough to be his forever. The fulfillment of his plan began when Jesus appeared. It wasn't because we had earned his attention that he decided to make something out of us, but just because he is merciful. His plan works through baptism and through the Holy Spirit that our savior Jesus offers us. He re-creates us so that we are holy by sharing his own life ("justified by his grace"). Because we are holy as he is holy, we have a claim (as "heirs in hope") on eternal life with him, with the Father, with the Holy Spirit.

Today we celebrate the birth of our savior. Through the human life that began at Jesus' birth, he offers us ultimate safety. Sinfulness cannot have the last word in our lives as long as we are in touch with him. Nothing can do us ultimate harm. Even the worst tragedies that can befall us in this earthly realm are secondary and subordinate to his love for us.

Through the human life that began at Jesus' birth, he offers us worth and value. He makes us worth preserving. Even the most insignificant of us has a mission that has eternal implications. Our life is no longer our life, but his life, too, a life that God meant to extend to every place and time through the collaboration of all those who would accept Jesus in faith. God will never throw us away because we are as precious to him as his own Son. He has determined to save us.

And it's all free. We don't have to achieve salvation. We don't have to earn it. We don't have to make ourselves worthy of it. In fact, what our savior offers us is so far above our human efforts that any idea of winning it by our own efforts is absurd if not downright blasphemous. Yes, we have to respond to Jesus' offer of salvation. We have to be willing to accept what he wants to give us and what he wants us to be. But the salvation that he gives us is ultimately his doing and not ours. It's all from his graciousness. It's all gift.

Jesus was the best Christmas gift that was ever given. And he is given to us.

FOR DISCUSSION AND REFLECTION

How am I precious to God?

From what threats or dangers does salvation in Christ deliver me?

Christmas, Mass During the Day (ABC)

Hebrews 1:1-6

The readings for the Mass during Christmas day are all concerned with the identity of the Christ whose birth we are celebrating. The Old Testament reading alludes to the redeemer of Jerusalem, the bringer of salvation, the restorer of Zion. The Gospel reading, from the prologue to the Gospel of John, is one of the most profound theological passages in the New Testament. In it, the author of John describes Christ as Logos, as the Word that the Father addresses to his people for their salvation. The second reading is another theological treasure, the beginning of the Letter to the Hebrews.

This book of the New Testament is a message of encouragement to Jewish converts who were growing weary of the demands of Christian life. In the introduction, as sonorous and symphonic a passage as we can find anywhere in the Bible, the author gives an overview of his whole message and leads the readers into the first important section of his message.

He contrasts what has been with what is. In the past, God spoke to his people in fragmentary ways: through dreams and visions, through natural phenomena, through historical occurrences. Now God's revelation has reached its definitive, final, climactic stage. He has spoken to us through his Son. This Son stands at the beginning and the end of creation. Because he is the full image and reflection of the Father, he is the pattern on which God created the universe. But this Son is also the redeemer and so has been taken up into glory by the Father and is now the goal toward which all creation is directed. He is the heir of it all. It all belongs to him. The glory of the Son, mediator of creation and liberator from sin, is greater than the glory of the angels. The text now cites several passages from Scripture that are interpreted to signify the superiority of the Son over the angels. This is an important initial point in Hebrews because the old covenant was thought to have been delivered through the ministry of angels, and the first section of Hebrews will demonstrate that the Son and his covenant are superior to them and therefore to the covenant they represented.

It's important for us to be clear about the nature and mission of Christ. Christ is the only-begotten Son of the eternal Father, Lord and God as the Father is. He is the full reflection of the Father's glory, the mirror image of the Father, as it were, everything the Father is except that he is Son. Because everything that exists somehow reflects the reality and variety of God, it is all somehow an expression of the Son. He is the mediator of creation.

The mission of the Son in the world is unification, to bring back to the Father the humanity that had been fragmented and dispersed through the selfishness of its own sin. He was to live a human life as God meant human life to be lived. He was to provide not only a model that the rest of us could imitate, but a whole new kind of being that we could share. Redemption does not consist so much in behaving like Christ as in being in Christ.

When our text says that, in these last days, God "has spoken to us through the Son," it doesn't just mean that God gave us new information that we didn't have before or that he said things that he hadn't been able to express before. The finality of revelation that we have in the Son consists in the reality of God that is offered for us to share through the humanness of Christ. There is no more to be revealed because we have been offered the very fullness of God. The final time is here because God has done for us all that even God could do. There is nothing more to come.

All this is another way of saying that the revelation that is constituted by the gift of the Son is final, definitive, exclusive, compulsory. Living in Christ is not one way of salvation among many others. It is the one, unique access to himself that God the Father has given to us. To be saved or redeemed means to be freed from our sinfulness and to be made holy in God's sight. There is only one kind of holiness, and that is to share the life of God as presented to us in Jesus. A virtuous life, generosity to those in need, attentiveness to God in prayer—these are all important things, but they do not of themselves constitute salvation or holiness. The only source of salvation and holiness is sharing in the life of the Lord Jesus, the Son whom God "made heir of all things and through whom he created the universe."

God offers us salvation through the Church (its Scriptures, its sacraments, its teachings, its community), because through the Church God offers us Christ. This is not to say that those outside the Church are necessarily removed from the possibility of being saved. In response to their search for God they, too, can be brought to share the life of Christ in ways that only God knows. But the fact remains that salvation comes only through Christ and that Christ comes only through the gift of the Father. That gift is what we celebrate on Christmas.

FOR DISCUSSION AND REFLECTION

Why do I need Jesus in my life?

What would the world be like if God had not given us his Son?

The Holy Family of Jesus, Mary and Joseph (A)

Colossians 3:12-21

The feast of the Holy Family has a somewhat checkered history. It was first inserted into the annual liturgical calendar by Leo

XIII in 1893 and observed on the third Sunday after Epiphany. When Pius X revised the Missal, the feast of the Holy Family was suppressed. Then, in 1921, Pius XI put it back into the calendar to be celebrated on the first Sunday after Epiphany. In the liturgical reforms that followed Vatican II, it was reassigned to the Sunday after Christmas.

The Gospel readings for this feast are about the childhood of Jesus, while the other readings are about the virtues of family life.

Our reading for Year A can be used in all three years of the cycle, though optional second readings are provided for Years B and C. This reading is from the letter to the Colossians.

In this section of Colossians Paul is instructing his readers about the practicalities of Christian life. In verses 5-9 of chapter 3, he has provided them with a list of sins and faults to be avoided, things to be taken off like dirty clothes. Then, in verse 10, he tells them what they are to put on: a new self which is Christ.

This is where our reading begins. It is in three parts. The first part (verses 12-14) continues the clothing metaphor. Paul gives the Colossians a list of qualities that they are to "put on," which will constitute a sort of uniform by which they can be identified. Christians are to be sympathetic, kindly in judgment, humble, gentle, patient and forgiving toward one another. Their basic moral style should be marked by love, the virtue that holds all the others together (and, one might add, gives the basic tonality to the whole ensemble).

Next (15-17), in a lyrical and carefully balanced passage, Paul writes of the ultimate foundations of all Christian behavior: the Lord Jesus and gratitude. They are to cultivate in their hearts the peace of Christ, and be grateful. They are to be taught by the word of Christ and respond to what they have learned with songs of gratitude. They are to do everything they do under the auspices of Christ and give "thanks to God the Father through him." The life of Christians together is to be the life of Christ, a life of thankfulness.

Finally we have a very specific list of directives for family life. Wives, husbands, children, parents are to defer to one another and care for one another in the context of the will and presence of the Lord. (In the full text of Colossians this passage continues with similar directives about the relationship between slaves and masters.)

Some people who listen to this passage may be distracted from its central message by verse 18: "Wives be subordinate to your husbands, as is proper in the Lord." This verse has a countercultural tone for us twenty-first century Americans. Scripture scholars tell us, however, that, in this passage, Paul is not setting out an unchangeable plan for familial relations, but is instructing his readers to follow the social customs of their times in a particularly Christian way, that is, "in the Lord." The issue is not who is supposed to be the boss in the family, but how Christ is to be expressed in all of their relationships with one another. (If Paul were laying down once and for all rules about the specifics of family life, verses 22 and following would be teaching us that families are supposed to have slaves! Moreover, those who find this text jarring might want to consider that there have been times in our western civilization when what Paul says about husbands ["Love your wives"] sounded just as countercultural as what he says about wives sounds to us.)

The central message of our reading is that we are to be loving and considerate of one another because of the presence and life of Christ in us and that this presence and life should make us consistently and habitually grateful. This is the secret of Christian family life and of all other interpersonal relationships.

Living together in the family of faith is not a matter of searching out and getting close to people we find interesting or attractive. It's not a matter of offering appropriate responses to their human gifts. Rather, it's a matter of being Christ to one another, of seeing Christ in others, and of reaching out to others in the Christ who lives in us.

And all this is to take place not in a context of burdensome demand or of fear of punishment if we don't shape up. It's to take place in a context of gratitude, of gratitude for the presence of the Lord in those around us, of gratitude for the presence of the Lord in us.

Gratitude is always appropriate in Christian spirituality because everything we are and have is gift, and gifts call for gratefulness. But on this feast of family—Jesus' family and our own—a little extra gratitude for what we have received and what we are able to give in our relationships with each another seems particularly fitting.

FOR DISCUSSION AND REFLECTION

In what ways is the Lord manifested in my family?

How much gratitude is there in my relationships?

The Holy Family of Jesus, Mary and Joseph (Optional B)

Hebrews 11:8, 11-12, 17-19

For the feast of the Holy Family the lectionary provides a different gospel for each year of the three-year cycle of readings, as well as standard Old Testament and apostolic readings that can be used in all three years. It also provides optional first and second readings for Years B and C. Our selection from the letter to the Hebrews is the optional selection for Year B. The introduction to the lectionary (no. 95) tells us that the Gospel readings for this feast are about Jesus' childhood, while the other readings are about the virtues of family life. Our optional reading for Year B is about faith.

We catch sight of faith in the longer form of the gospel as we hear about Simeon, whose trust in God's promise that he would see the Messiah is fulfilled. We see faith in Anna the devout woman who spent her years in the temple confidently "awaiting the redemption of Jerusalem."

Faith moves to center stage in the reading from the letter to the Hebrews. This "letter" is a message of encouragement to a group of people who were weary with the demands of Christian life. (We will be reading at some length from this book of the New Testament later in Year B's "Ordinary Time.") The selection provided for us today is from a section of the letter in which the author is inviting his readers to take heart from the example provided for them by Old Testament models of faith. We read the part that has to do with Abraham, whom the First Eucharistic Prayer calls "our father in faith."

Faith is a complex concept in Scripture and Catholic teaching. It includes belief, that is, accepting as true what God has revealed to us and what his Church teaches, but it also involves the commitment of ourselves in response to God's initiatives in our regard. It has overtones of confidence, hope and expectation. At the beginning of the chapter from which we read today, the author of Hebrews describes faith as "the realization of what is hoped for, and the evidence of things not seen." Not surprisingly, scholars are not in complete agreement about what this means. It seems clear, however, that what is involved in the faith that our author talks about is deep-seated confidence in God resulting from insight into the reality of the invisible world of God and into God's goodness and reliability.

Our text speaks of the faith of Abraham in three contexts. God called him to leave his home and go to an unknown new land that would be given to him for his own. Abraham goes with confidence because of what he has learned about God. Secondly, because of what Abraham knew about God, he trusted in God's promise to give him a son even though he was an old man and his wife was long past childbearing. Although he was as good as dead, he became the father of numberless descendants. Abraham's insight into the realm of the divine and his confidence in God's generosity reached its highest point when he showed his willingness to sacrifice his son at God's command. He knew that God could and would bring that son back from the dead if necessary. Abraham was a man of faith.

What has faith got to do with our families? It's what makes them Christian families.

When a man and a woman pledge themselves to each other for life in the sacrament of matrimony, they do so with the confidence that God will be part of their relationship until death parts them. Marriage is not just an act of faith in the partner, but in God as well.

Because of what their faith teaches them about the worth and dignity of each human life, they can be sure that their children will be as precious to God as they are to themselves. When their children are baptized, the parents take joy in the realization that these children are extensions of the life of Christ, each gifted with his or her own part to play in God's providence.

When hard times come in the family—sickness, uncertainty, misunderstanding—the family members can all take confidence in the ongoing care of the Lord whom they have come to know in faith, a God who can bring amazing consequences out of the least promising situations.

Faith doesn't make everything clear and easy in our families. Not everything was clear and easy in Abraham's family, and Mary and Joseph in today's gospel seem to have been troubled ("amazed") about what Simeon had to say about the infant Jesus. We don't get to understand everything right now. More often than not we don't get to see in detail how God is going to take care of us. But because we know God, because we have entrusted ourselves to him, because we know how he operates, because we are people of faith, we are confident that our family history will have a happy ending. That's what we celebrate today.

What role does faith play in my family?

Have I experienced God at work in my family's history?

The Holy Family of Jesus, Mary and Joseph (Optional C)

I John 3:1-2, 21-24

Each of the Gospel readings provided for the feast of the Holy Family in the three-year lectionary cycle provides an incident from the childhood of Jesus. For Year A it is the flight into Egypt; for Year B the presentation of the Child in the temple; for Year C the finding of the child Jesus in the temple. Each of these Gospel readings deals with the relationship of Jesus to Mary and Joseph and each of them teaches us something special about his identity.

The second (optional) reading for Year C, from First John, has to do with identity also, but its subject is our identity. In this letter the rambling, wise old author repeats the lessons of wisdom that his life in the Lord has taught him. Today's reading is from the beginning and the end of chapter 3, where he is talking about the implications of our being children of God.

First of all, at the beginning of the chapter, he says that being children of God is a gift we have received from a loving God. It's not something that the world sets great store by, because God isn't important to the world. But being God's children is not some sort of inert prize that God has given us. It is something that grows and develops to an extent that will only become clear at the end of time when God himself is fully revealed.

The verses from the end of chapter 3 deal with certain practical implications of our relationship to God as his children. Certain standards of behavior are expected of us and the observance of those standards brings with it a certain level of contentment and confidence because we know that we are striving to do what pleases God. The behavior that we are called to is contained in two basic commandments: Believe in Christ and love our neighbor. Those who do this remain in a family relationship with God and God remains in them through the Holy Spirit that is conferred on them.

It's important for each of us to know who we are, because if we lose sight of who we are, our lives are without direction and we merely drift through them. Most of us know our parents and families. We have memories of our own growth and development. We are aware of the people to whom we relate in our present life. All this contributes to our identity. It tells us who we are.

But there are other elements to our identity that are not so obvious, elements which we might overlook, but which are nonetheless more important than other facets of our identity that are more clear and present to us. The most important feature of our identity is that we are children of God, not just in the sense that God is our creator, but in the sense that God has given us his own life to live through Christ and the Holy Spirit. We belong to the Lord. We belong with the Lord. Our association with the Lord is what gives meaning and direction to our life now and what will constitute our fulfillment and happiness for all eternity. Everything else is secondary to that. Everything else is less important.

This fundamental spiritual identity that we have received from God offers direction for the way in which we are to spend our life. The most important thing for us is to believe in Jesus. This faith (which is not just a matter of accepting certain truths but also of committing ourselves to the Lord Jesus) is what keeps us in touch with our source and goal. If we reject faith, we are no longer children of God, and we are condemned to wander through our life on our own. The second primary commandment is that we love our neighbor, that is, that we extend ourselves to want and to do good to all those who are God's children and so are our brothers and sisters. Just as God looks after the world and the human beings he has created, so must we do also because we share God's life. Loving runs in the family. One might say it's God's family business.

Christian life can get tense and complicated. Often it seems that the Church demands so much of us, that the moral code we are called to observe gets so complicated. We never seem able to grasp fully what Jesus teaches us. There are always further implications of his life and preaching to learn and assimilate. Our relationship with an increasingly complex world around us seems itself to grow ever more complex. Who are we, anyway? Where are we supposed to be going?

Identity questions can get very painful. Yet our identity is clear: We are children of God, brothers and sisters to the Lord Jesus. Living out the implications of that is what constitutes our Christian existence. God has given us some basic directions ("Believe in Jesus and love one another"), and following those directions will keep us in touch with our identity and its demands.

The important thing to remember is that it's all gift. We don't have to work hard to make ourselves children of God. We simply have to strive as God has commanded us to respond to the identity that we have already received.

FOR DISCUSSION AND REFLECTION

How do I experience and express my identity as a child of God?
How does my faith affect my relationships with the people around me?

Solemnity of the Blessed Virgin Mary, the Mother of God (ABC)

Galatians 4:4-7

The octave day of Christmas has been celebrated under various headings in the history of the Church. For some time its title was the Feast of the Circumcision. Our Episcopalian brothers and sisters call it the feast of the Holy Name of our Lord Jesus Christ. Beginning in 1968 the popes have designated January 1 as a World Day of Prayer for Peace. Originally, however, it was a Marian feast, the oldest Marian feast in the Roman liturgy. In the renewed liturgical calendar it is the Solemnity of the Blessed Virgin Mary, the Mother of God.

On this day we celebrate relationships: the relationship between Jesus and his mother, between Jesus and the Jewish people, between Jesus and us, between ourselves and Jesus, between ourselves and the Holy Trinity.

The Gospel reading is the same reading we heard at the dawn Mass on Christmas, with the addition of the verse about Jesus' circumcision, the cultic act that made him a member of the people of Abraham. This ritual relationship serves as the jumping off point of the second reading from Paul's letter to the Galatians.

Apparently some Jewish Christian missionaries had come to Paul's converts in Galatia and were telling them that, in order to be true followers of Christ, they had to observe certain elements of the Jewish law, including circumcision. Paul replies that the Jewish law was a temporary expedient in God's plan that had no power in itself to gain God's favor and blessings. It was a kind of training program that would come to an end when God's plan reached its final stage in Christ.

In the verses that immediately precede our second reading, Paul uses an image from the social customs of his time. A rich man would appoint in his will a guardian for his son who, in the event of the father's death, would administer the son's inheritance until he came of age. Even though the son was entitled to vast wealth, he was no better than a slave. Paul goes on to say that, until God's people came of age, they, too, were slaves, subject not only to the Mosaic law but to the constraints of sin that are so powerful in the world.

This is where our reading begins. Paul tells the Galatians that God sent his Son, born at a certain specific time of a certain specific woman, to end the time of slavery. Through Christ, we are no longer slaves but have become sons and daughters of God. We are adopted into God's family and so are able to speak intimately with the Father through God's own Holy Spirit who now lives in our hearts.

Our salvation is a matter of relationships: Jesus' relationships and our relationship to him. Jesus is the only begotten Son of the Father, yet, through the humanity that he took from his mother, he became a human being, one of us. He spent his life as a Jew, subject to the demands of the Jewish law, starting with circumcision. But he didn't just relate to his own people, but to all of humankind. He came to save and free us all. When he becomes our brother he invites us to become his brothers and sisters, brothers and sisters to the man Jesus, but also brothers and sisters to the Jesus who is God. We become members of God's household and live in the community of Father, Son and Holy Spirit. The temporary and provisional demands of the Jewish law are now irrelevant and the powers of our sinful world have no more control over us. We are free of all that because we are now relatives of God, members of God's household. We can address God as "Father" just as the Holy Spirit of Jesus does.

In our culture, our social standing does not depend on the family we are born into. Being lucky enough to be born to wealth does help some, of course, and having parents who care for us and raise us well is important. But being born into nobility or prominence of some sort doesn't really matter much. What really matters is what we achieve for ourselves, what we "make of ourselves." In the context of our salvation, it's just the opposite.

We can observe all the moral laws we want and spend our whole lives struggling to be religious, but it doesn't mean a thing unless we somehow belong to the right family, the divine family of Jesus, the family of Father, Son and Holy Spirit.

The linkage between us and Jesus is our humanness. We are capable of sharing the divinity of Christ because he was willing to share in our humanity. We can become his relatives because he became our relative. That overlap provides the contact point between God and us that God used to free us from slavery and give us an eternal inheritance in his household. That saving humanity of Jesus was the gift of Mary. Our human link with Jesus is on his mother's side.

Today we don't just commemorate the fact that a woman named Mary happened to be the mother of Jesus. We celebrate Mary and what we celebrate is that it was she who made it possible for us to become relatives of God.

FOR DISCUSSION AND REFLECTION

How do I celebrate Mary's role in my salvation?

How does my relationship with Jesus involve relationships with other people?

Epiphany of the Lord (ABC)

Ephesians 3:2-3a, 5-6

The feast of the Epiphany celebrates the call of the gentiles to salvation. In the Gospel reading we hear how the magi came, not without difficulty, to offer homage to the infant Jesus. They were from a far distant land, out of nowhere, as it were, but, through God's guidance, they were led to the "newborn king" in Bethlehem. Somehow this child was of immense importance to them. In the Epiphany narrative, Matthew teaches us that Jesus is the one source of salvation and that this salvation is intended for the whole world. There is one plan of salvation and it applies to everybody. Epiphany celebrates the unity and universality of God's plan.

That's what our apostolic letter talks about. The letter to the Ephesians (which we will read at length later in this year of the lectionary cycle) is about the Church. In the section we read on this day, Paul is talking about his role in preaching the good news, and, in that context, enunciates and underlines the themes of the feast.

He says, in effect, "I, together with other spokesmen for God, have been given a mission for your benefit. That mission is to make public the secret of God's plan that has been revealed to us. It is something that has not been manifested until now. That secret plan, now made known to us, is that salvation—belonging to God's family, being members of the body of Christ, becoming eligible for the gifts that Christ offers—is directed to the gentiles as well as to the Jews."

There is one salvation, salvation in Christ, and that salvation is universal. Everybody is called. Everybody qualifies. Nobody is excluded from God's offer of intimacy. That's what we celebrate at Epiphany: the one call of all people of all times to share in the one saving life of Christ.

"That's nice," we think. "It's good of God to include us twenty-first century American Catholics in his plan of salvation." But working out the implications of the unity and universality of salvation for twenty-first century Americans is not without its challenges. The main challenge, the main obstacle to the proper assimilation of what we celebrate today is particularism, the tendency to let narrower and smaller realities get in the way of our appreciation of and response to God's universal plan for salvation. We tend to forget that the flip side of God's inclusion of us in his plan is the inclusion of everybody else as well.

One manifestation of unhealthy particularism is nationalism. Our nation is better than your nation. Defending our rights is more important than anything else. The love and care we are invited to have for others who have been called to share God's life, that is, all of humankind, takes second place to national interest. We see signs of this when our country enters an armed conflict. Almost spontaneously we presume that we are right and "they" are wrong. One wonders sometimes whether most of us do not see ourselves as Americans first and Christian believers second. This is not to say that patriotism has no place in the Christian life, but that our love for our country has to be practiced in the broader context of our love for God.

Then there is the ecumenical question. Thanks to human error, differing approaches to theology and historical circumstances, including nationalism, the one Church of Christ is divided into many particular Christian denominations. Vatican II teaches us that the Church founded by Christ "subsists in the Catholic Church" (*Lumen Gentium*, no. 8) but it acknowledges a relationship with other Christians "who do not profess the faith in its entirety or do not preserve unity of communion with the successor of Peter" (*Lumen Gentium*, no. 14). It points out elsewhere (*Unitatis Redintegratio*, no. 1), however, that, while "many Christian communions present themselves to men as the true heritage of Jesus Christ, ... their convictions clash and their paths diverge as though Christ himself were divided. Without doubt, this discord openly contradicts the will of Christ." A divided and particularized Christianity is not part of God's plan. It is almost impossible to imagine how a reunited Christianity could come about, yet that is what we are expected to work and pray for.

Finally, there is the particularism of the parish. The parish is the most common unit of the Church's corporate life, but it is necessarily part of something bigger: the local diocesan church and the Church universal. Often Catholics seem to think that the whole plan of salvation is centered in their congregation, and that concern for the wider Church is optional or even counterproductive. Sometimes we seem so attentive to the demands of our parish that we have no energy left to pay attention to the Church.

God's call, God's salvation, God's Church is more embracing than we sometimes think. The feast of Epiphany invites all of us to widen our horizons.

FOR DISCUSSION AND REFLECTION

What difference does the universality of God's call to salvation make to me?

How does my parish look beyond its own immediate interests?

The Baptism of the Lord (A)

Acts 10:34-38

The feast of the Baptism of the Lord is not an ancient celebration in the calendar of the Western church. Originally Jesus' baptism was celebrated together with the miracle at Cana on January 6. These two events constituted subsidiary themes to the adoration of the Magi. They were further expressions of the overall theme of the manifestation of Jesus' divinity and power. A separate observance of Jesus' baptism was assigned to January 13, the octave day of Epiphany, in 1960. In the liturgical reforms of Vatican II, the celebration of the Baptism of the Lord was assigned to the Sunday after January 6. If Epiphany happens to fall on that Sunday, the Baptism of the Lord is celebrated on the following Monday.

The second reading for this celebration in each of the three years of the lectionary's cycle (unless the optional readings for Years B and C are used) is a reading from the Acts of the Apostles. Though large sections of Acts are used each year in the first readings for the Sundays after Easter, this feast is the only time that Acts is used as a source for a Sunday's second reading.

The reason is that this reading from Acts 11 is the only time that Jesus' baptism is referred to in the New Testament outside the Gospels. (Some scholars think that Acts 1:22 is also a reference to the baptism of Jesus by John, but this does not seem to be certain.)

In our reading we find Peter preaching to the gentile Cornelius and his household. Peter and Cornelius have been brought together by visions from God. Peter now enunciates the basic lesson that God seems to be teaching them: Persons of every nation are included in God's will for salvation.

Peter hastens to observe that God's project of salvation was proclaimed to the Jews, all over Judea and Galilee, by Jesus. The proclamation started with Jesus' baptism by John when God identified and equipped Jesus as the Messiah. (This is the significance of Jesus' being "anointed...with the Holy Spirit and power.") After that initial manifestation, Jesus engaged in a ministry of healing and exorcism.

Our liturgical reading ends here, but Peter's speech in Acts goes on to describe how Jesus died and rose from the dead and how the significance and power of Jesus' ministry has continued to be announced by his apostles.

It would not be incorrect to say that the feast of the Baptism of the Lord is the feast of continuity. Its placement at the closure of the Christmas season and at the beginning of Ordinary Time reassures us that the Jesus whose birth we have just celebrated is the same Jesus who preached the saving plan of the Father through his public ministry. Peter's assurance to Cornelius that "every nation" is "acceptable" to God suggests that we, too, are being addressed by the same Savior who was identified as Messiah by God's voice as he was being baptized by John in the Jordan.

It's all of a single piece. It all hangs together. It all constitutes one continuous story: Jesus' birth, his baptism, his ministry, his death and resurrection, his proclamation by his first followers, his offer of himself to every nation through the agency of his Church. It's all part of God's one project of salvation.

Jesus and his Father are as much concerned about our salvation, here and now, as they were about the salvation of the first Jew and gentile believers back then. Jesus is Messiah for us as he was for them. The public ministry that began with the baptism of Jesus still continues through the agency of his Church. There is a great, overarching continuity of ministry and mission being exercised by God on our behalf.

But we are not passive recipients in all this. We are also workers in the project. Because each of us shares the one, continuous life of the risen Christ, we also share his mission. We are called, as the apostles were, to be witnesses to his presence, his power, his providence for us. Together with each other, together with Christ, all believers constitute the one body of the Church that is the body of Christ. We, too, like Christ, have been anointed "with the Holy Spirit and power."

Some Christian believers seem to have the impression that only the ordained or only those who engage in formal, professional ministry are responsible for carrying on the mission of Jesus. They think that the rest, the vast majority of the Church's embers, are there to take advantage of what the Church and its ministers offer them, to go shopping in the vast spiritual supermarket into which God has invited them. This is not authentic Christianity. Real faith and real commitment involve continuity with Christ, that is, consciously being part of the ministry of Jesus, deliberately carrying out the mission to which he was called, sharing in the mission of his Church. The public life of Jesus that began when he was baptized by John still continues—in us.

FOR DISCUSSION AND REFLECTION

Where do I find the ministry of Jesus in my life?

How do I participate in the Church's continuation of Jesus' ministry?

The Baptism of the Lord (Optional B)

I John 5:1-9

The feast of the Baptism of the Lord is a kind of overlap celebration. We again see John the Baptist, whom we last met on the Third Sunday of Advent. We mark the closure of Jesus' hidden life that began at Christmas, and continue the manifestation theme of Epiphany. And we begin Ordinary Time, that part of the Church's year in which the Gospels present to us the public life and preaching of Jesus.

When Jesus received baptism from John it was a sign of his association of himself with sinful humanity, but also the sign of the beginning of his public participation in the religious life of his time. It marked the official, public beginning of his ministry of salvation. The importance of the occasion was marked by the Spirit descending upon him in the form of a dove and by the voice from heaven that proclaimed that Jesus was God's beloved Son.

The optional apostolic reading for Year B is from the first letter of John, which we will be hearing from again six times on the Sundays after Easter. It's a somewhat rambling and repetitious letter, and the selection for today is a difficult passage. Of passages like this, Saint Augustine says that if they "were not cloaked in mystery, they would never be searched in earnest. And if they weren't searched in earnest, they would not be opened up with such pleasure" (Sermon 8.18). Let's now search in earnest.

This passage seems to have been chosen for today because it alludes to the baptism of Jesus. Its author presumes that his readers are familiar with the Gospel of John.

The first part of the reading is about faith and love. We are made children of God through faith in Jesus. If we love our Father, we should also love the children who are like him. This love, both of the Father and of the Father's children, is marked by keeping the commandments. These commandments are not a burden, but a means of our overcoming the sinfulness of the world even as Jesus overcame the sinfulness of the world. We are victorious because he was victorious.

But how do we know he was victorious? Because God has testified to his victory and that's a testimony we ought to accept. And how did God testify to the success of Jesus' mission? For one thing, there was the witness of the Spirit who proclaimed Jesus' sonship at his baptism. But there was more to Jesus' mission than the public announcement of it when he was baptized by John. Jesus also carried out his mission in his saving death for us, a death whose meaning was expressed when Jesus "delivered over the Spirit" to the world (see John 19:30), and when, together with his sacrificial blood, the living water that he had promised (see John 7:38) came forth from his side (see John 19:34). Here, then, are three witnesses to the authenticity of Jesus' mission from the Father: the Spirit, the living water and the self-sacrificial blood. These witnesses certify and validate the work of Jesus in conquering sin. They are witnesses that call for our response of faith, a faith that makes us children of the Father.

The earthly ministry of Jesus stretched from his baptism by John until his human death, in both of which God's Spirit participated. In his death, Jesus "delivered over the Spirit" to those who would believe in him. This gift of the Spirit that arose out of the death of Jesus is still conferred on believers of today "through water and blood," that is, through the sacraments of baptism and the Eucharist. The saving mission of Jesus continues and the sign of its continuation is the ongoing gift of the Spirit in his sacramental ministry of today. Spirit, water and blood still give witness to God's will to make us his children, called to love one another in him.

One of the lessons inherent in the Church's observance of "Ordinary Time," which begins with the celebration of Jesus' baptism, is that the ministry of Jesus is still going on. As we listen to the Gospel readings from Mark (with some supplementary passages from John) during this Year B, we need to be aware that it is not just an account of past happenings that is presented. It is

Jesus addressing himself to us, inviting our response of faith as he invited the response of the people of his time. Our live letter today, which serves as a commentary on the gospel reading, invites us to a renewed appreciation of that ministry of Jesus that began with the baptism of John and ended on the cross. The Spirit that testified to the sonship of Jesus is the Spirit that is offered to us to enable us to give continued testimony in our lives to Jesus and to his ongoing work of salvation. Jesus' gift of life in baptism and his gift of himself in the Eucharist are the means by which Jesus extends his mission to us and enables us in turn to carry it on as his brothers and sisters in our heavenly Father. This celebration of the beginning of Jesus' public ministry is not just about Jesus. It's about us, too.

FOR DISCUSSION AND REFLECTION

How do I carry on the mission of Jesus?

How are baptism and Eucharist signs of Jesus' victory over the sinfulness of the world?

The Baptism of the Lord (Optional C)

Titus 2:11-14, 3:4-7

The feast of the Baptism of the Lord is a pivotal celebration in the Church's liturgical year. It marks the conclusion of the hidden life of Christ (which we have commemorated during the Christmas season) and the beginning of his public ministry (which we will relive with him during Ordinary Time).

The birth, life, ministry, death and resurrection of Jesus were all directed toward our salvation, toward delivering us from our natural, inherited subjection to sin, toward giving us a new value that God would treasure forever. The optional second reading that the lectionary offers us for Year C is about salvation.

This reading is from the letter to Titus, a short book of the New Testament from which only two readings are selected for public proclamation in the liturgy. The first (2:11-14) is used at midnight Mass on Christmas, the second (3:4-7) at the dawn Mass on Christmas. Our reading for the Baptism of the Lord in Year C is a combination and repetition of these two readings.

The letter to Titus (whether authored by Saint Paul personally, or by one of his disciples) encourages Titus to be careful about the kinds of people he assigns to leadership in the church and to promote healthy relationships among the various groups that constitute church membership. The two separate passages that make up this Sunday's reading give the reason why Titus should be so careful in choosing fellow workers and so diligent in encouraging cooperation among church members: it's all connected with salvation. These two passages (which form our Sunday reading) offer the theological underpinnings for the advice that Titus is given.

There is a certain parallelism between the passages, and a degree of repetitiousness, but they form a single teaching about salvation that seems to be expressed in four points. First, salvation has come into our midst with Jesus, a salvation directed toward everybody. It is a salvation that involves liberation from sin and the constitution of a new chosen people, characterized by goodness. Second, what Jesus came to bring us is gratuitous. We don't earn it or deserve it. It comes with baptism, through which Jesus gives us the Holy Spirit as a gift, a gift that makes us holy. Third, the salvation that Jesus gives demands certain kinds of behavior: the rejection of deliberate sin and the pursuit of an ordered life in our relationships with ourselves, our neighbor and the Lord. Finally, although we have already received salvation, there is still more to come, a further gift that will be given us when Jesus comes in glory at the end of time and we enter the fullness and finality of life in heaven with him.

It may well be that salvation is the central, fundamental,

basic, all encompassing truth of Christian revelation, the elemental reality that explains everything, the chief energy source that drives all Christian activity and directs it toward its proper end.

Jesus was born to bring salvation to all humanity. He lived, taught, died and rose from the dead to carry out that mission, to enable all of us to share in his life, human and divine. He instituted his Church to continue the offer of salvation to all human beings of all times and places.

If bringing salvation was the fundamental purpose of Jesus' life, accepting salvation and cultivating it in ourselves is the basic purpose of our lives as Christians. Just as everything that Jesus did was directed toward our salvation, so everything we do is supposed to be directed toward accepting that salvation, toward sharing it with others in our world, toward participating in its final, definitive manifestation in the eternal glory of Christ.

Salvation isn't just one more thing in our lives as believers, one more item on the Christian agenda. Salvation is the agenda. Bringing salvation to humankind, offering us a chance to reverse the choices made by our first parents, giving us the opportunity to live the life of God through our sharing in the life of Christ: that's the agenda of salvation; that's the agenda that Christ came to carry out. Our agenda as Catholic Christian believers is also the agenda of salvation, not earning it but accepting it, not giving it (together with other religious values) a high prority but making it the main priority of all. The agenda of salvation is what impels us toward avoiding sin and living a virtuous life, not in order to keep the rules and make God pleased with us, but in order to be consistent with the saving life of Jesus with which we have been gifted. The agenda of salvation involves reaching out to others to share our faith and hope and love with them, not because we feel obliged to do so, but because the life of Christ impels us to do so, because the life and energy of Christ within us make us both saved and saving.

The Baptism of the Lord, straddling both Christmas and

Ordinary Time, reminds us of what the birth and public life of Jesus were all about: salvation. It reminds us of what we are all about, too.

FOR DISCUSSION AND REFLECTION

What does salvation mean to me?

How do I respond to it?

PART THREE

Lent

First Sunday of Lent (A)

Romans 5:12-19

Lent is a season of particularly intense spiritual effort in the life of the Church. Before anything else, it is a time of final preparation for those who will become members of God's people through baptism at Easter. But it is also a time for penance and change of heart for those who are already members of the Church. In addition to that, Lent provides, especially in its closing weeks, an orientation toward the celebration of Christ's passion, death and resurrection.

The Gospel readings, especially in Year A, have been chosen to illustrate the various facets of conversion and initiation. The Old Testament readings give us an annual overview of God's dealings with humanity and the first chosen people before the coming of Christ. The second readings, our live letters, serve to illustrate one or both of the other two readings.

This Sunday's second reading is clearly intended as a commentary on the first reading. In the first reading we hear about the sin of Adam and Eve. In the second reading Paul teaches us about the implications of that sin and about our salvation from it in Christ. (Almost all of Paul's letter to the Romans is concerned somehow with salvation. Romans is a formal overview of Paul's teaching about this fundamental aspect of our faith, a survey course addressed to a local church he had not yet been in personal touch with. We'll be hearing a lot from Romans later this year.)

Our reading begins with an explanation of the meaning of what Adam had done. Adam deliberately disobeyed God's command. He sinned. This sin destroyed the special relationship that Adam and Eve had enjoyed with God. It killed it and so brought into the world not only sin but death as well, both physical and spiritual death. Everybody participates in this death not only because of their descent from Adam but also because of their own individual sinfulness.

In a short digression, Paul now points out that those who are not aware of God's directives, for example, people who lived before God gave the Law to Moses, are not technically guilty of "sin" (which involves deliberate disobedience to a command) but are still subject to death that Adam's sin brought about.

Then Paul begins to talk about the undoing of Adam's sin by lining up parallels and contrasts between Adam and Christ. Sin and death entered the world through one man, Adam. Grace and new life entered the world through one man, Christ. But there is a difference between what Adam brought and what Christ brought. Adam was involved in one sin that brought condemnation to many. Christ had to deal with many sins (the sins of all the world, in fact) in order to restore life in God. In Adam we have sin and the destruction of God's life in us. In Christ we have reconciliation and new life. What Christ did was greater than what Adam did because Adam, through disobedience, brought destruction and slavery while Christ, through obedience, brought new life and freedom.

Paul's message is an important one as we begin the observance of Lent. It is a simple message, but one that we all have to assimilate. The message is that we all need salvation and that salvation comes through Christ Jesus.

Those not yet baptized need to be incorporated into the Church in order to share the saving life of Christ, the life that constitutes salvation. Those who are already in the community need to refocus their awareness of their ongoing need of life in Christ and of their ongoing vulnerability to the effects of sinfulness that remain in them. We all need to be aware that our liberation from what Adam inflicted on us, that is, a state of false independence and phony self-sufficiency, can only come through God's gift and that that gift has been provided for us through the lifelong obedience of Christ to his Father's will. (Those who have not had an opportunity to know Christ can be saved, too, but even their salvation comes through Christ.)

If we forget about our need for salvation, or begin to act as if we can provide salvation for ourselves, we are headed right back into the valley of solitude and death that Adam entered when his sin got him expelled from Eden. This is why we need a season of Lent each year: to remind us of who and what we are, where we have come from and where God wants us to be headed.

Salvation and the need for salvation are among the most central and basic aspects of our Christian faith. They provide the rationale for the incarnation of the Second Person of the Trinity, for his life and death. They enable us to have some understanding of why God has provided us with revelation, the sacraments, the loving support and encouragement of our fellow Christians. Salvation and the need for salvation provide the justification for our struggle to enter the heavenly kingdom where those who share Christ's life will live together forever.

If we don't understand salvation and the need for salvation, we can't understand redemption. In fact, we can't understand very much at all.

FOR DISCUSSION AND REFLECTION

How do I experience a need for salvation?

How do I experience salvation in Christ?

First Sunday of Lent (B)

I Peter 3:18-22

The Church's liturgy offers us three basic and recurrent themes or agenda items during the season of Lent. Lent is, first of all, a time of final preparation for those who will be baptized at the Easter Vigil. It is also a time of repentance and re-focusing for those who have already been baptized, a call for them to renew their baptismal fervor. Finally, it is a season for getting ready to celebrate once more the central events of the mission of Jesus: His suffering, death and resurrection. Baptism, repentance, Christ's death and resurrection: That's what Lent is all about.

In the liturgical readings for this season, the gospels highlight various aspects of these three themes. The Old Testament readings have not been chosen to complement the gospels, as is the case for the rest of the year, but rather to provide a more or less independent survey of the history of salvation, a review of the interventions of God in human history that led up to redemption in Christ. The readings from the letters of the apostles, the Introduction to the lectionary (no. 97) tells us, "have been selected to fit" the other readings "and, to the extent possible, to provide a connection between them." However, while our live letters are intended to straddle or link the other two readings during Lent, they sometimes have a way of inclining more to one of them than to the other. Our reading for this Sunday, for example, is more closely connected (via the allusion to Noah and the flood) with the Old Testament reading than with the gospel.

The first letter of Peter was written in Rome by Peter or one of his followers and is intended to offer encouragement to Christians in distant provinces of the Roman Empire who were finding difficulty in the profession of their faith. Most scholars look on it as a baptismal sermon cast in letter form. (The Church reads at greater length from First Peter on the Sundays after Easter in Year A.)

In the section we read today, the author is calling on his listeners to find encouragement in the risen life of Christ that they share. He is apparently quoting and commenting on an early formula for the profession of faith.

This profession of faith seems to have proclaimed Jesus as the one whose unique suffering and death put sinners back in touch with God. His life continued in the Holy Spirit. He proclaimed his triumph over sin to "the spirits in prison," and took his place in heaven to rule over the angels. Jesus' ministry was a cosmic event.

"The spirits in prison" is thought to be a reference to the wicked angels who had relations with earthly women (see Genesis 6:1 and following) and whose sinfulness led God to send the great flood. Jews of the first century seemed to have looked on these fallen angels as the origin and source of heathenism. Christ's "preaching" to them was to announce their final defeat, the ultimate annihilation of their power.

The author uses the connection with Noah to speak of baptism. Noah and the few others chosen by God were saved by the water that kept the ark afloat. Likewise, Christians are saved by the water of baptism, which is not a means of ordinary cleanliness but a bath that offers believers the opportunity to live without sin through their association with the triumphant risen Christ.

This is a difficult and complex Scripture passage, but several things are clear. In the general context of the letter, the author is calling on his readers to live nobly and courageously. Here he invites them to take confidence in the awareness that they have been delivered from evil as Noah was, that their deliverance comes through the cosmic triumph of Christ, and that this deliverance calls on them to serve God with a clear conscience, without sin. This reading, therefore, deals with the basic Lenten themes of baptism and detachment from sin.

There is no power in creation that can separate us from God. Whatever the powers of evil may be, we have been delivered from them through the baptismal washing that unites us to the risen Christ. Our own weaknesses and vulnerabilities are now secondary because we live in the Christ who overcame the primeval forces of evil and who now reigns in heaven. We are called to be aware of what Christ has done for us, to take courage in it and to live in accordance with what he has made us to be.

Traditionally Catholics have the practice of "doing something for Lent." It may be denying ourselves some minor pleasures or giving more attention to prayer or reaching out more energetically to those in various kinds of need. This is all well and good. But the real essence of Lent for those of us who are already baptized is a renewal of heart, a re-focusing on the basic meaning and implications of our existence in the Lord. This Sunday's reading offers us some basics to reflect on.

FOR DISCUSSION AND REFLECTION

How do I see Christ as deliverer in my life?

How does being baptized make me courageous?

First Sunday of Lent (C)

Romans 10:8-13

During lent our live letters again enter into relationship with the other readings. We no longer have a series of selections from one single letter for several weeks in a row as we have in Ordinary Time. Instead, the second readings are sometimes chosen to highlight the first reading which, for the first five weeks of Lent, is a review of Old Testament salvation history. Sometimes they highlight the Gospel reading that is concerned with the Lenten themes of baptism, repentance and preparation for the observance of the passion, death and resurrection of Jesus.

Today's second reading reflects the theme of the first reading. In this week's first reading from Deuteronomy we learn that worth in God's eyes was constituted by being a member of the Jewish people and by deliberately attaching oneself to the history of that people, being or becoming a participant in what God did for them. In our second reading, we learn that, with Christ, a new criterion of identity or membership came into play.

In this part of Romans Paul has been reflecting on the relationship of Jews and gentiles with God's plan of salvation. No longer is observance of the rules and regulations of the Old Law required for salvation. Now it is faith in Christ that makes us acceptable to God. This is not to say that Jews are excluded from saving grace and holiness, but that access to salvation comes to us all through the acceptance of Jesus as Lord and Messiah. Paul seeks to demonstrate his point by citing passages from the Old Testament to show that God's present plan was already foreseen in the former covenant.

As our passage begins he quotes Deuteronomy (30:14) to the effect that God's approach to us, his word, is not something far away but already in our mouths and in our hearts. Then he says that the word that Deuteronomy was speaking of was the word of faith in Christ that he, Paul, had been sent to proclaim. If we believe in our hearts what Paul preached about the death and resurrection of Jesus and openly profess the belief that Jesus is Lord of heaven and earth, we shall be saved or justified. That's how salvation comes to us!

Then he offers another quote, this one from Isaiah (28:16), which he had already used at the end of chapter 9: "No one who believes in him will be put to shame." This quotation says two things: first, that it is *belief* that brings security (that is, salvation); second, that belief brings security (that is, salvation) *for everybody*.

It is this second idea that Paul develops now. Belief in the Lord Jesus is the source of salvation for *everybody*, Jew and non-Jew alike. The same Lord enriches *all* believers. You don't have to be a Jew to be saved, but if you are a Jew, your salvation comes in the same way it comes to the gentiles: through faith.

Finally, by way of summary, still another Old Testament quotation (Joel 3:5) that reflects Isaiah: it is calling on the name of the Lord that brings salvation for everyone without exception.

This reading from Romans, chosen as a commentary on the Old Testament reading for this Sunday, is also highly appropriate for the first Sunday of Lent. Lent is a time of rededication and redirection for Christian believers and of final preparation for those who will enter the Church at Easter, and this reading is about the very fundamentals of our Christian life.

We are not Christian believers because we have carried out certain ritual observances nor because we observe certain rules and regulations. We are Christian believers because of our faith in Christ, that is, our acceptance of the truth of his teaching and our response to his offer to us of participation in his life here and hereafter. We are Christian believers because we acknowledge that Jesus is Lord. It is this commitment of ourselves to him in mind and heart that gives our life its basic meaning and direction. Everything else about us is secondary.

But being in Christ is not just a private and secret arrangement between us and him. It is a relationship that we are called to profess, to manifest in ways that other people can see and hear, that other people can imitate. We profess our faith in lots of different ways. The most basic is our membership in the new people of God that we call the Church. We also profess our faith by the way in which we carry out its demands in our social life, in our work, in our recreation. Our willingness to talk about our faith with non-believers and to let them perceive what the lordship of Jesus means to us are also ways in which we profess our faith. Each of us probably also has his or her own special ways of proclaiming our faith, connected with the specifics of our individual human existence. But external profession must be there if the faith that is in our hearts is to have any meaning.

Lent is a time of reflection and renewal for Catholic Christians. It's a good time to think about what we believe, and how we believe, and why we believe. It's a good time, too, to review the ways in which we profess what we believe.

FOR DISCUSSION AND REFLECTION

What does it mean to me to say, "Jesus is Lord"?

In what specific ways do I profess my faith?

Second Sunday of Lent (A)

II Timothy 1:8b-10

This Sunday's first reading is concerned with God's call of
Abraham, a call that would entail leaving the home he knew and
moving ahead toward the promises that God was making to him.
The Gospel reading for this Sunday shows us Jesus transfigured
on the mountaintop in the presence of his principal followers. Our
second reading bridges the two themes of vocation (our calling by
God) and of the manifestation of Christ.

In this reading from Second Timothy we have Paul (or
someone writing in his name) offering encouragement to a junior
apostle.

The reading begins with a sentence that sums up the
preceding paragraph in which the author has been encouraging
Timothy to be confident and courageous in his proclamation of
the gospel.

Timothy has reason to be confident, the text says, because
his calling to salvation and holiness does not depend on his own
resources, but on the planning and generosity of God. This is a
long-range plan that God prepared "before time began." It was a
plan that would find fulfillment in Christ Jesus. This plan has
now been made public through Jesus' manifestation of himself.
Jesus' work consists in bringing us into a new kind of unending
life and in destroying the former kind of life that was bounded by
death. Jesus does this through the proclamation of the gospel.
This reading from Second Timothy is deeply appropriate for the
Lenten season of preparation for baptism (for those entering the
Church at Easter) and of repentance and change of heart (for
those of us already members of the community of faith). It
continues the instruction that began last Sunday about the nature
of salvation and holds up three aspects of salvation for our
reflection.

First and foremost, our salvation consists in a holy life, that
is, a godly life. Being saved means being created again in a new

likeness to God. It means expressing and extending the life of God in our individual earthly existence. This life of God comes to us through our incorporation into the life of the risen Christ. The gospel that brings us "life and immortality" is the announcement of the presence of God in our midst through the life and ministry of Jesus. This is what God had in mind for us "before time began" and what is now being made clear and accessible to us through the saving initiative of Jesus. The transfiguration of Jesus that the apostles witnessed on the mountaintop was a preview of the transfiguration that all of us would be called to share through Jesus' gift of himself to us through faith and baptism.

The second aspect of salvation that this live letter offers us is the insistence that the newness of life in Christ that constitutes salvation comes to us as a gift from God and not "according to our works." Obviously we have a part to play in our own salvation, but that part consists in response, not initiative. When we strive to follow God's law in moral behavior, when we pray, when we reach out in generosity to our brothers and sisters, when we strive to improve the tone and vigor of our personal spirituality in times of penance, we are not achieving salvation for ourselves. Rather, we are responding to the salvation that God is either offering us or has already bestowed on us.

It's important that we stay aware of the gratuitous nature of salvation, because, if we don't, if we begin to think that we can deserve it, we are saying false things either about ourselves or about salvation. If salvation is a share in God's life, we simply cannot deserve it. It's totally beyond us, even as God is totally beyond us. God is not something we can reach out and harvest like an apple from a tree. To think that God is Someone or Something that is subject to acquisition by our human efforts is nothing less than blasphemous. Conversely, if we are able to earn salvation for ourselves, then it must be something considerably less awesome than Jesus and his Church lead us to believe. Everything that human effort can achieve on its own is tainted by sin, blighted by selfishness. Look at how limited and transitory the greatest human accomplishments are. Look at how everything human beings carry out is capable of being turned around for our own destruction. If human effort can buy or earn salvation, we need to ask ourselves whether that kind of salvation will prove to be worth the effort.

The third aspect of salvation that this reading offers us comes at the very beginning. "Bear your share of hardships...with the strength that comes from God." We live in a sinful and selfish world. God seems strange and distant to many people, and men and women who are reaching out in faith and commitment often seem to be living in a dream world. The circumstances in which we live make it difficult to profess the gospel. Then there are the elements inside each of us—inclinations to sin and selfishness, prejudices that make it hard for us to think correctly, superficiality that makes the things of God unappealing—that make responding to God a real struggle. Today God's word assures us that God loves us so much that he will see we have the strength we need in order to accept his gifts to us.

FOR DISCUSSION AND REFLECTION

How would my life be different if I had not been called to faith by God?

How do I perceive God's call to salvation on a day-to-day basis?

Second Sunday of Lent (B)

Romans 8:31b-34

The Gospel reading for the Second Sunday of Lent for each year of the cycle of readings is about the Transfiguration. It's as if the Church wants us to be quite clear about who Christ is and where our association with him through baptism is going to lead us.

The reading from our Old Testament survey of salvation history is about the sacrifice of Abraham and the deliverance of Isaac.

Our live letter links the other two readings and comments on them both. It speaks of God's Son who was revealed by the Father in the Transfiguration, but who was not spared as Abraham's son was. It alludes to Jesus' Resurrection, just as Jesus himself did as he and his disciples were coming down the mountain. Underlying the message of our reading is the obedience of Christ that had been prefigured by the obedience of Abraham.

In these four verses from the eighth chapter of his letter to the Romans Paul sums up everything he has said so far. He has been teaching the Romans about the need for salvation from God to overcome human sinfulness. This salvation is offered to us through faith in Christ that involves our incorporation into Christ's death and resurrection through baptism. Because of our life in Christ, we are freed from the law of achievement that only served to highlight our sinfulness.

Now comes our passage, a conclusive passage that is a kind of hallelujah chorus about the significance of salvation in our lives.

We've got it made! There is no longer any conceivable obstacle to our final well-being and salvation. If God has given us his very own Son, obedient to the point of death to benefit us all, there can be nothing more we need. Who can possibly contend that we are still guilty of something if God has acquitted us of everything? The Christ who died for us and who now, gloriously risen, holds the place of honor in heaven is there speaking in our favor. What have we got to worry about?

One of the biggest challenges for twentieth-century American Christians is to believe in the enormity and generosity of God's love for us. We tend to be achievers. We want to get things done and we want to do them ourselves. We are inclined to think that we have to earn our way into God's love and that if we keep enough rules and pray hard enough and do enough penance and perform enough kind actions for other people, we will be all paid up and God will then owe us salvation and eternal happiness. But that isn't the way it is.

Our salvation is God's gift to us. We don't—we can't deserve it. We can't earn it. We can't force God to give it to us. All we can do is accept it by our willingness to become incorporated into the life, death and resurrection of Christ through faith and baptism. And this willingness isn't our doing, either. It, too, is God's gift. Christ is the achiever of salvation. We can only be recipients. But once we have accepted salvation in Christ, Paul tells us today, everything else is taken care of.

That doesn't mean that, once we have accepted Christ, anything goes and that there are no behavioral expectations. We are still expected to live in accord with the demands of morality and serve our brothers and sisters in love and stay close to God in prayer. But all these things are consequences of the gift of Christ's life in us, not its cause. We are called to consistency, to living in accord with the life of Christ that we share. Moreover, the life of Christ in us is not some sort of bus ticket that we can put in our pocket and forget about until we get to the end of the line. It is a relationship, and relationships are capable of development and ever greater depth. We must live up to God's gifts, but we must also increase our appreciation and assimilation of them.

The abundance of God's gifts doesn't guarantee an effortless life, either. Because we participate in Christ's life, we are also called to participate in his self-giving obedience. We are called to share his cross. Carrying out the implications of Christian life and salvation can be very demanding. It has led some to martyrdom. Even the more pedestrian aspects of Christian consistency can require struggle: praying when we don't feel like it, being honest when we could easily cheat, exercising patience when we have every reason to blow our stack, forgiving somebody who has done us wrong. The crosses we are called to carry come in various sizes. They are no less crosses for that reason. But the bottom line is that just as the obedience and cross of Christ are irreversibly connected with his resurrection and eternal glory, so our struggles to remain faithful are connected with sharing in his final victory.

The basic orientation and significance of our life is assured through our share in the life of Christ. Everything else is derivative and secondary. God loves us. God is for us. What else matters?

FOR DISCUSSION AND REFLECTION

What am I afraid of? Why?

Why do I strive to follow God's will in my life?

Second Sunday of Lent (C)

Philippians 3:17-4:1

The gospels of the first two Sundays of Lent have the same subject in each of the three cycles of readings. The First Sunday is about the temptation of Jesus, the second about his Transfiguration, each as presented by the synoptic evangelists. It's as if the Church wants us to be clear about the subject matter of the Lenten season: struggle against the powers of evil and transformation into a new way of being. Both of these themes illuminate the meaning of the Lenten agenda of baptism (for new members) and of the need for personal change of heart (for old ones).

Our live letter for this Sunday serves as a commentary on the Gospel reading. It's about the future transformation of Christian believers. At this point in Philippians Paul is bringing to a close an energetic, even shrill passage aimed at false teachers in the Philippian church. Scholars are not unanimous in identifying these teachers, but it seems likely that they are Judaizers, that is, people who claimed that Christians were bound to observe the demands of the Law of Moses. Paul spent most of his ministerial career combating this error.

This Sunday's reading (in the longer form that the lectionary gives us), at its start, gives the Philippians direction about their behavior. The same guidance is repeated at the reading's end. In between we have two brief descriptions, one of the Judaizers and where their teaching leads, the other of the Christian way of life and its outcomes.

Paul starts off by telling the Philippians that they should imitate him and those who behave as he does. What might sound arrogant becomes understandable if we recall that Paul was convinced that Christ lived in him, and that this life of Christ came to him as a gift. In effect, he is telling them to be Christlike.

Next comes a description of those who are not Christlike. It pains Paul to acknowledge that, by setting up ends and means other than those set forth by Christ, they are being hostile to the redemption that Christ's death won for us. Their concern for Jewish food rituals makes their stomach their god. They find glory in the mutilation of their bodies that comes with circumcision, something of which they should rather be ashamed. Their orientation is earthly and they are headed for destruction.

"But *our* citizenship is in heaven." We Christians are awaiting the final, transforming act of salvation in which our earthly bodies will share Christ's glory, in which all creation will be united with God through the saving power of Christ.

Finally comes the conclusion in which Paul recalls his affection for the Philippians and repeats the direction he had given earlier: *This* is the way to be firm in the Lord.

What has all this to do with us? We may not be tempted to engage in the ritual practices of the Jews, but we do need to hear about transformation. Jesus isn't finished with us yet. We still have something to look forward to. And that which we have to look forward to will not come when we want it, but when Christ's plans reach fulfillment. Without doubt, we have to collaborate with those plans, but Christ is the principal agent of their execution and we have to wait for their realization until he is ready.

We're not very good at waiting, especially when the waiting involves trust in someone we can't see and the expectation of outcomes that we don't fully understand. We want what we want, and we want it in a hurry. Prepackaged food, condensed books, quick trips with drugs or alcohol, hasty sexual encounters without responsibility for long-term results: it all reveals a common mind-set; it's all directed toward immediate satisfaction on terms set up by us.

Yet that's not what the Lord has in mind for us. The Lord offers better plans, deeper fulfillment. He offers us a share in his risen life, the same life that he showed a sample of to his apostles in the Transfiguration, the same life that Paul encouraged the Philippians to pursue.

Our collaboration in the implementation of those plans consists in receptivity, not the passive receptivity of the sponge, but the active receptivity of a child responding to the guidance of its parents as it matures. The Lord has taught us how to assimilate ever more deeply the life whose beginnings he gave us in baptism. That assimilation involves certain standards of behavior. It involves ongoing prayer. It involves nourishing Christ's life in us by study and reflection. It involves participation in the sacraments. Above all it involves faith, the commitment of ourselves and our human existence to the life and love of the Lord Jesus.

There are plenty of distractions to our commitment, plenty of by-ways in which to stray, plenty of things that are immediately much more appealing than the future glory of heaven. That's why we need to hear about transfiguration every year. That's why we need Lent.

FOR DISCUSSION AND REFLECTION

What kinds of transformation do I look forward to?

How do I cooperate with God's plans for me?

Third Sunday of Lent (A)

Romans 5:1-2, 5-8

The introduction to the lectionary (no. 97) tells us that the Gospel readings for the Third, Fourth and Fifth Sundays of Lent for Year A are all concerned with the theme of Christian initiation. For that reason, they are to be used in Years B and C in Masses where there are "elect," that is, persons who will be baptized at the Easter Vigil. The Old Testament readings for these Sundays carry forward the account of the history of salvation "from its beginning until the promise of the New Covenant" (*ibid.*). The second readings are supposed to "fit" the first and Gospel readings and to serve as a connection between them. Our live letter for this Third Sunday of Lent certainly does that, as we will see.

But there is still another theme at work in our second readings for Year A. In one way or another these readings are all concerned with salvation, with the meaning and qualities of justification/uprightness/righteousness/justice/sanctification/reconciliation/liberation/redemption. They provide a kind of mini-course in soteriology (the study of salvation).

The reading for this Sunday is from Romans, Paul's theological masterpiece. He has been pointing out to his readers that Abraham was justified because of his faith, not because of his observance of the law. So also we are justified by our faith in the dying and rising of Christ.

Our reading now provides an overview of some of the

principal results of this justification that comes through our faith.

We are now in a relationship of calmness and tranquility with God. This comes to us through Christ, through whom we are also put in touch with God's generous gift of himself ("grace"). In addition to that we have hope, the right to expect that, when our salvation reaches its final fullness, we will share in the glory of God.

All this comes to us through God's love for us. This love is expressed through the Holy Spirit who has been given to us by the Father and through Christ's death for our salvation. Dying for somebody is a rare thing, although one person might die for the other if the other were particularly virtuous. But Christ died for us when we were still sinners, still helpless, still ungodly. That's how much he loved us.

This reading from Romans is about God's generosity. The salvation that God so liberally gives us includes peace, grace, hope, the presence of the Holy Spirit in our hearts and the love of Christ in spite of our unworthiness.

Our passage gives some further meaning to the first reading, in which we see God being generous to his first chosen people in the desert in spite of their lack of faith and hope in him. It also throws some theological illumination on the Gospel reading about the Samaritan woman to whom Christ related so magnanimously and to whom he promised a whole new kind of relationship between God and God's human creatures ("worship...in Spirit and truth"). These three readings teach us that generosity has been characteristic of God's relationship with those he loves for a long time. Generosity is an essential ingredient of God's plan of salvation.

There are two further lessons for us as individual believers in this passage from Romans. First of all, the reading reminds us once more that we cannot earn or deserve God's attention. We become eligible for salvation not because of our observance of any moral code or ritual regulations. We become eligible for salvation by our acknowledgment of our own helplessness and by our willingness to accept the new life that Christ offers us in spite of our own unworthiness. Being saved means being willing to be loved by a generous Father who does more for us than we can ever imagine or appreciate.

The other main lesson for us in these verses is that faith and salvation and the generosity of God involve hope. Hope is the confident expectation of future good. Hope means that there is still more to come.

Our salvation is already present and active in our lives. Even now we live the life of the risen Christ. Even now the Holy Spirit has been given to us. But in many ways, we are still in a state of transition, of potentiality, of negative or positive development.

We can move in the direction of negation. We can change our minds about being willing to accept what God offers us. We can return to our sins. We can take for granted or overlook what God has given us and live a life of superficiality.

In a more positive direction, we can strive to develop what God has given us. We can respond deliberately and consistently to what God's generosity has made us to be.

The virtue of hope assures us that the negative potential that still remains in us need not have the final word. It also reminds us that, no matter how receptive we have been to God's gifts in the past, God's giving never stops. There is always more to look forward to until we have been definitively taken into God's glory.

This reading invites us to celebrate the unmerited abundance of the salvation that God offers us.

FOR DISCUSSION AND REFLECTION

How do I experience the abundance of God's love for me?

What role does hope play in my life?

Third Sunday of Lent (B)

I Corinthians 1:22-25

On the Third, Fourth and Fifth Sundays of Lent, it is always permitted to use the readings from Year A of the lectionary cycle because of the connection of these readings with the preparation of the catechumens for baptism. But the Church also provides proper sets of readings for Years B and C, for use *ad libitum*, presumably for congregations where there are no catechumens or where the various ritual stages of the catechumenate are observed at other Masses.

For Year B, the Gospel readings on these three Sundays are from John. They deal with the third basic theme of Lent, that is, Jesus' coming glorification through his passion, death and resurrection. The Gospel for this Sunday is about the cleansing of the temple and the Jewish leaders' demand for a sign that would validate his authority for behaving in this way. Of course Jesus had already begun to offer signs of his messianic mission at the wedding feast of Cana, the account of which immediately precedes our gospel passage, and now he offers the promise of his resurrection after the temple of his body had been destroyed. But that wasn't the kind of sign the leaders had in mind. They wanted the big, cosmic event that would compel everybody to believe in Jesus whether they wanted to or not, an incontrovertible demonstration that left no room for choice or faith. They were daring him to convince them of the value of his credentials. They wanted Jesus to conform to their criteria of proof.

This demand for reducing the gospel message to the requirements of ordinary human thought patterns forms the subject of the reading from First Corinthians. At Corinth there were some who found other Christian preachers more appealing than Paul. These others seemed to have a greater depth of wisdom than the plainspoken Paul. So Paul takes out after those who seemed to be demanding more proof than he himself had offered them.

He tells them that the demand for demonstrations of cosmic power ("signs") and for profound human wisdom is unbelievers' talk. That's not what we Christians are all about. All we have to offer is Christ crucified, a dead criminal. This presents problems to the Jews and is unpersuasive to the philosophically minded Greeks. But believers realize that what God has done is to turn everything upside down. What looks like powerlessness is really the strength of God and what seems to be absurdity is the wisdom of God. And what God offers us in the power and wisdom that is Christ far surpasses human categories of strength and understanding.

As Paul plays out these contrasts between believers and unbelievers, between human wisdom and the foolishness of God, between human power and God's weakness, he is recalling to our minds the virtuosity of God who effects our redemption through apparently inadequate and inappropriate means. Christ expresses the power of God by giving himself away for our salvation. Christ expresses the wisdom of God by concluding his life as a criminal outcast.

Like the Jews who wanted signs and the Greeks who wanted philosophical speculation, we might have wished that God had done things differently. Faith might be easier if God's plan of salvation had been a little more in accord with our ordinary human way of doing and explaining things. God might have done a better job of convincing us, of proving things to us. But God is neither a magician out to impress the crowd nor a logician who works in argumentation. God is a lover and lovers don't always act predictably.

Of course there is a rational dimension to our faith. It's not a hodgepodge of disconnected and fanciful elements. There is a fundamental consistency to it that has kept theologians busy for millennia. But, in order for it to make sense, we have to accept the basic premise that there is a "foolishness" about God that is wiser than human wisdom and a "weakness" that is greater than human strength.

But there's still something more. Just as we have to try to understand salvation on God's terms, terms in which apparent weakness is really strength and apparent foolishness is really wisdom, so we have to accept salvation on God's terms. Just as the strength of Christ lay in his gift of himself on the cross, so our strength in him lies in our own self-giving to him and to those he loves. Just as the wisdom of Christ consisted in his willingness to end his life as a criminal outcast, so the wisdom in our life lies in our willingness to imitate his humility and acknowledge that the real worth of our life does not consist in what we can achieve for ourselves but in what we can give away with and for him. There's nothing wrong with being powerful and wise, as long as we define the terms the same way God does.

As we prepare during these weeks of Lent to walk once more to Calvary with Christ, it's good for us to recall what that really involves.

FOR DISCUSSION AND REFLECTION

Where do I find power and wisdom in my life?
What signs do I look for from Christ?

Third Sunday of Lent (C)

I Corinthians 10:1-6, 10-12

The Gospel reading for this Sunday presents us with a deeply Lenten lesson. Jesus tells his listeners that it's not just people who suffer catastrophes of one kind or another who are in need of repentance and a change of heart. We all need to struggle to become what God wants us to be, and if we do not bring forth the fruit that God expects of us, we all face final rejection.

The Old Testament reading continues this year's survey

course on salvation history. It shows us Moses being called by God to liberate his people from slavery.

The second reading is connected in part to the first, in that Paul refers to the events of the exodus that God had spoken to Moses about. But the principal referent for this reading from First Corinthians is the gospel. It's about our need to continue to strive for the fulfillment of our salvation.

In this section of First Corinthians, Paul has been talking about Christians eating meat that had been sacrificed to idols. Generally there's nothing wrong with that, he says, but we have to be careful not to end up practicing idolatry.

Our passage is a warning about overconfidence, about being so sure of ourselves, so assured of God's care for us that we fall into the very sins that God is trying to free us from.

As our second reading begins, Paul is using the story of the exodus as an example for the Corinthians. He reminds them that their "ancestors" in faith (the children of Israel) were all rescued from Egypt by being covered with a cloud. They all went through the waters of the Red Sea. These experiences were a kind of baptism that molded them into one people.

They all ate the manna God sent and drank of the water from the rock that God provided for them. The water was given to them on more than one occasion, so that it was almost as if the rock was wherever they were! This eating and drinking was an image of the eucharistic food and drink that Christ would give and of Christ's ongoing care for his people.

In spite of all this, most of them sinned and never made it to the Promised Land.

Now Paul draws the parallel with his Christian Corinthians. All this happened, he tells them, as a lesson for you. (Here the lectionary omits some verses in which Paul warns them of the dangers of falling into idolatry as the Israelites did.) He reminds them of the results of the Israelites' refusal to accept the plans that God had for them. They suffered death because of their grumbling. All this is directed toward you, Paul says. What went before was a lesson directed toward those (that is, to you) who would live in the last phases of the history of salvation. Don't be overconfident in what you have received. You could end up lapsing into unfaithfulness.

The point here is that just as the Israelites had something quite like sacraments in God's care for them and still perished in the desert, so also Christians can be lost in spite of what they have been given in baptism and the Eucharist. Having received the life of the risen Christ is not a guarantee that Christians will finally enjoy what that life is supposed to lead to.

The sacraments are not infallible means of salvation that have their effect whether we respond or not. True, each time a sacrament is celebrated, the action of God is there. But if the one to whom the sacrament is addressed is not receptive, the sacrament cannot have its effect. Likewise, even if a sacrament is fruitfully received, the recipient still needs to live out the implications of what God gives in the sacrament if the sacrament is to have any long-term results.

God will not save us in spite of ourselves. The sacraments through which God offers us salvation are not magic, automatically effective in us no matter what our state of mind and heart. We have an important part to play in our salvation. Moreover, we are all susceptible to idolatry, to wandering off in the service of false gods, to setting up goals for ourselves that are not the goals of God. That's why we have to "take care not to fall," even when we think we are "standing secure."

This task of "taking care" involves ongoing analysis of the motives for which we do what we do. It involves continuous contact with the Lord through prayer and reflection. It involves nourishing our faith through the reading of Scripture and of other sources of strength and direction. It involves regular participation in the Eucharist. It involves being honest and realistic about our own sinfulness, willing to ask God's pardon in the sacrament of reconciliation. All this is involved in the change of heart to which the season of Lent invites us. All this is part of what Jesus calls for in this Sunday's gospel.

God is neither a stern taskmaster eager to punish on any pretext, nor a rich uncle thoughtlessly handing out presents to his relatives. God is a loving Father who is serious about our salvation and expects us to be serious, too.

FOR DISCUSSION AND REFLECTION

Where is there danger of overconfidence in my life?

Where do I look for assurance and a sense of security?

Fourth Sunday of Lent (A)

Ephesians 5:8-14

The gospel for this Sunday is John's complex and thoughtful narrative about Jesus' cure of the blind man, the man's washing in the pool, the tensions that the miracle caused for its recipient and his family, the cured man's acceptance of Jesus in faith. This particular reading was clearly chosen for its relevance to the Lenten theme of initiation: those who enter the community of faith are freed from their darkness and are welcomed into the light of Christ. The second reading seems to be intended as a commentary on the gospel. (It also has some relevance to the first reading, however, in which Samuel is told to listen to God's instructions rather than trusting his own instincts, since God sees in ways that are different from the way humans see.)

Our passage from Ephesians comes from the last section of the letter in which the author is giving practical moral directives to his audience. He has warned them about impurity, greed, silly talk and personal relationships that could be dangerous to their faith. In the verses that constitute our reading he offers them a basic rationale for moral behavior and a general conclusion or two, all based on the image of salvation as light and illumination.

One of the fundamental results of faith (and salvation) is becoming "light in the Lord." Before you were saved, the author says, you were darkness. But you have to live consistently with what God has made you to be, consistently with being light. That means that you have to produce the products of light: "every kind of goodness and righteousness and truth." It also means that you have to learn the ways of the Lord.

Just as light is in opposition to darkness, so also persons of faith have to be opposed to the sinfulness in the world around them. The shameful sins of the pagans (presumably sexual sins in particular) have to be exposed for what they are by believers, by those who are light.

To conclude the passage, the author quotes what seems to be an early Christian baptismal hymn that assures us that being in Christ involves light and life.

This passage contributes an informative image to the little treatise on salvation that our live letters have been giving us during these weeks of Lent: salvation brings us light and also makes us light.

In order to tease out some of the implications of what our text is offering us in this image, we need to reflect a bit on what light is and does in our natural world. (Using images is helpful in teaching because it frees the teacher from dependence on abstractions and technical terms, but also because images have manifold meanings that say a lot in a simple way.)

Light is a symbol of understanding. Intellectual grasp of something is called "seeing the light." When God's word tells us that salvation is light, it means that living in the Lord enables us to understand things in a new perspective, God's perspective. When God's word tells us that we "are light in the Lord" it is telling us that we have the ability and the responsibility to help others understand themselves and their existence as God does.

Light also symbolizes life and energy. Just about everything we are familiar with in the natural world thrives on light and atrophies without light. The most vigorous houseplant will die if we put it in a dark basement. Salvation (grace) involves a whole new level of living. It involves having the life of the risen Christ as the underpinning of our present human existence. It means acting with the energy of the Holy Spirit who comes to us with the life of Christ. The difference between living on our own and living the life of God is like the difference between a plant in full sunshine and a plant in a lightless cellar—only much more so, of course.

But we don't just receive light and salvation. Scripture tells us that we "are light." We are agents of life and energy to others, instruments of God's salvation. This doesn't apply just to priests and Church ministers, it applies to everybody who has received the light of Christ.

Light also suggests cheerfulness, joy, emotional well-being. We are gloomy when we are in the dark. Psychologists have recently described and learned to treat a pervasive sadness that affects some people who live in parts of the world where there are long seasons of short daylight. Salvation is a source of joy and well-being, too. It offers us the security of knowing that everything is well with us, that we are heading in the right direction in our life, that what lies ahead of us is a happiness far greater than even the best and most fulfilling experiences of this earthly existence. And the brightness that we experience as a result of salvation is something we are called to share with others.

Understanding, life, energy, joy: they all come as part of salvation. They are gifts that we receive and gifts we are called to share. It's good to be enlightened. It's good to be light for others.

FOR DISCUSSION AND REFLECTION

How does grace enlighten me?

How do I enlighten others?

Fourth Sunday of Lent (B)

Ephesians 2:4-10

This Sunday offers us another reading from John's Gospel on the subject of Jesus' glorification through his passion, death and resurrection. Jesus tells Nicodemus that his being "lifted up" would become the source of eternal life to everyone who believes in him. Here and elsewhere (see John 8:28 and 12:32) Jesus seems to use this phrase to signify not only his physical elevation above the earth on the cross, but also his resurrection and final glorification in heaven. The evangelist goes on to explain that this "lifting up" of Jesus is God's gift, a gift that brings life, liberation and illumination to all who would respond to him.

Our second reading is a commentary on the gospel passage. It comes from the letter to the Ephesians which, as we will see later this year, is about the Church, about oneness in Christ and about the Church's universal mission. In chapter 2, Ephesians is dealing with the generosity of God's plan of salvation. Our passage is connected with the Gospel reading through its reference to our being raised up with Christ and through its insistence that salvation is God's gift.

Our text points out that the same things that happened to Christ have happened to us through our association with him. We were dead because of our sinfulness. God brought us back to life with Christ and raised us up with him and brought us triumphantly into heaven with him. Why? It was not to reward us for our virtuous works, so that we could brag about what we had done. It was because of his mercy, his love, his grace, his kindness, his generosity. (It's almost as if the author can't find enough words to describe the motivating force of what God did. Note that "grace," which occurs three times in our passage, has overtones of undeserved benevolence.) God did all this for us as a kind of demonstration of the boundlessness of his generosity and so that we could carry out as extensions of Christ the plans that God has in mind for the world.

Two things require our attention in this passage. One is that the author looks on our life in Christ as "realized eschatology." That is to say, becoming a believer, beginning to live the life of Christ is not a question of starting off on a new way of life to give God a chance to see how we work out so that he can then decide whether we belong in heaven or not when our earthly life is over. No, the big questions of our life have already been answered. It's all settled. Just as we share Christ's death and resurrection here and now, so also we share his glory in heaven here and now. We already have a place in heaven, we already belong there simply because we are joined with the risen life of Christ. However— and this is the second point that we have to be attentive to—our claim on life in heaven, our actual citizenship there does not entitle us either to take credit for ourselves or to sit back in leisure on the pretext that we have already arrived. Our participation in Christ's passion, death, resurrection and exaltation in heaven is totally and exclusively gift. This is a point that the author of Ephesians makes over and over again in our passage. We have no claim on achievement. Nor can we let our Christian life develop into a kind of spiritual effortlessness and euphoria because we have already reached our goal. On the contrary, because our lives, even here on earth, have been so infused with the life of the risen Christ, we are called to strenuous moral effort, to the hard work of carrying out the agenda that God planned for the risen and glorified Christ to bring to completion through us. The salvation brought by Christ is not a past event. It's something that is still going on, and, because we are in Christ, we are participants in bringing it to completion.

Most of the New Testament is about salvation in one way or another. We have already begun to see how often the subject comes up in our live letters. Today our reading again offers us some of the basics about salvation: salvation comes from Christ alone and consists in our being made participants in the life of the risen and glorified Christ; there's no way we can earn salvation, but we are called to respond to its consequences in us;

salvation is not merely an event of the past nor just a promise for the future but a present relationship with Christ that determines the meaning of our life today by its association with his once-and-for-all death and resurrection and with his never-ending, on-going glory in heaven.

When the Church calls us during these weeks of Lent to be attentive to the significance of baptism for the Church and for us, to refocus and rekindle our own baptismal fervor, to prepare to celebrate again the central events of the life of Jesus, it is calling us to be attentive to salvation. Salvation is what Jesus is all about, what the Church is all about, what we are all about. Without salvation, nothing makes any sense.

FOR DISCUSSION AND REFLECTION

In what circumstances am I tempted to look on salvation as a personal accomplishment?

Has my baptism—my sharing in the life of Christ—made any difference in my life today?

Fourth Sunday of Lent (C)

II Corinthians 5:17-21

The primary definition of "reconcile" in the dictionary is, "to restore to friendship or harmony." The component elements of the word mean to conciliate again, to make things or persons compatible again. "Reconciliation" (together with other words like redemption, new life, grace) expresses what God did and does for us when he gives us salvation.

The Gospel reading for this Sunday of Lent is about reconciliation, about the restoration of harmony between the wayward son and his loving father. This deeply moving parable is

obviously chosen for this season in order to invite us to intensify
our process of personal renewal and change of heart. It calls us to
seek reconciliation with our heavenly Father to whatever extent
reconciliation is needed.

The second reading is an explanation of certain aspects of
the salvation and forgiveness that are implicitly offered to us in
the gospel parable. While its general subject is Paul's ministry,
which he felt constrained to defend in the face of the Corinthians'
skepticism about it, it also speaks about reconciliation. In fact,
"reconciliation" and related words occur no less than five times
in these five verses.

The passage begins with a general statement: something new
is happening and that something is that we are created over into
the life of Christ. This life supersedes everything that has
happened previously. (There may be a slight connection here with
the first reading, which is concerned with the ending of the first
phase of the Israelites' journey to the Promised Land.)

This new creation into Christ is God's doing. God has brought
us back into contact with himself through Christ and in Christ.
Our sins no longer keep us separate from God. The proclamation
of this offer of reconciliation, the responsibility for seeing that it
gets presented to those to whom it is offered has been entrusted to
Paul and his fellow workers. They speak for God. They are
"ambassadors for Christ," channels of God's call to salvation.

Then he enunciates the content of the message he has been
called to deliver for Christ: "Please be reconciled to God."

Finally, by way of summary, he proclaims the basic truth
once more: Jesus' faithfulness made up for our sins; he carried
out what we should have been doing all along; the result is that
we can now share his life, a life that is nothing less than the life
(and therefore the holiness) of God.

At least three things call for our attention in this reading.
The first is that God *appeals* to us to accept reconciliation. God's
ministers *implore* us to be reconciled to God. It is not the case
that God sets up an opportunity of salvation for us, tells us about

it, and then stands by quietly while we decide whether to accept it or not. God pleads with us to receive his gifts. God is like the father in the parable who can't do enough to make his wandering son feel welcome.

The second thing that calls for comment is that, although reconciliation (or salvation, or redemption) is a clear and definite thing (either you share the life of Christ or you don't), it is not a once and for all thing. Nor is it something that is exactly the same for everybody. God calls us to a relationship. Relationships can be broken off. Relationships admit of varying degrees of intensity. Reconciliation, therefore, is an ongoing project. We have to be attentive to it as a fundamental element in our lives. Otherwise we run the risk of being distracted by less important matters and of allowing the relationship to shrivel up and die. And we also have to work at deepening and strengthening it.

It is significant that, although the Corinthians had been baptized and therefore had begun to live the life of Christ, Paul still implores them to "be reconciled to God." Reconciliation is not an inert possession but a way of being in touch with God.

There is still another aspect of reconciliation that we need to be aware of as we work through these Lenten weeks of change of heart. It's an aspect that is not explicit in this reading from Second Corinthians, but that is part of Paul's teaching nonetheless. Being reconciled with God, coming to share the life of the risen Christ, also involves being reconciled with our brothers and sisters in the Lord. It is simply not possible to say that we love the Lord if we do not love those beloved by him. It is profoundly inconsistent to attempt to embrace the Lord while rejecting others who share his embrace. This means that, as we examine the quality of our state of reconciliation with God and work to intensify it, we must also look at our relationships with the women and men around us. Reconciliation belongs in every aspect of our lives.

Today God says to us: "Please be reconciled with Me. Please repent. Please get back together with your brothers and sisters.

Please come home. I'm waiting for you."

FOR DISCUSSION AND REFLECTION

What would my life be like without new creation in Christ?

With whom do I need to be reconciled?

Fifth Sunday of Lent (A)

Romans 8:8-11

The Gospel readings for Lent and the readings from the Old Testament are on different tracks. The gospels are about initiation, in view of the reception of new Christians at the Easter Vigil. The first readings provide an overview of God's relationship with his first chosen people. The second readings, our live letters, sometimes relate to the Old Testament reading, sometimes to the gospel. Sometimes they act as a bridge between the other two readings. Yet they still teach us about the nature and the effects of salvation.

On this Sunday, however, all three readings seem to be in harmony. They all have to do with life. The reading from Ezekiel has to do with God's promise of restoration in the homeland for his people and comes at the end of the account of the prophet's vision of dry bones coming back to life. The gospel is about Jesus bringing his friend Lazarus back from the dead. The reading from Romans deals with our life in Christ and its implication, both for now and for the future.

Chapter 8, from which our reading is taken, is a climactic chapter in Romans. Paul brings to a conclusion his long treatment about our need for salvation and the nature of salvation with an extended discourse about two ways of life: the way of the flesh and the way of the spirit.

They cannot please God, Paul says, who are "in the flesh," that is, who are self-centered, striving for personal self-sufficiency. (Note that "flesh" for Paul does not necessarily mean our physical body, but a fundamental orientation of our will in which we deny our dependence on God.) Believers, however, are not "in the flesh" but "in the spirit," that is, in a particular relationship with God, seeing that the Spirit of God dwells in them. Having the Spirit in us is essential if we are to belong to Christ.

If we do belong to Christ, our body may still be vulnerable to the mortality that sin brought with it, but our spirit will be alive. Indeed, we can look forward to the full and final resurrection of our bodies from the dead at the end of time, provided only that the Spirit who raised Christ from the dead remains in us. We will live in Christ forever.

Life is one of those things that we know about more or less instinctively, but which we have a difficult time enunciating with any precision. We can tell the difference between a dead body and a living body, but we can't always verbalize that difference.

When I was a seminarian, one of our philosophy professors defined life as "immanent activity." That which can express itself in actions which originate from within itself, actions which somehow contribute to the well-being of the self is alive. That which does not have the ability or resources to do anything of itself and for itself is not alive.

There are all kinds and levels of life. In our own personal existence we have the action of the cells of our body that enable us to keep producing tissue and energy. We also have an emotional and intellectual life through which we relate to the wonders of the persons and the world around us, a relating that results in our own growth and development as well as in the growth and development of those whose lives touch ours.

In our second reading today Paul reminds us that, as believers, we have a certain special level of life in the Spirit of Jesus. We foster and develop that life by striving to live "in the spirit" rather than "in the flesh." Yet that level of life will be changed into a still deeper kind of living when the Spirit's power brings us to final resurrection.

Being alive means being like God. God is essentially vitality and activity, always expressing the divine being in self-animation and interior movement. But being alive is also being like God because God is the source of life in others, in plants and animals and angels, and every kind of life is somehow an expression of God's life. God is the One who can bring a whole people back to life when they were as dead as a field full of bones or who can raise a friend after he has been dead for days. Our physical and emotional lives are one kind of reflection of the interior being of God. A more full and exact reflection of God's life is our sharing of the life of the risen Jesus, a life that will find its most complete and definitive expression when we are united with the life of Christ and the Father and the Spirit after human history has reached its completion.

Over the last few weeks our live letters have been telling us about salvation, about its origins in faith, about how God gives it to us freely and without any deserving on our part. We have heard how salvation brings us peace and hope in spite of our sinfulness. We have learned to appreciate it by looking on it, last week, as light and, this week, as life.

As we approach the annual solemn celebration of the death and resurrection of Jesus, it's good for us to recall what all that was and is about. It's about salvation. It's a great gift for us to be saved. It's a great gift for us to be alive.

FOR DISCUSSION AND REFLECTION

How many kinds of life do I experience?
How do I know that I am alive?

Fifth Sunday of Lent (B)

Hebrews 5:7-9

Once again our Gospel reading is from the Gospel of John and
once again it deals with Jesus' passion, death and glorification.
The request of the gentile Greeks to be put in touch with Jesus
seems somehow to have indicated for him that his public ministry
was near its end. He begins to reflect on what lies ahead of him:
glorification that would arise from suffering and death, pain from
which he might have wished to be freed except for its redemptive
value. A voice from heaven offers him reassurance and the
passage ends with Jesus promising that his being lifted up (that
is, his death and resurrection) would draw sinful humanity to him.
Note that the element offered by the Gethsemane scene in the
other evangelists—Jesus being troubled at what lay ahead of
him—is presented here in the Gospel of John.

Our live letter is a commentary on the significance of the
Gethsemane scene and on the significance of Jesus' suffering for
our salvation.

In the portion of the Letter to the Hebrews from which our
reading is taken, the author is explaining how Jesus is a more
effective high priest than were the priests of the Old Law. He is
constantly interceding for us in heaven, yet he is able to
sympathize with our weaknesses and limitations, having shared
them himself in his humanity.

In this Sunday's passage we hear about Jesus' humanity in
greater detail, specifically about his dread at the suffering that
lay ahead of him as he faced the end of his life and about his
willingness to be obedient to what the Father asked of him. He
offered "prayers and supplications," which resulted not in his
being dispensed from the need to suffer and die, but in his death
becoming a source of new meaning for human life. Although he
was the fully divine Son of God, he still needed—in his human
nature—to learn and express human obedience, even when that
obedience demanded suffering and humiliation. It was that

obedience that became the source of salvation for those who would be willing to be conformed to him.

There are two things that are important for us to be attentive to as we move toward the culmination of Lent in Holy Week.

The first is that Jesus' sufferings were real and that they were his sufferings. Matthew, Mark and Luke all show us Jesus praying in the garden to be freed from the terrible ordeal that he knew was facing him. It wasn't some pageant that he was about to take part in, but one of the most excruciating and humiliating methods of criminal execution that human ingenuity had been able to devise. This Sunday's gospel shows us Jesus being troubled at what the end of his public ministry involved. Jesus knew he was going to suffer and he really did suffer. Some early Christians found the idea of Jesus' suffering and death so repugnant that they held that these sufferings were mere appearances and didn't really touch or affect him. The Church quickly rejected this idea as heretical. Jesus really suffered. Jesus really died.

Yet the significance of his death is not to be found so much in the intensity of the suffering that surrounded it, but in the obedience that inspired it. This obedience is the second thing to which it is important that we be attentive. Our first parents had sinned in wanting to do things their way, in spite of what God had asked of them. Original sin was a sin of disobedience, and it destroyed the special relationship that had existed between God and humanity. The restoration of that relationship required obedience, the willingness of someone to carry out God's will even if the immediate result was rejection, misunderstanding, suffering, agony and death. This is the meaning of Christ's life and death. Here was one who was fully human, yet fully God, and who was willing to offer his Father human obedience even if that obedience cost him his human life.

Jesus redeemed us because everything that he did throughout his life was done out of reverence for and response to his heavenly Father's love for his human creatures. He lived a human life as God had intended it from the beginning, a life of obedience. Because that human life was lived in the context of human sinfulness, it resulted in Jesus' rejection and death. But its value does not lie in the pain and suffering that accompanied it, as if the Father somehow needed to watch his Son being tormented. The value of Jesus' life—and his suffering and death—lies in the obedience and reverence that his humanity offered to the Father through it all. It wasn't the degree of Jesus' pain that saved us, but the depth of his obedient dedication, even when that obedient dedication brought him suffering and death.

We are saved by Jesus because, through baptism, we share in his risen life, a life that is the Father's response to his obedience. Our life in Christ is to be a life of obedience, too, not to earn our salvation but to be consistent with it.

FOR DISCUSSION AND REFLECTION

Has God's call to obedience ever caused me to suffer?

What role do Christ's sufferings play in my life?

Fifth Sunday of Lent (C)

Philippians 3:8-14

The first reading for this Fifth Sunday of Lent provides the conclusion to this year's mini-course in salvation history. The readings we have heard from the Old Testament have taught us about the basic identity of God's people, about God's approach to Abraham and Moses, about the conclusion of the people's wandering as they entered the Promised Land. This final piece is from the Israelites' time of exile and God is promising to bring them home again and relate to them in a new way: "Behold I am doing something new."

The Gospel reading is the narrative of the woman caught in adultery. Jesus responds to her situation in a way different than his enemies expected, in a new way, that is, with forgiveness rather than condemnation. But that doesn't mark the end of the encounter. He does not condemn her, but he also insists that she go and not sin again.

The second reading for this Sunday relates to both other readings. It describes the new relationship that God has given us in Christ, but also makes clear that there is more to our encounter with the Lord than just accepting what he offers.

The reading is from the third chapter of Philippians that we heard from three weeks ago. This chapter is a passage of vigorous warning to the Philippians to beware of false teachers who wanted to involve them in the observance of Jewish law. Just before our passage begins, Paul has been telling them that, although he had enjoyed many advantages in the context of Judaism, none of it was of any advantage in comparison with having Christ.

As our reading begins, Paul enlarges his frame of reference. It's not just Judaism that was of no profit to him. *Everything* is worthless, *everything* is loss, *everything* is rubbish compared with knowing Christ, that is, experiencing, absorbing, being permeated by him. This relationship with Christ is not something that Paul claims to have achieved by his observance of the old laws. It consists, rather, in sharing the holiness (righteousness) of God through God's gift in faith. This faith and knowledge of Christ are aimed at being in touch with Christ, with his death and resurrection in the hope that he, Paul, will eventually share definitively in that resurrection.

But it's not over yet, he says. Paul acknowledges that he has not taken over Christ but has been taken over by him, but that doesn't mean that he has attained full maturity. There is still something else to be gained. Having abandoned his Jewish past, he continues his present efforts ("my pursuit") and strains forward in faith toward the goal of receiving the fulfillment that God has promised in Christ Jesus.

This is an extraordinarily rich reading. It teaches us about the basic elements of Christian life.

Our faith gives us a whole new level of living. Through no merit of our own, we are grafted into the life of the risen Christ. Everything in the world is of secondary importance, or even detrimental to us, apart from this basic relationship with the Lord.

But having begun to live in Christ does not mean that we will necessarily reach full participation in his life in heaven. This newness of life demands some effort on our part. It demands an ongoing struggle to assimilate the life of Christ into our life, to bring ourselves into ever greater conformity with him and with his faithfulness to the Father even though that faithfulness involved the cross. This newness of life demands our dedication to a clear set of priorities, to an awareness that some things are more important than others, that some things which might seem attractive to us are really "rubbish," while others that might seem unappealing and demanding can lead us into a more mature relationship with the death and resurrection of Jesus.

All this is not without effort. Making choices is not necessarily easy or fun, because every time we choose one thing, we implicitly reject others. And sometimes we wonder whether the choices we have made were the right ones. Yet we must "strain forward" in our "pursuit" just as Paul did.

In addition to giving us a miniature view of all Christian life, this reading also touches the basic themes of the Lenten season that is now moving toward its close. It invites us to participation in the death of Jesus in view of a participation in his resurrection. It speaks to us of the new life of faith that we have received from God and that our catechumens will enter at the Easter vigil. It calls us to ongoing change of heart, to continuous repentance in response to what we have already received and in anticipation of what is still promised to us.

Today, God's word reminds us Christians who we are and what we must still become, where we are and where we are going. It also reminds us that we are not there yet.

FOR DISCUSSION AND REFLECTION

What constitutes "rubbish" in my life?

What's most important to me now? To what do I look forward?

Palm Sunday of the Lord's Passion (ABC)

Philippians 2:6-11

Every year the Church's liturgy offers us two readings of the
account of the passion and death of Jesus: one on the Sunday of
Holy Week (which the new lectionary calls "Palm Sunday of the
Lord's Passion"), the other on Good Friday. These are long
readings because each of the evangelists offers an extended
treatment of what happened to Jesus in his last days on earth.
The evangelists recount the events of those days at great length
because they were so important to the story of Jesus' life and
mission. And the Church has us read the accounts twice in one
week because what happened to Jesus is so important to us.

What's important for us in the passion narratives is not just
coming to know the sad facts of the end of Jesus' life, but
grasping the significance of those facts in Jesus' life and in our
life. What do the passion and death of Jesus really mean?

The answer to that question comes in this Sunday's second
reading from the letter to the Philippians, a reading that the
Church assigns to this Sunday each year of the three-year cycle.

Paul is encouraging the Philippians to be humble and
generous to one another. They should imitate Christ, he says. Now
comes our reading. The reading seems to be an early Christian
hymn that Paul cites (and embellishes a bit) in order to make his
point. If you want to imitate Christ, you have to know what Christ
was and is all about.

Christ was God's Son, equal to the Father, but he didn't see that as something to be hung on to at all costs. He became a human being in order to offer the Father humility and obedience. He carried obedience to its most demanding extreme in his willingness to die the death of a criminal. Because he was God, his humility and obedience were unique, totally surpassing anything that human beings had been capable of before. In view of that, the Father raised Jesus in his humanity to a position of honor that demands reverence and adoration from everyone everywhere ("in heaven, on earth, and under the earth"). All creatures are called to acknowledge the gift of universal dominion that the Father has conferred on Jesus because of his humility and obedience.

The implications of the hymn for the Philippians are clear: If you want to share in the glory and the kingdom of Jesus, you have to participate in his humility and obedience.

But the hymn also offers us an explanation of Jesus' suffering and death. It tells us that Jesus didn't take advantage of his being God's Son in order to escape any part of his human mission. His mission was to exemplify and demonstrate what love and service to the Father are all about, and thus to exemplify and demonstrate the purpose and goal of every human life. In his affection for his friends and followers, Jesus showed how God's love translates into human love. In his concern for the poor, the outcasts, the sick, the sinners, Jesus demonstrated that the love of a human being for God entails a universality of love for all those whom God loves. In his faithfulness to his mission in spite of rejection and hostility and hatred and even death, Jesus taught that nothing in human existence is more important than humble and obedient response to the loving will of God. The life of Jesus was a life of obedience, obedience to what God asked of him in the human mission he had taken on. That obedience is what brought him into conflict with the powers of his time. That obedience brought him to the death of a criminal. The humiliation and suffering and death of Jesus were a direct result of his life. The significance of the passion narratives, therefore, does not lie merely in the facts they preserve, but in their reflection of the humility and dedication and obedience of Jesus that lie behind the facts and that were the reason for their occurrence.

Our mission and Christ's mission are the same: faithful obedience to the implications of God's love for us and for all his human creatures. This is what we committed ourselves to when we accepted the life of Christ in baptism. We may not be destined to suffer public humiliation and the death of a criminal. But we are called to deal with the demands of faith in a godless society. We are called to be loving and generous to other human beings who may not be loving and generous in return. We are called to be faithful to the commitments we have made in marriage or parenthood or priesthood. We are all called to put absolutely everything we have into the acceptance of God's will in our lives, even when his will is dark and painful and frightening. We are all called to absolute obedience to the Father, cost what it may. Our life plan is to be the same as Christ's life plan, and the passion and death of Christ show us what that life plan can involve.

Jesus is not our Savior because he suffered a lot. Jesus is our savior because he showed us and taught us and enabled us to carry out the obedience and humility that all human life was meant to express.

FOR DISCUSSION AND REFLECTION

How do I participate in the passion of Christ?

What does it mean to me to say, "Jesus Christ is Lord"?

PART FOUR

Easter

The Resurrection of the Lord, the Easter Vigil (ABC)

Romans 6:3-11

The Easter Vigil is the high point and center of the Church's liturgy. In this long ceremony of watchfulness and reflection and waiting, all the themes that we have been hearing and reflecting on during the season of Lent are brought to their clearest enunciation and their final expression. The first seven readings give us a reprise of the Old Testament history of salvation and of its orientation to a new covenant, a new set of blessings. The gospel narrative of the Resurrection brings us to the conclusion of what we have been experiencing together during Holy Week. After the gospel will come baptism and the other rites of initiation, toward which the elect have been moving during these weeks and from which those who are already members of the Church receive orientation for their ongoing life of grace.

The reading from Romans combines several of these themes. It is a reflection on salvation (which we have heard a lot about during Lent in the second readings), placing it in the context of baptism and of Jesus' death and rising to new life. It has been suggested, in fact, that this reading ties the whole vigil together and enunciates its meaning, expressing in words what the lights and the bells express in symbol.

Paul has been telling the Romans how salvation has overcome human sinfulness and that, although sin has been pervasive and powerful in human history, grace and salvation have "overflowed all the more" (5:20). Now he addresses a potential objection: If salvation has been greater than sin, does it follow that we should continue to sin so that salvation can be still more abundant?

This is where our reading begins. It is a rather rambling and repetitious treatment of the relationship between sin and salvation, which Paul explains by drawing a parallel between baptism and the death and resurrection of Jesus. It's helpful to remember that, when Paul speaks of baptism, what he has in mind is adults being baptized by immersion, by being pushed fully under the water, which thus becomes a kind of tomb for the one being baptized.

Baptism, Paul says, is a kind of death that unites us to Christ's death. But if we are united to Christ's death, we are also connected with his Resurrection. When we come out of the water, we have a new kind of life in us just as Jesus did when he came out of the tomb.

Our sharing in Christ's death through baptism releases us from our connection with sin since dead people are no longer inclined to or involved in sin.

Paul now repeats: If we have died with Christ (through baptism) we will live with Christ. Just as Christ won't die again, neither will we. Jesus' death broke the dominion of sin in human affairs. He is no longer involved in the world of human sinfulness as he had been during his earthly life. His life is totally in God. Because of our association with Christ, what applies to him also applies to us, including victory over the power of sin.

This weighty reading does not invite us to conclude that, once baptized, we are no longer able to sin, nor that sinning doesn't make any difference once we have come to share Christ's life. Its point is that sinning doesn't make sense any more. Because we have shared the death and rising of Jesus through baptism, the self-seeking and false independence of sin are simply inappropriate and alien to us. We've got other things to give meaning and direction to our lives, namely, the life of the risen Christ. Sin is part of our past, part of what we left behind when we died with Christ.

In the course of teaching the Romans why salvation doesn't constitute an invitation to keep on sinning, Paul also manages to enunciate a triple connection between the death and rising of Jesus, salvation, and entering and coming out of the waters of baptism. (Scholars point out that this is the longest treatment of baptism in all of Paul's letters.) All three realities come together in a kind of dynamic heavenly convergence. Being baptized, sharing the life of Christ, and being saved all happen at the same time. Each involves and reflects the other two.

All three are involved with the annual Easter Vigil. All three are constitutive of the life of each Christian believer. Our Christian life is based on our being saved, which consists in sharing the life of Christ, which has its origin in us through the waters of baptism. Baptism incorporates us into the life of the risen Christ, which makes us holy, justified, saved. Because we share Christ's death and resurrection through baptism, we participate in the salvation that he came to bring. Through this triple exercise of God's re-creating power we receive the source of our Christian life, the pattern for its development, the initial stage of the goal toward which it is directed. It all fits together.

Easter is not just concerned with something that happened to Jesus a long time ago. It's also concerned with something that is still going on in us now.

FOR DISCUSSION AND REFLECTION

How do I see sin as inappropriate and alien my life?

What does living Christ's risen life mean to me?

The Resurrection of the Lord, the Mass of Easter Day (ABC)

Colossians 3:1-4

The lectionary offers us a wide range of choices for the readings for the Masses on Easter Day. The Gospel reading can be the empty tomb narrative from John 20 or the Emmaus story from Luke (for a Sunday evening Mass) or a rereading of the Gospel from the vigil. For the second reading, two possibilities are offered, one from Colossians and one from First Corinthians. Here we offer some reflections on the reading from Colossians.

In this letter, the author is dealing with a local church that had been incorrectly taught that, in addition to faith in Christ, salvation also demanded attention to certain angelic powers and involvement in specific ascetical practices. The letter's message is that Christ is all that's required to receive what God wants us to have.

The reading offered for Easter day comes just before the section of the letter that is concerned with moral behavior. It offers the principles that were to govern the everyday practical lives of believers. Its message is really quite simple.

The text reminds the readers that they have been made participants in the death of Christ, and therefore sharers in his resurrection, that their life is now enfolded into the life of the risen Christ and that they would share his glory when his final manifestation takes place. In view of that, there is a certain mind-set that is appropriate for them and certain goals for them to pursue more in harmony with Christ's glorious life in heaven than with the earthly pursuits of unbelievers. "Seek what is above. ...Think of what is above."

This text highlights and summarizes the themes that we have been dealing with during the season of Lent.

The Resurrection of Jesus wasn't just something nice that the Father did for Jesus in view of the faithfulness and obedience that Jesus expressed in his suffering and death. It was the Father's response to the whole life that Jesus had led. Here was, at last, a human life in accord with what the Father had wanted from human beings from the beginning. Moreover, this life was the human life of God. It was therefore too good, too precious, too important to come to an end on the cross. It would continue, a human life of a human Jesus, but in a new mode that admitted of no diminution or suffering, in a way that could be shared by those who were willing to accept it.

Our attachment to the life of Christ takes place through our

baptism. When we accept baptism into Christ, we are gifted
with his life. We give up what we have been and take on his
faithfulness and obedience as well as the new mode of being that
was his as a result of his Resurrection. As our live letter puts it
for this Sunday, "you have died...you were raised with
Christ...your life is hidden with Christ in God."

But there are some expectations. Because we come to share
the life of the risen Christ through baptism, we are expected to
live in accord with the implications of that life. Those
implications include things like love for our brothers and sisters
in Christ, the selfless giving of ourselves to the service of our
heavenly Father, respect for our bodies which are now
instruments of the risen Christ. It is not the case that we earn our
salvation, our participation in the life of the risen Christ by
"being good." It is rather that we respond to what we have been
given and maintain and deepen our salvation by living in accord
with the risen life of Christ that we have received. "Seek what is
above....Think of what is above."

Final preparation for baptism and entrance into the Church,
renewal of baptismal fervor on the part of long-time members,
getting ready to celebrate the suffering, death and resurrection of
Jesus—that's what Lent has been about. And each of these three
agenda items for Lent finds its fulfillment on Easter, in the
celebration of Jesus' new and glorious life, a life that still
continues. Those who were baptized at the Easter Vigil now have
a new dimension in their life, a dimension constituted by the life
of the risen Christ. The long-term members who have kept Lent
conscientiously have been gifted with renewed energy by their
participation in the journey of the Church's new members and by
the renewal of their own baptismal commitment. All of us who
have reflected on the life context of Jesus' suffering and death, on
the meaning of what he endured in his final days find ourselves
enlivened and encouraged by a new appreciation of the
significance of the Resurrection, a new perception of our
salvation by Jesus, a new energy in carrying out the implications

of what Jesus accomplished for us.

Easter is the greatest liturgical feast in the calendar. On this day we celebrate the fullness of the life of Jesus and his desire to share that life with us. We celebrate the meaning of our life in him. And we celebrate the eternal glory that will be ours in company with him.

FOR DISCUSSION AND REFLECTION

How do I direct my life to "what is above"?

How does the life of the risen Christ manifest itself in me?

The Resurrection of the Lord, the Mass of Easter Day (Alternate)

I Corinthians 5:6b-8

The lectionary provides two second readings to choose from for Easter Day, one from Colossians, the other from First Corinthians. The latter was the reading for Easter in the pre-Vatican II liturgy, and it is that one that is the subject of these reflections.

Chapter five is in the part of First Corinthians that deals with the disorders in the church of Corinth that had been brought to Paul's attention "by Chloe's people" (1:11). Among these sinful situations was that of a man who had married his stepmother. This constituted incest, a scandalous breach of morality, yet the Corinthians were tolerant of the arrangement, presumably out of a false broadmindedness that they thought was consistent with the freedom offered by the gospel. Paul orders them to excommunicate the offender. This is where our reading begins.

Paul wonders whether the Corinthians are unaware of the danger their tolerance puts them in. After all, he says, "a little yeast leavens all the dough." This seems to have been a kind of proverb. Paul uses it in a similar context in Galatians (5:9). In order to understand the thrust of the proverb, we need to recall that, for the ancients, there was something impure, unclean, corrupt about yeast. Its mysterious action had a sinister element about it. That's why, in times of special purification, pious Jews got rid of yeast and of dough that had undergone leavening by yeast. Paul is saying here that the misbehavior of the incestuous man is like yeast that could infect and corrupt the whole community if left unattended.

He goes on to remind the Corinthians that they themselves are "unleavened," purified by their association with Christ. Consequently, they should clear out any of the old leaven that is still around, that is, their pagan ways that are no longer appropriate.

The mention of unleavened dough calls the Passover to Paul's mind. (Cleaning out the yeast was part of the Passover celebration.) He tells the Corinthians that they are in a Passover situation, a time of celebration that involved the sacrifice of Christ, imaged by the Passover lamb. Given the ongoing celebration of the new Passover brought about by Christ, they were to purify themselves by getting rid of the old leaven and live lives characterized by consistency with their real, true newness of life in Christ.

The Church gives us this reading on Easter not to remind us that inappropriate marriages within a family are wrong, but to teach us about some of the implications of being a Passover people, involved in the ongoing acceptance of and response to the self-gift of Christ. This self-gift was expressed by his sacrificial death. Its acceptance by the Father was expressed by Jesus' Resurrection. Our salvation consists in participating in this new Easter life of the Lord.

Paul calls us to Easter consistency, to a life that is in accord with what we have become in Christ who died for us and who rose from the dead.

This Easter consistency consists, first of all, in our personal and individual extension of the life of the risen Christ. Just as

Christ was free from sin and so offered a perfect sacrifice, just as Christ was freed from corruption and so lives again forever, so we are called to lead lives of sinlessness and to reject anything that might lead us into spiritual decay.

But what Paul has to say is not just concerned with individual behavior. It also reminds us that the life of each of us has its effects in all the others. As the community of believers, we are, as it were, one mass of dough, all of us kneaded together into the one life of the risen Christ. Sinfulness and corruption on the part of any of us brings with it the danger of corrupting all the rest.

Easter is a complex feast. It marks the end of our Lenten period of repentance and reform. It brings new members into the community of faith. It recalls for us the final outcome of the life and ministry of Jesus. It offers hope and reassurance to all who believe in Christ. But, at the same time, it also makes demands on us. It reminds us that the gifts we have received demand a fitting response from us. The risen Christ is the source of our Christian existence. But he is also the exemplar of Christian life, the model that we are to assimilate, the life and energy that we are to extend to others. True Christian life is a life that is consistent with the risen Christ who is in us. It is a life that has implications for all the other women and men who live in Christ.

The basic behavioral lessons of Easter are twofold. One is that each of us who has been remade in Christ owes him a Christian life. The other is that each of us owes the life of Christ to all the others. We each live in Christ ourselves. We all live in Christ together. Consequently, we must not be involved with anything that would bring corruption or sin to us or to those whose lives are involved with ours. "Clear out the old yeast."

FOR DISCUSSION AND REFLECTION

What needs to be cleared out of my life to make it more pure?
How does what I do affect others?

Second Sunday of Easter (A)

I Peter 1:3-9

With this Sunday we begin a series of more or less consecutive readings from the first letter of Peter. This letter is addressed to members of Christian communities scattered throughout the Roman provinces of Asia Minor. It is attributed to the authorship of the apostle Peter, but scholars think that the high quality of the Greek in which it is written make it unlikely that it was dictated or written down by a Galilean fisherman. Perhaps Peter used an editor. It is also possible that the letter was composed by a disciple of Peter's writing in his name. We don't know much about the specific purpose of the letter, the situation of the addressees, or the date when it might have been written.

The letter is clearly intended to provide encouragement to its readers who seemingly found themselves in a difficult situation. It is a Christian exhortation about life in the world based on reflections about the meaning of faith and baptism. Its teaching applies to every member of the contemporary Church, but it is particularly appropriate material for those who were baptized or received into the Church at Easter.

This Sunday's passage is in three parts. It starts off with praise and thanksgiving to God for the believers' new birth through baptism. This new birth gives us reason for confidence in the future ("hope") by reason of our association with Christ's Resurrection. Because of our faith, the new birth gives us a sure and unswerving claim to participation in God's family. Finally, the new birth constitutes our salvation, already begun but destined for final manifestation at the end of time.

All this provides reason for joy and gladness, in spite of the difficulties in which the believers find themselves. Their faith may have to be tested like gold in the fire, but, if it is genuine, it will be a source of ultimate validation when Jesus returns in glory.

Finally the author acknowledges that their relationship with

Christ is based on their faith and love, not on visible human contact with Jesus. This initial association will develop into joyful fulfillment when salvation reaches its completeness at the coming of Christ.

Everything that the author of First Peter says about the condition of the first recipients of his letter also applies to us. Our association with Christ is not based on immediate personal contact with Jesus, but on faith. While our salvation has begun in us through the new birth of baptism, it has not yet reached its final fullness. We still have growing and developing to do. Finally, like these early Christians, we live in a context of trials and temptations that test our faith.

Scholars think that the "various trials" to which the author refers are not a formal, state-sponsored persecution, but rather the more ordinary sufferings of scorn and social rejection that would naturally be aimed at men and women who involved themselves with this new and unknown religion.

The kinds of trials that we face are similar to theirs, though not exactly the same. Our religious faith does not result in our being arrested and put to death, as happened in times of deliberate persecution. Nor do we routinely experience open contempt or insult because of our membership in the Church. What our situation offers is more a matter of indifference and disinterest. Our culture says to us: "If you want to believe all that stuff, go ahead. It's your business. But see to it that you don't involve us with it. We don't want to hear about how religious faith is supposed to influence society. We don't care about sin and salvation because we're too busy with other things. Religion is a nice hobby for those who are interested, as long as it is kept for one's private entertainment."

This kind of attitude is dangerous because it is contagious. If we are not careful, we can find ourselves dragged into this mind-set that is all around us. We can find ourselves ever more distracted from our religious faith by the false values that the world holds up and the mass media glorify: success, comfort, security, power, constant amusement. We can also feel threatened by the realization that people of obvious religious commitment are looked on by many as rather strange, as outsiders to the world's real business, as not really involved with the important things of life. We may find ourselves feeling left out as we feel the constraints of our faith that lead us away from participation in the world of casual sex, elastic honesty, sanctioned selfishness. It's a difficult and dangerous world that we live in, and we need to be conscious of that.

We also need to be conscious that the trials we experience here and now are only transitional stages in our journey toward final fulfillment in the glory of Christ. Our faith and our hope carry us forward. The new life we have received in baptism is only the beginning of "an inheritance that is imperishable, undefiled, and unfading."

FOR DISCUSSION AND REFLECTION

What makes me most glad to be a Christian believer?

What trials to my faith have I experienced?

Second Sunday of Easter (B)

I John 5:1-6

For the Sundays of the Easter season in Year B the Church gives us a series of readings from the first letter of John.

This book of the New Testament is not really cast in the form of a letter. It is more like a sermon or an exhortation. The text does not name its author, but early Christian tradition saw that its style and content resembled that of the Fourth Gospel, and so attributed the letter to the presumed author of the Gospel, John.

First John seems to reflect a somewhat later stage of the Church's life than John's Gospel. In the Gospel, the enemies are "the Jews," outsiders to the Church, successors of the Jewish leaders who rejected and eventually killed Jesus. In First John the opponents about whom the author writes seem to be believers who have moved away from the sound doctrine of the Church community and are proposing false teachings, teachings that undermine the reality and meaning of the humanity of Jesus, teachings that seem to deny any connection between faith and personal moral behavior.

First John is both a simple and a difficult work. Its language is uncomplicated and straightforward, so much so that students of biblical Greek find themselves able to handle it early on in their studies. It's generally the first book of the New Testament that they read. At the same time, it is repetitious and rambling and elusive. The author seems to talk in circles and what he has written cannot be clearly divided into thematic sections. More often than not, it's hard to determine what he is talking about and how one part of the work relates to the others. One is inclined to suspect that the author of First John would not have received a high grade in a course on Greek prose composition!

We are able, though, to identify the general themes of the treatise. It is about faith (including the true humanity of Jesus), about love (God's for us and ours for God and one another) and about obedience to the commandments (moral behavior).

The reading for this Sunday is from the last chapter of First John. One might have expected that a semi-continuous reading would start from the beginning of the book! It may be that this reading from the end of the book was chosen to begin the series because it addresses all the themes that will appear on the upcoming Sundays of the Easter season. More likely it was chosen for this Sunday because its insistence on belief fits in particularly well with the gospel narrative about Thomas and the risen Christ, which is also about belief. (We have already seen this reading from First John once this year on the feast of the Baptism of the Lord.)

The reading tells us that faith is the foundation of a whole chain of consequences. To believe that Jesus is the Son of God is to have been born of God, to have become his children. This, in turn, involves loving God and therefore loving his other children (others who believe in him). We express our love by keeping the commandments, which in turn constitutes victory over the forces of evil that are in the world. Faith, therefore, and its consequences lead to overcoming everything that might stand in the way of God's love for his faithful. The object of this faith is Jesus, both divine and human, who really died a real human death. The benefits of his saving death are offered to us in the Holy Spirit through the sacraments of baptism and Eucharist.

The fundamental point of this reading, and perhaps of the whole of First John, is that faith has implications. Faith has consequences. Faith is not merely the theoretical acceptance of a series of theoretical truths about God, Father, Son and Spirit. Faith is not merely signing on to the conclusions of a course in dogmatic theology. Faith involves personal commitment to a person, Jesus Christ. This commitment brings with it relationships with God the Father and with the Holy Spirit. Because the person of Jesus had a human nature and a human history yet is a divine person, commitment to him means that we relate to the world and its history in a different way than we would if God had remained distant and unknowable. Because those who believe in Christ share his risen life, our relationship with him includes a relationship with all others who believe in him. Because the risen Christ calls all women and men throughout the world to participate in salvation and grace and glory, we who live in Christ have some responsibility for presenting to them God's offer of eternal life.

God's love as expressed in Jesus' saving life and ministry has brought everything into unity in him. There is no aspect of the world—from electrons to galaxies, from microbes to mastodons, from unborn children to rocket scientists—that is unaffected by the love of God, untouched by Christ's death and resurrection. So also there is no aspect of the world that is alien and indifferent to us who profess faith in Christ. Because we are in Christ, everything that is connected with Christ is also connected with us. Everything and everyone to whom his life is significant has meaning for us. Everything and everyone for whom his life is a blessing calls for a response from us. We are all involved in the one life of Christ, all involved in the victory of God's love.

FOR DISCUSSION AND REFLECTION

How does my faith in Jesus affect my life?

What difference would it make to me if Jesus were not really human?

Second Sunday of Easter (C)

Revelation 1:9-11a, 12-13, 17-19

Although the lectionary readings for the Sundays after Easter have no relation to one another on any given Sunday, they are all somehow connected with the Resurrection of Jesus. The Gospel readings for the first three Sundays give us the narratives of Jesus' post-Resurrection appearances. The Gospel for the Fifth Sunday of Easter is about the good shepherd, the risen Christ looking after his flock. For the last two Sundays we have Gospel readings from Jesus' last supper discourse in John's Gospel in which Jesus encourages his followers to look beyond the events of the next few days to a more distant future.

The first readings for these Sundays are about the results of the Resurrection in the young Church as described in the Acts of the Apostles. These are offered in "a three-year cycle of parallel and progressive selections," as the lectionary's introduction puts it (no. 100).

The second readings are a series of readings from books of the New Testament that "fit in especially well with the spirit of joyous faith and sure hope proper to this season" (*ibid.*). For Year C we have readings from the last book of the New Testament, the Book of Revelation. This book deals with the ultimate outcomes of the life, death and resurrection of Jesus.

Revelation is a book whose intent is to offer encouragement and hope to its readers in time of tribulation. The tribulation may have been a persecution, or, more likely, a time of rejection and alienation during which Christians were being excluded from ordinary society because of their refusal to take part in the worship of the emperor that was expected as part of ordinary civic life. The encouragement that Revelation offers comes in the form of visions and narratives that deal with God's involvement in the present world and with his future triumph in the world still to come. It's important to be aware that Revelation is not intended to give us a set of specific predictions about the future, but rather to remind us of ultimate salvation and ultimate victory that began with the Resurrection of Jesus. It is a difficult book, not so much because its content is obscure or enigmatic, but because the means that the author uses to communicate his message (for example, symbolic colors, garments, numbers) are not the means that we would employ for the same purpose.

The first part of Revelation consists of letters from God to seven local churches. Their general message is that God knows what is going on here in our world and that he has expectations about the behavior of Christian believers. The reading for this second Sunday of Easter is the introduction to this first part of the book. It comes immediately after the verses that give the title of the book and its opening salutation.

The author introduces himself as John, in exile for the faith but a sharer with his readers in adversity and in hope for the final kingdom. (Scripture scholars hold that this John is not the same as the author of the Fourth Gospel.)

He tells how he was called by a heavenly voice to write down the visions that he would see. This heavenly voice belonged to the triumphant Christ, standing in heaven in the midst of lampstands that signified the local churches, dressed in a way that identified him as both priest and king. When John collapses in reverential fear, Christ encourages him and speaks of himself as Lord of history, risen from the dead, ruler of the living and the dead. He calls John to write down what he would see: an explanation of both present and future. (Notice how often we have words such as "as though," "like," "as" which indicate that what John describes is not to be taken literally, but as a sign of deeper realities.)

In the context of Revelation as a whole, these verses are introductory material. Nonetheless, they have a message for us. They remind us that Christ is now in eternal glory, awesome beyond the capabilities of human language to describe.

We all have images of Christ. We think of him in many different ways. Sometimes we imagine him as he must have been when he walked the roads of Judea and Galilee. Sometimes we think of him as he described himself: the good shepherd, the sower of the seed of God's word. Perhaps we picture him as the judge of living and dead, the Lord of the Sistine Chapel's last judgment. Or maybe we think of him as the cosmic Christ, Lord of the universe, as he is portrayed in the great mosaic in the National Shrine in Washington. We all have one or more favorite pictures of Christ. That's not inappropriate. We should have many images of Christ in our minds because the reality of Christ is too rich and too complex to be expressed in one image. Christ is both God and man, temporal and eternal, infinitely merciful but all just, one who suffered the death of a criminal yet reigns as Lord of heaven and earth. We can never capture his full reality in any single image or concept. Today's reading reminds us of certain dimensions of Christ that we must not forget. He is Lord of all and judge of all, yet he reaches out to us and tells us not to be afraid.

What dimensions of Christ are most important to me?

If I were an artist, how would I picture Christ?

Third Sunday of Easter (A)

I Peter 1:17-21

In the wider context of faith and baptism, the author of First Peter quickly turns his attention to Christian identity and Christian behavior. In the passage that immediately precedes this Sunday's reading, he tells his readers that, since they have been delivered from their former pagan ignorance, they must now conduct themselves as obedient children of God. He addresses to these new converts the direction that God gave to his first chosen people: Be like me, "Be holy because I am holy" (Leviticus 11:44 and 19:2).

In our passage he teases out the implications of this direction and gives some explanations for it.

First and foremost, since they are now in a relationship with a God who will judge each person with impartial justice, and since they have not yet reached their final state of perfection, they must conduct themselves "with reverence." (The Greek word used here means "fear," but it is clear that the author does not want to inculcate an attitude of servile subjection but of filial attentiveness and awe in the presence of God. The readers are being invited to behave in accord with who and what they are as God's children, and in accord with who and what God is.)

Why are they to conduct themselves this way? The text gives three reasons.

First of all, because they have been set free from the constraints of their former pagan beliefs by the blood of Christ. (That is to say they are precious enough to God to have been brought into contact with him through the faithfulness and self-sacrifice of Christ. Their freedom has not been paid for by mere money!)

Secondly, because their salvation was part of a plan that was in God's mind since "before the foundation of the world," but which only now has begun to be revealed and fulfilled "for you." (The saving work of Christ was not some spur-of-the-moment thing, but a carefully arranged undertaking that calls for a careful and generous response from those who have benefited from it.)

Finally, they must conduct themselves in a godly way because they relate to God through the Resurrection of Jesus. Because they share the glory of the risen Christ, they are directed toward the glory of God.

This passage addresses one of the basic questions of human existence: How are we to behave? Practically everybody agrees that human beings should conduct themselves in a moral way, that they should pursue virtue, that they should do good and avoid evil. But what constitutes good and evil? What does it mean to behave in a moral way? In what does a good life consist?

There have been lots of answers to these questions in the history of human thinking. At times, religious leaders have taught their followers that being good simply means obeying the rules that God has set out for us, whether we understand them or not, whether they mean anything or not, and that if you are obedient you will earn happiness and if you are disobedient you will be punished. Others have thought that a good, happy, moral life consists in the pursuit of tranquility, in avoiding pain and upheaval, and that whatever contributes to interior peace of the individual is what constitutes goodness. Still others have seen morality as a system of behaviors that human beings have agreed on so that they can live together in some degree of security. Being good means not harming your neighbor so that, in turn, your neighbor will not harm you.

Each of these approaches to morality has elements of truth, but none of them reflects the full import of authentic Christian morality. The basic principle of true Christian morality is the directive that is inherent in this Sunday's live letter: respect what you have become, behave in accord with what God has made you to be.

Christians look on morality, on "doing the right thing," as a consequence of the salvation that we have been given through Christ. We follow the directives of moral behavior not because of what we hope to get out of such behavior, nor because of what we hope to avoid, but because of what we are. We are women and men who have been brought into a family relationship with God through the life, death and resurrection of Jesus. This is a long-term undertaking on God's part, and it has not yet reached its completion either in each of us individually nor in all of us together. We live in an interim state now. But the way we are to live during this time of our "sojourning" (as our text puts it) is determined not by extrinsic regulations but by what we are: children of God.

Christian morality is not a matter of observing lots of rules. It's a matter of living consistently with what we know God is and with what we know God has made us to be. It's a matter of reverencing the relationship to which God has called us. It's a matter of authentic self-awareness and of gratitude.

FOR DISCUSSION AND REFLECTION

What role does fear play in my life?

What motivates the behavioral choices that I make?

Third Sunday of Easter (B)

I John 2:1-5a

The Introduction to the Lectionary tells us that the first letter of John was chosen to provide the second readings for the Sundays of Easter time because it fits in "with the spirit of joyous faith and sure hope proper to this season" (no. 100). These readings, therefore, were generally not chosen to illuminate or highlight either the gospel or the first reading, but to reflect the general atmosphere of the Easter season.

This Sunday's reading is from the beginning of chapter 2 and has to do with sin and forgiveness. In his usual rambling and spiraling fashion, the author has already been dealing with these matters and will continue to deal with them throughout the rest of the work. Behind it all is his concern for the dissidents in the church community who seem to have been convinced that the essence of faith was to have special knowledge about Christ that rendered unnecessary any concern about personal moral behavior.

At the end of chapter 1, the author has been insisting that we are all sinners in one way or another, but that Christ offers us forgiveness. Now, at the beginning of our Sunday reading, he nuances (and repeats!) what he has just said. His point in speaking about the universality of sin and the availability of forgiveness is not to encourage or play down sin. His point is rather to remind us that the ministry of Jesus has won forgiveness for sin and that the risen Christ makes intercession with the Father for us sinners. Of course it is important for us to "know" him, but knowing him involves not just abstract information, but also the observance of his commandments. It is simply inconsistent, and therefore false, to say that we are in touch with Christ unless we do what he tells us. Yet if we do observe his commandments, "the love of God is truly perfected" in us. (It is not clear whether this last phrase is speaking about God's love for us or our love for God. Perhaps it involves both: Keeping the commandments deepens and brings to fulfillment the loving relationship that Christ has established between God and us.)

Our faith in Christ, the relationship with the risen Jesus that we entered through baptism, has certain specific consequences. It involves believing the full truth about Jesus, human and divine, but it also calls for behavior that is consistent with our faith relationship, consistent with the life and teachings of Jesus.

Some of the people of John's time seem to have played down the demands of Christian moral behavior on the grounds that, once one has reached a certain level of knowledge, nothing human makes any difference—whether it be the humanity of Christ or the details of our day-to-day human conduct. In our time, people are more likely to sidestep the demands of Christian morality on the grounds that God isn't really interested in all the details of our daily life. All that matters is feeling good about Jesus and feeling good about ourselves. Everything else is irrelevant because "God understands."

Of course God understands, but what God understands is that our relationship with Jesus makes demands on us just as Jesus' saving mission to us made demands on him. Catholic Christian morality ("being good") is not a matter of earning God's love by our behavior, but of responding to the love of God we have already received. It is not a matter of keeping a whole complex system of rules, but of living consistently with the life of the risen Christ that is in us through baptism.

Over the centuries, Catholic Christian thinkers have spent lots of time and energy reflecting on the implications of our life in Christ. Just about every detail of every possible human behavior has been scrutinized to determine what is virtuous and what is sinful. Sometimes, when we lose sight of the basics, it seems that Christian life is surrounded with regulations and prohibitions and that we are supposed to apply most of our attention and energy to avoiding sin. In fact, the commandments of Jesus that John speaks about are relatively simple. We find them expressed elsewhere in First John (2:6; 3:23) and in John's Gospel (13:34; 15:12): believe in Jesus Christ, love one another as he loves us, live as he lived. That's all Jesus asks of us. Of course, the implications of those commands reach into every aspect of our life, and are supposed to color and direct everything we are and do. No detail of our life is too small to serve as an expression of our faith in Christ or a conduit of our love for one another in him.

No detail of our life is too insignificant to reflect the life of the Lord Jesus.

Faith—knowing Christ—makes demands and offers possibilities. It demands loving as he loves and living as he lived. But it also makes that kind of loving and living possible through his risen life that we share.

FOR DISCUSSION AND REFLECTION

Are the commandments of Jesus good news or bad news to me?

To what extent do I love others as Christ loves me?

Third Sunday of Easter (C)

Revelation 5:11-14

Like last Sunday's second reading from Revelation, this Sunday's also gives us an image of Christ. In chapters 1-3, the author has recounted the letters from God to seven local churches of Asia Minor. Now he proceeds to record the visions he experienced and was ordered to share. By way of introduction to these visions, he shows us, in chapters 4-5, a convocation of the heavenly court.

First of all, at the beginning of chapter 4, we see God seated on his throne of glory. The atmosphere is filled with thunder and lightning, like the atmosphere of Mt. Sinai when God gave the commandments to Moses. Around God's throne are twenty-four elders, a circle of priestly kings who are nonetheless subject to the King of kings. Also present are "four living creatures covered with eyes in front and back." These represent the elemental powers of the cosmos. The living creature and the elders are pictured offering adoration to the One on the throne.

Next we see a scroll in the hand of God, his complex plan for the world. But who is there to implement the plan? Now there appears the lion of the tribe of Judah, the offspring of David, the lamb slain, yet endowed with power. This complex image represents the risen Christ. (As regards the image of the Lamb, recall how John the Baptist pointed out Jesus to his followers in John 1:29, how Isaiah described the Servant of God as "a lamb led to the slaughter" in Isaiah 53:7 and how Paul spoke of Christ as "our paschal lamb" in I Corinthians 5:7.) Only the Lamb is able to carry out what is determined in the scroll. The elders and the living creatures fall down before him in worship. This is where our Sunday reading begins.

Now countless angels join the living creatures and the kingly elders to proclaim the worthiness of the Lamb to receive every kind of reverence and recognition. (Lovers of Handel's Messiah will recall the glorious music that the composer provides for these verses.) Next the circle of praise widens to include every creature in the universe crying out honor and glory to the Lamb. The elders and the living creatures confirm the worship of all creation with their own Amen.

The purpose of chapters 4-5 is to offer Revelation's readers hope by recalling the heavenly foundations of their salvation. It also provides the background setting for the visions in which God's plans for the future of heaven and earth will be manifested.

As presented to us in the lectionary, the reading does not give us the full context of John's prefatory vision. It only shows us the Lamb being worshiped by the celestial beings in heaven. Perhaps the intent is to invite us to reflect a little about how we ourselves offer our worship and honor to the risen Christ here on earth.

If one were to ask a random sample of people what prayer is, most of them would probably answer that it is talking to God. If you pressed a little further, they would probably say that prayer is talking to God to ask him for things. "When all else fails, pray!"

Prayer is much more than that. Our traditional Catholic Christian spirituality teaches us that there are four purposes for prayer: to ask God for things, but also to express our sorrow for sin, and, perhaps most importantly of all, to offer to God our praise and our thanksgiving.

God is not a kind of rich uncle, approached only when we need something. To view God that way is to acknowledge our own immaturity, as if the only word in our vocabulary were "Gimme!" To be sure, God wants us to acknowledge our needs in his presence, but he also wants us to acknowledge our sinfulness and our unworthiness of his love and care. Even more than that, God wants us to keep ourselves attentive to all the wonderful things that he has done for us in the past and continues to do for us with each passing minute. We can never run out of things to be grateful for.

But perhaps most important for our prayer life is the prayer of praise, the acknowledgment of the greatness and the excellence of God. Praising God doesn't mean offering him flattery, as if we had to keep God in good humor so that he will be nice to us. No, praising God means keeping ourselves aware of who and what God really is. This awareness results in a more intense prayer of thanksgiving as well as a more intense awareness of our need and unworthiness in relationship to God.

It's important for us to know how to praise God, because praising God is what we will be doing for all eternity in heaven. We will be expected to be able to join in with the kingly elders and the living creatures and the angels and everything in the universe as they offer blessing and honor and glory "to the one who sits on the throne and to the Lamb."

Maybe the reason why Handel's *Messiah* music for this passage is so deeply moving to us is because we have an instinctive intuition that some day we'll all be singing it together in God's kingdom!

FOR DISCUSSION AND REFLECTION

Do I offer praise and thanks to God? Why? For what?
What do I look forward to in heaven?

Fourth Sunday of Easter (A)

I Peter 2:20b-25

We continue our series of readings from First Peter. At the beginning of chapter 2 the author had given directions to the general membership of the Church about the demands of Christian life in the world. In this Sunday's reading he addresses a special category of Church members: the slaves. Probably a high percentage of early Christians were either very poor free persons or slaves, completely subject to the will of their masters and not unacquainted with mistreatment and cruelty. In our passage they are given some guidance about how to react to their misfortunes. (This passage comes to us out of order. According to the sequence of the full letter, it should follow next Sunday's reading. Probably it was moved up one Sunday because of the allusion to God as shepherd at the end of the passage which thus ties in with the gospel for Good Shepherd Sunday.)

At the beginning of verse 20 (not included in our reading), the author tells Christian slaves that being patient under suffering that they deserve is not meritorious. However (as our passage begins) if they are patient when they suffer undeservedly, that is, for doing good, this makes them pleasing to God. It wins them God's approval for two reasons.

First of all, because patiently suffering injustice is part of their Christian calling and makes them similar to Jesus. Here the author quotes one of the suffering servant songs from the book of Isaiah (53:9) which Christian tradition saw early on as foretelling the mission of Jesus. He suffered to show us that the innocent and upright person does not respond to unjust treatment by insults and threats. Instead, he entrusted himself to the justice of God, who would bring about final vindication.

But there is more to the suffering of Jesus (and therefore to the unjust suffering of his disciples) than giving an example of patience. Jesus' suffering also brought about salvation for us. Although innocent, he suffered what would have been appropriate for a sinner. He made up for the wrongdoing of sinners and thus gave them a chance to live in his righteousness. We had all gone astray in our sinfulness, but the suffering of Jesus healed our wounds and brought us back to the health and safety of God's flock. (Implied here is that the innocent suffering of the mistreated slaves somehow made them participants in Christ's work of salvation.)

There are several levels of question and subject matter in this reading. Some readers will find themselves wondering why the author doesn't just tell his readers that slavery is wrong and that they should not put up with their servitude. Of course, he couldn't and it wouldn't have made any difference if he had. His purpose was not to undo the evils of the society in which he found himself, but to give some practical guidance to people who needed it here and now.

That's what this passage is about at its most obvious level. How should Christian slaves conduct themselves? Obviously they shouldn't misbehave so that punishment was called for. But if they were punished unfairly, should they resist the wrong that was being done to them in view of their new life in Christ? The author says no. Take what comes to you, he seems to say, and make the best of it because it somehow makes you like Jesus.

Underneath all this is one of the most basic questions of all: the suffering of the innocent, whether "the innocent" be a mistreated first-century slave, or a prisoner in a Communist gulag, or the victim of a flawed judicial system, or a virtuous man or woman suffering a painful and incurable disease, or an abused spouse, or the victim of a drunk driver. Why do the innocent suffer? Why does God let things like that happen?

There's no full and final answer to that question, but this passage of God's word gives us some elements to ponder. First of all, we are not to look for full and final justice here and now. Even the Son of God had to endure pain and derision until the final intervention of "the one who judges justly." The world is a sinful and unjust place, and only God can finally remedy that.

Secondly, the most virtuous and perfect human being who ever walked the earth, Jesus, Our Lord, did not live an effortless and painless life. When God became a human being, he came into an existence that he knew would bring suffering and insult. We can't fully understand that, but we know that—if we are supposed to be like Jesus—suffering will be part of our life, suffering that we are to endure without recrimination.

Finally there is a "pay-back" dimension to human suffering. None of us can say that we deserve to be fully free from pain. We have all overstepped our boundaries again and again. We need to be brought back to where we belong. We have to pay the price of our sins. The only one free of the debts of sin was Jesus, who nonetheless suffered, not because of his misdeeds but because of ours.

There is an inherent element of mystery to the suffering of the innocent, an imponderable dimension that involves injustice and sin, but that also involves the Lord Jesus and salvation.

FOR DISCUSSION AND REFLECTION

To what extent have I suffered injustice?

Is there any sense in which my sufferings are salvific like Jesus'?

Fourth Sunday of Easter (B)

I John 3:1-2

The author of this exhortation has been addressing his listeners as "children." The term occurs no less than five times in the first two chapters. It is not a judgmental term, or a means of talking down to the work's addressees, but an expression of pastoral love, parallel with the term "beloved" that the author also uses.

At the beginning of chapter 3 our author pulls himself up and offers some reflections about the meaning of the term that he has been using so freely. "Children" is more than a term of affection. It also indicates a profound spiritual reality.

Our text teaches us that it is God's generosity that enables us to be called his children. It's not something that we can earn or deserve. Moreover, it's not just a matter of being called God's children but of actually being his children. To be God's children is something really special. It is a great distinction, but a distinction that is of no interest to the world because the source of our filiation, God our Father, is of no interest to the world. But what we are now is only a beginning. Just as Christ will come again in glory at the end of time in a form that surpasses our keenest imagining, so we who now share with Christ the likeness of sonship will be changed and glorified, too. We will see and know his final exaltation and mirror it in ourselves.

What does being children of God involve? First of all, there is nothing in created reality that does not somehow reflect the richness and glory of God. It has all been made in his image and is thus somehow God's offspring, somehow God's child. But the filiation—being God's son or daughter—that we speak of in the context of Christian faith is something more than that, something beyond the likeness of a creature to its creator.

The filiation that we have with God through faith is an analogue, a parallel to the filiation that exists between Father and Son in the Holy Trinity. Obviously as creatures—and creatures scarred by sin—we cannot participate in the fullness of self sharing that constitutes the relationship between the divine persons of the Trinity. But we can and do share some aspects of it.

First of all, there is likeness. Just as the Son is the full image of the Father—God from God, light from light, as the Creed puts it—so we are remade in baptism into the image of the risen Christ. We are no longer just a single dreary human individual, remote from God and turned in on our self. We are participants in the saving life of the risen Christ, the life that embraces all believers on earth, the life that offers praise and intercession to the Father in heaven. Our life has a whole new dimension and meaning because it is an extension of Christ's life.

Next, just as Father and Son in the Trinity share with the Spirit the energy that created and redeemed the world, so our life, remade in the image of the Son, involves participation in the ongoing process of creation and redemption. We are not just images of the Son, but his collaborators, working with him to make the world what God intended it to be, offering his love and salvation to our sinful and unredeemed fellow human beings. With that in mind, it's easy to see that Christian morality, the appropriate behavior of God's children, is more than avoiding sin, more than keeping lots of rules. Appropriate behavior for God's children consists in carrying out God's plans for creation, God's program of redemption.

Obviously these relationships of likeness and action between ourselves and the Son involve loving. Loving is the giving of the self to the benevolence of the other. When, through baptism, God makes us his children, we enter into a whole new level of giving and receiving. It is no longer the love of creator for creature and creature for creator. It is the love of Father for Son, expressed through the Holy Spirit. It is a love that enfolds us into the deepest life of the Trinity. When we become children of God through faith in Christ, we are loved as members of God's most intimate family. In return, we are invited to love God not just as creator and judge, but as father and brother.

But there's more. When our life reaches its conclusion and we stand before God in judgment, the main issue will not be the extent to which we kept all God's rules. The main issue will be whether we are in a filial relationship with God or not. If we are, we will be taken into the company of the Lord for all eternity, not as a pay-off for the good we have done, but simply because we belong.

The idea of divine filiation—being children of God—sums up the whole content of First John. Everything the author says about faith, about love, about Christian morality is summed up when he reminds us that we are children of God.

FOR DISCUSSION AND REFLECTION

What effect does being a child of God have on my daily life?

How does it matter whether those around me share filiation in Christ?

Fourth Sunday of Easter (C)

Revelation 7:9, 14b-17

In chapters 6-16 of Revelation, John offers his readers a series of visions of cosmic conflict in which the powers of evil struggle against the goodness and power of God. Ultimately, of course, God will triumph. Just after this portion of the book begins in chapter 6, there is a kind of interlude in chapter 7. Chapter 7 (in verses 1- 8) shows us God sealing his elect with his protective sign to preserve them from harm in the coming crisis. Then (in verses 9-17) we see these elect in their state of final triumph in heaven. Our reading is from this portion of the chapter.

The elect are not a small and exclusive group, but a "great multitude" beyond numbering from every possible grouping on earth. They are in their state of final fulfillment, standing before the risen Christ ("the Lamb") dressed in the white garments that signify joy and carrying palm branches that signify victory.

One of the elders explains the vision to John. These people are those who have survived tribulation. Their claim to be in the presence of the Lamb is the association of their struggles with his blood. (Note that these persons are not necessarily those who have given their lives as martyrs, but those whose struggles have put them in touch with the sacrifice of Christ. Jesus had foretold that his followers would have to take up his cross if they wanted to follow him. See Matthew 10:38.)

Their reward is to stand in unending worship in the presence of the Lamb. He will shelter and deliver them from every need, every want, every suffering. The Lamb will become their shepherd, leading them to the water that signifies their sharing in his life. God will take away all sorrow from their hearts. (Notice how, in these few verses the risen Christ is referred to as Lamb, as a tent offering protection and as a shepherd. No one image can fully express the relationship between Christ and his elect.)

This vision describes the future of those who are faithful to God in spite of present suffering. It describes how Christ cares for them and protects them and comforts them in every conceivable way. It shows how things will be at the end for those who exercise faithfulness and perseverance now.

There are three important elements inherent in what John the visionary teaches us in this passage. First of all, there is the element of struggle. Being a follower of Christ is not some sort of effortless state in which we simply sit back and wait to be gifted by God. No, being faithful to Christ means being like Christ. It means offering ourselves up for the benefit of our brothers and sisters just as Jesus did. It means making ourselves vulnerable to those who reject Jesus and who reject what he stands for. Those who persecuted him are likely to do the same to his followers. There are lots of reasons why being faithful involves struggle.

The second element that we need to be attentive to is fulfillment. All who are faithful, the "great multitude...from every nation, race, people, and tongue" will be sheltered and comforted by the risen Christ, freed from every frustration, dryness, hunger, weariness. All sources of suffering will be removed from them. Christ will recompense them for their efforts with abundant and eternal salvation. "God will wipe away every tear from their eyes."

However (and this is the third important element in the vision), all fulfillment and all salvation comes from Christ. The faithful are qualified to join in the praises of the heavenly court not because they were moral virtuosos who exercised superhuman virtues that God is now obliged to reward but because they have washed their robes (steeped their lives) in the blood of the Lamb.

It is their participation in the heavenly life of the Lamb, the risen Christ, that brings them fulfillment. It is Jesus' death that brings salvation and Jesus' risen life that brings happiness.

Heaven is not a pay-off for the wonderful things we may have done in our lifetime, but Christ's final, definitive, irreversible gift of himself. The heavenly celebration is the final outcome of his life, death and resurrection. Our struggles have meaning only to the extent that they keep us in contact with him. Our fulfillment consists in being made eternally like him. He is the beginning and the end of it all, the substance in which it all consists.

There is one more thing that is not an explicit part of this vision, but which forms the kernel of the preceding vision and which needs to be mentioned here. The Lamb enthroned does not wait indifferently for us until our time of effort is ended. What he has prepared for us in heaven is the conclusion and fullness of the care and love that he already offers us here and now. Heaven has already begun here for those who accept Christ's gifts and who serve the Lamb with joy and confidence. That's part of what we celebrate during this Easter season.

FOR DISCUSSION AND REFLECTION

In what ways have I suffered for my Christian faith?

How do I experience the risen Christ's care for me here and now?

Fifth Sunday of Easter (A)

I Peter 2:4-9

This Sunday's passage from First Peter jumps us back to the initial section of the letter in which the author was talking about the implications of faith and baptism. Our reading comes at the end of that section and deals with Christian identity. Who and what are we who have been led to faith and baptism?

The passage is in three parts, two of which use the image of stones to describe Christ and his Church, the third of which speaks more directly of the believers as God's people.

Christ is a living stone, our text says, and we are living stones, too. We are called to join ourselves to Christ in order to form with him "a spiritual house," a kind of temple that somehow images the old temple in Jerusalem. This spiritual house is a living community that engages itself in "spiritual sacrifices," that is, in prayers and action that proclaim the glory of God. This new edifice, built up through Christ, had already been alluded to by the prophet Isaiah when he was talking about a bright future for the dynasty of King David (see Isaiah 28:16).

Next we see the negative side of Jesus as cornerstone. Those who reject faith in Christ will discover that he is an obstacle in their path, a hindrance that will cause them to stumble. Here the author cites Psalm 118:22 (where the psalmist is talking about Israel's rejection by more important political powers) and Isaiah 8:14 (where the prophet is dealing with the corrective measures that God would take against the wickedness of his people). The implication here is that rejecting an association with Christ, refusing to be part of his spiritual temple, brings with it spiritual destruction.

Last of all in our passage, the author describes the people of faith, those called out from darkness, in more direct terms. He uses terminology from the Old Testament that had been used to describe God's relationship with the Israelites, thus suggesting that Christ's faithful are God's new chosen people. They are chosen by God (see Isaiah 43:20-21) to offer priestly service and worship to God in Christ (see Exodus 19:6). They are "a holy nation," that is, set apart for God (see Exodus 19:6), God's very own people (see Malachi 3:17).

There are several important teachings for us in this passage. First of all is the centrality of Christ. Our worth consists in our association with him. On our own, of ourselves we are nothing. Christ is the central reality to which we must relate. Association with him or detachment from him are the criteria by which the ultimate significance of a human life is judged. Unless we are built into Christ, we are nothing.

This passage also makes clear that our relationship with Christ is not to be a merely private affair. It is true that each individual human being is precious to God. Yet we relate to God in faith in the context of everybody else who has accepted God's gifts. Faith and baptism and Christian identity are essentially communitarian. We are all in Christ together. As a single community of faith we all form together a single temple that is based on the one Christ. A spirituality of individualism is simply not authentically Christian.

Just as participation in Christ's "spiritual house" cannot be individualistic so also it cannot be passive. No member of the community of faith is called merely to receive. We all have the responsibility to carry on the mission of Christ, to offer praise and service to the Father through him. That's why the text calls us all "a royal priesthood." It's not that there is no need for a ministry of ordained priests among God's people, but that we all share in the priestly work of Christ through the communion with Christ that comes to us with baptism.

Finally, because there is only one Christ and only one "spiritual house" founded on him, so also there is only one full and complete expression of that house. There is only one community of faith that is the true Church. Our faith teaches us that that community "subsists in the Catholic Church" (see *Lumen Gentium*, 8). The Council goes on to say that many elements of sanctification and truth can be found outside the visible structure of the Catholic Church. These elements, however, are gifts properly belonging to the Church of Christ and so possess an inner dynamism directed toward Christ's one Church (*Lumen Gentium*, 8).

It is a very rich reading that the Church gives us here. Each part of it calls for further reflection and exploration. Yet it is an answer to a simple question: Who are we?

The cornerstone of our life of faith is that we are sharers in the life of Christ. This sharing we hold in common with all other followers of Christ. We form one people with them. Our membership in this holy people demands our participation in the priestly mission of Christ as well as the expression of our faith by membership in Christ's Church. It is to all that that God calls us.

FOR DISCUSSION AND REFLECTION

How do I see myself as a component of God's edifice?

In what ways do I experience the Church as "a chosen race, a royal priesthood, a holy nation"?

Fifth Sunday of Easter (B)

1 John 3:18-24

Back to the commandments again! Only this time the author of First John does not deal with the commandments as God's challenge to us or as agenda items that flow from our being children of God. In this reading he speaks of God's commandments as a source of security and reassurance in the context of our relationship with the community of faith.

The unorthodox Christians against whom John is writing had ideas about Christ and about Christian living that were different from those shared by John's community. Both sets of beliefs could not be true. If you espoused the wrong beliefs, you were separated from Christ and his people! How can you tell if you really belong? John does not set out to offer a technical theological "proof" for the instructions he gives his readers. He simply offers them a principle: if you keep the commandments you belong to the true community of faith. That's what this Sunday's reading is about.

He has been talking about the implications of the

commandment to love one another. Loving one another involves laying down our lives for one another just as Christ laid down his life for us. At the very least, love means reaching out to our brothers and sisters when they are in need. This is where our reading begins.

Real loving is not a matter of theory or words. It's a matter of practical doing. But this practical doing also enables us to verify our standing as Christians. If we are uncertain sometimes about this standing, we can be confident if we find ourselves doing what God commands, since God's commandments can only lead to righteousness, because God knows what he is doing. If we don't have any question about our standing, keeping the commandments will enable us to maintain security in God and find confidence in our prayer. The commandments being referred to here are faith in Christ and (one more time!) love for our neighbor. If we keep the commandments, we remain in touch with God, God remains in touch with us, we receive God's Spirit, and (by implication) we remain part of the community of God's children. (This mention of the Spirit leads the author in the next few verses, at the beginning of chapter 4, to point out that the acknowledgment of the true humanity of Jesus Christ is a sign of the presence of the Holy Spirit.)

This passage offers us two important teachings. The first is a hard-nosed reminder that loving our neighbors includes actually doing something for them. It means getting our hands dirty. It means giving up time for them. It means making sacrifices. The kind of love that John is talking about is not a way of feeling but a practical orientation of life and action. Love involves giving ourselves away for the good of someone else. It is a matter of decision and will rather than emotion. That is why we can sacrifice ourselves for the love of somebody we don't even like!

The second teaching is about the demonstrative aspects of Christian moral behavior. We have to be very clear about the fact that keeping the commandments does not earn us salvation. There is absolutely nothing that we can do, no matter how generous or how heroic, that will make us worthy to share the life of Christ or that will constrain God to take us into the interior life of the Trinity. God's life is too far above us to be accessible to our own efforts.

We have seen, however, that sharing that life (through God's gift) involves some consequences, carries with it some implications. If we share truly Christ's life, certain kinds of behavior must necessarily follow. What John tells us today is the reverse of that principle: if we can verify certain kinds of behavior in our lives, we must be sharers in the life of Christ. What we are to look for in ourselves to verify our union with Christ is authentic and true faith in him and practical, effective love for our fellow human beings. If that's there, we have no need to wonder about the fundamental direction of our lives, no need to torment ourselves with questions about whether God is pleased with us, no need to be afraid that, when our life is over, we will be found deficient.

This reassurance and security that John offers us are not intended to encourage arrogance or self-satisfaction. The issue is not what we accomplish, but our response to what God has accomplished in us. Our ability to relate to the Father in Christ and our capacity to give ourselves generously to the service of our neighbor are not our achievements but God's gifts. The confidence that we are able to have in him as a result of our keeping his commandments is based on our conviction of his love for us and not on any awareness of our own natural worth or personal virtue.

God does not like to toy with his children, to keep them in suspense about his care for their well-being, about his presence in their lives. He keeps telling us how we stand with him. He lets us know where we stand through what he has put into our hearts: faith in Christ and love for our neighbor.

FOR DISCUSSION AND REFLECTION

Whom do I love? What does that love involve?

How do I know if my faith in Christ is true and authentic?

Fifth Sunday of Easter (C)

Revelation 21:1-5a

The first three readings from Revelation offered us images of the heavenly Christ: ruler of the churches, saving Lamb, protector and rewarder of the faithful. Now the lectionary takes us to the last chapters of Revelation and gives us two Sunday readings about the final state of redeemed creation and then, to complete the series, provides the conclusion of the book for the Seventh Sunday of Easter.

This Sunday's reading from the beginning of chapter 21 gives us a general overview of how things will be when the conflicts have ended and God's enemies have been destroyed. It is a lyrical passage that deserves to be set to music and sung by a choir of a thousand voices!

"Then I saw" indicates that this is a new vision, distinct from what had gone before. John the visionary sees "a new heaven and a new earth," not all creation cast aside and substituted with something different, but the old creation, renovated and purged from the age-old stains of sinfulness. The sea is an image of chaos and evil and it is completely done away with.

Now to fill this new creation there comes a city from heaven, sent by God, beautiful as a bride on her wedding day. (In 19:7 Revelation speaks of the wedding feast of the Lamb and, in the image of the bride, seems to be referring to the Church.) In this heavenly city on earth God is to dwell with his human creatures. (The idea of living together includes more than God appearing to his people or even protecting them from their enemies. It has overtones of permanence and immediate personal intimacy. God will settle down and be close to us forever.) Everything that made the previous kind of earthly life painful will be removed. Death and sorrow and pain will all be things of the past when this new world order begins.

Finally, we hear the voice of God himself: "Everything is fresh and new and it's all my doing."

This passage gives us the full and fundamental message of Revelation: God is going to win in the end and everything is going to be OK. All this has been the accomplishment of the Lamb, who had come forward in chapter 5 to carry out God's plans for the world and who, in the intervening chapters, had confronted and defeated all God's enemies.

What this message calls for from us is not mindless optimism, but deep spiritual conviction about the power of God, a conviction based on the victorious salvation brought about by Christ. God will win in the end because the end will be the full development of what has already begun in the resurrection of Jesus.

His Resurrection makes the old categories irrelevant: selfishness, sinfulness, burning out, getting old, losing our way, undergoing death—all this is over thanks to our new life in Christ. It is not a matter of throwing away or destroying the basic human contexts in which we have lived, but of imbuing them with newness, with new life and new meaning that come from the risen life of Christ. He is the source of a new hope for those who believe in him, the source of a new identity which is, at the same time, both ours and his.

Being part of this new heaven and new earth, being a citizen of the new Jerusalem in which we will live side by side with God is not something that we achieve or earn by our human efforts. It is all God's doing. It is God who makes all things new.

Yet our role is not simply passive waiting, hiding out in a cave, as it were, until the conflict is over and it's time to march in the victory parade. Our part is more than that, and it's a part that nobody can perform for us. God looks to us for ongoing receptivity, for ongoing assimilation of the life of Christ whose beginnings we received in baptism. God wants us to become ever more capable of living in the new Jerusalem, ever more in harmony with the kind of life that he will share with us there.

This is not an effortless undertaking. It requires resistance to the evil that is all around us, that infects our minds and hearts and directs us in destructive directions. It requires resistance to our own sinful inclinations, those inherited tendencies that make us want to look out for ourselves first, that make us settle for immediate short-term satisfaction instead of waiting for what God has in store for us later. Maturity in the life of Christ can also demand patience with our fellow believers who so often seem to hinder us more than help us. It can even call for forbearance with the Church on our part, with that community of believers which itself is always in need of purification and renewal. All this can cause us sadness and pain and tears. It can cause us to undergo many kinds of death in our earthly life's span. But in the end our efforts will be assumed into the life of the risen Christ in the new creation, not as a reward for what we have accomplished but as God's definitive gift to us.

A saintly friend of mine used to say, "We are an Easter people and 'Alleluia' is our song." "Alleluia" because God will make all things new in the risen Christ. Even us.

FOR DISCUSSION AND REFLECTION

What needs to be made new in my life and my world?

What causes the tears in my life? How can I allow God to wipe them away?

Sixth Sunday of Easter (A)

I Peter 3:15-18

At the end of chapter 2, the author of First Peter addressed directions about Christian behavior to the slaves in his audience, as we saw in the reading for the Fourth Sunday of Easter (A). Following that, in the full text of the letter, came directions for spouses, then some general principles of Christian behavior. Now he instructs these new Christians about how to deal with suffering.

Just before our passage, the author tells his readers not to be afraid if they are mistreated because of their faith. Rather (as our passage begins), in the forum of their hearts they should venerate or reverence Christ as their Lord. Exteriorly they should be ready to explain their way of life to non-Christians. This dialog should be conducted with courtesy for the questioner and with reverence for the God whose initiatives are being explained. Believers should conduct themselves in a way that makes mistreatment and slander inappropriate. Their behavior should offer their opponents no pretext for punishment. If mistreatment and punishment are inflicted, it must not be for any evil they have done.

After all, Christ was totally innocent of wrongdoing, yet he suffered, and, in so doing, brought salvation to the world. But suffering was not the last word for Christ. He was brought "to life in the Spirit" by his Father (a life that his followers were presumably invited to share).

We have already seen that these new Christians to whom this letter is addressed were not suffering full-fledged persecution and torture and death. Those things had not yet begun. What they were suffering was insult and defamation and vilification. They were resented because their faith made it inappropriate for them to live like their pagan neighbors. They were "different," and "different" people are often suspected, despised and made unwelcome.

First Peter's advice to them is not to withdraw from the world, to betake themselves into separatist defensiveness. On the contrary, they were to be ready and willing to enter into association with their pagan neighbors, to speak with them about their faith and their commitment to Christ. This communication should take place in an atmosphere of cordiality and friendship. They were to be conspicuously gentle. Arrogance, aggressiveness, belligerence were not to be part of the mix. They were to invite interest rather than to provoke animosity.

This advice of First Peter to these unidentified early believers is still good advice for us today. Our situations are similar. We live in a mostly pagan world, a world whose goals and values are different from our own. We may not like to admit it, but most of the world around us has different ideas than we do about success and failure, about the purpose of our existence, about sexuality, about marriage and family life. Things that horrify us, such as abortion and assisted suicide, are taken for granted and looked on as a basic human right by our contemporary American society. Our enunciation of other values, our protests against what is nothing other than murder are not kindly received by the world around us. We don't get arrested or punished for what we believe and say, but it certainly doesn't make us popular in many circles. We are looked upon as antiquated, unhelpful, retrograde, socially irresponsible, if not downright subversive.

In a context like this, there are some choices that could be made. We could take ourselves out of the mainstream of society and live apart from the rest of the world, waiting for the wrath of God to descend on everything around us. But that has never been the Christian option.

We could also stand up and fight, spending our lives in open opposition to and defiant rejection of the world in which we live, preferring even to die for our beliefs rather than live in a context of sinfulness. There have been some such persons in the history of the Church, men and women who went around trying to provoke civil authorities into making them martyrs. But people like that have never been proposed as a model for everybody.

There is another option, the option of quiet and determined witness. God wants us to live in the real world, a world populated by blasphemers and sinners. This was the world that Christ lived in, the world he came to save. We are to live here not as participants in all the world's sinfulness and vanity, but as women and men who look to a further horizon. We are called to be conspicuous not by our pushiness or pugnacity, but by our goodness and love toward those around us, by our reverence for the Lord we serve. God expects us to know what we believe and why, to be clear about how we are called to behave and why. And all this is not to be held in secret like a hidden treasure, known to only a few. It is rather to be proclaimed as a gift intended for all, a gift whose beauty and worth we are skilled at describing. We believers of today, like the believers of old, have been gifted with a wonderfully full way of living, with magnificent future expectations. To us, as to them, God's word speaks: "Be ready to explain the reasons for your hope to anybody who asks."

FOR DISCUSSION AND REFLECTION

In what ways have I suffered because of my faith?

How do I communicate the good news of Christ in my life?

Sixth Sunday of Easter (B)

1 John 4:7-10

The last two readings from First John that the lectionary gives us are about love. This Sunday's is principally about God's love for us (and happens to fit nicely with the Gospel reading for this day). Next Sunday's is about our love for one another. However, as usual in this book of the New Testament, the author does not present a clear, linear treatment of a clearly identified theme. Everything he talks about is mixed up with something else. This is due in part to the writer's limited literary skill, but also to the fact that the things of God are not generally clear and linear, but tend to be linked together in such a way that one thing necessarily leads to another. We can start anywhere we please and eventually reach every aspect of God's revelation.

If this Sunday's reading were to be rewritten in a clearer and more logical way, it might turn out to be something like what follows. One of the most basic characteristics of God is loving, the giving of one's self. God has shown his love to the world by sending the Son to make up for our deficiencies ("expiation for our sins") and reunite us to himself. Our love for one another is a response to God's initiative of love in our regard and is a consequence of the life of Christ we share thanks to his redemption of us. Just as godliness and loving and self-giving are all linked together in God, so also they are linked together in us. Loving is a sign of knowing God and being like him. Not loving is an indication of detachment from God and dissimilarity to him.

There are three pivotal points of Christian revelation inherent in this short selection from First John.

The first is that God is a God of love. In the history of human thought and human religious experience, people have looked on God in many different ways. Some have seen him as the benevolent clock maker who wound things up and walked away, leaving creation to unwind according to the plan he set for it, but not taking any day to day interest in it in the meantime. Some have seen God as the fierce warlord who will lead his people to victory over their enemies provided they have made appropriate sacrifices to keep him happy. Some, closer to home, have seen God as the bookkeeper who keeps careful watch on us, scrupulously noting down all our good and bad deeds so that he can close out our account quickly and efficiently when we finally stand before him in judgment. The real God, the Father of our Lord Jesus Christ, isn't like any of that. He is a loving Father who cares for his creatures, who invites them to be like him, who goes to great—some say ridiculous—lengths to insure their eternal happiness in his company.

The second pivotal point of Christian revelation presented in this Sunday's reading is that God has intervened in human history. At a certain specific point in time, God determined to clean up the mess that human beings had made of the world he had given them. He came into their midst in the person of God the Son who became a specific human being and lived in a specific place and spoke specific words and experienced certain specific events in his lifetime. Jesus is not some faceless everyman, an abstraction based on philosophical speculation about human nature or about God. Jesus is a real, distinct, one of a kind human being who entered human history as an expression of God's love to carry out a clearly defined mission of salvation.

These two truths of revelation are among the most fundamental realities that distinguish Christian belief from every other religious faith, every other religious philosophy. Belief in and commitment to a loving and a saving God, a God who became and remains part of human history, are essential components of the Christian faith.

The third pivotal point of Christian belief (and life) that this reading provides is something that has already appeared in our live letters, but which bears frequent repetition. It is a consequence of God's love and God's project of salvation. Our love for God, our service to God, our obedience to God are not ways of compelling some positive response from God, but themselves derive from the action that God has already taken on our behalf. In sending his Son to be our redeemer, our loving Father has taken the initiative. Anything that the most godly and most generous of us can offer him is a response, an answer to God's prior undertaking. The gift of ourselves that we offer to God, the sharing of ourselves that we offer to our brothers and sisters is all derivative from God's previous gift of himself to us. "This is love: not that we have loved God, but that he has loved us." Any approach to God that does not take that into account is simply erroneous.

It all hangs together, not just in the foggy prose of the author of First John but in our grasp of Christian revelation: faith, love, obedience to God's commandments—not three disjointed articles of belief but one consistent insight to guide us to salvation.

FOR DISCUSSION AND REFLECTION

How do I experience God's love for me?

How have I responded to God's gift of salvation in Christ?

Sixth Sunday of Easter (C)

Revelation 21:10-14, 22-23

In last Sunday's reading John gave us a general overview of the end time, when God will be definitively victorious over his enemies, when God will dwell with his elect, when all creation will be made new again.

This Sunday's reading elaborates and interprets one element of what we saw last week: the holy city, the new Jerusalem. As edited for the lectionary, the reading shows us the origin and nature of the city, its beauty and its purpose.

First of all the city is imbued with godliness. It comes from God's heavenly abode and is "holy," that is, godlike. It even looks like God, gleaming with God's indescribable brilliance. (Note that John says its radiance was "like that" of jasper and crystal.)

Next comes a series of descriptive items, all of which have for their purpose to express the beauteous perfection of the city. Six times in all we have the number twelve, the number of fullness and completion (like the number of months in a year). There are twelve angels stationed at the twelve gates inscribed with the names of the twelve tribes of Israel. There are twelve levels of foundation inscribed with the twelve names of the twelve apostles of the Lamb. With three gates on each side, the city is cubical in shape, that is, it has a perfect geometrical form. The mention of the twelve tribes of Israel and of the twelve apostles of the Lamb acting as foundation seems to indicate that the city is to be viewed as the continuation, indeed the conclusion, of God's plan of salvation that began with the Israel of old and that reached its final stage with the apostles' proclamation of the risen Christ.

Thirdly, the reading gives us the purpose of the city: to provide a means of contact between God and his elect. There is nothing in the city that is not holy, nothing that needs to be shut out by the walls of a temple. There is no sun or moon there because there is no darkness, no alternation of day and night. Within the city, God and the Lamb are everywhere, constantly providing brightness and life. Everything is imbued with the power and the majesty and the sacredness of God and the Lamb.

This holy city is an image of the Church. Just before our reading begins, in 21:9, the angel says to John, "I will show you the bride, the wife of the Lamb." As we saw last week, the bride of the Lamb is the Church. As Revelation moves toward its conclusion, the victorious kingdom of God, the triumphant Church and the living presence of God all meld into one in the image of the heavenly Jerusalem.

This reading invites us to give some thought to a fundamentally important question about the Church, that is, the relationship between the community of the faithful here and now and the full and final kingdom of God still to come. Put succinctly, the relationship is one of "already but not yet."

The Church, this community of believers that we experience here and now, is the beginning of the final victory of God over evil, the start of a people who will dwell in glory with God for all eternity. God's project of salvation that began with the patriarchs of the Old Testament and was proclaimed in its final form by the apostles and their successors is embodied in the Church, the

Church that will reach its full maturity as the new Jerusalem. No further suffering and death of Christ is necessary for human redemption. No further instruction and guidance will come from God to lead us where he means us to be. Everything we need to reach final glory has already been provided for us. We are already equipped to become citizens of the heavenly Jerusalem, already counted in the census of its citizens.

But we are not yet there. We have not yet reached the point when everything will be expressed and provided for us in the universal, all-uniting presence of God. We are still on the road. We still need sacraments and Scripture. We are still called to repentance and change. We still vary in fervor and dedication from day to day. We still need help from each another. We are still called to provide help for each other. We have to put up with the sinfulness of the world (and the Church!) around us, and the world around us (and the Church!) has to put up with us.

There are two pitfalls that we have to be careful of as we deal with the "already but not yet" of the Church. One is to write the Church off as irrelevant in our pursuit of eternal happiness, to forget that the Church of now will become the Church of then, to overlook the fact that, with all its faults, the Church is even now the bride of the Lamb, even now offering salvation from Christ. The beginnings of the new Jerusalem are already in our midst.

The other pitfall is to forget that the Church we have now has not reached its final fulfillment. We need to acknowledge the present limitations of the Church, its leaders, its members. We need to acknowledge that its final perfection will not and cannot come from us. It can only come "down out of heaven" from God.

The Church of now lives in hope and repentance and it looks forward to the state in which it will exist in gratitude and fulfillment—in the city of the Lamb.

Does the light of the Lamb shine in my life here and now?

What elements of the Church of now do I find particularly indicative of its future glory?

The Ascension of the Lord (A)

Ephesians 1:17-23

Many people look on the feast of the Lord's Ascension as the commemoration of a change of address for Jesus. He had been living on earth for a while, but at a certain point he moved back to heaven where he had come from. That's one way to look on the Ascension, of course, but there is more to it than that.

Jesus' being taken up into the clouds was an expression of the Father's pleasure in the mission of Jesus. In answer to his life of faithfulness and self-sacrifice, the Father exalts Jesus above all creation and establishes Jesus' glorified humanity permanently in his own presence.

Likewise, although Jesus would no longer be present to his followers as he had been before, his saving activity would continue in the life of the Church, a life that was just beginning to unfold. Ascension has to do with Jesus, but it also celebrates the Church.

The passage from Ephesians that is read in Year A (and which may also be read in the other two years of the cycle), is concerned with Jesus' exaltation and with the Church. The passage comes soon after the opening salutation and a long passage of praise and blessing. It is immediately preceded by the thanksgiving that was a conventional part of letters of that historical period. But the thanksgiving is brief and leads into our passage in which Paul prays for the recipients of the letter and introduces the main topic of the letter, the Church. It is a reading that is complex in content and structure. It practically cries out for grammatical diagramming and theological explanation.

The author (Paul or one of his disciples) first prays for knowledge for Ephesians, for a grasp of spiritual realities. This knowledge would bring enlightenment. This enlightenment that is being prayed for would be concerned with three realities, that is, with an awareness of the hope that is connected with our call to faith; with a consciousness of the gifts that come to us as followers of Christ; with an appreciation of the power of God that we share through faith.

Now the text goes on to describe how God has exercised his power. He raised Jesus from the dead and gave him the position of honor in heaven. Jesus Christ is superior to all the powers of the cosmos both now and for all futures, temporal and eternal. Christ is at the summit of everything and has been established as head of the Church. The Church is nothing less than the body of Christ, a body that will continue to grow and develop until it manifests the full life and holiness of its Head.

Put simply, this passage prays that the readers may become aware of God's power expressed in the exalted Christ and in the life and growth of the extension of Christ that is the Church.

One might say that this reading describes what it means to be a member of the Church. Being a member of the Church involves sharing in the exaltation that the Father conferred on Jesus as a result of his human ministry. But it also means sharing in the earthly expression of the glorious risen Christ, sharing in his body, the Church.

The last verse of our reading speaks of the Church as "the fullness of the one who fills all things in every way." This suggests that, while the Church will never be anything different from the body of Christ and while all fullness of godliness and grace already dwells in Christ, the Church is not yet finished. It is still being filled with the glory of Christ and is growing toward the stage when it will be a complete expression of the fullness of Christ.

This means that the Church has a history, a history that is still in the process of coming to completion. That history consists in the unfolding of God's plan for our salvation. In Christ, the Father's plan has reached its final stage. Christ's eternal glorification in heaven means that his work is done, that there is no more need for future earthly ministries on Christ's part. Salvation has been achieved. But it still has to be applied to specific women and men. It still has to be presented and responded to by various cultures in various times under various circumstances. God seems to want his saving love for us to be expressed in all the multitudinous contexts that make up human reality. Until it is, the body of Christ has not reached its goal, has not reached fulfillment. Its history is not over.

But God does not work at the history of the Church alone. Just as Jesus chose to need human collaborators for his ministry of salvation in his earthly life, so also he has chosen to need collaborators for the ministry of salvation that he continues from heaven. Each one of us has a role to play in the expression of God's love for us human creatures. Each one of us has a part to play, a contribution to make to the history of the body of Christ. The ascension is concerned with the final glorification of Christ. It is concerned with the growth of the body of Christ, which is the Church. And it is therefore concerned with us.

FOR DISCUSSION AND REFLECTION

Where do I see the saving power of God working in the Church?
How do I contribute to the future of the Church?

The Ascension of the Lord (Optional B)

Ephesians 4:1-13

On the feast of the Ascension of the Lord, we commemorate Jesus' return in glory to his Father after the conclusion of his earthly ministry. But the Ascension is not just concerned with

Jesus. It is also concerned with the Church.

The plan of salvation is now fulfilled. Everything that Jesus had intended to do is now accomplished. Humanity has been reunited to God in and through the self-giving and faithfulness of Jesus. But what Jesus accomplished still has to be applied to humankind. We still need to be transformed into Christ. We still need to assimilate his life into our own. And that's the task of the Church. Jesus' human mission is over and he will no longer be present with us as he was before, but the Church's extension of the mission of Jesus has just begun. This is why the Gospel readings for all three years of the lectionary cycle are concerned with Jesus' definitive sending his apostles out to preach the good news throughout the world.

It is appropriate, therefore, that the second reading in all three years of the cycle is taken from the letter to the Ephesians, whose principle subject is the Church. (We will be reading at some length from Ephesians later in this year's Sunday cycle.)

The optional reading for Year B is from the portion of the letter that is concerned with behavior. There are three parts to the reading.

First of all, the author encourages the readers to pursue unity in the Church. Oneness is what life in Christ is all about, oneness in the faith community, oneness in the Trinity. It is in this context of unity that he calls for attitudes and actions that will promote unity: humility, gentleness, patience, willingness to bear with others' faults, eagerness to preserve the unity and peace that are the gift of the Spirit. This is the kind of behavior that is in accord with the Christian vocation that we have received.

Now the author wants to talk about diversity, about the various kinds and degrees of gifts that Christ gives to his followers. He introduces this section with a quote from Psalm 68 (which is a victory song for God). The author comments on God's victorious "going up" and applies it to Christ. The Son who had come from heaven has now returned there in order to exercise divine generosity by giving gifts to humankind.

Finally, in the third section of our reading, the text lists some of the gifts that Christ gives. Some people are called to be apostles, others prophets or evangelists or teachers. But the purpose of all these different gifts is the same: to enable the members of the Church ("the holy ones") to carry out their "work of ministry." This work, this calling that is given to all the members of the Church, is to express the reality of Christ and extend his work, his generosity, his love, his presence until the body of Christ (which is the Church) reaches the full extent of the growth that Christ has in mind for it. That maturity of the body of Christ also involves knowledge and unity of faith for us all.

This reading from Ephesians teaches us that we are all called to help the Church reach maturity. There are several implications to that call.

The first is that the Church is much more than a convenience store where we come to get goods and services as we need them. Our participation in the Church is not just a matter of receiving. We are all called to give, to participate in the execution of the plan that the glorious Christ wishes to unfold from his place in heaven. We all have a job to do in bringing about "the full stature of Christ," the total fulfillment of his project of salvation.

The second implication to our call to help the Church reach maturity is that we must all be dedicated to the same Christ and all extend ourselves to one another in the one life of the one Christ that we share. Selfishness and isolation in our relationship with the Lord, a "me and Jesus" mind-set, is simply inappropriate to our Christian vocation. We are to be united with one another even as we are united with Christ.

Yet this does not mean that we are all called to be the same. Each of us is called to reflect and extend the saving plan of Christ but none of us can reflect Christ is his fullness. We cannot all be everything or do everything. Christ calls "some as apostles, others as prophets, others as evangelists." We could extend the list to include parents and statesmen and scholars and social workers. We are not all the same, but we are not, for that reason, unimportant to one another. The fullness of Christ needs the contributions of each of us. For that reason we are called to respect not only the gifts that we have received, but also the gifts and capabilities of our sisters and brothers in the Lord.

As Christ ascends to the right hand of the Father he leaves behind a Church gifted both with unity and with diversity in him, a Church whose final goal is full maturity in him.

FOR DISCUSSION AND REFLECTION

How do I contribute to the full growth of the body of Christ?

Which is more demanding for me, the unity of the Church or its diversity?

The Ascension of the Lord (Optional C)

Hebrews 9:24-28, 10:19-23

The feast of the Ascension marks the end of Jesus' earthly mission. He now returns to his heavenly Father. But what Jesus accomplished during his years on earth still has to be applied to humanity. That's the task of the Church, and so the feast of the Ascension is concerned, at least in part, with the mission of the Church. That's why the second reading from the first chapter of Ephesians (provided for Year A) is permitted on this feast in all three years of the cycle. That's also why the optional reading for Year B is also from Ephesians (chapter 4) and is also about the Church.

But there is another aspect to the feast of the Ascension, that is, the permanence of redemption. It is that aspect that we hear about in the optional reading that is offered for Year C, from the Letter to the Hebrews.

This reading is from the section of Hebrews in which the author is demonstrating the superiority of Jesus' priesthood and sacrifice to what had been available under Jewish law. (Recall that the purpose of Hebrews was to offer encouragement to Jewish converts who were growing weary under the demands of the Christian faith.)

The reading is composed of two sections. In the first section the author is contrasting the sacrifice of Christ with the rite of the Jewish Day of Atonement, the only day when the high priest entered the Holy of Holies of the Jerusalem temple. Jesus' sacrifice is not offered in a reproduction of heaven (like the sanctuary was), but in heaven itself. He actually appears before God to intercede for us. Likewise, his sacrifice was not one that had to be repeated every year. It was a one-time event that marked a definitive turning point in human history ("at the end of the ages"). If Jesus' sacrifice had to be repeated, it would mean that he had to keep dying over and over again. (Note how carefully structured the passage is: not made by hands...but heaven itself; not repeatedly...but once and for all.) Now comes a parallel with ordinary people: Just as each of us dies once and then faces judgment, so also Jesus dies once (for our sins), but he comes back not to face judgment but to bring salvation.

The next section of the reading is from the section of Hebrews in which the author draws practical consequences from his comparison of Jesus and the Old Law. The sacrifice of Jesus makes it possible for us to enter the heavenly Holy of Holies with him. We should be confident about our future access to heaven since we have there in Jesus "a great priest over the house of God." Having been cleansed in the waters of baptism, we can approach God with trust. The commitments we made at baptism and the reliability of him to whom we made the commitments make it possible for us to live in unwavering hope.

Today's feast, as illuminated by this reading from Hebrews, teaches us that there was an end to the visible, earthly life of Jesus. At a certain point his redemptive ministry among us reached a conclusion, and he returned to where he had come from. But the salvation he merited for us persists because the self-offering of Christ persists in the presence of his heavenly Father in heaven. The sacrifice of Jesus was not time-bound or only partially effective like the sacrifices of the Jerusalem temple. It was a "once for all" offering of himself that will continue forever.

The mission of the Church is to proclaim the sacrifice of Christ and make it accessible for men and women of other times and places. But what the Church proclaims and offers is not a new sacrifice, not a new ministry on Jesus' part, but the same self-gift, the same self-offering that he made during his earthly life now continued and universalized in heaven. The salvation that the Church offers is not only the saving action of Jesus in the historical past, but also the saving gift of himself for his human brothers and sisters in the heavenly present.

Christ has left the spotlight at the center of the earthly stage on which he played out the redeeming events of his earthly life. But he continues to control the action of the drama from the timeless sanctuary of heaven.

In view of all this, we are called to confidence, to trust and to hope. If we maintain the contact with the living Christ that began for us in baptism, the outcome of our earthly life is guaranteed. We will enter the sanctuary of heaven with Jesus to spend an eternity of happiness with him there. We belong there because that's where our priest is, and a priest and his people belong together.

Christ died for our salvation. In response to his death, his heavenly Father brought him back to life, to a new kind of life that will never end. Christ is still living for us, still loving us, still liberating us. That's what we celebrate on the feast of Ascension.

FOR DISCUSSION AND REFLECTION

How do I express confidence in Christ's ongoing redemption?

Which parts of my life in Christ require repetition? Which parts are unchanging? Why?

Seventh Sunday of Easter (A)

I Peter 4:13-16

This reading is the last of our six-week series from First Peter. The author has been speaking about the final judgment that is soon to come (verse 7) and will return to that subject after the verses that constitute our section (in verses 17-19). That is the context in which he returns still again to the question of suffering as he moves toward the conclusion of his letter.

He calls on these new believers to face their sufferings with rejoicing when their suffering reflects the suffering of Christ. Present rejoicing will be increased when Christ's final glory is revealed. Such suffering constitutes a blessing and involves our being enfolded into the glory of God.

Of course sufferings that are inflicted on people as a result of their own misdeeds are not a source of glory. Such sufferings are unworthy of a member of the family of faith.

But if our faith is the cause for our suffering, we have nothing to be ashamed of. In fact, we should glorify God if being identified as a Christian is what gets us into trouble. (It is worth noting that the label "Christian" appears only three times in the New Testament: Acts 11:26, Acts 26:8 and here. Each time it seems to be a name given to members of the community by outsiders and to have a connotation of contempt. "Christians" were "them," and not nice people like "us." Being called a Christian was not a compliment. The very name involved disparagement.)

Whatever suffering these Christians were experiencing, it certainly was of concern to the author of First Peter. We have heard about it on three of the last five Sundays. But our reading for this Seventh Sunday of Easter puts suffering into a new light. The important words in our reading are "rejoice," "glory" and "blessed." Suffering is a cause for rejoicing if it links us to the suffering of Christ. It qualifies us for a share in God's own glory and enables us to offer glory (that is, praise and honor) to God. To suffer abuse for the name of Christ (that is, to experience the insult of being called a Christian) is really a blessing.

Our passage offers us a chance to reflect a bit on the meaning that Christians are invited to find in suffering. First of all, it's important to remind ourselves that there are many kinds of suffering: physical pain, emotional unbalance, social rejection, personal embarrassment. Sometimes suffering comes as a result of something that we ourselves have or have not done. Sometimes it arises out of causes that we cannot determine.

Our Christian faith does not teach us that any suffering is good in itself (unless, perhaps it is the suffering we are made to experience as a result of our own misdeeds, the sort of suffering that our text excludes from being a source of blessing). But our faith does teach us that there can be a dimension of value in our suffering. This value comes from the opportunity that our sufferings give us to tie into the sufferings of Christ.

The sufferings of Christ, however, were not salvific because they were sufferings, but because they were expressions and consequences of Christ's faithfulness to his heavenly Father. It is not the case that the Father took pleasure in the suffering of Jesus and therefore pardoned our sins. The heavenly Father took pleasure in the dedication and consistent self-giving of Jesus that persisted even when it brought Jesus suffering and death.

Our sufferings, therefore, have value not because they are sufferings, as if God is most pleased with us when we are most in agony, but because they are reflections of and participation in the faithfulness of Christ. Patient endurance, persistent trust and hope in God's love for us, the willingness to forgive: these are what make our sufferings meritorious because these qualities are what make our sufferings like Christ's. The issue is not whether and how much pain (of whatever kind) we are asked to endure, but how we endure, how we respond to the suffering.

The call to rejoice in our suffering that we hear in this Sunday's text is not a call to be happy because we are in pain. It is a call to be happy because the pain we are asked to bear is an opportunity to be like Christ, and being like Christ is more important than being without suffering.

Our passage also gives us a chance to do a little reflecting about what it means to be a Christian. We don't have to endure the same sort of scorn and insult that was directed toward our ancestors in the faith. Most of the time, it doesn't make much difference to the people around us whether we are Christians. Much of the time, they can't even tell whether we are Christians or not! The whole idea of Christian faith has, as it were, become watered down and trivialized by our culture so that it's of about the same importance as what color socks we wear. And yet, over the course of the family history of our faith, being a Christian has cost people their lives, has motivated people to leave behind everything they had, has led people to devote themselves to the most thankless of human tasks, has guided people to almost superhuman heights of mystical experience and theological speculation. Maybe this reading can invite us to reflect on what the name of Christian means to us.

FOR DISCUSSION AND REFLECTION

Can I find reasons to rejoice when I experience suffering?

What difference does my being a Christian make to the world around me?

Seventh Sunday of Easter (B)

I John 4:11-16

This Sunday's reading follows immediately on last Sunday's in First John. Not surprisingly, there is a great deal of repetition in the two, but, whereas last Sunday's emphasized the meaning of God's love for us, this Sunday's underlines the significance of our love for God.

If we want to be in touch with God, the author says, if we

want to know and see God, if we want to experience God's love for us, we have to love one another. That's what godliness is all about and that's how we express godliness in human terms. If we are in touch with God through love, the Spirit will be in us. But there is more. God's sending his Son to save us is a particular expression of his love for us, and so we also remain in touch with God through our acknowledgment of Jesus as savior. Love is what keeps God in touch with us and us in touch with God. Through love he remains in us and we in him.

One of the recurrent themes of First John (in addition to faith, love, keeping God's commandments) is the theme of "remaining in." More than a dozen times in this short treatise the author speaks of God remaining in, abiding in, being in union with us and of us remaining in, abiding in, being in union with God. The outcome of our faith in Christ and of our love for God and for one another (the basic demands of Christianity) is that God remains in us and we in God. "Remaining in" is what Christian life is all about.

"Remaining in" is another way of expressing the reality of grace and of our sharing the life of the risen Christ. When we are baptized, our human existence is raised to a new level. It is no longer just we ourselves, in our individual human personhood, who live this particular human life. Christ lives it with us. He enters the fabric of our life and we enter the fabric of his. Our life is his and his life is ours. He, true God and true man, "remains in" us and we in him.

This is what constitutes salvation or redemption: participating in the ongoing life of the risen Christ. Obviously this participation is a gift. It's not something we can ever earn or deserve. God has to give it to us, and God has given it to us through Jesus' life and death and resurrection whose outcomes he extends to us now through the sacraments of the Church.

But we have our part to play in salvation, too. We have to accept the gift that God offers us. The initiation of that acceptance is expressed by our reception of the sacrament of baptism when we (or others in our name if we are infants) profess our faith in Jesus as Son of God and Savior. We continue to deepen and assimilate God's gift of salvation throughout our lives by our participation in and response to the saving action of Christ that is offered to us in the other sacraments.

But living a Christian life, cultivating the salvation that God has given us, "remaining in" Christ, demands more than receiving the sacraments. It also requires living consistently with the life of Christ that we have received, living in accord with Christ's godliness. The life of Christ which constitutes our godliness can and should determine and color every aspect of our individual human existence. The Christian life consists in each of us expressing in our concrete human circumstances what Christ would do if he had his way here. Our Christian life is supposed to speak out the presence of Christ that abides within us. Moral theologians and spiritual guides have thought and written volumes about the details of Christian life, about the specifics of letting Christ live in and through us. But it's all summed up in John's repeated exhortation to love. We express God when we express love because God's most obvious characteristic is love. We express Christ when we express love because his life was and is a life of love. We extend Christ's life when we love our sisters and brothers because love for his sisters and brothers was and is the guiding force of his life and mission.

Sharing the life of Christ, God and man, through faith and love is what constitutes a Christian life. But it is also what constitutes eternal happiness. When our earthly life is over and we are united definitively with the risen Jesus, we will enter a life that is totally different from what we experience now. But it will also be a life that is totally the same, because its basic constituents—living in Christ Jesus and loving in Christ Jesus—will not change. They will remain.

"Remaining in"—God remaining in us and we remaining in God through Christ—is what we are called to now and what lies ahead of us in heaven. We accept and carry out that "remaining in" through faith in Christ, human and divine, through love for God and neighbor and through carrying out the commandments that flow from faith and love. That's what First John teaches us.

FOR DISCUSSION AND REFLECTION

How do I remain in God? How does God remain in me?
Where do I see God in my world?

Seventh Sunday of Easter (C)

Revelation 22:12-14, 16-17, 20

This Sunday brings us to the end of our series of readings from Revelation. Indeed, it brings us to the end of the New Testament, to the last words of the Bible.

The final part of chapter 22 constitutes a kind of epilogue to this book of comfort and reassurance. It comprises a set of warnings, exhortations and words of encouragement. John the visionary brings his readers back from the new creation that is the kingdom of God and plants us once more in the here and now, but in a here and now that is enriched by contact with the eternal risen Christ. (The speakers in this part of Revelation are many, and it is not always clear who is speaking at a given moment.)

Our passage begins with the voice of Jesus, announcing himself in images (Alpha and Omega, and so on) that were earlier applied to "the Lord God" (see 1:8). He announces the theme of this reading: "I am coming soon," and says that his coming will bring with it a just recompense to each person according to what he or she has done.

Next a few lines of commentary, perhaps from John: being blessed at the time of the coming of Jesus will consist in having washed one's robes and in having access to the tree of life and so to the heavenly city. (These seem to be allusions to the sacraments of baptism and Eucharist.)

Christ speaks again, identifying himself by means of messianic titles and assuring the reader that the message presented in this book of visions is really from him.

Now two more voices are heard from: the Church and the Spirit of Jesus that inspires the Church speaking in response to Jesus' promise to come. "Do come!" they say. Then the text invites the reader to join in praying for the coming of Jesus and to come forward to receive the gift of eternal life.

Jesus repeats his promise one last time and the voice of the author expresses again the prayer of the Church: "Yes! Come, Lord Jesus."

The recurrent motif of this reading is "Come." In these verses Jesus twice promises to come and the elect pray for his coming three times. It is worth noting that Jesus had already promised his coming in 22:7, before our reading begins, as well as in 2:5, 2:16, 3:11 and 16:15. One might say that the coming of Jesus is the recurrent theme of the whole book. In addition, scholars tell us that the last line of Revelation, "Come, Lord Jesus," (which also occurs in I Corinthians 16:22 and in the Didache, an early handbook of Christian spirituality) is a reference to the liturgy, a quotation from the basic Christian prayer.

The lesson for us here is at least twofold. First of all, we are supposed to long for the coming of the glorious Christ at the end of time. Those to whom Revelation was first addressed probably saw this as self-evident. They lived in an atmosphere of social rejection, of isolation from the culture of their time and it was only natural for them to look forward to something better. For them Revelation offered reassurance. For us it offers challenge, challenge to be mindful that the comforts and satisfactions and diversions that form such a great part of our earthly existence must not be allowed to constitute our final end, the goal toward which our life is directed. It would be easy indeed to allow ourselves to get so distracted and drugged by the world around us that we forget about its provisional nature. Revelation calls us to an awareness that the best is yet to come, and that it will come only with the Lord Jesus.

The second lesson that our reading offers us lies in the very last line. In New Testament times as now, direction toward our final end is to be found in the liturgy. The first readers of Revelation and the Corinthians to whom Saint Paul wrote looked forward in their eucharistic celebrations to the coming of Jesus. Our liturgy today does also. At the central moment of our Church gathering we remind ourselves that "Christ will come again." We promise to proclaim his death until he comes in glory. When we participate in the eucharistic re-presentation of the sacrifice of Jesus in the Mass, we are called not just to recall the past self-offering of Jesus, nor to be grateful for his presence in our midst now. We are also called to look forward to the final fulfillment when the pains and the distractions of this world will have given way to the final glorious manifestation of God's love in his heavenly kingdom. The liturgy involves the eternal, risen Christ, and so it reminds us that our faith is a faith with a future.

Obviously all God's blessings do not lie in the future. Already here and now we enjoy his presence in Scripture and sacrament, in the lives of the saints in our midst. But that's only the beginning. We live in hope of more to come, in confidence that the love of the Lord will lead us farther than we can even imagine. We find reassurance in looking forward to Christ's final gift of himself to us in his kingdom. "Come, Lord Jesus."

FOR DISCUSSION AND REFLECTION

How is longing for the coming of the Lord part of my life?

Does my participation in the liturgy have a future orientation?

Pentecost Sunday (A)

I Corinthians 12:3b-7, 12-13

The fundamental reading for Pentecost is Acts 2:1-11. In that
reading, which is mandatory for each year of the three-year cycle,
we hear how the Holy Spirit came upon the apostles and sent
them out to preach the gospel of Christ to every people
throughout the world. There are many peoples and many
languages, but only one Christ, one gospel, one Spirit. This feast
has to do with the unity and the diversity of the Church.

Our live letter for this day shows us unity and diversity in
practice. The Corinthians were a difficult group of new
Christians. The Holy Spirit (the same Spirit that had come upon
the apostles at Pentecost) had given them spectacular gifts. Some
of them were charismatic preachers. Some were healers. Some
were prophets. The trouble was that these gifts became a source
of competitiveness in the young Church. The community was in
danger of splitting up as its members vied with one another in
asserting the particular value of their individual gifts. In our
passage, Paul finds it necessary to remind them that the Church
is not a conglomeration of individuals, but rather the one body of
Christ under the direction of the one Holy Spirit. The gifts of
individuals were to be appreciated in the context of the unity of
the Church. (Note the recurrence of the word *same* in the first
part of the reading, and of the word *one* in the second.)

Our passage begins by situating the gifts of the Spirit in the
context of faith. If you don't confess the lordship of Jesus,
whatever gifts you may have are not from the Spirit of Jesus.

Next Paul comments on the variety of the Spirit's gifts,
directed toward various kinds of service for the community,
bringing about various effects. None of us deserves any of them.
They are all freely given gifts of the Spirit, of the one Spirit of
Jesus. And although the manifestation of the Spirit may vary from
individual to individual, the purpose of the gifts is one: the
development of the common good of the community.

The following verses of our reading describe the community. It is one body, the body of Christ. It has many parts (and, by implication, the many parts have many functions), but these many parts constitute only one body, which is animated by one Spirit. Ethnic and social differences in the community (Jews and Greeks, slaves and free persons) are irrelevant in the context of the one body and one Spirit.

Pentecost is a good day to reflect a bit on the unity of the Church. We are members of the one Church because we have opened ourselves to the full holiness of Christ which he offers us in baptism and the other sacraments. We are members of the one Church because we have all accepted the full teaching of Jesus expressed in the community of those who believe in him. We are members of the one Church because we have each accepted our specific part in the one visible community of faith that includes our fellow parishioners, but also the pope and the bishops and all believers throughout the world. Holiness, teaching, community: these are the elements that make the Church one because they are all various aspects of the one ministry of Christ and are therefore manifestations of the one Spirit of Jesus. Each of us has his or her own assortment of gifts. Each of us expresses his or her own personal emphasis in our response to our gifts. We are all different. But we all constitute one body enlivened by one Spirit.

There are two important teachings here. The first is that we are not free to pick and choose among the elements that make up the basic realities of the Church. We can't, for example, take baptism and reject the Eucharist, or accept the parish and write off the diocese. The Church is not ours. The Church is Christ's and we can no more remake the Church to suit ourselves than we can remake Christ and the Spirit into a pattern we find more appealing.

The second lesson is that, if unity in holiness and belief and community is going to mean anything to us, we have to keep it high in our consciousness. It's easy to get annoyed with the Church. There are so many imperfect people in it, people whose priorities and emphases are different from our own. It's easy to get discouraged with the Church, whether it be the Church universal or our local parish. Its leaders seem to move so slowly—or so fast. If we lost sight of the basics, we run the risk of seeing only the surface of the Church. And then it's easy to walk away from the real unity of the real Church into a foreign land of our own making. We have to base our faith on an awareness of the elementary unity of the Church—one body of Christ enlivened by one Spirit—and not on the Church's secondary features, be they ornaments or flaws.

There is an ongoing tension in the Church between unity and diversity. The abundance and variety of the Spirit's gifts makes for diversity. The oneness of the Spirit makes for unity. Overemphasis on either weakens the body of Christ and frustrates the work of the Spirit.

FOR DISCUSSION AND REFLECTION

What do I appreciate most about the diversity in the Church?

What do I appreciate most about the Church's unity?

Pentecost Sunday (Optional B)

Galatians 5:16-25

The Christian feast of Pentecost celebrates the coming of the Holy Spirit on the apostles, which energized them and enlightened them and impelled them to set out into the whole world to bring the news of the salvation that God had effected through Jesus. But Pentecost was also a Jewish feast. It commemorated God's gift of the law on Mount Sinai to Moses and the Jews.

In view of that, it's appropriate that our second reading for Pentecost in Year B is from Paul's letter to the Galatians, because Galatians is about the relationship between Jewish law and

Christian salvation. Paul's basic point in Galatians is that the Mosaic law is ineffective for gaining divine favor and that salvation comes to us through Christ as a gift that constitutes freedom from the detailed constraints of the Jewish law. Toward the end of the letter, Paul deals with the practical moral consequences of this Christian teaching. This Sunday's reading is taken from that part of the letter.

Paul is dealing with three intertwined subjects here. One is the Law, the complex of commands that God gave to Moses whose purpose, according to Paul, was not to bring salvation but to provide religious and moral norms that the Jews were, in fact, unable to observe. The second subject of our passage is the flesh which signifies not just bodily or sexual matters, but the whole human creature, mind and body, left to itself and dominated by natural, earth-oriented tendencies. The third subject that Paul treats here is the Spirit, the love and energy of Father and Son who is given to believers at their baptism and who serves as enlightenment and impulse for our implementation of the life of Christ that is in us.

Paul begins with a basic principle: If you live as the Spirit directs, you will not have to gratify the demands of the flesh. This is not to say that we are free to do whatever we please, since the flesh and the Spirit are hostile to each other and cannot both be responded to. One excludes the other. Then Paul lists "the works of the flesh." In one way or another, all these moral deviations are acts of selfishness, putting ourselves ahead of God and our neighbor, making our wants the center of our existence. This kind of behavior, he says, is simply incompatible with the kingdom of God. On the other hand, there are the acts and habits that result from the Spirit living in us. These are all outgoing, self-sacrificing qualities that extend the love of God beyond our personal sphere and send God's love into the wider world. The law is irrelevant in this context, Paul says, because those who have the Spirit are not obliged by the law and because the law is concerned with sins rather than virtues. If we belong to Christ, the flesh is dead in us, as dead as the crucified Christ. If we belong to Christ, we live in the Spirit and must conduct ourselves accordingly.

To say that we have received the Spirit is not to say that all moral and spiritual struggle is now foreign to us. The basic direction of our lives is oriented by the Spirit, but our flesh (in the Pauline sense) still clamors for recognition. Spirit and flesh are not "opposed to each other" merely as abstract ethical principles, but as potent energies in our day-to-day existence. There are times when some of the items on Paul's list of the works for the flesh seem more than a little attractive to us, at least when they are dressed up in their more appealing costumes. These are times when the items on the list of the fruits of the Spirit seem totally unattractive. Yet we know that the Spirit of Christ is more powerful than the flesh and that the outcome of our moral struggles is guaranteed as long as we stay in touch with the Spirit, if we "follow the Spirit."

And how do we "follow the Spirit" in practice? We follow the Spirit by maintaining a relationship with Father, Son and Sprit through prayer, not just in times of trial but as part of the ordinary fabric of our daily life. God should be our constant friend and companion rather than vice-president in charge of crisis management. We follow the Spirit by cultivating a sense of confidence in the Spirit's presence and guidance in our lives. This doesn't mean running away from making decisions or refusing to take responsibility for ourselves, but living in the assurance that the Spirit is part of the ordinary processes of our moral life. We follow the Spirit by being attentive to the moral quality of the elements of our life. Which of the options that confront me are good? Which are bad? Which one will bring the kingdom closer to me? Which will bring the kingdom closer to my world?

Pentecost marks the end of the Easter season. Now we enter Ordinary Time when we walk with Jesus through his public life and through his ongoing ministry that reaches to the end of time. It's good to know that we are accompanied by his Holy Spirit.

FOR DISCUSSION AND REFLECTION

In what ways do I struggle with the flesh (in the Pauline sense)?
In what aspects of my life do I experience the action of the Holy
Spirit?

Pentecost Sunday (Optional C)

Romans 8:8-17

The public coming of the Holy Spirit upon the apostles is
recounted in Acts 2:1-11. This selection constitutes the first
reading for Pentecost Sunday in all three years of the cycle. The
Gospel reading for Year A (John 20:19-23) is the account of
Jesus' private meeting with the apostles after his Resurrection,
during which he bestows the Holy Spirit on them and gives them
the power to forgive sin. This reading may be read in Years B and
C, too, or it can be replaced by readings from John's last supper
discourse in which Jesus promises to send the Holy Spirit to his
disciples. For the second reading the Church has provided, in
Year A, a reading from First Corinthians (12:3b-7, 12-13) in
which the Spirit is described as the source of unity in the Church.
This reading, too, can be repeated in the second and third years
of the liturgical cycle or it can be replaced (in Year B) by
Galatians 5:16-25, which speaks of the relationship between the
Holy Spirit and Christian behavior. For Year C there is an
optional second reading from Romans 8:8-17. It's as if the
Church, aware of how much there is to say about the Holy Spirit,
gives its ministers the choice of offering to the faithful the basics
each year or of giving them a richer fare by means of the optional
readings.

Our reflection deals with the optional Year C reading from
Romans. This part of Paul's letter deals with the relationship
between justification (that is, salvation) and Christian life.

Our reading has three parts. First, Paul speaks of the distinction between flesh and spirit, a favorite subject of his. In a context like this, flesh does not mean physical skin and muscles ("a pound of flesh"), nor sexual misbehavior ("sins of the flesh"). Paul uses the term "flesh" to signify our whole moral and spiritual attitude toward God when we were, or are, in a state of separation from God. It involves isolation, self-interest, hostility in our relationship with God. Its opposite is "spirit," which Paul now describes.

He says that those who are detached from God ("in the flesh") cannot please him. But Christian believers are "in the spirit," that is, God's own Spirit, God's own life lives in them. We belong to God because Christ's Spirit is alive in us. Because of this, we are righteous and alive even when our body (tainted with hereditary sinfulness) dies.

Having proclaimed the basic reality of our relationship with God (that is, that God's Spirit dwells in us), Paul speaks of two results of that indwelling.

First of all, the Spirit gives us a new life. The same Spirit that caused Jesus to rise from the dead is also in us. It gives its own life to our bodies. This means that we have to live, not as if we were still detached from God (that is, "in the flesh"), but in accord with the Spirit of God in us. Sinfulness and selfishness ("the deeds of the body") will lead us to spiritual death unless we destroy them through our adherence to the Spirit.

In the third part of our reading, Paul gives us the second result of the Spirit's life in us: we enter into a whole new relationship with God. We are no longer servants, motivated by fear of punishment, but sons and daughters. We can speak to God with the same term that Jesus used: Abba. We become intimates in God's household. We belong there because we are not servants or guests, but members of the family. If we imitate the faithfulness of Christ, the glory that faithfulness brought to him will also be ours.

Pentecost is the feast of the beginning of the public and

universal proclamation of the good news of Christ's salvation. It is called "the birthday of the Church" and the Holy Spirit is called "the soul of the Church." However, the Holy Spirit is not merely the driving force of the Church at large. The Spirit is also the determinant element of the life of each and every Christian believer. Because of the Spirit that is in us, we live the life of the risen Christ and we share Christ's relationship with Father and Holy Spirit.

The Spirit in us, who brings us the life and glory that are shared by Father, Son and Holy Spirit, is what makes us members of the Church. It's not because we have kept the rules of Christian behavior that we belong, nor because we believe all the doctrines that the Church calls us to believe. Those are not unimportant matters. But the basic reality is the gift of the Holy Spirit that comes to us with baptism, the gift that gives us a whole new level of life and a whole new kind of relationship with the Father.

Pentecost, the coming of the Holy Spirit upon the followers of Jesus, is not just something nice that happened a long time ago. The coming of the Holy Spirit is something that still happens today every time a new member is initiated into the Church. Moreover, it's something that persists throughout our earthly life in Jesus and that prepares us for life in heaven with the Lord in an eternal family reunion.

FOR DISCUSSION AND REFLECTION

In what ways do I see myself as a daughter or son of God?
What difference does the Holy Spirit make in my life?

PART FIVE

Ordinary Time

Second Sunday in Ordinary Time (A)

I Corinthians 1:1-3

The weeks of Ordinary Time in the Church's calendar begin on the day after the celebration of the Baptism of the Lord. During these weeks the second readings for Sunday are composed of extracts (which the lectionary refers to as "semicontinuous readings") from the Pauline letters, the letter of James and the letter to the Hebrews. These readings have no connection with the first readings or the Gospel readings.

To begin each year's ordinary time, we have a series of readings from Paul's first letter to the Corinthians. This is a long and complex letter, which the people in charge of putting the lectionary together apparently thought would be too much for a single year. Consequently we have seven readings from First Corinthians in Years A and C, and five in Year B, making this the book of the New Testament that provides more second readings than any other.

First Corinthians is a very intense letter because the Corinthians were seemingly very intense people. Scripture scholars describe them as conceited, stubborn, over-sensitive, argumentative, infantile and pushy. There were lots of problems in this young Church, some of which Paul had heard about from personal reports from the community's members, some of which had been sent to him for comment by the community itself. Practically all these issues are concerned with Christian identity and church unity. One might say that the question to which Paul addresses himself in this letter is: "What does it mean to be church?"

This Sunday's live letter reading consists of the greeting that constitutes the very first verses of the letter. The epistolary conventions of Paul's time called for a letter to open with greetings preceded by the name of the sender and of the addressee: "X to Y, greetings." The greeting section of First Corinthians is much more elaborate than that because Paul wants to offer teaching to the Corinthians right from the beginning.

He begins with his own name, but hastens to add a rationale for their acceptance of what he is going to say: he is an apostle of Jesus Christ and has been called to this responsibility by God. He mentions Sosthenes, who is otherwise unknown and who is not mentioned again in First Corinthians. Apparently this was a Christian who was known to the Corinthians and who was with Paul when he was composing the letter.

The letter is addressed to "the church of God that is in Corinth." Paul goes on to describe what "church" involves. Its members are those who have been called to holiness by being in Christ Jesus. They are connected with believers everywhere else who profess faith in Jesus.

Finally he wishes them "grace and peace." This phrase is used in every one of Paul's letters. It puts together the standard words of greeting in Greek and Hebrew and constitutes a prayer that the fullness of God's generous blessing would come upon the community to which it is addressed.

In these few words in this most conventional part of the letter, Paul is giving the basic orientation of the whole letter, the fundamental context in which his teaching is to be received. He is giving a description of the Church. The Church is one and holy because its membership is constituted by the shared holiness of the one Christ. It is catholic, that is, universal, because it includes "all those everywhere who call upon the name of our Lord Jesus Christ." It is apostolic, because it is proclaimed by those who have been called by God to be apostles. This community offers grace (a participation in God's life) and peace (the fullness of his blessing) to its members. In one way or another, all the rest of First Corinthians will be a commentary on these three verses.

There is a lifetime of material for reflection here, but we will content ourselves with just two sets of observations.

First of all, being in the Church means being made holy by the act of God, an act expressed in the sacrament of baptism. We do not earn holiness or achieve it. We receive it as the free gift of God. This holiness consists in sharing the life of the risen Christ. From our first day as members of the Church, we are all "saints" (one of the standard terms that Paul uses to refer to members of the Church) because we have Christ's life in us. This is not a sainthood that comes as the result of our spiritual and moral efforts, but a participation in God's holiness that calls for certain types of behavior on our part by way of response. We act like Christians not in order to become holy but in order to be consistent with the holiness we have already received.

Secondly, this holiness involves "grace and peace." The word "grace" has overtones of joy. It suggests God's generosity, God's intervention in our lives. "Peace" in the biblical sense means more than the absence of war. It suggests a harmonious working together of all the elements of the reality in which God has placed us.

Holiness, grace, and peace: that's what being a Christian believer involves.

FOR DISCUSSION AND REFLECTION

In what ways do I see myself as holy?

How and where do I experience grace and peace in my life?

Second Sunday in Ordinary Time (B)

1 Corinthians 6:13c-15a, 17-20

Ordinary Time begins on the day after the celebration of the Baptism of the Lord, so that feast takes the place of the first Sunday.

With this Second Sunday of Ordinary Time the second readings, our live letters, come into their own. Up to now in the Church's year these readings have been selected for their relationship to the season of the year or to the gospel. Now we launch into a series of more or less continuous readings of the various apostolic letters without any relationship to the Gospel readings, which themselves constitute another series of semi-continuous readings. The two series are not connected.

For the next several weeks, therefore, we will be reading through Paul's first letter to the Corinthians. But we don't begin at the beginning! Because this letter is quite long and deals with such diverse issues, it is spread over all three years of the cycle. The first part of it is read in Year A, the last in Year C. We read the middle of it this Year B.

The first letter to the Corinthians is divided into two main parts. In the first part, Paul addresses some of the disorders in the Corinthian church that had come to his attention through people who had visited there. (The Christians of Corinth seem to have been a rather wild group!) In the second part, he answers some questions that had been addressed to him by the Corinthians themselves. Today's reading comes at the end of the first part.

Paul seems to have been told that the Corinthians were taking his teaching about Jewish dietary laws—that every kind of food was lawful—as applying also to sexual behavior. They were engaging in fornication, perhaps with the cult prostitutes in the pagan temples. After all, isn't sex just one more physical need like eating and drinking?

Paul answers in our text. Sexual activity is not just satisfying one more appetite, but a commitment of our whole person, our whole body. Thanks to our incorporation into Christ, our bodies are now one with his and will be raised up as Christ's body was. Misusing our bodies is to misuse the body of Christ. Moreover, the Holy Spirit dwells in us, and so we are temples of the Spirit and are not free to do with ourselves as we please. Because we have been redeemed by Christ, we belong to God. Our bodies are to serve God's purposes, not our own. Sexual promiscuity is not appropriate for the Christian believer.

Sexual promiscuity was not an ancient aberration confined to the misguided Christians of Corinth. It's with us still. Our culture seems to regard sex pretty much as they did, as one more appetite to be satisfied. And our culture does not put a high value on delaying the satisfaction of appetites until their satisfaction is appropriate. In fact, the world around us seems to presume that everybody is sexually active all the time and that whatever kind of sexual activity is attractive to an individual is therefore acceptable. Similarly, much of the commercial world seems to believe that the best way to sell its products is by presenting them in the context of sexual activity. It won't sell if it's not somehow sexy.

This all makes a certain kind of sense if we presume that human beings are nothing more than bodies. The demands of the body need to be satisfied as quickly and as efficiently as possible and the only limit in the satisfaction of bodily needs is that we not hurt other people (although even this limit seems to have its limits).

For us Christians it's different. We know that we are not just bodies, but human persons beloved by God and redeemed through the suffering and death of Christ. We know that we are members of the risen Christ, that his Spirit dwells in us, that our final destiny is eternal life when we will be raised from the dead as Christ was. And all of this is not some sort of spiritual parenthesis deep inside us, but a complex of realities that exists and expresses itself here and now, on this earth, in the context of our earthly life and our earthly bodies. Our bodies can be demanding and troublesome, but they are the vehicles of God's presence to us and to the world around us. They are the means through which the glory of God works and manifests itself. They demand respect.

There is a great deal of Catholic Christian teaching about sexuality, about specific sexual behaviors, about the dignity and purpose of sex in marriage. Sometimes people look on these teachings as check lists of restraints or as unenlightened doctrines of a former age. But they all make sense if we remember who and what God has made us to be: not our own to do with as we please, but purchased by Christ to be members of his body and temples of the Holy Spirit. The real issue isn't sex. It's our Christian identity.

FOR DISCUSSION AND REFLECTION

How does Christ's life in me affect my behavior?

What sexually oriented TV commercials, billboards and other ads have I seen recently? What was my reaction?

Second Sunday in Ordinary Time (C)

I Corinthians 12:4-11

On the Sundays in Ordinary Time we have an ongoing series of readings from one of the Gospels. In Year C the Gospel is Luke's (prefaced on the second Sunday by a reading from John that describes the beginning of Jesus' public life). These Gospel readings are illuminated by the readings from the Old Testament. The second readings during this season are selections, more or less in order, from the apostolic letters in the New Testament. They are independent of the first readings and the Gospel readings.

The first book we have such selections from in Year C is First Corinthians. We hear from First Corinthians at the beginning of Ordinary Time each year in the three-year cycle. Apparently those who put the lectionary together thought it was too long and too complicated a letter to be surveyed in one year.

The basic structure of First Corinthians consists of Paul's comments on disorders in the local church at Corinth (chapters 1-6) followed by responses to some questions from the Corinthians (chapters 7-10). Next comes material on liturgical questions (chapters 11-14) and on the Resurrection (chapter 15). It is not clear whether these last two sections are the result of what Paul had heard about the disorders at Corinth or of questions that the members themselves had addressed to him. In any case, it is from these final sections that we will read over these next seven Sundays, on the first three Sundays from chapters 12 and 13, on the next four from chapter 15.

The section on liturgical questions starts with Paul's teaching about how women were to dress in the liturgical assembly and continues with his instruction about behavior during the celebration of the Eucharist itself. Then (in this Sunday's reading) we hear about spiritual gifts.

Probably most of us would have found it troubling to attend Sunday Mass in Corinth. The Corinthians seem to have set great store by ecstatic and charismatic practices, gifts given to individuals that enabled them to speak foreign languages or pray aloud in highly personalized ways. This isn't the sort of thing that most of us are used to at Mass! In addition to that, they seem to have thought that having these gifts (especially the gift of speaking in tongues) was a sign of spiritual superiority. People with special gifts were thought to be better or more important than the others. This is what Paul addresses in our reading.

First of all, he emphasizes that all these spiritual gifts, whatever their purpose, are from one and the same God, one and the same Spirit. (The words "same" and "one" occur eight times in these eight verses.) They are all given for the well-being of the community. Then he lists some of the gifts: wisdom (understanding God's plans) and knowledge (being able to teach so others can understand); faith, a special level of confidence in God that enables the recipient to do healings and other wonders; prophecy and discernment, speaking and interpreting tongues (all concerned with speaking out in God's name). Whatever the gifts, they come from God and are given for God's purposes.

Paul teaches, therefore, that God's generosity is manifold, expressing itself in many ways. Yet it is not aimed at making some people better than others, but at strengthening the Church at large.

What does all this have to do with us? Most of us do not speak in tongues or bring about miraculous healings. But we are all gifted by God. Our gifts may be a little less spectacular than those of some of the Corinthians, but they are real gifts nonetheless. The ability to comfort people in sorrow or help people to pray better, skill in teaching about the faith, the capacity to chair a meeting or lead a discussion group, helping children to grow up as believing Christians, a special zeal for social justice: all these are gifts that God gives to the members of his Church today. And there are many more! Each of us has his or her share of them. They are all gifts and they all come from the same loving God. And they are all directed not toward the building up of the ego of the one who has received them, but toward the building up of the life and energy of Christ in the Church.

The Church is not a warm, quiet context in which I can be with Jesus, quietly and alone. It is a living community of ordinary people, saints and sinners, brilliant and silly, attractive and repulsive, all of whom need the gifts God offers us through our fellow members. The Church is not a spiritual convenience store where we go shopping for what we want, and drive away when we have what we came for. The Church is a living community in which each of us has the right to be supported by the others, in which each of us has something to offer for the well-being of all. It's not just priests and bishops who work for the well-being of the Church. We are all called to make our contribution out of the gifts that the one God has given to each of us.

FOR DISCUSSION AND REFLECTION

What spiritual gifts have I received?
How am I using them to build up the Church?

Third Sunday in Ordinary Time (A)

I Corinthians 1:10-13, 17

These verses begin the main body of First Corinthians. In this
first main division of the letter, Paul addresses the fundamental
problem that lies behind almost everything else he will have to
say to the Corinthians, the problem of divisions within the
community, which, in turn, is rooted in the question of ecclesial
identity. What is important in being a Christian believer?

Paul begins with a solemn exhortation "in the name of our
Lord Jesus Christ" that they not allow their community to be
fragmented. In three different ways he urges them to pursue
oneness of speech, of mind and of purpose.

He is quick to explain why he admonishes them in this way.
He has heard from members of the household of Chloe (perhaps
some of her domestic slaves who had come from Corinth) that the
community was infected with "rivalries." Nobody seems to know
for sure the specific nature of these contentions. Apparently they
were not serious enough to have caused the community to have
split apart, but they were serious enough to be of concern to Paul.

The community seemed to have divided itself into factions,
each of which claimed a particular loyalty. Some members
belonged to "Paul's group," some to Apollos's, some to Cephas's,
some to Christ's. (Apollos was a Jewish convert from Alexandria
conspicuous for his learning and eloquence who had come to
Corinth from Ephesus. Cephas is the apostle Peter, whose
relationship with the Christians of Corinth is not known.) It may
be that these groups were constituted by people who had been
baptized by Paul, Apollos or Cephas, or who were particularly
charmed by the approach taken by the particular preacher. Those
who claim to be in Christ's group may be those who have not
given their allegiance to any of the other groups.

In any case, Paul goes on to say that the important thing is
not who baptized you, but who saved you. It is the one, undivided
Christ who is savior and who died for us. Paul and Apollos and

Cephas are all secondary to Christ. That's what the Corinthians needed to remember.

In the verses omitted in our lectionary reading, Paul recalls that he didn't personally baptize very many of the Corinthians, so that there were less grounds for a faction to be formed in his name. As our reading draws to its conclusion, we hear Paul saying that his responsibility was not the formal administration of baptism (which he apparently left to someone else) but the sober, unadorned proclamation of the gospel of Christ's death.

Factionalism and division in the Church is not something that was confined to first-century Corinth. It is still with us today in more than one way.

Most parishes of any size have their share of liberals and conservatives, of social-action types and charismatic types, of people who will struggle mightily against moving a statue to a different place in church and others who don't care whether there are any statues at all. A certain amount of this small-time difference of taste and orientation is understandable and tolerable. There is enough variety in our Catholic faith to allow for differences of emphasis. But these differences of emphasis become destructive when they become so important that they overshadow more important things, like the nature of our life together in Christ and our common need for Christ's love and salvation. There is real danger in making secondary things primary.

But divisions in the Church are not confined to these parochial tensions. There is also the reality of full separation between various groups of people who claim to be followers of Christ. We have grown so used to having Catholics and Presbyterians and Methodists that we begin to think that that's the way things are supposed to be. But they're not. Vatican II (*Decree on Ecumenism*, no. 1) teaches us that this kind of division "openly contradicts the will of Christ, provides a stumbling block for the world, and inflicts damage on the most holy cause of proclaiming the gospel to every creature." These rifts are due to overemphasis or underemphasis on one or more aspects of Christ's gospel, to errors on the part of individuals, to historical circumstances. In most cases everybody involved has to assume a share of responsibility for the fragmentation of the Church.

Putting things back together is an urgent task, but not an easy one. The Council's *Decree on Ecumenism* (no. 4) calls for sensitivity, dialogue, study and prayer. Above all, it calls for everyone to examine his or her "own faithfulness to Christ's will for the Church."

A common thread of all these forms of factionalism, whether it be that of the Corinthians, or of parish members, or of whole church communities divided from one another, is the desire for independence, to go off on our own and insist on our own priorities. And that's not what is important. What is important is belonging to Christ and subjecting ourselves to his will.

FOR DISCUSSION AND REFLECTION

How have I experienced factionalism and division within the Church?

How can I contribute to healing the divisions of Christianity?

Third Sunday in Ordinary Time (B)

I Corinthians 7:29-31

In chapter 7 of this first letter to the Christians at Corinth, Paul begins to answer some questions that had come to him by letter from Corinth. The Corinthians wanted Paul's advice about marriage and divorce and celibacy. In addition, they wanted to know whether it was permissible to take part in dinner parties where meat was served that had been sacrificed to idols. They may also have asked about problems they were having in their liturgical assemblies and about some matters relating to the resurrection of the dead. (These last two items are dealt with in the readings from First Corinthians that the lectionary gives us for next year.)

As we read these, and other New Testament texts, it is important to be aware that, at this early period of the Church's history, Christians generally believed that the second coming of Christ, the final and full realization of the kingdom, was imminent. It might come any day now. This assumption plays a large part in the letters to the Thessalonians, for example, but it is also at work in what Paul has to say to the Corinthians.

Our text for today comes toward the end of Paul's treatment of marriage, virginity and widowhood. He has been telling the Corinthians that there is no one best state of life that everybody has to adopt in order to be ready for Christ's coming. They should answer God's call where it finds them. Now he offers a bit of more general advice about appropriate Christian attitudes in a world still in transition toward the kingdom.

We don't have much time, he says. The important thing is not whether we are married or not. The important thing is not emotional well-being or economic prosperity. The important thing is to be aware that our present world is provisional and that it is passing away to make room for a whole new kind of world that will be inaugurated when the Lord comes in glory.

The fact that Paul's teaching to the Corinthians is based on a presumption that the second coming is very near, a presumption that the passage of time since then seems to have proved incorrect, does not mean that what he has to say is irrelevant to us. For one thing, the fact that the second coming did not occur in the middle of the first century does not mean that it will not occur at the beginning of the twenty-first century. Over and over again in the gospels Jesus tells his followers that the time of the coming of the Son of Man is unknown and that they are to be prepared for it at any moment, like servants awaiting their master's surprise return (see Matthew 24:36-44; 25:13; Mark

13:32; Luke 12:40). Settling down in comfort because we think the Lord won't be here for a while is simply not in accord with the teaching of Jesus.

But apart from the final coming of Jesus to take the whole world to himself and remake it in glory, there is also the coming of Jesus at the end of our individual lives. None of us can guarantee that we will be around tomorrow, or an hour from now. We know this in theory, yet we sometimes act as if we had plenty of time at our disposal to arrange things as we wish, forgetting that the Master may come when we least expect him.

Paul's warning to the Corinthians, then, also applies to us: "The time is running out."

We need to be clear about what Paul is saying here. He is not saying that the quality of Christian marriage is unimportant or that God doesn't care whether we are happy or sad here and now or that it doesn't matter how we carry on our business affairs, or whether we work at all. He is not saying that we are supposed to disregard the circumstances in which we and others find ourselves in our day-to-day existence. After all, appropriate love of ourselves and care for our brothers and sisters and justice in our dealings with others are as much a part of Christian teaching as is the second coming. The point that Paul is making is that all this, important as it may be, is temporary and provisional. Our earthly life is not without significance, but its significance is relative.

This little reading invites us to examine our priorities, not just in theory but in practice. What aspects of our life seem to take up most of our attention? What are we willing to make sacrifices for? How much of our energy goes to making ourselves comfortable, physically, emotionally, socially? I am inclined to suspect that many of us pay lip service to the lordship of Jesus in our lives, but in practice we carry on as if the *really* important part were the things that Paul tells us not to be so concerned about.

Maybe the best thing that could happen to us as we read this bit of Paul's live letter to the Corinthians would be a healthy discomfort as we realize that it is addressed to us.

FOR DISCUSSION AND REFLECTION

What would I change in my life if I knew the world would end tomorrow?

What things are so important to me that their absence would render my life meaningless?

Third Sunday in Ordinary Time (C)

I Corinthians 12:12-30

This Sunday's long second reading follows immediately on last Sunday's in First Corinthians, even as next Sunday's follows immediately on this Sunday's. It is unusual to have such a long selection (nearly two whole chapters) without interruption, even in a "semi-continuous" series of readings. Those who prepared the lectionary must have thought that the teaching in these chapters is important, important enough to be read in full.

Last Sunday Paul was emphasizing that all the spiritual gifts that Church members receive are from the same God, the same Spirit and that they are all aimed at building up the one Church. This Sunday, he deals with another aspect of God's gifts: their multiplicity and variety.

The reading starts off with a general principle: just as there is a variety of parts in the human body, so also there is a variety of membership in the body of Christ which is the Church. Jews and gentiles, rich and poor: they were all baptized into one body, they have all been gifted by the same Spirit.

Now Paul gives an extended reflection on the variety and unity of the human body. Every part belongs, every part is needed no matter what its function. Without the multiplicity of parts and functions the body could not survive. Yet it remains one body whose various parts need each other in order for the body to function. Moreover, there is a kind of balance among the parts of the body, such that weak parts (like the eye, perhaps) are more necessary, the "less honorable" and "less presentable" parts (perhaps feet or genital organs) are always adorned with clothing. Somehow it all balances out so that no part of the body is useless or without honor. Each part contributes to the unity and beauty and health of the whole. Each is needed.

Now Paul returns to his explicit consideration of the variety of gifts in the one Church: "You are Christ's body, and individually parts of it." Obviously there are all kinds of gifts, some (like being an apostle) of obvious importance. Others ("assistance, administration") may seem less prestigious, but are not, for that reason, unneeded by the body of the Church. Not all of us can be apostles or prophets or healers or speakers in strange languages, but we each have something to contribute. The Church needs all the gifts of the Spirit.

Last Sunday's and this Sunday's live letters offer us two sides of one important lesson, the lesson of unity in diversity.

First of all, we are one in the life of the risen Christ that we share. That life of Jesus that we call grace is the primary reality that makes us Christians, that gives fundamental direction to our lives, that unites us in our journey to final fulfillment in the glory of heaven. Everything else is secondary to that. Everything else derives from that. If we forget about the one life of Christ that we all share, if we lose sight of the one Lord that makes us into his one people, nothing else makes any sense. Compared to the importance of our sharing the life of Christ, all other gifts and distinctions we may have are insignificant.

But that's not to say that we are all the same. We share the sameness of the one life of Christ, to be sure, but each of us is called to express and respond to that life in his or her own way, a way that not only constitutes our personal individuality, but that also enables us to participate uniquely in the life of the Body as a whole. You don't have to be the pope in order to be important in the Church, any more than you have to be the head in order to be important in the body. What a body it would be if we were all heads and there were no hands and feet! We all need each other and we need each other in our own personal uniqueness.

One example of what can happen if we undervalue individuals' gifts is clericalism (with its opposite, anticlericalism). Clericalism is a mind-set that sees worth and value only in those members of the Church who are ordained. "If a priest didn't say it, it can't be true. If a priest didn't do it, it can't be any good." Anticlericalism, on the other hand, is a mind-set that sees all deficiency and evil in the Church (and elsewhere) as having its source and power from the ordained. "It's the priests' fault if there are poor people in society. If people commit sins, it's because the priests haven't taught them any better." Obviously the Church needs ordained ministers. That's how Christ established the Church to work. But a vocation to ordained ministry is not the only gift that the Spirit gives, and sometimes those who feel they have been left out because they are not ordained can give the impression that they think that diversity in the Church is a matter of oppression rather than abundance.

We all share the one life of the one Christ, but we all share it in a particular tonality. We're not all heads or hands or feet, but we all have something to offer to the health of the body.

FOR DISCUSSION AND REFLECTION

What do I contribute to the life of the body of Christ, the Church?

What would the Church be like if everybody were just like me?

Fourth Sunday in Ordinary Time (A)

I Corinthians 1:26-31

In last Sunday's reading we heard Paul admonishing the Corinthians because of their factionalism, because some considered themselves better than others on account of their dedication to one or the other leader of the local church. He concluded that passage (in verse 17) by reminding them that the real kernel of the gospel is the unadorned proclamation of Christ's death on the cross.

In the verses that come between that reading and this Sunday's reading (that is, verses 18-25), he reminds his readers that their fascination with power and wisdom is not a sign of a healthy faith. All that Christians have to rely on is a dead criminal, Christ crucified. Christ constitutes a power and a wisdom that surpasses human categories of strength and understanding.

Now, in this Sunday's reading, Paul suggests that they consider their own experience if they want to know about how God's wisdom and power work. They have been called to faith by Christ through the preaching of Paul, but it wasn't because they were well-educated, or influential, or members of the upper class. On the contrary, the vast majority of them were uncultured, powerless, common people according to the world's criteria. But it was precisely for that reason that God paid attention to them. By calling people like them to membership in his Church, God shows how insignificant are the wisdom, the power and the nobility of the world. God chooses "nobodies" to show what he thinks of the "somebodies."

Paul continues with a general principle: None of us can claim personal importance or independent worth in relation to God. Nobody can pretend that salvation is his or her individual achievement. Whatever we are in relation to God is God's gift to us, given through Christ who has become our wisdom and who has conferred his salvation ("righteousness, sanctification, redemption") on us. To conclude our passage, Paul cites the prophet Jeremiah (9:23) to the effect that if we want to brag about something, it should be about God's care for us and not about our own worth.

What Paul tells the Corinthians in this passage is a central principle, a basic insight of his preaching and, indeed, of all Christian doctrine: salvation (being in touch with God, sharing his life through Christ and the Spirit) is a gift, not an achievement.

That lesson is not just relevant to the Corinthians, those fractious folks who were so captivated with their own insights and their own spiritual accomplishments. It's also something that we need to hear.

We twenty-first century Americans, just like our forefathers, prize independence and self-sufficiency. We like to think that, given a little bit of luck, we can make our own way through life, that the biography of each of us can be a success story. If we get a fair shake, we will all be able to feel good about ourselves. We are at our proudest and best when we have overcome the challenges that face us with our own resources, without anybody having to bail us out. The qualities that we tend to prize most are those associated with personal initiative and individual autonomy. "I did it for myself, and I did it my way."

The trouble is that, while that may be the way things work in the world of human affairs (although even that is questionable), it certainly isn't the way things work in God's affairs.

For one thing, what God gives us when he saves us is so far above our natural abilities that we can't even understand it adequately, much less provide it or earn it for ourselves.

For another, we are sinful people. We start with a negative balance, a balance of selfishness and pride that we can never pay off on our own. The harder we try to pay off the negative balance with our own resources, the deeper into debt we fall because the idea that we can redeem ourselves from sin by our own efforts is itself sinful.

The fact of the matter is that the only source of salvation, the only entrance to eternal life with God is through the wisdom and power of God. It is God's strange, paradoxical, astonishing initiative that gives us final worth. By human standards, it doesn't make much sense for God to be interested in us at all. We're just not worth his trouble. By human standards, God's outreach to us, foolish and weak and sinful as we are, just doesn't compute. Yet God reaches out to us anyhow and all he asks in return is that we be aware of what's really going on. He asks that we be willing to give credit to where credit is due: to the love and self-sacrifice of the dead criminal, Jesus, who died for our salvation.

People like to be remembered after they die. That's why we have tombstones on which we record the dead person's birth date and death date. Sometimes people arrange to have their achievements recorded there, too (war veteran, parent, author). For the Christian believer, there is only one really important fact that is worth remembering: that we were and are loved by God.

FOR DISCUSSION AND REFLECTION

How has God's initiative played out in my life?

What can I take credit for in my personal salvation history?

Fourth Sunday in Ordinary Time (B)

I Corinthians 7:32-35

Today's passage is another summary passage, like last week's, but it is more deliberately focused on the specific questions that the Corinthians had addressed to Paul.

In the community of Corinth, there seem to have been two basic currents of opinion about sex and marriage. One group seems to have held that unlimited sexual freedom was a sign of salvation, parallel to the dietary freedom that came with liberation from the observance of Jewish law. Paul had learned about this second hand, and we heard him addressing it two weeks ago at the end of chapter 6. The other current of opinion seems to have held that all sexual activity, even in marriage, was sinful. Uncertainties about this view seem to lie behind the questions that Paul is answering here in chapter 7. Is it all right to get married? Is it all right to stay married? Are we all supposed to be celibate? What about widows? What state of life are we supposed to be in so as to be most ready for Christ's coming?

Paul himself was unmarried and he saw advantages for the service of the Lord in remaining so. But he was very clear about not wanting to recommend his situation for everybody (see 7:7 and following). He was also quite aware that marriage can be the source of lots of affliction, but was not, for that reason, ready to say that it was wrong to get married (see 7:28). In view of "the present distress," that is, the impending advent of the Lord, it seemed a good thing for everybody to remain as they were (see 7:26).

Now, in our text, he sums up. What's important, he says, is not to spend your time worrying about your state of life. I want to spare you that. There can be cause for anxiety in every state of life. Married people can be all caught up in trying to respond to the (legitimate) demands of their spouses and families and find themselves distracted from the attention they owe to God. But unmarried people, too, can find causes for anxiety in their attempts to make themselves pleasing to the Lord. I don't want to lay down specific directions for any of you or force you into different states of life. The important thing is for each of you to look for the Lord in the situation in which you find yourselves.

What Paul is telling us here is that there is no one, single right state of life for all Christians. Obviously each of us has to search out the life context that seems most in accord with the gifts that we have been given, most responsive to what God seems to be asking of us. But we don't have to spend our whole lives wondering whether we have made the right choice, whether God might not have been more pleased if we were something other than what we are.

Religious celibacy has always enjoyed high regard among Christians. Religious celibates are women and men who have freely renounced marriage "for the sake of the kingdom," in order to give themselves fully to the immediate service of the Lord and to act as accredited witnesses to the provisional nature of earthly goods and values. Their life does not suggest that other ways of living are wrong or without value in God's sight, but merely that there is more to Christian living than the here and now. The rest of the Church needs their testimony.

Marriage is not some second best, for those who can't make it as celibates, but a true and proper vocation in itself. Sacred Scripture looks on the dedication of Christian marriage as a symbol of Christ's love for his Church (see sections beginning with Ephesians 5:25 and 29) and Catholic tradition refers to the Christian family as the "domestic Church" because of its important role in fostering the faith of its members and providing a context in which the fundamentals of Christian life are taught and learned.

There is another group of Church members who often do not receive appropriate attention, that is, women and men who are not religious celibates but who are not married, either. Often the circumstances of their lives make both of the more ordinary options unavailable. They are not, for that reason, outcasts. They serve God and the Church and their fellow Christians in their own particular ways and are precious to the Lord for that reason. (Somewhere there ought to be a special memorial shrine to all the unmarried aunts and uncles who "stayed home" to take care of Mom and Pop.)

There is one constant requirement, though, in this variety of acceptable options for Christian life, and that is relationship to Christ. However we decide to spend our "pre-kingdom" years, the decision must not be made exclusively on the basis of personal likes and wants. There are selfish celibates and selfish married people and selfish unmarried people. They may have chosen the right state for themselves, but for the wrong reason. All right choices involve "adherence to the Lord without distraction." Bloom where you're planted, but be sure you're blooming for the Lord.

FOR DISCUSSION AND REFLECTION

How does my life reflect a call from God?

If I had my life to live over again, what would I want to be different?

Fourth Sunday in Ordinary Time (C)

I Corinthians 12:31-13:13

In chapter 12 (from which we read last Sunday and the Sunday before) Paul has been dealing with unity and diversity in the Church, with the diversity of gifts in the context of the unity of the body. In chapter 14 (which is not used at all in the lectionary) he offers a long dissertation on the implications of the gift that the Corinthians seem to have prized most of all: speaking in tongues. In chapter 13, assigned to be read on this Fourth Sunday in Ordinary Time, he seems to sidestep the whole discussion of specific gifts and their contribution to the life of the Church and gives his attention to something much more fundamental, something that sums up and surpasses the more limited charisms the Corinthians were so fascinated with. This chapter gives us the so-called hymn to love.

Before we examine the text, it is important to be aware of what Paul is talking about here. The love he is talking about is not primarily the love of the Father for his creatures, nor of Christ for his human brothers and sisters, although God's love provides the model and foundation for all other loves. The love that Paul is talking about is not a matter of emotion or sentimentality, of feeling good about somebody else. The love that Paul is dealing

with in this chapter consists in good will aimed at the welfare
of another, in wanting and doing what is beneficial for the
other.

Our passage begins with a topic sentence (from chapter 12)
that ties what will come with what went before: here's something
better than what we have been talking about. This is what you
ought to be pursuing.

Then Paul writes of love from three different perspectives.
First of all, all other gifts and virtues are worthless without love.
Whatever charisms of tongues, or deep knowledge, or faith, or
heroic self-sacrifice I may have, they don't amount to much
without love, without generosity toward our neighbor.

Next, he offers some characteristics of love, fourteen of them
in all, some positive (what love does), some negative (what love
does not do). Love is willing to bear hardships without complaint,
to ease others' pain. It is not self-centered, boastful, easily
offended. It is not judgmental or suspicious or cynical.

Finally, he deals with the permanence and maturity that
characterize love. Love is not some transient and partial gift that
serves only a limited purpose like prophecy or speaking in
tongues or having great knowledge. It carries us beyond spiritual
infancy to full and lasting maturity in the Lord. Compared to
other gifts, love leads us to see things immediately and directly
instead of looking at an image in a mirror. (Note that in Paul's
time most mirrors were of polished metal and not very efficient.)
Love makes us ready for our final and eternal relationship with
God, able to know God even as God knows us. In the last
analysis, love is what's important, even more important than the
basic gifts of faith and hope.

In these two chapters of First Corinthians Paul has been
talking about the most fundamental components of Christian life.
The first is oneness in the life of Christ that we share (each
exercising his or her own personal mix of gifts, to be sure). The
second is love for our neighbor which gives meaning and
direction to whatever gifts we may have to offer to the Church and

which prepares us for our final union in Christ with Father and Holy Spirit in heaven.

These two basic components of Christian life are not distinct and separate. It is the life of Christ in us that impels us to offer love and service to our neighbor. Love expresses our likeness to him. Living our life in Christ consists in giving ourselves away in love for the well-being of others, just as Jesus did. If there is no love and generosity in our lives, one could rightly wonder whether Christ is really in them, in us. Love is the way we demonstrate that living in Christ Jesus is really what we are all about. Without hard-nosed, practical, patient loving, any claims we might think we have to faith and hope, to being religious, to standing well with God, to living in the Lord Jesus are mere pretense, spiritual gongs and cymbals.

Another way to look at these two realities (Christ's life in us and our love for each other) is in the context of Christian maturity. To live one's life for the benefit of others involves understanding what the life of Christ was and is. Jesus was and is not about pettiness and self-serving and whining about our needs. Holding grudges and fostering the memories of past hurts is not what Jesus gives us to imitate. Jesus was and is about giving himself away. The extent to which our life is a life of self-giving is the extent to which we are really like Jesus, really mature in him. Do you want to know how grown-up you are in the life of faith? Ask yourself how loving you are.

FOR DISCUSSION AND REFLECTION

What does love mean to me?
What/whom/why/how do I love?

Fifth Sunday in Ordinary Time (A)

I Corinthians 2:1-5

In response to the divisions that had occurred in the local church of Corinth as a result of the members' enthusiasm for the gifts of one or the other church leader, Paul has reminded them that human talents and human standing were not the basis for their faith. They have been saved by the power of Christ and not by any contribution that any of them brought to the relationship with God.

In this Sunday's reading he applies the same sort of argumentation to his own apostolate in their midst.

He brought them "the mystery of God," the proclamation of God's secret plan of salvation for his human creatures. But the mystery was not offered to them in the trappings of lofty words or deep human wisdom. Paul deliberately limited his presentation of the gospel to the unadorned truth about Christ and his saving death. That's all he needed to know about and that's all he shared with them.

He proclaimed the gospel not with the confidence of a professional wordsmith, but with the reverential fear that was appropriate to someone who knew he was doing God's work. He didn't try to use methods of human persuasion on them. He merely showed them what the Spirit offered and the result was the miracle of their faith, their community, a result that could be attributed only to the work of the Spirit and not to the effectiveness of human eloquence or human wisdom.

In this passage Paul makes it clear that, in his preaching, he wanted his hearers to pay attention to what he said, not to how he said it. The results of his proclamation can be attributed only to the power of God, not to any gift or talent on the part either of the speaker or of his hearers. What counts is the redemption wrought by Christ crucified and the disbursement of that salvation through the power of the Spirit. Nothing else is really important.

Just as the Corinthians did not deserve salvation because of their sophistication and human excellence (which they didn't even have to any great extent!), so Paul was not a successful evangelist because of his impressive oratory and philosophical profundity.

Does all of this mean anything to us? I believe it means a lot to us.

First of all it means that the ministers of the gospel who serve God's people today must rely on the power and presence of God for the success of their work just as Paul did. The main agent of their work is the Lord, just as the Lord was the main agent in Paul's work. They are called to give witness to the Lord, not to entertain their hearers or impress them by the quality of their presentation.

This does not mean that ministers of the gospel don't need to cultivate human skills for their ministry. God does use human means to carry out his will. The fact that it is God who touches hearts doesn't mean that therefore the priest doesn't need to prepare his homilies! All of us who proclaim the gospel have to make ourselves as effective an instrument of God's power as we can be. But it is still the Lord who uses the instruments that we provide. It is the Lord who is the principal agent, the main doer, no matter how humanly skilled or how humanly talented the human proclaimer may be and whatever success is forthcoming is the Lord's success and not ours.

The fact that God is the main agent in calling people to life in Christ also has something to say to people who are not professional church ministers. Often those who see themselves as "ordinary people" in the Church act as if only priests or professional religious educators are responsible for proclaiming the gospel. That's not the way God intends it to be. If God can use the limited talents and abilities of his professional ministers, God can also use the talents and abilities of other members of the Church. You don't have to wait until you have a doctorate in theology or until you have done extensive training in homiletics in order to share the good news of God's love with other people.

Every member of the Church is called to bear witness to the gospel, to let other people see and know what it means to be a disciple of Jesus. Parents do this all the time simply by living out their faith in ways that their children can see and eventually understand. Friends evangelize each other when they share their lives and activities and each gradually comes to discern what makes the other tick. We announce the gospel to the people we work with as they come to know why we do what we do and what our personal values are. When we stand up for what we believe in opposition to those who disagree with us, we are giving witness to our faith and inviting our opponents to consider our point of view. We are all called to evangelize.

The Spirit of God is the principal preacher of Christ's gospel. He can use professional ministers of religion for his purposes and he can use "ordinary people." He can use human skills and talents to get his message across, or he can do without them. All that the Spirit requires is our willingness to be his instruments.

FOR DISCUSSION AND REFLECTION

Who is the most effective minister of the gospel I have ever known? What are/were his/her gifts?

How do I experience the power of God working in and through my life?

Fifth Sunday in Ordinary Time (B)

I Corinthians 9:16-19, 22-23

In the eighth chapter of this letter, Paul has been answering the second question that the Corinthians had posed to him: was it appropriate for Christians to take part in dinner parties where the meat that was served may have been sacrificed to idols? (In a pagan city like Corinth, much of the food consumed could have passed through pagan religious ceremonies before it found its way into the marketplace.) Paul tells them that, since there is no reality to pagan gods, eating meat sacrificed to them has no religious meaning for a Christian believer. At the same time, some less sophisticated believers could be scandalized by even this apparent, though remote, participation in pagan rites. It would be better for the "knowledgeable" believers to forego their "rights" out of respect for the tender consciences and spiritual needs of their brothers and sisters.

At the beginning of chapter 9, Paul intends to strengthen his teaching about sensitivity to others' needs by invoking his own example of giving up his "rights" for the sake of the spiritual well-being of those he serves. He wants to make the point that he has the right to be provided with a living for preaching the gospel, but instead has chosen to support himself and not take any recompense from his young Christian community. This practice of his seemed to have been a source of contention in the church of Corinth, and so Paul's simple example turns into a complicated defense of his own mission and of his approach to that mission. Paul seems to have been very sensitive on these matters. We find similar defenses of his apostolate in the second letter to the Corinthians and in the letter to the Galatians.

Apparently some people said that the reason why Paul did not accept any payment for his services was because he really wasn't a true apostle and so didn't have a right to payment anyway. He defends his apostolic calling at the beginning of chapter 9 and then goes on to offer a whole series of reasons why he could lay claim for sustenance on the Corinthians if he wished. He has rights just like everybody else, and is free to invoke those rights, but he freely chooses not to exercise them. In our passage for today he explains why. The explanation is typically complicated and passionate.

I don't preach the gospel because I have chosen to do so, he says, but because I have been called by God. I am under obligation to him. If I preached on my own volition, the preaching itself would be my reward. But it wasn't my idea. God gave me a job to do, a "stewardship." Doing what the master demands doesn't merit any special "reward." If there is to be a reward, there has to be some further, spontaneous quality to my service, and that quality is my willingness to give up the support that might otherwise have come to me as part of my service. I have chosen to forego my "rights" and offer the gospel free of charge as a little something extra for God. I don't have to do this, but I do it in order to be as accessible and available as possible to those to whom I preach, to be their slave, as it were, their companion in weakness and limitation and need. It makes the gospel more credible, and gives me a better chance to share in its blessings.

Most priests of today would resonate in several ways with Paul's devotion to his calling, his response to the "stewardship" he had been given. First of all, the vast majority of priests are happy in their priesthood and they wouldn't want to be doing anything else. They might prefer a different assignment, but not a different vocation.

In addition to that, priests of today, like Paul, find fulfillment and strength in the people they serve. The greatest blessing they find in their ministry is the men and women to whom they minister. People vary from parish to parish and their needs and sensitivities are different at different times. But priests know that their people need them and appreciate them and respond to them and this constitutes one of the major gifts of their priestly ministry. They are happy to serve, and find ever greater happiness in their service. Their priestly ministry provides its own reward. Their share in the promises of the gospel is "becoming all things to all in order to save at least some."

All this is not to say that contemporary priestly ministry is effortless or without problems. After all, Paul had his problems, too. Sometimes questions arise about working conditions and retirement, about the way assignments are made, about how certain situations ought to be addressed. Sometimes priests find themselves in conflict with certain members of their flock, who seem to go out of their way to make things difficult. Paul experienced that, too. But in spite of all this, like Paul, they continue to preach the gospel because they have been called to preach it and they are grateful for the call.

FOR DISCUSSION AND REFLECTION

What priests do I admire? Why?

How does the ministry of priests enable all the members of the Church to preach the gospel?

Fifth Sunday in Ordinary Time (C)

I Corinthians 15:1-11

The fifteenth chapter of First Corinthians is totally concerned with the Resurrection—Christ's and ours. It is not clear whether the Corinthians had addressed questions to Paul on this subject or whether he had been informed of erroneous doctrinal trends in their midst. It does seem clear, however, that some of them were saying that, whatever may have happened to Christ, there was no such thing as resurrection from the dead for others. This might have been because they simply could not imagine how any kind of bodily existence could be possible after death, or because they disdained everything bodily and were willing to content themselves with the survival of the soul, or because they thought that the Resurrection was a purely spiritual experience that had already taken place in them at baptism.

This chapter is divided into three parts. The first (which constitutes our reading for this Sunday) offers the basic Christian doctrine about the Resurrection of Jesus. The second (which we hear from next Sunday) deals with the implications of denying the Resurrection. The third part (which provides readings for the Seventh and Eighth Sundays in Ordinary Time) teaches about the nature of a resurrected body.

This Sunday's reading begins with a reminder of the fundamental importance of the Resurrection of Christ for Christian faith. Paul tells the Corinthians that the Resurrection of Christ is the source of their salvation and that, if they have lost their belief in it, their whole faith is vain. Without the Resurrection of Christ, everything collapses.

Then he reminds them of the content of the basic preaching that he had given them, a preaching that contained the very kernel of Christian revelation, the fundamental content of all Christian belief. In accord with the plans that had been intimated through the Hebrew Scriptures, Jesus died for our sins and was buried. (The burial confirms the reality of his death.) Then he "was raised from the dead." (The Greek tense used here signifies an action in the past whose reality continues into the present. It could be properly translated, "He has been raised and is still with us." This construction is used no less than seven times in First Corinthians 15.) Then the risen Christ showed himself to his followers: Peter, the twelve, five hundred of the brothers at once (some of whom are still available for verification), James and, last of all, to Paul.

Never one to overlook a chance to defend himself, Paul now gives us an overview of the nature and outcomes of his apostolate. His calling was different from that of the other apostles. He has worked harder than they, though the results came from God's grace rather than his own efforts. But the bottom line is that all the apostles, including Paul, have preached the same saving truth about the Resurrection of Jesus.

There are two important aspects of the Resurrection of Jesus that we need to be aware of before we can discuss the meaning of the Resurrection for us. The first is that the Resurrection was not just Jesus coming back to life again to take up his previous life where he had left off (as Lazarus and the widow's son in Naim presumably did). No, the risen Jesus lived a whole new kind of life, a kind of life that Paul will have more to say about next

Sunday. Secondly, the Resurrection of Jesus was not an occurrence that took place a long time ago to which we relate as we relate to other events of the past. No, the Resurrection of Jesus, his new life, continues now. The risen Christ is still with us. The risen life of Christ is still going on.

Why, then, is the Resurrection of Jesus important for us? For one thing, the Resurrection of Jesus assures us that the life and ministry of Jesus are still going on. The man who walked the roads of Judea and Galilee, who taught about the love of the Father, who remained consistent in his love and dedication to the Father, who maintained his generous openness to God's will—that man is still alive, still with us, still carrying on his redemptive activity in and through his new, post-resurrection life.

For another, the life of the risen Christ extends itself to us. We share it through the grace of baptism, we express it in our own individual human existence, we assimilate it ever more deeply by our response to his generosity. If Christ had not risen from the dead, we would be able to relate to him only as an ideal, as a historical figure of the past, not as our living Lord in the present.

Finally, the Resurrection of Jesus and our sharing in his life constitute a promise of a new and different life for us when we finally share fully in his kingdom. Body and soul we will be enfolded into his life with Father and Holy Spirit. All that we are will be assumed into him. If there were no Resurrection, no risen Christ, we would have no reason to hope for anything more than we already experience. What a grim prospect!

FOR DISCUSSION AND REFLECTION

What aspects of the Resurrection of Jesus do I find most appealing?
What does the Resurrection of Jesus have to do with my attitudes toward my body?

Sixth Sunday in Ordinary Time (A)

I Corinthians 2:6-10

Two Sundays ago Paul reminded the Corinthians that, if they were saved, it was not because of their own merits, their own status and wisdom, but because of God's generosity. Last Sunday he told them that the success of his own preaching was not due to his own rhetorical skill, still less to his human wisdom. Wisdom, speculative sophistication, has not been a source of salvation for the Corinthians nor a source of evangelical success for Paul.

In this Sunday's reading Paul continues to talk about wisdom, only now it is God's wisdom.

In spite of all that has been said to put human wisdom in its proper place, there is a wisdom that is involved with salvation—God's wisdom. This is what Paul offered to those who would be saved ("those who are mature"). This wisdom is different from earthly sophistication, different from the alleged profundities of those in charge of the world, whose authority is already being diminished.

God's wisdom is his plan of salvation, worked out long ago, directed toward the final glory of humankind, not previously manifested. God's wisdom (his secret plan for redemption now revealed to those who accepted Christ) has not been grasped by "the rulers of this age." (By "the rulers of this age" Paul may mean the secular officials who were responsible for Jesus' death, or the cosmic powers of evil who exercise control over the world, or the cosmic powers working through human instruments.) If these rulers had known what God was up to, they never would have crucified Jesus. (Paul seems to be suggesting here that God's wisdom tricked the powers of the world into cooperating with his plan of salvation by crucifying Jesus. They would never have helped bring the plan of salvation to fulfillment in this way if they had realized what they were doing.)

Next it sounds like Paul is citing Scripture: "What eye has not seen, and ear has not heard...," yet these words are found nowhere in the Bible. Perhaps he is making reference to some well-known bit of rabbinic writing. In any case, the point is clear: what God has prepared for those who love him, what God has revealed to us through the Spirit far surpasses any human capacity to grasp or even imagine. These insights come to us only through the Spirit who alone has access to the innermost thoughts of God.

The main point of this passage is that the Spirit confers on those who are saved some degree of understanding of God's plans. God does not treat us like children who are given direction but not explanation. We are more mature than that. We are provided with some fundamental insights about the meaning of the life, death and resurrection of Jesus and about our salvation. This level of understanding is not based on our own speculative skills. It is given to us by the Spirit as gift. We are wise with a wisdom that far surpasses anything that human ingenuity or penetration could reach.

But the fact that God has given us some degree of wisdom does not mean that we therefore understand everything. We always remain infinitely beneath God's level of providence and planning. While we accept with gratitude the understandings that his wisdom has made available to us, there always remains a vast degree of mystery, whole realms of the unknown. This calls for a posture of reverence in the face of the fullness of God's plans, for a sense of awe in the context of God's wisdom, for faith and confidence about what God has not revealed to us arising from gratitude for what God has revealed.

Catholic theology teaches us that, thanks to God's revelation and our own intellectual capabilities, we can know and speak about God in ways that have real meaning. We do know something about God and about God's plans for human salvation. To say that God loves us and that God has redeemed us is not to talk nonsense.

At the same time, God is greater than anything that human intellect can grasp about him. God is beyond anything that our limited human language can say about him. Whatever we think or say about God always has to be qualified by a strong awareness of the inadequacy of human thought and language. The wisdom that God shares with us about our salvation is only a faint glimmering of the full reality, not because God doesn't know what he is talking about, but because we are so limited in our capacity to receive what God wants us to know. If God seems to stammer sometimes in his communication with us, it's because stammering is all we are able to grasp.

Human wisdom cannot answer all our questions about our relationship with God, and we are wasting our time if we think that it can. Even God's wisdom cannot answer all our questions here and now, simply because God's wisdom surpasses our capacity to understand. God leads us to a certain degree of awareness about what he has done and continues to do for us, but God also wants us to be aware that there are whole universes of wisdom beyond what we are given. We don't have to understand everything. As a matter of fact, we can't.

FOR DISCUSSION AND REFLECTION

How has the mysterious wisdom of God been active in my life?

How much of God's plan must we understand in order to carry out God's will?

Sixth Sunday in Ordinary Time (B)

I Corinthians 10:31-11:1

After his fiery defense of his own ministerial style in chapter 9, Paul returns to the question of eating meat sacrificed to idols. He tells the Corinthians that they have to beware of overconfidence in eating idol meats, lest they back into idolatry unaware and find themselves substituting banquets of evil for the table of the Lord.

He also addresses the question of the spiritual harm that might be done to believers by a Christian's taking advantage of the freedom his own conscience offers. The other's conscience is important, too. Now, in our text, (the last from First Corinthians this year) comes another summary passage.

There's a general rule at play in this context of what we are permitted to eat and drink, Paul says, and that is to be mindful of the requirements of God's glory. Don't make problems for anybody. Try to behave in a way that shows the most concern for the most people without always invoking your own rights and preferences. That's what I do and I do this because this is what Christ did.

Here Paul is referring to his own practice of accommodating himself to the sensitivities of those with whom he is dealing. He didn't flaunt his freedom from Jewish law when dealing with Jews. He didn't invoke dietary scruples when eating with pagans. By not taking advantage of options that were rightfully his, he tried to avoid causing problems for believers. Paul behaved as he did in imitation of Christ. For the sake of our salvation Christ became a human being, he lived poor, he died on the cross. He didn't have to do any of that, but he did because he wanted to save us. Like Christ, Paul was concerned for the ultimate well-being of others rather than with his own prerogatives, and he calls for a similar attitude on the part of his Corinthian converts.

There are two ways to look at what Paul is saying here. The first is to examine its negative implications. "Don't be so concerned with your own rights and privileges that you end up giving offense to people." Beware of causing scandal.

In our ordinary way of speaking, scandal denotes circumstances or actions that offend propriety or established moral norms. "He left his wife and children and eloped with the teenaged girl next door. What a scandal!" In theological parlance, however, scandal means behavior that causes other people to be shaken in their faith or their religious observance. Scandal may be sinful behavior that causes others to sin. But sometimes the behavior may not be wrong in itself, yet cause problems for others. An easy attitude about the Sunday Mass obligation may cause harm to more strict observers, even as scrupulously exact devotional practices may elicit distaste in other members of the community. Sometimes even the tone and vocabulary we use when expressing our opinions can offer offense. Scandal is action that puts stumbling blocks in the path of others' path to God.

To avoid scandal doesn't mean that we have to spend our whole lives worrying about what other people might think about what we do, but it does demand that we be aware that what we do and say may have consequences beyond what we intend.

(There is also another kind of scandal that theologians have identified. It is called pharisaical scandal. It is a pathological mind-set that causes those affected with it to be determined to be offended. Whatever the other person does or says constitutes a cause for dismay, outrage, disillusionment. Bishops and parish priests are often the targets of this kind of scandal. This is not what Paul is talking about here.)

On the more positive side, Paul is reminding us that we share responsibility for the spiritual good of those around us. We have something to contribute to the glory of God. Little sacrifices of our legitimate personal tastes and preferences can contribute to the salvation of our brothers and sisters, believers and non-believers alike. Keeping quiet when we could rightly lodge objections, going the extra mile in religious observance beyond what is strictly called for, being willing to forego our own devotional preferences for the sake of the community—all these are relatively small things, things to which we are not strictly obliged. Yet they may constitute important contributions to somebody else's relationship with the Lord, important steps in somebody else's salvation. Being a Christian believer is not just a matter of tending to my own needs and seeking "my own benefit." It's also a matter of looking out for the benefit "of the many, that they may be saved." We are all called in these matters to be imitators of Paul, and thus imitators of Christ.

There isn't much idol meat in the markets these days. We don't have to worry a lot about the implications of going to dinner with pagans. But that doesn't mean that the advice that Paul offered the Corinthians has no significance for us.

FOR DISCUSSION AND REFLECTION

How have I been scandalized by another member of the Church?
What efforts do I make to avoid giving spiritual offense to others?

Sixth Sunday in Ordinary Time (C)

I Corinthians 15:12, 16-20

The erroneous opinion that some of the Corinthians seem to have held, namely that, whatever may have happened to Christ, there is no such thing as resurrection for the rest of us, has some implications. Paul discusses some of those implications in this Sunday's live letter. He begins with a logical dilemma that requires careful attention if we are to follow it.

If you say that there is no resurrection from the dead, you cannot say that Christ rose from the dead. But if, as we believe, Christ did rise from the dead, then you cannot say that there is no resurrection. Either Christ rose from the dead, and there is, therefore, resurrection from the dead, or he didn't and then there is no resurrection for anybody. You can't have it both ways.

Then the text speaks of three consequences that would follow if there is no resurrection and Christ has not been raised from the dead.

The first consequence is that salvation from our sins is an illusion and our conviction that we are saved is mere fantasy. (The main penalty for sin is death. We were condemned to die because of our turning away from God. Christ's triumph over sin, therefore, must necessarily involve a triumph over death. If Christ and those who follow him are condemned to die at the end of their earthly lives without hope of anything further, then the forgiveness of sins that Christ supposedly won for us has no meaning. We are no better off than we were before.)

The second consequence if there is no resurrection has to do with the fate of the followers of Christ who have already died. (The earliest Christians were looking for the second coming of Christ to take place quite soon. Christ would then take the faithful to eternal happiness with himself. That raised a problem about those believers whose earthly life had ended before Christ's coming. That's the problem that Paul alludes to here.) If there is no such thing as future resurrection, then those who have already died are simply dead. They have missed out on the coming of Christ and there is nothing more for them to look forward to.

Thirdly, if there is no resurrection from the dead, there is a significant consequence for all of us, and that consequence is that our life is meaningless. We have been cheated by our commitment to a Christ who cannot save us. We must continue to fight a losing battle against sin without hope of victory. Religious beliefs like this can only arouse pity. It's better to be a pagan!

Now Paul draws his conclusion: as a matter of fact Christ did rise from the dead, and so there is resurrection! Moreover, Christ's Resurrection is not just an event of personal importance to him. It marks the beginning of a whole new kind of human life, the initiation of a vast harvest of which we, too, will be a part.

Paul has been talking to the Corinthians about how things would be if there were no resurrection of the dead. We accept the idea of resurrection, but it's important for us to be aware of the positive side of the three consequences that Paul lists.

First, because Christ has risen from the dead and because there is therefore resurrection, we can be confident that Christ has triumphed over sin and that we are saved. In Jesus we see that death is no longer the last word, and so sin has somehow been overcome. Because we share the life of the risen Christ through baptism, sin has been overcome in us. The resurrection of the dead is not merely an event of significance that lies ahead of us in the future. It's something that colors our whole human existence now.

Secondly, because of the reality of the Resurrection and of Christians' participation in the life of the risen Christ, our loved ones who have gone before us in death are not simply dead. They are still alive because they are still in Christ. They await the final manifestation of Christ at the end of time, but in the interim they remain dear to him and to us. As the Church's liturgy prays, "For your faithful people, Lord, life is changed, not ended."

Finally, our Christian faith in the Resurrection constitutes grounds for real hope, real joy, real happiness even in this life. Granted, Christian life can be demanding. It often seems that our faith requires a lot of us. Perhaps it also seems that other people, untrammeled by an awareness of their responsibilities to a loving and saving God, can live more freely and easily than we do. But our faith in the ongoing life of the risen Christ, our conviction that we will share that life not only here and now but in the final kingdom with Father, Son and Spirit gives meaning and direction to our lives that non-believers cannot share. We know we are important to God and we know that that importance will last forever.

At every Eucharist we celebrate the death and rising of Christ. In that celebration, we also celebrate our own present and future. Easter, the feast of resurrection, isn't just about Christ. It's about us, too.

FOR DISCUSSION AND REFLECTION

Is there any reason whatsoever for faith and hope if there is no resurrection?

What meaning could resurrection have for those who do not believe in Christ?

Seventh Sunday in Ordinary Time (A)

I Corinthians 3:16-23

Paul continues to deal with the factions that were so much a part
of the church of Corinth. In the verses that immediately precede
this Sunday's reading, he speaks of the collaborative effort that is
required in the construction of a building. The various fellow
workers all make their contributions and the various contributions
are tested to determine their quality. But everybody is working
together to erect a single building, so everybody must work
carefully.

Now, as this Sunday's reading begins, Paul draws another
conclusion from his image. "*You* are the temple of God," he tells
them. What's being built up by the efforts of all these
collaborators is nothing less than a home for the Holy Spirit, a
home constituted by themselves, by their church community.
Those who, through their divisiveness or lack of dedication
undermine this building ("which you are") will be punished,
because the building belongs to God and is therefore holy.

Next Paul returns to the theme of wisdom that we have
already heard him dealing with over the last two Sundays. He
cites the book of Job (5:13) and Psalm 94 (verse 11) to underline
the futility of merely human wisdom and to remind the
Corinthians still again that human philosophical insights are
foolishness in God's sight. They would do much better, he says, to
pursue God's wisdom, which is foolishness in the sight of the
world.

Now comes another conclusion, this one based on an
apparently well-known philosophical maxim that Paul turns to his
own purposes. The maxim is something like, "All things belong to
the wise." There's no need for the Corinthians to invoke their
relationship with ("boast about") Paul or Apollos or Cephas as the
source of their own importance. They don't belong to Paul or
Apollos or Cephas. On the contrary, Paul and Apollos and Cephas
belong to them because of their sharing in the wisdom of God. In

addition, the world and life and death and the present and the future are all theirs, too. They, in turn, all belong to Christ who belongs to the Father.

Paul has been talking about the dangers of partisanship for two and a half chapters now, and will go on talking about it through the end of chapter 4. His basic teachings have become clear by this time: what's important is not whether you "belong to" Paul or Apollos or Cephas. What's important is whether you belong to Christ or not. Human sophistication, the pursuit of profound philosophical wisdom that makes you seem better than others is a waste of time. What's important is the wisdom of God expressed in the death and resurrection of Christ. All the big names of the local community are really the agents of the one God and are supposed to be working together on one task: building up the temple of the Holy Spirit. The building of the temple is what's important, not who contributes what to the construction.

Divided communities and factionalism have not been limited in the Church's history to the early church of Corinth. They are with us yet, and probably have always been part of the Church's life. Most contemporary Church leaders have had to deal with tensions between liberals and conservatives, between those who can't let go of the old liturgy and those for whom the liturgy must be always new, between those who would have the community limit its energies to worship and those who would have the community engage itself exclusively in social action projects. Personalities have their followers today as they did then: Fulton Sheen and Mother Angelica versus Karl Rahner and Andrew Greely. Even organizations that are set up to reduce tensions in the Church (such as Cardinal Bernardin's Catholic Common Ground Initiative) become the source of new tensions.

All this happens because people lose their perspective. In the twenty-first century as in the first century what's important is that we belong to Christ, that we share his life, that we look forward to sharing the final kingdom with him. Everything else is secondary. People in positions of ministerial leadership are not there in order to be idolized by the "ordinary" members of the Church but to serve them. The ministers "belong to" their people and not vice versa. The kind of hymns we sing on Sunday may have some importance to the spiritual development of the congregation, but not nearly as much importance as the self-giving of Christ that constitutes the center of the Eucharist in which we participate. The place of the tabernacle in the church building is not nearly as significant as the place of the love of Christ in the parish community. First things need to come first, and whenever secondary things are put first, the result is tension and disorder in the community.

Everything in the Church is there for the salvation of its members. It all belongs to all of them. It is all God's gift to them. There is no point in their wasting their attention and energy on anything less than what God offers.

FOR DISCUSSION AND REFLECTION

What does it mean to say that Church leaders or ministers "belong to" their people?

How do I see myself as "belonging to" Christ and the Father?

Seventh Sunday in Ordinary Time (B)

II Corinthians 1:18-22

The semi-continuous reading of Paul's second letter to the Corinthians that we begin today gets short shrift in the Church's lectionary. It is interrupted when Lent and Easter time take over from the Sundays in Ordinary Time. Then, when Ordinary Time begins once more after the Easter season, the first three Sundays of it are superseded by Pentecost and the feasts of the Holy

Trinity and Corpus Christi. We never get to read all eight portions of Second Corinthians that the lectionary offers. We just get pieces of it. In a sense, that's not inappropriate because some scholars think that Second Corinthians is itself a collection of pieces, of briefer letters sent to Corinth over a certain span of time and later gathered together, perhaps by Paul himself, into one document.

The general context of Second Corinthians is tension and misunderstanding. The Corinthians themselves seem to have been demanding and insecure, but the young church had also been visited by other Christian missionaries who differed from Paul in their approach to the gospel and who seem to have been quite free about sowing doubt and confusion in the minds of the Corinthians about Paul's character and methods. Hence this letter is a long and defensive explanation by Paul of certain specific happenings and of his apostolate in general. Because so much of the letter is concerned with words and actions that are not fully explained, it is sometimes difficult to understand the points that he is making. Reading Second Corinthians is like listening to one side of a family fight.

In today's reading from chapter 1, the issue is Paul's promise to make several visits to Corinth and then not showing up. Later he will explain that his change of plans was determined by his conviction that a visit would not have been timely or helpful to the Corinthians, but here he is addressing a wider issue: his own credibility. It seems that the hostile element at Corinth took Paul's change of plans as merely one more sign of his character and his ministry: vacillating, inconstant, unsure. They saw him as one who talks out of both sides of his mouth, whose yeses and nos were indistinguishable and undependable. So now, at the beginning of his explanation about the unmade visits he has to defend his basic reliability and consistency.

My ministry deals with Christ, he says, as does the ministry of Silvanus and Timothy, my colleagues. We are not indecisive or unclear about what we preach. We preach the decisiveness and clarity of Christ who is the unique fulfillment of all God's promises. Christ is God saying "yes" to us even as our response to Christ is saying "yes" to the Father through him. You ought to have confidence in us when it comes to relating to Christ, because we have been appointed by God and because we have received the Spirit as a kind ʃ ˡᵒʷⁿ payment on the full messianic benefits still to c[...]

clear, and unequivocal and[...]

Paul's defense of his s[...] hrist is God's a[...] interesting issues for us. F[...] ovidence for us. We, too, love and care, the express[...] stitutes the beginning of have received the Holy S[...] m. The basic outlines of our final fulfillment in C[...] s no reason for us to wonder meaning in our life are [...] are supposed to be headed. what we are all about ar[...] nd we have said "yes" to In Christ, God has said[...] God.

    Yet all too often w[...] aren't really convinced of all that. Many of our prior[...] concerned with Christ. We spend a lot more time[...] ut the details of job and family and personal econom[...] an we do about the presence and action of Christ i[...] ur personal relationships are more concerned with[...] n than with sharing Christ's love with others. Our cul[...] at importance on "feeling good about yourself," and[...] ut more energy into pursuing that goal than into [...] and appropriating the self that Christ has imparte[...] attention to the presence of Christ in prayer and com[...] ip frequently takes second place to dealing with th[...] emands of ordinary life or to an extra hour's sleep[...] It's not that we have walked away from Christ or gi[...] hristian beliefs, but that the strong "yes" of faith tha[...] ands of us has degenerated in practice to, "Ma[...] t too much trouble."

    Clarity and[...] and single-mindedness were part of Paul's basic character as an apostle. If those traits were not obvious to the Corinthians, it was because they really didn't understand him, or chose not to understand him. Clarity and consistency and single-mindedness are supposed to be part of our character as Christian believers. If they are not, it may be because we really haven't understood Christ.

FOR DISCUSSION AND REFLECTION

What elements in my life indicate that I have offered a firm "yes" to Christ?

What elements in my life indicate that my commitment isn't all that it should be?

Seventh Sunday in Ordinary Time (C)

I Corinthians 15:45-49

Having dealt with the centrality of Christ's Resurrection to our faith and with some of the consequences of denying the resurrection of the body, Paul now deals with two more items that seem to have been troubling the Corinthians. The first was the question of the nature of the risen body. What will it be like? This is the subject of this Sunday's second reading. The other question, how will the resurrection take place, will be dealt with in next Sunday's live letter.

Apparently the Corinthians had trouble imagining any kind of body other than what they experienced here and now, which simply rotted away after death. In a rather grumpy way (see "You fool...," in verse 36) Paul offers two parallels, two comparisons to help them see that there is more than one kind of body, more than one kind of life.

In verses 36 to 44, just before our text, Paul offers them the example of a seed that seemingly dies and then comes back to life as a plant. One kind of life form gives way to another. Similarly, when we die we are "sown" as one kind of body, a natural one, but we are raised as another kind, a spiritual one.

Our Sunday reading gives another parallel, this one concerned with two kinds of life arising from two kinds of people.

Paul speaks of two Adams, one, the first man, the other (Christ) the final man, and he lines up the similarities and differences between them. The first Adam was alive in a natural way, but the second Adam was alive in a way that offered life to others. The natural life of the first Adam was "earthly" and preceded the spirit-filled ("heavenly") life of Christ. People who are like the first Adam are "earthly" and people who are like the heavenly Adam (Christ) are "heavenly." Just as we are all like the earthly Adam in our present existence, so, in due time, we shall all be like the heavenly Adam.

Our relationship with Adam gives us an earthly body. Our relationship with Christ will give us a "heavenly" one. We will be like the risen Christ just as we are like the earthly Adam. One kind of life will succeed the other. Paul does not go into great detail about the nature of our risen body, but he assures the Corinthians that its principal element will be likeness to Christ.

The nature of a risen body is not a hot issue for us contemporary Christians. Yet there are at least two important facets of this question that we need to be clear about.

The first is that our salvation, our eternal worth depends on our likeness to Christ. That likeness is what constitutes resurrection and final fulfillment. But the likeness we are dealing with here is not mere imitation of somebody else's actions. We do speak of and encourage Christ-like attitudes and behavior. But that could be a matter of merely pretending to be something or someone we are not. The likeness to Christ that constitutes our resurrection, our salvation, our redemption is a real sharing in the risen life of Christ. We are like him not because of certain words or actions modeled on him, but because of his eternal risen life that becomes operative in our life.

This participation in the life of Christ is what the Christian tradition calls grace. It is given to us in baptism, and we are invited to assimilate and develop it throughout our existence in time. Being in Christ, living the risen life of Christ is not some sort of legal fiction in which God pretends that we are like Christ. It's not a reward that we receive for being good. It's a gift that we cannot deserve and that consists in really sharing in, really living the risen, glorified, eternal life of Christ. Nothing else makes us holy in God's sight or worthy of his attention to us.

The second facet of Paul's teaching about the nature of the risen body that is important for us to be attentive to is that we do not yet fully and definitively share Christ's risen life. "We shall bear the image of the heavenly Adam," he says. The final transforming action of God on our behalf is still in the future.

We do share the risen life of Christ now through grace. Our transformation into him is real. But it is a transformation that is partial, contingent, vulnerable, mingled with other levels of life. It is not the case that, once having received the life of Christ through baptism, we are home free and no further effort is required. On the contrary, one might say that the real struggle of the Christian life is just beginning when we are graced with Christ's life. It is the struggle to appreciate what we have received, to act in accord with what God has called us to be, to understand and respond to the incomprehensible depths of God's goodness and generosity to us. Our resurrection from the dead begins with baptism, but it doesn't come to conclusion until we are finished with this life and definitively transformed into the second Adam.

FOR DISCUSSION AND REFLECTION

What does being like Adam mean to me?

What does sharing the life of Christ mean to me?

Eighth Sunday in Ordinary Time (A)

I Corinthians 4:1-5

Almost since the very beginning of his letter to the Corinthians Paul has been dealing with the divisions in the community, divisions based on the presumed superiority of one church leader over another. He chided them for claiming to "belong" to Apollos or Cephas or Paul. Last week we heard him tell his readers that, far from the faithful "belonging to" one of these leaders, the leaders belonged to them! Now he is drawing this first major topic of the letter to conclusion with a general description of the function and significance of all the church leaders.

He tells the Corinthians that they should look on the leaders (Apollos, Cephas, himself) as servants *of Christ* and managers *for God*. The leaders are neither employees of the faithful nor independent entrepreneurs. They work for God and no one else.

If you work for somebody in a position of trust, it's up to that somebody alone to evaluate your performance. Paul does not see himself as subject to the evaluation of the Corinthians nor of any other human agency. It is not even his own evaluation of himself that counts. He doesn't think that he has done a poor job in his apostolate, but that alone does not mean that he has been successful. The only one who can evaluate him properly, the only one who can pronounce on the quality of Paul's service is the Lord, the master for whom he has been working.

Our reading draws to a close with a comprehensive conclusion for the Corinthians: it's not up to them to judge or evaluate Paul or Apollos or Cephas or anybody else. The meaning and quality and success of anyone's life can only be determined by God, at a time chosen by God. When God is ready to judge he will make known the final worth of each person. It will be from God that the true appreciation of our value will come.

There are two important teachings in this reading, one about the ministers of the Church, the other about each and every one of its members.

The important part of a Church minister's service is not how well he or she responds to the expectations of those who are being served, nor even the abilities and talents that the minister brings to his or her service. Whatever the ministry may be (bishop, priest, deacon, catechist, parish manager, youth minister or whatever) its success and effectiveness depend on how well it corresponds to the will of God for that specific exercise of ministry. The reason is that it is not the personal talents of the minister that carry out the ministry, but the grace and action of God. The minister is an instrument of God and is successful to the extent that he or she is faithful to God and open to God's activity working through the minister's instrumentality. If the sacraments are celebrated, if God's word is proclaimed, if the community is built up, it is principally and primarily due to the intervention of God and not to the abilities of God's agents.

There is a "givenness" to God's activity in our midst. You take what you get. God can use whatever ministers are at hand to carry out his purposes. This is not to say that the ministers don't need to prepare themselves to be God's agents, nor that the people they serve have no right to expect certain levels of competency in their church ministers. But it does mean that what really counts is God's doing and not ours and that human judgments about the effectiveness of Church ministers can be wildly wide of the mark.

This Sunday's reading also reminds us to be cautious about judging others in general. "Do not make any judgement," Paul says. Jesus was clear about this, too: "Stop judging that you may not be judged" (Matthew 7:1). It is wrong for us to judge our brothers and sisters in the Lord because we know so little about what really drives the other that our judgments are almost certain to be incorrect.

We may be able to judge behaviors and try to restrain actions or omissions that are harmful to society. We know theft when we see it, for example, and theft is something that we can't tolerate. But we cannot fully judge the subjective guilt or degree of responsibility of the thief unless we can weigh motives, individual freedom, extenuating circumstances and the like, simply because we don't have all the information. Only God has all the information, so we have to leave to him final judgment about the worth of a person's life, whether the person be a criminal on trial or a troublesome neighbor or a seeming paragon of virtue.

There's still another reason why we should leave judging to God. It is not just that God alone has all the information that is required to make a final judgment about somebody's ultimate value. It is also that judgment needs to be tempered by love and mercy, and nobody loves human beings more or is more inclined to be merciful to them than our loving and merciful God. We are much more valuable than we—or those around us—think. Only God realizes how valuable we are and that's why it makes sense for definitive evaluations to come from him alone.

FOR DISCUSSION AND REFLECTION

On the basis of what criteria do I evaluate those who serve me in the Church?

Would I prefer to be judged by human beings rather than by God?

Eighth Sunday in Ordinary Time (B)

II Corinthians 3:1b-6

At the end of chapter 2, Paul abandons his treatment of specific events and their explanation, and launches into a long digression on the nature of his ministry and his qualifications for it. The liturgical readings for today and the next four Sundays of Ordinary Time are from this part of Second Corinthians.

Although the connection of this digression with what precedes it is not totally clear, we still find traces of the work of the Corinthian critics that we have seen before. They seem to have been complaining that Paul presented himself in Corinth without appropriate documentation, without letters of recommendation that would attest to the authenticity of his apostolate and his previous activity. Moreover, he hadn't received any recommendation from them to present at the next stages of his apostolate.

Paul doesn't want to have anything to do with such things. He says in our reading that he has no need of letters of recommendation to or from the Corinthians. Their very existence as a Christian community is enough to recommend him. That, and Paul's affection for them, give abundant testimony to anyone who wants to understand that Paul's work is authentic apostolate. Moreover, this "letter" constituted by their faith is not a piece of paper written on in ink like the credentials of other preachers. It's not even a set of stone tablets like the Ten Commandments that Moses received. Paul's "letter of recommendation" is Christ's doing, written by the Holy Spirit on their hearts and his. Paul says that that's all the certification he needs. Of course this qualification for mission and the confidence that his successful preaching instills in him are not based on his own achievements. They come from God through Christ. God has established him as minister of a new covenant of life that replaces the ineffective written covenant of the old law. Paul's apostolate is God's doing.

Paul's defense of his own importance as an apostle and his grateful awareness of his success invite us to reflect about what importance and success mean for us. The two concepts are related, but they have different overtones.

Importance is a state of being, being of significant worth or influence. There are lots of reasons why people are considered important. It can be because of their credentials, generally accepted testimonies to their talents and abilities, like having Ph.D. or M.D. after one's name. It can be because of the office they hold. The president of the United States is important. It can be because of the resources they have at their disposal. "Of course he's important. He owns half the town." Sometimes people are important because of the value they are given by others. A movie star is important to his or her fans and children are important to their parents.

Success is more concerned with outcomes. A successful person is one whose efforts have yielded positive and desirable results. She worked her way through college and law school and is now managing partner of the biggest firm in the city. She's a success. He has taught for twenty years and has published seven learned books. He's a successful scholar. They worked hard and raised five wonderful children. They're successful parents.

Importance and success are not bad things. Today's reading shows us that Paul himself had some interest in them. We all want to be important in some way because being important involves the recognition of our worth and if there is no context in which we are important, nobody to whom we are important, it means that we are without worth. We all want to be successful, too, because success involves using our talents and gifts to better ourselves and others and if we are totally unsuccessful it means either that we had no abilities to start with or that we have wasted them. We are all persons of worth and ability, made so by God, and it is not inappropriate to want to have that worth acknowledged and see that ability produce results.

But we have to determine very carefully where we want to find importance and in what context we want to pursue success. How significant are superficial importance and transitory success that have nothing to do with our fundamental calling as children of God? Being rich and famous won't do much for us when we stand before a Father who isn't impressed with such things. Being fabulously successful, gaining the whole world, in fact, won't be of much consequence if we haven't given adequate attention to the main project and purpose of the life the Lord has given us.

The real secret of importance and success is that we are not the owner of our life but its steward. Like Paul, we are ministers of the Lord, his servants called and gifted by him to carry out his plans. No testimonial to our importance, no evidence of our success is of any value whatsoever unless it is certified by its origin in the Lord's generosity and its usefulness for his purposes.

FOR DISCUSSION AND REFLECTION

What is important in my life? Why?

What have been my greatest successes?

Eighth Sunday in Ordinary Time (C)

I Corinthians 15:54-58

Last Sunday Paul taught the Corinthians about the nature of the risen body, about its likeness to the risen Christ, the heavenly Adam. In this Sunday's reading Paul is dealing with the "how" of the resurrection: what's going to happen when it takes place?

He describes the resurrection in verses 50-53. That which is material and corruptible cannot have a place in the realm of immortality. A transformation is required, an intervention of God. The instant of fulfillment will come suddenly and with grandeur, like an unexpected trumpet blast. At that moment, those who are already dead will rise incorrupt, since they have already been changed by God. Those who are still alive will undergo a similar kind of change to bring them into incorruptibility. It will be something like putting on different clothes when that which is mortal will be clothed in immortality.

Next, in our reading for this Sunday, Paul engages in a kind of lyrical reflection on the significance of this change, when perishable existence is replaced by immortal life.

That transformation, he says, constitutes the fulfillment of prophetic declarations from the Hebrew Scriptures. He cites, rather freely, it seems, Isaiah 25:8 ("He will destroy death forever"), and Hosea 13:14 ("Where are your plagues, O death, where is your sting, O nether world?"). He applies these quotations to the redemptive work of Christ. Sin brought death as a consequence, and the law of the former covenant brought not redemption but a deepened awareness of sin. Thanks to the faithfulness and dedication of Christ, humanity, in and through him, has now overcome sin and so there will be no more death. We have defeated our enemy. We are called to thanksgiving.

By way of conclusion to this chapter on the resurrection from the dead, Paul teases out some of its consequences. We who follow the Lord need to be consistently faithful and firm in our service of him, being aware that all our efforts to live up to Christ's gifts in us will not be useless, but will find their fruitfulness in our final, full participation in his resurrection.

This is a passage about hope and consistent dedication. Hope assures us of God's love and generosity still to come. Granted, in baptism we have been given a sharing in the life of the risen Christ and our lives have meaning in him. But our life here and now can be terribly flat, superficial, distracted. It is hard sometimes to keep in focus where our real value lies. In addition to the dangers of tedium and dullness, there are more acute episodes that can force our attention away from living in the Lord, episodes like serious illness, like significant misunderstandings with a friend, like the break-up of a marriage, like difficulty in finding any meaning or comfort in our faith and in our efforts to stay in touch with the Lord. We find ourselves wondering, "Is this all there is? Is this present state of uncertainty and struggle the best that God can do for me?" The answer, of course, is no. We have been redeemed and gifted by God, but the final act of God's generosity is still to come when all that we are is definitively transformed by our being clothed with his glory once and for all. We can still look ahead in hope to the joyful call of God's final trumpet.

But hope does not authorize laziness. We are still called to contribute our own efforts to God's plans for the final resurrection. It is not that we have to qualify for resurrection by our good deeds or that we have to bribe God to continue his benevolence toward us by our efforts at virtue. It's rather an issue of consistency, of exerting our own efforts to live up to what God has already made us to be, and to make ourselves ever more receptive to what God has in store for us in the future. We are to be "fully devoted" (that is, dedicated) to the work of the Lord, knowing that the Lord will not allow our efforts to be without effect.

This reading brings to a close the lectionary's survey of First Corinthians. In the short last chapter (that we do not hear from in the Church's liturgical readings) Paul talks about his project for a collection for the Christians in Jerusalem and about his travel plans. He offers greetings to a whole series of individuals, signs the letter personally, and prays for his readers: "The grace of the Lord be with you. My love to all of you in Christ Jesus."

This is an important book of the New Testament, the only one from which the Church gives us serial readings each year. Maybe that's because First Corinthians deals with so many issues that are still current: divisions in the Church, marriage questions, liturgical disputes, the ultimate direction of it all. We need to hear that many of our "contemporary" issues are two millennia old, that there has always been tension in the Church, that we are always in need of guidance and encouragement. And we need to be reminded how much we need the grace of the Lord and the love and guidance of the Lord's apostles.

FOR DISCUSSION AND REFLECTION

What do I look forward to as my future from God?

What relationship does my life today have to that future?

Ninth Sunday in Ordinary Time (A)

Romans 3:21-25, 28

Year A of the lectionary cycle might well be called the year of
Romans because of the broad use that is made of this great letter
of Paul throughout the Sundays of this liturgical year. On three of
the four Sundays of Advent and on three of the five Sundays of
Lent the second reading for Mass is taken from this Letter to the
Romans. In Ordinary Time, beginning with this ninth Sunday, we
have sixteen Sundays in succession on which we hear consecutive
readings from Romans. This is the longest continuous series from
one book in all the second readings.

The Letter to the Romans was written by Paul when he was
on his way to Jerusalem to deliver to those in need there the
collection that he had been taking up in the churches he had
previously evangelized. When he had finished in Jerusalem, he
intended to go on to Rome and make that city his headquarters
for missionary campaigns in the farthest reaches of the earth, that
is, in Spain. (As things turned out, Paul did go to Rome but as a
prisoner, awaiting trial by the emperor's court. We don't know
whether he ever did get to Spain.) Paul had had no previous
personal contact with the Christians of Rome, so he felt the need
to introduce himself to them as a first step to eliciting their
cooperation in the planned evangelization of Spain. For that
reason he seems to have thought it necessary to give them an
overview of what he had been teaching in the churches in Asia
Minor.

The Letter to the Romans is the longest of Paul's letters. It is
a quiet reflection on the basics of the Christian faith. In this
letter, Paul can say what he wants to say without the necessity of
dealing with the local problems and abuses he had to address
with the Corinthians and the Galatians.

The overall subject of Romans is salvation. In the first
section of the letter he explains why salvation is necessary. Then
he goes on to deal with how we are saved and the results of

salvation. Then comes a section about the meaning of salvation by Christ in the context of God's prior relationship with the Jews. At the end of the letter there are several chapters on the practical moral implications of salvation.

This Sunday's reading comes after the long first section in which Paul has been saying that both Jews and gentiles have detached themselves from God through their sinfulness (in spite of the natural knowledge of goodness that God had given to them all, in spite of the gift of the law that God had given to the Jews). They have put themselves into a state of unholiness, of idolatrousness, of sin.

Our Sunday passage begins with a big adversative conjunction: "But now," or "However." In contrast with man's natural state and apart from the law that God gave the Jews, the holiness of God has been made available. The offer of this holiness was predicted by the law and the prophets, and all believers share in it "through faith in Jesus Christ."

This salvation is intended for everybody. Just as every human being is naturally in a state of detachment from God, so every human being is "justified" (that is, saved or made holy) through the redemption that Christ achieved through his dedication and generosity toward his heavenly father on our behalf. Jesus made up for the sins of the rest of humankind.

Last of all, in this reading, we have a clear enunciation of Paul's most basic teaching, the kernel of the gospel he preached: justification comes by faith, apart from the works of the law.

For Paul the works of the Jewish law implied religious observance in such detail and in such attentiveness that God would be compelled to grant salvation to the observant. Paul teaches that that's not how it is. Salvation comes as grace, as gift. Our part is not to earn or deserve it (which we can't do anyhow). Our job is to accept salvation, respond to it and commit ourselves to the ongoing generosity of God. This is what Paul refers to as faith.

The matters that Paul deals with in Romans in general and in this passage in particular are fundamental to Christian belief. The implications that are inherent in these truths are what give sense and direction to every Christian life. The way these teachings are absorbed and interpreted constitute the way in which various groups of Christians relate to God. Some groups of believers have seemed to say that "salvation by faith alone" means that all and any human efforts are simply irrelevant. Others have seemed to emphasize the need for human response to God's initiative to the extent that they appear to be saying that we can force God to save us. The truth of the matter is that salvation is a gift that cannot be earned, but a gift that can only be assimilated by human response and human effort. There is no authentic faith that does not involve human effort in good works. There are no effective good works that are not founded in faith. And there is no salvation without God's ongoing initiative at every step of the way.

FOR DISCUSSION AND REFLECTION

Whom do I see as responsible for my salvation?

How do I practice faith?

Ninth Sunday in Ordinary Time (B)

II Corinthians 4:6-11

Paul continues to reflect on his apostolate. In the background are the criticisms of his enemies at Corinth: that Paul is arrogant and boastful, yet weak and unreliable, his work plagued by problems and failures. He hardly seems to be the right material for an apostle!

Paul begins today's passage with an allusion to his call to be an apostle, his encounter with the risen Christ on the road to Damascus. The God who called light out of darkness at the creation has also illuminated him so that he, in turn, could manifest to others the bright glory of God offered to humankind in Christ. Of course, his calling is not based on his own merits or abilities. God chooses unlikely instruments in order to demonstrate his own power, a power that prevails over human limitations. Paul says that he has experienced affliction, perplexity, persecution and oppression, but in every case God has brought forth liberation, hope, support and safety. Further on in Second Corinthians (6:4-10 and 11:22-33), he will speak in greater detail about his adversities: beatings, imprisonments, riots, shipwrecks, the dangers of travel, betrayal by those who should have been his friends. Here he generalizes. His own sufferings parallel those of Christ. Just as the sufferings of Christ led to his unending risen life, so also Paul's sufferings will serve as instruments to bring the life of Christ to those to whom he ministers.

Paul is a unique figure in the history of the proclamation of the gospel, yet all of us are called to a service similar to his. As Christian believers we share the responsibility to transmit the glory of God that shines forth from the face of Jesus. Most of us will not have to endure beatings and imprisonment and the dangers of first-century travel, but we are called nonetheless to proclaim the Lord Jesus in our families and our jobs, in our friendships, in our willingness to be known as committed Christian believers. We don't have to deliver formal speeches or write letters in order to do that. We simply have to be what God has made us to be, to stand up for our Christian beliefs, and be willing to acknowledge God's gifts to us in a way that other people can see and understand and find attractive. Jesus called his followers to let their light shine before others so that the others would be led to glorify our heavenly Father (see Matthew 5:16). The light that we are called to share is the same light that Paul transmitted.

But we are weak and limited! So was Paul. We are all "earthen vessels," like the numberless, indistinguishable oil lamps and cooking pots that archeologists find: ordinary, fragile, without any claim to special worth. And most of the time our performance as transmitters of God's light is pretty ordinary, too. We have all experienced perplexity and affliction and failure in our life for the Lord. Our efforts to deepen our own relationship with God often seem fruitless and our outreach to others seems weak and ineffectual. We don't see much result from our Christian witness. We know that somehow our life in the Lord is connected with the sufferings of Jesus, but we don't see much evidence of resurrection. Most of us probably find it hard to think of ourselves as apostolic ministers in the lineage of the great Saint Paul. Yet that is what we are called to be, in ways different from his ways, yet no less urgently, in spite of our limitations.

It's important for us to remember that there is a reason why God uses earthen vessels in his work. If God were to choose only deep thinkers and highly skilled communicators and women and men of conspicuous sanctity to do his work, the impression could be given that God needs such talent in order to get his work done. He doesn't. It is the power of God that gets the work done, that gets the proclamation delivered, that gets the light transmitted. God uses unpromising tools for his work—and all of us are unpromising, all of us are earthen vessels in the context of what God wants to accomplish—so that we do not lose sight of the principal agent and begin to think that he needs our contribution. "The surpassing power" is "of God and not from us."

God doesn't call us to his service because he can't do without what we have to offer. God's call to his service is one more of his many gifts to us. What a privilege to help transmit the light of the glory of God shining through the face of Christ! How sad it would be to decline the gift to which we are called because we know we are unworthy and unsuited. If only the worthy and the capable responded, God's gifts would go begging, his generosity would be frustrated—and there never would have been a Saint Paul.

God is like a musical virtuoso who can deliver unforgettable performances on inferior instruments. If we are hesitant to let him perform with us because of our awareness of our own limitations, we are denying him the opportunity to exercise his virtuosity and denying others the gifts that he wants to offer them through us.

FOR DISCUSSION AND REFLECTION

How does "the glory of God on the face of Christ" shine in my life? How has God used my limitations to gift others?

Ninth Sunday in Ordinary Time (C)

Galatians 1:1-2, 6-10

This Sunday initiates a series of six readings from Paul's letter to the Galatians. This is one of the most energetic and passionate books of the New Testament, a live letter indeed.

The Galatians had been pagans and were converted to the Christian faith by the preaching of Paul. After Paul had left the Galatians to continue his mission elsewhere, he learned that there had been a follow-up by other Christian preachers. These follow-up preachers had been causing trouble among the Galatians by telling them that Christian belief required observance of certain features of the Jewish law, things like circumcision and dietary restrictions and the observance of certain Jewish feast days. They told the Galatians that what Paul had preached to them was a watered-down form of Christianity intended to win converts without really initiating them into the full requirements of faith in Christ. Moreover, they said that Paul himself wasn't really a full and authentic apostle since he had not known and followed Jesus as the "real" apostles had.

In response to all this Paul writes to the Galatians to defend what he had taught them, to clarify the basic import of salvation in Christ, and to reassure them about the validity of his own apostolate. Given the nature of the attacks made upon his teaching and his apostolate, it's not surprising that he reacts vigorously. In fact, his defense of his teaching and his work shows us Paul at his most energetic, his most passionate. You can almost hear him shouting at the Galatians.

This Sunday's passage is from the beginning of the letter, where he is so upset and so defensive that he almost forgets to say hello.

"This letter is coming to you," he says, "from Paul and his colleagues." He hastens to point out that his calling to be an apostle is not from any merely human source but from Christ and from the Father who raised Christ from the dead. Paul is not some kind of apostolic interloper but the real thing, an authentic apostle of Christ.

He omits the thanksgiving section that appears at this point in his other letters and immediately takes out after the Galatians. "What's wrong with you that you would abandon the one true gospel that I taught you for the sake of some other counterfeit teaching? The people who are teaching you things different from that which I taught are leading you astray! No matter who it may be, even an angel from heaven, if they try to get you to believe something different from what you learned from me, to hell with them!" Then, just in case they didn't understand the first time, he tells them again: "If anyone preaches to you a gospel other than what you received [from me], let that one be accursed."

Now he slips into sarcasm. "You can see how hard I'm trying to win converts with cheap grace. I'm addressing you like this so that you will be won over by my easy words." In fact, if he were merely trying to gratify his audience, he wouldn't be a real servant of Christ.

Why all this fuss? The issue here is not the observance of some minor or optional pious practices. The issue is the source of salvation. Paul wants to make it quite clear to his recent converts that we do not qualify for redemption and salvation by being Jewish or observing Jewish religious practices, but by accepting the gracious gift of Christ. Salvation comes from him, and if we think it comes from anywhere else, we are simply not in touch with the way things are. There is no other way to be saved than through Christ, and if we try to find another way, we will end up accursed, beyond the pale of the saints.

Sometimes people today try to find ways to salvation outside the self-sacrifice and generosity of Christ. They want to earn it or deserve it by carefully chosen and scrupulously observed religious practices, by special prayers and rites, by insisting that everything has to continue to be done the was it was before. If we do not say the right words and perform the right religious actions, God cannot possibly see any good in us. Others look for salvation from belonging to the right race or the right nationality. For example, in time of war we are sometimes encouraged to believe that God loves us more than he loves our enemies. Still others expect salvation from their own individual selection of religious beliefs. "I do what I think is right and I know that's enough for the Lord."

The simple fact is that all salvation comes from Christ, from receiving and responding to the gifts that God offers us in Christ Jesus. If we look for salvation from any other source, we are, at best, wasting our time and, at worst, engaged in some kind of more or less sophisticated idolatry. It may seem that the matters that Paul was dealing with the Galatians about are old and irrelevant theological controversies. But they're not. They are concerned with the very basics of our salvation, with the fundamental nature and meaning of our eternal destiny.

FOR DISCUSSION AND REFLECTION

In what or in whom do I place my hope for salvation?

Is my practice of Christianity more a matter of achieving or of receiving?

Tenth Sunday in Ordinary Time (A)

Romans 4:18-25

Last Sunday, our reading from Romans taught us that justification (a relationship with God constituted by our sharing in God's holiness) comes by faith. It is a gift and is not and cannot be earned by our human efforts.

This Sunday's reading teaches us what faith entails, and Paul uses as the prime example of faith the experience of Abraham, whom the Jews reverenced not only as the father of God's people, but also as the just man *par excellence*. Throughout chapter 4 Paul is making the point that the relationship between God and Abraham was a gift from God that Abraham was able to receive because of his faith. The relationship began before God commanded Abraham to circumcise himself and his family, and so it began before God gave his law to Abraham. Consequently, it was faith and not observance of the law that made possible Abraham's acceptance of God's gift.

Today's reading is the conclusion of chapter 4. Here Paul describes Abraham's faith in greater detail and goes on to apply Abraham's experience to our own access to justification.

Abraham's faith consisted in confident hope beyond any reasonable expectation that God's promise to make him the father of many nations would come true. Abraham's faith was unwavering it its conviction that God would give him a legitimate son, in spite of the fact that he and his wife were far beyond childbearing age. As far as having children was concerned, they were as good as dead. Abraham did not doubt God's promise. He was fully convinced that God was able to do what God had promised to do. This conviction made him strong and resulted in his being able to receive God's gifts.

But, our text continues, Abraham wasn't the only one who became able to receive God's gifts through faith. We, too, become qualified for God's gift of life through our faith. Just as Abraham believed that God could bring life out of his and Sarah's "dead" bodies, so we believe that God raised Jesus from the dead and made him the source of new life for us.

Most of us tend to look on faith as firmly believing "what the Church believes and teaches," as the traditional act of faith has it. Faith is indeed that, but it is something more than that, too. The *Catechism of the Catholic Church* put it this way: Faith "involves an assent of the intellect and the will to the self-revelation God has made through his deed and words" (no. 176). Faith involves both intellect and will, head and heart, knowledge and love, understanding and determination, belief and self-gift. Both elements have to be there if our faith is to be wholesome and real.

Faith as intellectual assent alone becomes an exercise in reasoning, a matter of comprehending things. This can be pretty chilly. It can reduce our relationship with God to enunciating the right words in the right order, to knowing all the answers.

Faith as a response of the will alone can degenerate into a kind of spiritual emotionalism, "feeling good about God." Religion becomes a way of giving ourselves away to vagueness and affectivity, so that it doesn't matter much what we believe, as long as believing warms our heart.

Abraham's faith was a matter both of knowing and of loving. He knew what God had promised him: to make him the father of many nations, to give him a legitimate son to carry on his line. There was no uncertainty about what God was saying. But he wasn't content just to know. He was confident that God would fulfill what he had promised. He committed himself to faithfulness to God. He accepted God's word with his head and responded to it with the full conviction of his heart.

Our faith has to be like Abraham's. We are called to know the Lord Jesus, called to grasp the truth of his being and his salvation. It matters whether or not Jesus was and is true God and true man. It matters that God is one nature in three Persons. It matters that there are seven sacraments and not seventeen. We have to know what our Christian faith is all about. We have to accept with our minds what the Lord teaches us and deepen our understanding of what that teaching means.

But we are also called to love of the Lord Jesus and to confidence in him. We are called to hang on to our love for him and dedication to him in good times and in bad, when we understand what is going on in our lives and when we haven't got a clue. Even if the whole world seems to be crumbling around us, even if God's promise of care and love for us seems absolutely ridiculous, we have to hang on to our dedication, we have to remain firm in our commitment just as Abraham did.

Knowledge of God and response to him, understanding and commitment to his openness to us: this is what constitutes faith. Faith enables us to accept God's gifts, and is itself God's gift to us. The person of faith—Abraham and every committed Christian—says to God: "I believe what you tell me and I trust in what you promise me."

FOR DISCUSSION AND REFLECTION

Have I ever known a person of deep faith? How did/does he/she relate to God?

How has my faith been tested?

Tenth Sunday in Ordinary Time (B)

II Corinthians 4:13-5:1

Paul continues his defense of his ministry, his attempt to get the Corinthians to appreciate his service to them, to lead them to understand that his failures, weaknesses and limitations are not indications that his apostolate is without meaning and value.

Paul begins this Sunday's reading by telling the Corinthians that it is his faith that leads him to preach to them, the same faith that inspired the psalmist to say, "I have spoken because I believed." He preaches to them with the confidence that they will share in Christ's Resurrection together with him. His ministry for them is aimed at enabling the love and favor of God to be more widespread and abundant, which, in turn, will result in greater thanks and glory to God. This requires an ongoing expenditure of himself and the experience of affliction. But that's only temporary and has to be looked at in the light of eternity. These efforts will result in ongoing renewal of himself and in glory in the eternal life to come. That's what he has to look forward to. God has better things in store for us in heaven than we have now, a permanent dwelling place for eternity when the provisional habitation we have now has been destroyed.

This passage about Paul's apostolate is relevant to the work of all the Church's ministers. But it also has applications for the life of every Catholic Christian believer.

Faith is the fundamental energy source of all Church ministers, of everybody who provides service to others in the name or the Church. Their belief in the goodness and generosity of God, their commitment of themselves to God in response to his love is what drives them to look out for the good of others, to serve as instruments of God's providence, to speak out in God's name. In dozens of different ways, the ministers of the Church express God's will and God's love, and the basis for it all is faith. Every priest, deacon, catechist, youth minister, visitor of the sick has at the foundation of his or her life's work the same declaration that Paul shared with the psalmist: I spoke, I worked, I ministered because I believed. It is not the minister's own insights and convictions and energies that drive his or her ministry, but authentic faith in the living God.

Most Church ministers have probably also shared the experiences of weakness and failure that formed such a significant part of the fabric of Paul's ministry. They work hard without visible results. Sometimes everything they do seems to turn out badly. They are profoundly aware of their own limitations.

Often enough Church ministers find themselves misunderstood by the people they serve, just as Paul was. Their intentions are misinterpreted. The outcomes of their ministry are downplayed. What they have not been able to do often seems to get more attention than what they have done.

Sometimes Church ministers ask themselves what they are actually accomplishing. They are tempted to evaluate themselves on the basis of numbers (how many people contributed to the collection, how many students signed up for class) or on the basis of immediate response by those they serve (what did the audience have to say). Yet in their hearts they know that the true results of their service are generally not visible. Just as the origin of their ministry is in their faith, so also the outcome of their ministry is in the faith of those they serve, in the increase of grace and thanksgiving that Paul mentions. Those kinds of results are humanly imponderable. The Church's ministers, therefore, can't count on visible results to keep themselves going. It's a matter of ongoing faith.

But it is not only professional Church ministers who speak out because of their faith. Every believer is called to share the gift of belief and commitment that he or she has received from God. We all have a vocation to witness to the goodness of God. You don't have to give homilies or teach classes or organize activities in order to do that. Simply being a person of visible religious commitment, a person of clear principles, a person conspicuous for generosity can serve as an expression of our faith. The willingness to be known as a defender of human life, as an opponent of pornography, as an enemy of racism, as someone interested in social justice: all this can serve as a witness to our faith, as an encouragement to others to want to share the gifts we have been given. Even something as ordinary as saying our meal prayers when we are eating out can constitute a quiet proclamation of faith. You don't have to be a professional to be led by faith to proclamation. One might also say that all persons of faith are professional proclaimers of it, and that the full-time

Church ministers are merely those who do it in specialized ways.

"I believed, therefore I spoke." That's why Paul ministered. That's why people engage in professional Church ministry today. That's why all Church members are called to proclamation. Because we have believed.

FOR DISCUSSION AND REFLECTION

How is my faith strengthened by the Church ministers who serve me? How are others strengthened by my faith?

Tenth Sunday in Ordinary Time (C)
Galatians 1:11-19

It is not totally clear what fault Paul's enemies were finding with his relationships with the Jerusalem apostles. It could have been that they were telling the Galatians that, although Paul may have received instruction from the other apostles, he had never really been authorized by them to teach converts that they didn't have to observe the mosaic law. Or it could have been that they alleged that he received teaching from them but deliberately falsified it by dropping their insistence on Jewish religious practice. In either case, they seemed to have been making the point that Paul was not loyal to the instruction he had been given.

In this Sunday's reading, Paul cuts the ground out from under the feet of his detractors. Whether he has been authorized by the Jerusalem apostles to preach what he preaches or whether he was being disloyal to them is irrelevant, he says, because the gospel he preaches didn't come through human agency at all.

This is where our Sunday reading begins. Paul tells the Galatians that what he preaches did not come through any human instrumentality. It came through a direct revelation from Christ.

(Paul is referring to his Damascus road experience which is narrated in the Acts of the Apostles no less than three times. See Acts 9:3-19; 22:6-16; 26:12-18. This conversion experience provided Paul with the basic insights that would constitute the fundamentals of his preaching mission.)

He then goes on to reject two sources that might have been responsible for his contact with the teaching of Christ if things had been different. First of all, he didn't come to know Jesus and his teaching through ordinary contact with Christian believers. In fact, such contact was impossible for Paul since he was so violently opposed to Christianity that he became an outstandingly violent persecutor of its adherents.

Secondly, he didn't learn about Christ from the apostles. He alludes to his calling by God, a calling that came to Paul as a prophetic calling had come to Jeremiah, set apart from before his birth (see Jeremiah 1:5). This calling involved God's revelation to Paul about his Son. It included a mission to preach the truth about Jesus to the gentiles. And what did Paul do then? Go up to Jerusalem in order to learn about Christ from the Apostles? Not at all! He went off to the gentiles in Arabia (presumably just east of Damascus) and immediately began his preaching mission there. It was only after three years that he got in touch with the apostles, and that was on a brief courtesy visit when he contacted only Peter and James. He certainly didn't learn his gospel from them!

Paul's point is not that he is a freelance maverick apostle who wants nothing to do with the rest of the Christian community and has no responsibility for preaching correct doctrine. It is rather that he received the gospel from the same source as the other apostles, namely, from the risen Christ whom he had seen even as they did. Both he and the Jerusalem apostles preached the same Christ who had offered himself to the original twelve in one context and to Paul in another. And, as Paul makes clear in the parts of Galatians that follow our text but which are not used in the liturgy, the authorities in Jerusalem later accepted Paul's mission with joy.

Does this have anything to say to us? It does indeed. It

reminds us that the center of our faith, the foundation on which everything must be built is the Lord Jesus, risen from the dead and still alive in our midst.

Sometimes there are fashions and fads in the Church. Certain devotions (for example, the nine first Fridays or pilgrimages to Lourdes or Medjugorje) become popular and the impression can be given that you're really not a person of faith unless you are involved with them. Certain personalities can find themselves in the limelight of Catholic consciousness (for example, Mother Teresa and Mother Angelica, Bishop Sheen and Padre Pio), and their devotees can seem to be making them the center of their attention. There's nothing wrong with special interests like these, provided they are pursued in the proper measure.

The important thing for us is the lesson that Paul taught the Galatians: it is the reality of Christ that is central. Everything else is secondary. And just as the reality of Christ was offered to the people of Paul's time by the apostles (whether apostles to the Jews or apostles to the gentiles), so also today the truth and fullness of Christ's revelation is offered by the successors of the apostles, the official teachers of the Church. Whether our popes and bishops are popular or not, whether they are charismatic and appealing or bland and drab, they are the apostles of today and Christ has guaranteed to provide his grace and truth through them and their ministry for the Church. They may have learned about Christ through more ordinary channels than Paul did, but what they offer us is no more of merely human origin than what Paul offered the Galatians.

FOR DISCUSSION AND REFLECTION

How do I see Christ in the teaching and practice of the Church?
How am I called to proclaim the gospel?

Eleventh Sunday in Ordinary Time (A)

Romans 5:6-11

Two weeks ago, in the first of our Sunday readings from Paul's masterpiece on salvation, we learned that salvation comes from faith, apart from the works of the Jewish law. Then, last Sunday, we heard about the nature of the faith that opens us up to God's gift of salvation. In the verses that follow last Sunday's reading, Paul begins a lengthy reflection on the results of God's gift of justification in our life. He tells the Romans that salvation/justification brings, first of all, peace, that is, the fullness of divine blessing expressed in a right relationship with God (see 5:1). In addition, salvation brings confidence that enables us to rely on God's care for us and even to find a positive side to our afflictions (see 5:2-5).

Now, in this Sunday's reading, Paul continues his list of the results of salvation and describes both the unfailing certitude of our new relationship with God as well as the basis on which that certitude rests.

Our reading begins with an account of how Christ accomplished our salvation. It was through his death, a death that made up for the unfaithfulness and selfishness of human beings up to his time. We were without any claim on God, that is, "helpless" and "ungodly." Yet Christ died for us anyhow. Paul remarks that giving up one's life for somebody else is almost beyond imagination, although, if the somebody for whom one's life is given up is a particularly good person, the self-sacrifice might make some sense. But that's not what Jesus did. He died for us before we had any goodness with which to claim his attention. He died for us when we were sinners and, in so doing, demonstrated his love for us.

Now Paul takes his argument a step further. If Christ loved us and saved us when we were God's enemies, how much more will he love us and care for us now that we have been redeemed! We are now not sinners, but people who are sharers in his life, justified, sanctified, saved. Our salvation began with Jesus' death. Its continuation is insured by our participation in his life. We no longer need fear that God is going to write us off or turn angrily away from our pride, rebellion and disloyalty. All this makes it possible for us to "boast of God through our Lord Jesus Christ," that is, to find security and worth for ourselves in the relationship of reconciliation that God has bestowed on us through the self-giving of Christ.

This passage reassures us that we have the right to hope in final salvation in view of what God has done for us through Christ's gift of himself for the sake of our well-being. We are now no longer sinners, no longer cut off from God through our participation in the sinfulness of humanity. We are saved, justified, made holy and this state in which God has placed us guarantees our final fulfillment.

Sometimes believers torment themselves by trying to discern whether they are really saved or not, whether God has really taken them for himself, whether God's goodness will continue to be active in their lives. This kind of doubt and questioning reveals a defective idea of redemption. The fact of the matter is that God loved us and cared for us even before we became sharers in his life. If God looked out for us when we were hostile and distant, God will certainly continue to look out for us after we have become extensions of the life of the risen Christ!

The trouble is that, despite what God has taught us about sin and redemption, many of us still think that we have to earn salvation and that, once God has embraced us with grace, we have to live in a constant state of anxiety that God will turn away from us again. We find it hard to accept how much God loves us. We are inclined to think that God loves as we sometimes love each other, conditionally and contingently, willing to love as long as the other proves him or herself lovable, always ready to withdraw our love when the other stops seeming worthy of it.

We are never worthy of God's love, either before or after we are justified. We are always inclined to sin, limited, constitutionally incapable of meriting God's love or of responding appropriately to it once it has been conferred on us. We have to take God's love as a gift we can never deserve and respond to it with the deepest level of gratitude of which we are capable.

We rely on God for our meaning and fulfillment, we "boast" in him, not in view of what we have achieved, but in view of the goodness that God has expressed toward us. That's all we have to rely on, but it's infinitely more than we can provide for ourselves! Will many be saved, or only a few? Is it hard or easy to be saved? Once we have entered the community of believers, can we be sure that we will persevere in our acceptance of God's gifts to us? These are all understandable questions, but they can only be answered in the context of God's free and unmerited love for us. There is nothing we can do to guarantee salvation for ourselves. All we can do is rely on God. But the God on whom we rely is the God who loved us even when we were his enemies.

FOR DISCUSSION AND REFLECTION

Why does God bother with us at all?

How do I "boast of God" in my life?

Eleventh Sunday in Ordinary Time (B)

II Corinthians 5:6-10

Paul had plenty of reason to be discouraged. He was aware of his personal limitations. He knew that his sufferings and failures were being interpreted as signs that his apostolate was not authentic. Prestigious personages in the Church were calling his whole ministry into question. But he didn't lose heart. In this Sunday's reading he talks to the Corinthians about the sources of his strength and energy.

Just before our passage begins, Paul has been talking about

the eternal life that God has prepared for us and about the Spirit we have received which constitutes a first installment of that life. That's why he is courageous. Granted, in this present life we are exiled from the Lord and are guided by faith rather than by immediate and clear sight. Yet we have a future home with the Lord, in view of which leaving our present dwelling place holds no fear. We are courageous because of where we know we are going. Our main task—whether here or in heaven—is to be pleasing to the Lord. Our success in that endeavor will determine what kind of reward we will receive at the time of judgment.

This reading offers two recurrent themes for our reflection. One is the "at home"-"away" combination. The other is courage.

Being "at home" means being where one belongs, where one is supposed to be, where one fits in. In these verses, Paul refers to the fact that we seem to have two homes. One is the here and now, our life in this world, in this body. We are more or less comfortable here because our surroundings are familiar and we know the people around us. Yet this is not our real and final home. In fact, as long as we are here, we are really "away" from where we finally belong. We are in exile in this world. Our real home is with the Lord. That's why Paul has no fear at the prospect of leaving the body and going "home to the Lord." It's where he and we belong!

The hazard for the believer, that which we need to fear is not passing from our temporary home here to the permanent one with God, but of making the present one into our final goal. God help us if we forget that we are "banished children of Eve," and settle down here as if this were all there is. We are called to busy ourselves in the service of Christ here and now, aware that our present home is only temporary and that where we really belong is "away" from here.

That brings us to courage. The dictionary defines courage as mental or moral strength that enables us to persevere, to withstand danger or difficulty. Courage is what enables us to hang in there, to soldier on in spite of the perils that surround us. The opposite of courage is discouragement, that is, lack of confidence, disheartenment.

There are plenty of reasons for us to be discouraged, just as there were for Paul. To begin with, there is the world we live in, a world that trivializes religious commitment, promotes consumerism, celebrates superficiality and cultivates violence. It's probably as pagan a world as the world Paul lived in. It's not a world that is going to give us much support in our pursuit of our real home.

Then there are the realities that we find in ourselves. How easily distracted we are from the real goals of our life. How difficult it is for us to pray regularly and well. How demanding it is to love the people around us. How easily we slip into accepting the values of the pagan world around us. How readily we begin to act as if the here and now were all that we have to be concerned about. How easily we forget that our real task is the service of Christ. When we look at what's around us and what's within us, discouragement does not seem to be an inappropriate reaction.

Yet we have the promises and the gifts of the Lord. The Spirit already lives in our hearts and constitutes the beginning of our future eternal life. We have the teachings of Christ and his Church (including the letters of Paul!) which guide us on our journey of faith. We have the sacraments through which the creating and healing hand of Christ touches our lives over and over again. We have the example of other Christian believers who guide us and strengthen us by sharing with us the gifts that they have themselves received. There's plenty of reason for us to be strong, to persevere in the face of danger both outside and inside us.

The important thing for us to realize is that the courage that keeps us going, the mental and moral strength that enables us to face both life and death is not our own doing. It's not something that we achieve or develop for ourselves. Like everything else in our relationship with God, it is a gift. And when we appear before "the judgment seat of Christ," the question will not be what we achieved, or how courageous we made ourselves, but how we utilized what we were given.

FOR DISCUSSION AND REFLECTION

What are the sources of courage in my life?
How have I used what I have been given?

Eleventh Sunday in Ordinary Time (C)

Galatians 2:16, 19-21

Paul makes clear in the last part of chapter 1 of Galatians that the church authorities in Jerusalem were pleased with his message to the gentiles. But then, at the beginning of chapter 2 he indicates that, some time later, there were tensions and misunderstandings between himself and some of the Jewish Christians, although his mission to the gentiles was never found to be totally inappropriate.

Now, in this Sunday's reading, by way of conclusion to Paul's reflections about past relationships with the Jerusalem apostles, we have a basic, general, fundamental statement about Paul's teaching about the relationship between justification (that is, redemption, salvation, sanctification) and the observance of the Mosaic law.

At first comes a general statement. We (that is, former observers of the Jewish law), have learned that justification does not come to us through the law but through acceptance of what Christ brings (that is, through faith). That's why we have accepted Christ: in order to receive from him alone that justification that the law cannot give.

Now he follows up with three more specific observations on the same theme. First of all, because it became clear that the law could not justify, he gave up living in the law and began to live in Christ. As far as the law was concerned, he was now dead.

Secondly, Paul says that the life he now lives in this world, here and now, is the life of Christ. This is the Christ who loved us and gave himself up for us on the cross. He has now risen from the dead and shares his new life with us through faith, that is, through our acceptance of his gifts to us.

Finally he observes that, if he were to maintain his commitment to the ritual law of the Jews, he would be implying that justification somehow came through the law. In that case the death of Christ would have been to no purpose and what Christ achieved for us would be made void.

The nature of justification is treated often in the New Testament, for example, here in Galatians, in Romans and in James, to mention the most obvious places. It was a matter that was treated often because of its fundamental importance.

Justification means being in touch with God, being acceptable to him. When we speak of justification (that is, redemption, salvation, sanctification) we are speaking of the way in which God has chosen to relate to us. We are talking about the sources through which our life receives sense and meaning.

The teaching of the New Testament is that justification (that is, salvation) comes exclusively from faith in Christ, from our willingness to receive the risen life that Christ offers us as a result of his faithfulness and self-giving to his Father. This acceptance on our part of what Christ offers us, this response to his saving action on our behalf is expressed in our commitment to him that is expressed in faith and baptism. Nothing else but accepting Christ in faith can bring us justification because justification (or redemption or salvation or sanctification) consists precisely in sharing the life of the risen Christ. There is nothing else that can constitute or establish an appropriate relationship between us and God.

This is not to say that the life of faith does not involve certain standards of behavior. Obviously we are called to be prayerful and chaste and honest and generous to our neighbor. (Notice that these kinds of actions were also included in Jewish religious observance in addition to ritual requirements like circumcision and dietary restrictions.) But this kind of moral and religious observance is not the cause of our relationship with the Father through Christ. It is the result of it. We are supposed to live lives of goodness not in order to persuade God to enter into a loving relationship with us, but because God has already entered into a relationship with us through Christ and faith. Living a virtuous life is a matter of living consistently with what God has caused us to be rather than of causing God to save us by reason of our religious and moral conduct.

One of the most basic truths of Christian belief is that justification is a gift, not an achievement. It's something that God does for us, not something that we earn from God. At the same time, justification calls for a certain kind of response, and we are not free to live a selfish and careless life just because God has loved us freely and first. Loving relationships require giving on both sides.

The whole history of the Reformation could be described as an argument over the meaning of justification. Some theological currents seemed to stress God's generosity to the exclusion of human involvement. Others seemed to stress human effort to the exclusion of God's initiative. The truth requires appropriate attention both to God's doing and to ours.

FOR DISCUSSION AND REFLECTION

What part does my personal behavior play in my relationship with God?

Why are people inclined to want to earn or deserve salvation for themselves?

Twelfth Sunday in Ordinary Time (A)

Romans 5:12-15

Our long series of readings from Romans continues. Last Sunday we heard Paul explaining how Christ's death for us when we were sinners provides us with a basis for ongoing confidence now that we share his life. This Sunday's reading offers a further reflection on the action of Christ based on a parallel between Christ and Adam.

Paul begins the passage with an account of how sin came to be in the world. It is the result of "one man," Adam, who let the destructive forces of sin loose in the world through his own act of selfishness. One of the principal consequences of this primeval sin was the entrance of death into the world, not just the physical death of the body, but also the death of the soul, that is, the destruction of the relationship that had existed between humanity and God. Death affected everybody, not only because everybody was deprived of the previous relationship with God, but also because everybody contributed his or her personal acts of sinfulness to the sinful state of the world at large.

Now Paul deals with the relationship of sin and death with God's law, the law that God gave to his people as a vehicle of their relationship with him. (Later on in chapter 5, Paul will explain that one of the results of the law was an intensification of sin that arose because people of the law not only did wrong but, through their awareness of the law, were conscious of their wrongdoing. It made their sin worse. That attitude toward the law is implicit in what Paul says here.) Sin was in the world before the law was given, but, although it was destructive both to the one who committed it and to those to whom it was directed, it was not attributed to the sinner the same way it would be after the law. There was still death, though, even for those who did not sin in deliberate defiance of a direct command from God as Adam did.

Now comes the connective with Christ: Adam serves as a kind of parallel with Christ. Both were figures of universal significance, and both exercised an influence that affected the destiny of "many," that is, of everybody.

But there is a difference. Christ's achievement was far greater than merely undoing the damage that Adam had done. The superabundant grace of God that resulted from the self-gift of Jesus left humanity in a far better situation than it had been in even before the sin of Adam. Jesus makes God's graciousness "overflow for the many."

As the Church reflected on what Paul says in this passage (and in the rest of chapter 5), its members began to understand better and better the situation of humanity before the coming of Christ, why human beings needed redemption, and what Christ had provided for us. This part of Romans gives us the foundation for one of the most basic doctrines of Christianity, namely the Church's teaching about original sin.

Before the coming of Christ, humanity was in a state of detachment from God. A relationship that had existed earlier had been broken and we were on our own. Every human being since Adam is born into this state of privation that we call original sin. Note that original sin is not a sin that each of us commits without knowing it. Nor is it something for which we will be individually punished. It is a state, not an item of individual behavior.

To be freed from original sin means to be liberated from the state of detachment from God into which we were born. In other words, if we are to come out of the state of original sin, it has to be because we enter into a new association, a new relationship with God. Entering such a relationship cannot be the result of our own efforts. It has to come from God and it can only come from God through God's gracious generosity. Specifically, we are freed from original sin when we begin to share the life of the risen Christ through baptism.

But our humanity continues to bear some of the scars of original sin even when we have entered the state of grace. Our nature is weak and inclined to evil, not because God has not taken us to himself after all, but because the all pervasive sinfulness of humanity has left us mutilated. No matter how close our relationship with God, we are still damaged goods. All of us know how easy it can be to do bad and how difficult it can be to do good.

This teaching about original sin developed over a long time. Some development occurred in response to the Pelagians in the fifth century who held that there wasn't really anything wrong with us and that all that Adam did was give us a bad example. Further development came in response to the early Protestants who claimed that original sin had damaged us so radically that not even God could bring us back except by a sort of legal fiction that covered over original sin but didn't cure it.

We Catholics believe that original sin is real, that God's cure for it is real, and that it all depends on the grace of Christ.

FOR DISCUSSION AND REFLECTION

How does the Church's teaching about original sin help me deal with the evil in the world?

What remnants of original sin do I find in myself?

Twelfth Sunday in Ordinary Time (B)

II Corinthians 5:14-17

Paul continues his defense of his ministry. He doesn't preach the gospel in order to make a good impression or to make a personal impact on those touched by his ministry. He is guided by something far more important than self-interest, and this Sunday's reading tells us what that is. Paul identifies the very center of his missionary effort and, in so doing, describes the very center of Christian life. It is the love of Christ.

At the beginning of our passage, he tells the Corinthians,

"It is the love of Christ that impels us." (The verb translated by "impels" in our lectionary version is rendered in other translations as "controls," "overwhelms," "leaves us no choice," "is the wellspring of our action." The point is that the love that Christ has offered him pushes Paul forward in his mission, almost as if Christ's love is too strong for him to resist.) This love sparked Paul's activity once he realized that Christ died for the benefit of everybody. In connection with Christ's death, everybody experienced a death. Likewise, just as everybody shares in his death, so everybody shares in his risen life. We live in and for Christ, not just in and for ourselves. All this means that human distinctions like race, rank, or social position are now no longer of any significance. Paul admits that at one time he even looked on Christ according to exclusively human criteria, that is, as a mere criminal, but he does so no longer. Through Christ a whole new manner of being has been given us. In Christ we have been created over again. Things are no longer the way they were before. Everything is fresh and new in him.

The love of Christ and its implications are what gave energy and direction to the generous and long-lasting apostolate of Paul. The love of Christ is what gives energy and direction to the lives of all those who believe in Christ.

Our salvation, our worth, our meaning does not depend on anything that we do for ourselves. It all depends on Christ's love for us, on the gift of his own life on the cross that made up for our sinfulness, on the sharing of his new life after the Resurrection that enables us to participate in the glory that his faithfulness earned from the Father. If Christ did not love us, if Christ did not share his risen life with us, we would be detached from God, left to our own devices, irretrievably bogged down in the old selfishness of Adam and Eve, forever incapable of attaining the only relationship that can bring us worth and happiness.

Sometimes Christians give the impression that they have to earn their salvation by being good, by being obedient to God's commandments. They seem convinced that, if they just try hard enough, God will owe them salvation. This is simply not Catholic

Christian belief. The only thing that can bring us salvation is sharing in the life of the risen Christ, and that sharing comes to us exclusively from the generosity and love of Christ. Yes, we do have to "be good" and obey the directions we have received from God. But that constitutes response to a gift, not work that earns a reward.

This is how the love of Christ drives us on as it drove Paul. Once we come to realize what Christ has done for us, how he gave himself up for us, how he now shares his risen life with us, the only thing that makes any sense is to love him in return, to let his involvement in our life become the driving force that impacts and directs every element that forms part of our lives.

This love of Christ for us makes all human distinctions, all marks of merely human importance secondary to the point of irrelevance. What difference does it really make if we are prominent or rich or popular or important in this temporary world? What really makes the difference is the love of Christ that is the driving force of our lives, that gives us eternal worth and meaning.

Likewise, the love of Christ is a source of constant renewal and energy for us. A relationship with God is a relationship that never grows stale. In and through Christ, God always has new gifts for us, new challenges that lead us ever more deeply into the life of Father, Son and Spirit. There is no place for boredom or disillusionment in a life that is imbued with the infinite variety of the creating Word of God, no occasion for loneliness when we are called to reach out to those around us with the loving embrace of Christ. The ups and downs of our own individual human existence are of secondary importance compared with the force and power of the ongoing life of Christ that pushes us forward toward eternal newness of life with God.

"The love of Christ impels us." The love of Christ for his apostle is what made sense out of the life and ministry of Paul. The love of Christ for each of his members is what gives sense and energy to our lives, too.

FOR DISCUSSION AND REFLECTION

How is the love of Christ in the center of my life?

How does Christ energize and renew me?

Twelfth Sunday in Ordinary Time (C)

Galatians 3:26-29

In the lectionary's progressive series of readings from Galatians, Paul has been defending his gospel and his apostolic teaching authority. In the section of Galatians that begins with chapter 3, he deals with faith and freedom and, in this Sunday's live letter, he talks about the benefits that faith brings us apart from the observance of Jewish law. Just prior to our passage he has been describing the law as a kind of disciplinarian or guardian whose task was to keep little children out of trouble until they could be trusted to act on their own. Through faith, he says, we have outgrown the need for what the law offered. This is where this Sunday's passage begins.

It is through faith (not the law) that we have become members of God's family, children of God. Through baptism (the necessary correlative of faith) we have been clothed with Christ. (Note that "being clothed with Christ" is not intended to suggest that our likeness to Christ is something like a sweater that we take off or put on according to personal preferences or circumstances. It rather suggests being "invested" with a new status or new dignity. Elsewhere, Ephesians 4:24, for example, Paul speaks of "putting on a new self.") He goes on to speak of two consequences of our being "clothed with Christ."

The first is that distinctions of culture, social status and gender that had served in the past to divide people and keep them apart are no longer relevant. Compared with the fundamental saving significance of our all being one in Christ, these other distinctions are no longer important. (Notice that Paul does not say that everybody is now the same or called to the same sorts of service in God's people, but that our likeness in Christ is more important than our human differences.)

The second consequence of our belonging to Christ, our being in Christ, is that we become children of Abraham. (Part of what was in question in the controversy about the observance of the Jewish law was how the gentiles could become beneficiaries of the promises that God made to Abraham. Here Paul suggests that Christ is the primary fulfillment of everything that had been promised to Abraham and that, therefore, we are part of Abraham's family because we are like Christ.)

The fundamental reality of Christian faith and Christian existence is our likeness to Christ, the sharing in his risen life that we call grace. Because we live the life of Christ, we are freed from our fundamental sinfulness. Because we live the life of Christ, we are qualified to enjoy the happiness of heaven. Because we live the life of Christ, we have come into the inheritance that God promised to the descendants of Abraham. Because we live the life of Christ we are brothers or sisters to everyone else who shares that one life of the one Christ. Everything that constitutes Christian faith or Christian life is somehow based on our sharing life in Christ. It's the key that gives sense and meaning to everything else. That's why Paul found it absolutely essential to stress life in Christ over observance of the Jewish ritual law as the source of salvation. (It is not without significance that the phrase "in Christ" occurs some 160 times in the Pauline writings.)

There are at least two important corollaries to this basic reality. The first is that salvation in Christ is a gift, freely given by God without merit on our part. Who could possibly earn or deserve a share in the life of God? What would it require for us to make ourselves worthy of living God's life? If we find it hard to understand how salvation is God's gift to us, it may be because we don't understand what salvation really is.

The second implication of salvation thus understood has to do with our relationship with our brothers and sisters in the Lord. If the source of our importance in God's sight is our participation in the life of his eternal Son, Our Lord, then that same life should be the source of others' importance in our sight. The people around us are not just other human beings with their personal or corporate characteristics ("Jew or Greek, slave or free, male or female"), but sharers with us in the life of the risen Christ (either in fact, if they are Christian believers, or in potential if they are not). We have to treat them accordingly. Their likeness to Christ (present or possible) is more important than anything else about them. This is the fundamental insight that lies behind Catholic moral teaching about how we are to relate to our neighbor, about care for the poor, about respect for human life in all its forms and in all its stages. We're not dealing with just another creature, or even just another man or woman. We're dealing with someone who has been (or can be) gifted with the life and dignity of Christ.

FOR DISCUSSION AND REFLECTION

How does my likeness to Christ help me to relate to other people?

What significance do cultural, social, or gender differences have in the context of Christian faith?

Thirteenth Sunday in Ordinary Time (A)

Romans 6:3-4, 8-11

At the end of last Sunday's reading, Paul proclaimed that the salvation brought by Christ is wider and deeper than the sinfulness brought into the world by Adam. In the verses that follow that reading and precede this Sunday's, Paul continues in the same vein and, in his zeal to highlight the vast abundance of Jesus' redemptive act says (in 5:20), "Where sin increased, grace overflowed all the more."

But this could give rise to misunderstanding, a misunderstanding that Paul was quite aware of. "Shall we persist in sin that grace may abound?" (6:1). Such a question might come from a naive member of the assembly who thought that becoming a Christian removed all constraints. It could also come, however, from Paul's judaizing opponents who might have wanted to show that Paul's dismissal of the Jewish law could only lead to moral chaos.

In any case, this Sunday's reading responds to the question. It just doesn't make sense for anybody who is a Christian believer to think that it's OK to go on committing sin. Paul explains why.

He tells his readers that they need to be conscious of what happens when we are baptized. We are baptized "into Christ Jesus," that is, we somehow begin to be him. When we are immersed into the baptismal pool it's like dying, like going into a tomb. When we come up out of the water it's like being raised from the dead. These actions present a parallel with Jesus' death, burial and resurrection, but they are not just symbolic. They also bring about what they signify. We become participants in the death of Jesus and in the new, risen life of Jesus that was the sign of the Father's acceptance of Jesus' gift of himself.

The second part of the reading reiterates this teaching. Just as Christ died and now lives and has forever escaped the dominion of death, so also we share Christ's life and will continue to share it because we have become participants in his death. But the domain of death is also the domain of sin. People who have come out of death are free of any relationship with sin. It no longer applies to them. This is the case with Christ who is now free from every threat or harm from sin that could arise from his contact with sinful humanity. He has a new kind of human life now. "He lives for God." The same principles apply to us. Because we have shared Christ's death and resurrection, we no longer have any relationship with sinfulness ("dead to sin") and live the life of the risen Christ that is totally directed toward union with God.

Christian life is not a matter of doing exactly as we please on the grounds that our sins have been forgiven. Nor is it a matter of observing a whole multiplicity of behavioral rules that membership in the Church imposes on us. Christian life is a matter of consistency, of living in accord with what Christ made us to be in baptism.

Avoiding sin has to be part of our Christian existence. Having been made sharers in the life of the risen Christ does not mean that we are no longer able to do wrong, no longer able to return to the dominion of sin and death that Christ freed us from. We are all experienced enough to know that, thanks to the lingering effects of original sin, sin can be very attractive to us. That's why Christian spirituality teaches us that we cannot afford to toy with circumstances that might lead us into wrongdoing. We must avoid the occasions of sin as well as sin itself.

But Christian life is much more than that. Living out our faith is not just a matter of not being bad or of avoiding sin. It is a matter of being good with the goodness of Christ, of living out in practice the life of Christ that constitutes our participation in the community of faith. Being a follower of Jesus is a positive thing. It means extending his love and kindness and generosity and compassion and forgiveness to every aspect of the world in which we live. And why do we do all that? Not because we are afraid of what will happen to us if we don't. Not because we are trying to model ourselves on some sort of external pattern that has been offered to us by the story of Jesus' life. We extend the virtues and values of Christ to the world around us because we are extensions of Christ. The risen Christ has been the source and direction of our lives ever since we were baptized. Just as he wants to live in us, so also he wants us to live in him and to make our lives into a continuation of his saving and redeeming human existence.

Sometimes people look on Christian life as an unending series of demands. There seem to be so many rules: do this; don't do that; keep away from such and such; be conscious of the many obligations that Christian faith brings with it. All that has its place, of course, but it's a pity if that's the only light in which we see our life as people of faith. Paul's words to the Romans are much more encouraging. He seems to be saying that, in the final analysis, there is only one rule, and that is to live consistently with the life of the risen Christ that is in us.

FOR DISCUSSION AND REFLECTION

How do I see myself as "dead to sin"?

How do I experience "newness of life"?

Thirteenth Sunday of Ordinary Time (B)

II Corinthians 8:7, 9, 13-15

For the moment, Paul has finished his treatment of the tensions between him and the Corinthians and his reflections on the nature of his ministry. Now he turns his attention to another matter, to something very dear to his heart: the collection for the Christians of Jerusalem.

Early on in his apostolic career Paul had been chosen to bring financial assistance from Antioch to Jerusalem at a time of famine (see Acts 11:27-30). Later, when the problems connected with Paul's mission to the gentiles had been discussed and dealt with, Paul had been encouraged to make responding to the material needs of the Christians of Jerusalem one of the elements of his ministry (see Acts 15:1-29 and Galatians 2:1-10). It was a mission that he undertook with earnestness and enthusiasm. He speaks of it in both letters to the Corinthians as well as in Galatians and Romans.

The young Church in Jerusalem was no doubt experiencing

hard times because of the suspicion, rejection and even persecution that it was suffering from official Judaism. Financial help would be welcome. At the same time, however, there were other reasons for generosity. It would serve as a sign of the oneness of the Church. Though gentile Christians and Jewish Christians were separate in general culture and in their manner of Christian religious observance, they were nonetheless one in Christ. Moreover, Paul's dedication to dealing with the needs of the Christians of Jerusalem could also serve as a sign of his personal respect for Jewish Christianity and might even diminish the hostility of those who were suspicious of his ministry and who seem to have been very interested in making Paul's converts suspicious of him, too. (We have seen evidence of the activities of such persons in our readings from Second Corinthians.)

In chapters 8 and 9 of our letter, Paul specifically addresses the collection. Our Sunday reading is from chapter 8. Chapter 9 may originally have been a separate note, written later than chapter 8, but appended to it when the various parts of Second Corinthians were brought together.

This Sunday reading has been edited to remove the specific details of the collection and the Corinthians' response to it while leaving the basic rationale for Christian generosity that Paul offers them—and us. The text offers three reasons for being generous.

First of all, the Corinthians had received many spiritual gifts as part of their conversion to Christianity. (Paul had dealt with some of the implications of these in chapters 12-14 of First Corinthians.) The exercise of generosity toward those in need would seem to be in keeping with the other gifts.

Next, the generosity of Christ, who gave up the richness of his being God for the sake of becoming poor for our salvation and our spiritual enrichment should elicit gratitude and generosity from us in return.

Finally, Paul tells the Corinthians that he is not asking them to impoverish themselves for the sake of the Christians of

Jerusalem. It's rather a matter of evening things up. Just as the Jewish Christians shared their spiritual riches with the gentiles, so the gentile Christians should be willing to share material abundance with the Jewish Christians. The result will be a kind of ecclesial balancing out. Paul cites God's directions to the Jews in connection with the manna in the desert: everybody ought to end up with more or less the same.

This Sunday's reading teaches us several lessons. One is that fundraising has been part of the Church's life from the very beginning. Another is that, while the specific pragmatic purpose for which the funds are raised is important, there are generally additional dimensions to the effort that may be equally significant. Third, Paul's appeal to the Corinthians suggests that giving itself has many dimensions. In this reading we hear him telling his converts that generosity ought to be a consequence of the other spiritual blessings they have received, that generosity makes them like Christ, that generosity is not a matter of depriving themselves of what they need but of engaging in the healthy give and take that is part of life in the Church catholic.

The basic truth is that our need to give is more urgent than the causes for which we give. Obviously our parish needs the support of its members. The missions need our help. The Holy Father depends on our annual contribution to the Peter's Pence collection. But we have a need, too, and our need is to be part of our parish, part of the Church's mission effort, part of the pope's concerns. We respond to that need in many ways, one of the most prominent of which is our financial giving.

Sometimes people say that their priest never talks about anything but money. I'm not sure that's ever really so, but even if it is, it may well be that when the priest talks about money, he's really talking about something a lot more spiritual, a lot more significant.

FOR DISCUSSION AND REFLECTION

Does my generosity depend on what the Church needs or on my need to be generous?

What do I get out of my giving?

Thirteenth Sunday in Ordinary Time (C)

Galatians 5:1, 13-18

The lectionary continues its semi-continuous series of readings from Galatians. In chapters 3 and 4 Paul has been speaking to the Galatians about the relationship between faith and freedom, about how commitment to Christ liberates them from the demands of observing the law of the Old Testament. Now, in chapter 5, he offers them practical advice about Christian living. (A section of practical moral guidance toward the end of Paul's letters is one of their standard components.)

This Sunday's live letter begins with a bridge verse that unites the two portions of the letter and then goes on to offer general moral principles. In the verses that follow this Sunday's reading, Paul will give a list of behaviors unacceptable for a Christian believer, followed by another list of virtuous outcomes of life in the Spirit.

First, then, the general statement that ties what he has been saying with what is now to come: Christ has freed us, he says, so that we could be free, but we have to be careful not to fall back into slavery. Paul sees submission to the observance of the Jewish law as slavery. In verses 2-12, which the lectionary omits, he points out one more time that an attempt to win justification through observance of the law, specifically through circumcision, is not compatible with life in Christ.

Now come the general moral principles. The first is that our having been freed by Christ does not mean that any and all kinds of behavior are acceptable. Rather, our freedom in Christ calls us to a new kind of service, the service of one another in love. Paul suggests that freedom involves a new kind of law, that of loving our neighbor as ourselves. If the Galatians keep on fighting with one another instead of loving one another, they will end up destroying themselves.

The second moral principle is that our freedom in Christ does not liberate us from all temptation. "The desires of the flesh," that is, the inclinations of our previous, unredeemed self, are still alive in us and we have to oppose those desires with the power that comes to us through the Spirit of Christ in us. Living in Christ is not a matter of following our human inclinations wherever they might lead us.

Finally, a one-liner that repeats what Paul has said so often in this letter: you are not subject to the (Jewish) law if you have accepted Christ and his Spirit.

This passage uses several terms that occur frequently in Paul's writings, and it's important that we be aware of their meaning for him and his readers.

"Freedom" refers to the state of being a citizen, of belonging, of having civil and social rights. Its opposite is slavery. When Paul speaks of freedom, he is using it more or less as a synonym for justification, redemption, salvation, sanctification. It is a state by which we are at home in the household of God, no longer subject to somebody else's rules and regulations (the slavery of the law) that determined our behavior without really being able to establish us as full and free members of the family of Father, Son and Holy Spirit. (It is not that Paul sees the Jewish law as simply bad, but as making demands on us that we could not fulfill because of our sinful nature and as calling for observances like circumcision that were simply not redemptive.)

Paul also speaks of "the flesh." We tend to think of the flesh as having something to do with sexual sins. For Paul the term has a wider meaning. It signifies our humanity insofar as it is still unredeemed. It suggests our inborn self-interested hostility toward God, our unhealthy self-reliance and selfishness. The flesh gives rise to the sorts of things that Paul lists in verses 19-21 (not included in our liturgical reading, but worth reading over and thinking about).

"The Spirit," on the other hand, is our new self in Christ, constituted by the presence of the Holy Spirit and governed by the Spirit's power and action in us. It is the Spirit that gives new dimensions of spirituality to our lives, new capacities for relating to the world and to other people, new potential for eternal life with and in Christ. Some of the outcomes of being in the Spirit are catalogued in verses 22 and 23, all of which are connected with love and care for our neighbor.

Paul's main theme in Galatians was one that does not seem particularly important and urgent for us: the Christian believer's deliverance from the demands of the Mosaic law. Yet in the process of dealing with this now irrelevant problem, he teaches about matters that are of crucial personal importance for each of us. He tells us about the implications of faith and freedom. He reminds us of our own limitations, even after we have been redeemed by Christ. He invites us to be attentive to the implications of our life in Christ. Best of all, he reassures us of the presence and the action of the Spirit in our lives.

FOR DISCUSSION AND REFLECTION

Where do I experience freedom in my life?

What elements of slavery are there in my life?

Fourteenth Sunday in Ordinary Time (A)

Romans 8:9, 11-13

We are still in the section of Romans that speaks of how we are saved and that outlines the major outcomes or results of salvation. One of salvation's major effects is liberation from the obligation to observe the law that God had given to the Jews. In chapter 7 and the beginning of chapter 8, Paul describes how the law, though good in itself, really served to raise the consciousness of sin in those who tried to follow it, although it was not able to free them from sin. It is only through the saving action of Christ that we are freed from our state of sinfulness and freed from the law that made us aware of our sinfulness. This comes about by our sharing in the Spirit of Christ.

As chapter 8 proceeds, we hear more about the influence of Christ's spirit in the lives of Christian believers. This is an important chapter in Romans, and the lectionary gives us no fewer than five readings in a row from it. (As we begin our reflections on the action of Christ's Spirit in the justification of the believer, it is important to note that some scholars find that the term "Spirit" in this context does not seem always to mean the third Person of the Blessed Trinity. Until Christian Trinitarian terminology reached its final state of clarity and precision, the word "Spirit" could sometimes mean the dynamic presence of God in the justified Christian, that is, the power that enlivened Christ himself. Consequently, the terms "God's Spirit" and "Christ's Spirit" could be interchangeable.)

As this Sunday's reading begins, Paul is drawing a contrast between being in the flesh and being in the Spirit. (Note that "flesh" here does not mean the physical material that forms our bodies, but a state of selfishness and consequent hostility toward God.) He reminds the Romans that they are freed from being in the flesh, but only if they have been enlivened by the Spirit of Christ. You have to have the Spirit of Christ if you are going to be Christ's.

This new life in Christ, the Spirit of God dwelling in the believer through grace, will give a new life even to our mortal, physical bodies at the end of time, even as it gave a new life to the dead body of Jesus.

If that is so, then we need have nothing more to do with "the flesh." We have no obligation to pay it any attention whatsoever. As a matter of fact, if we do continue to pay attention to "the flesh," we will revert to a state of being dead, whereas if we suppress the claims of the flesh ("the body") through the energy of the Spirit, we will live.

Implicit in what Paul says here is the awareness that God lets us make choices. We can choose to accept the salvation that Christ offers us, or we can choose to reject it. Once we have accepted new life in Christ, we can choose to persevere in it or we can choose to return to the ways of sinfulness. If we persevere in the life that Christ's Spirit gives us, we will enjoy the same kind of eternal risen life that he enjoys. If we choose to return to the ways of "the flesh" we will end up in detachment from God, that is, in an ongoing state of death. Salvation depends totally on God's loving initiative, but it also depends on how we choose to respond to that initiative.

It boils down to a matter of priorities, of what we determine as most important in our lives. We can embrace the way of immediate and consistent self-indulgence, the easy way, the comfortable way, or we can embrace faithfulness to the demands of the risen Christ, demands that are often difficult and not always immediately rewarding. The effects of these priorities will follow necessarily, automatically out of the choices we make.

It's worth noting that most of the time we express our priorities in the context of small things. We very rarely find ourselves in a situation in which we are faced with a monumental choice of lifetime importance. Most of the time it's a choice between doing some little act of kindness for somebody else, or taking care of ourselves; of spending some time in prayer or watching more TV; of facing up to a difficult situation or getting out of it by telling a little lie. Our priorities express themselves in our choices, mostly little choices. But these choices add up. If our choices are consistently in the direction of greater openness to the Lord and to our neighbor, the goodness of Christ that God has bestowed on us will grow and flourish. If our choices are consistently in the direction of selfishness and comfort, we will find that we are gradually becoming inconsistent with the Spirit of Christ that is in us. It's the little choices that count. It's the little choices that express our basic priorities. It's the little choices that lead us to big choices that ultimately determine whether we live according to the flesh or according to the spirit, whether we are going to have eternal death or eternal life.

FOR DISCUSSION AND REFLECTION

Do I perceive the action of the Spirit of Christ in my life?
What are my priorities? How are they expressed?

Fourteenth Sunday in Ordinary Time (B)

II Corinthians 12:7-10

In this final section of Second Corinthians (chapters 10-13), Paul returns to the same concerns he had addressed in the beginning of the letter: tensions between himself and the Corinthians, the accusations of his critics and the nature of his ministry. However, the difference in tone between these chapters and chapters 1-7 cause many scholars to think that chapters 10-13 originally constituted a separate letter.

The pretensions of his critics (whom he refers to as "superapostles") and their questions about his credentials elicit a strong, indeed a passionate response from Paul. Any title to distinction they might have also applies to him. He has worked signs and wonders even as they claim to have done. His efforts and sufferings in proclaiming the gospel surpass anything that they might boast of. He is as good as or better than any of them! He has even had revelations from God that are beyond the power of human words to describe. Nobody has more claim to respect than Paul!

Yet the important thing is not what the minister can claim for himself, but what God does through the minister. Here we arrive at this Sunday's reading. After the extended account of his sufferings and distinctions in the service of the gospel, Paul now speaks of another element in his life. In order to keep him from the pride that might have arisen from all these spectacular features of his apostolate, God sent him something to remind him of his weakness. We don't know what this affliction was—whether it was physical or psychological or connected with his relationships with other people—but it seems clear that it was something that Paul found embarrassing and hard to deal with, an instrument of the devil impeding his work. He prayed insistently, like Jesus in Gethsemane, that it be taken away, but God gave him to understand that he, God, could get his work done even with an imperfect instrument. The strength of Christ can work and indeed does work most effectively through human weakness. The bottom line is that human weakness is more important in Paul's apostolate than human strength, because it is in human weakness that the power of Christ is most clearly manifested. Paul is proud of his weakness and vulnerability because it is a vehicle for the strength of Christ.

What does all this mean for us? For one thing, it means that we don't have to be perfect for God to be able to use us for his providential purposes. Sometimes people hang back from offering themselves to God for his use. They don't see how God could possibly make anything of them for his purposes. They are too limited, too imperfect. As a result, their marriage, their family, their work, their friendships, the use of their leisure time are without a dimension of godliness that could easily be part of their lives if they were willing to accept their own limitations and rely on God's ability to work through their weakness.

There is a flip side to this lesson. Often when people are aware of their own quite real talents and abilities, they tend to rely on them alone, to the extent that there is no room for the power of Christ in what they do. An awareness of dependence and vulnerability is a necessary condition for Christ's action in and through our lives.

Another lesson that Paul's experience offers us is that we shouldn't look for perfection from those who minister to us in the Church today. Lay ministers and deacons and priests and bishops are all weak and limited. They—we—may not have some definite and specific disability as Paul seems to have had, but none of them is without faults, none of them limitlessly talented for every aspect of their ministry. Some of them find it hard to reach out to those they are supposed to serve. Some seem to have very little sense of practicality. Some do not seem to be particularly intelligent. Obviously they all try to make themselves as useful to the Lord as they can by developing the capabilities that God has given them. But none of them is totally successful. Each and every one is open to criticism. Yet they are not, for that reason, useless ministers of the gospel since, as Paul has taught us, the real source of life and vigor in the Church is not the human qualifications of the minister, but the power of Christ working through human weakness.

This Sunday's passage is a reprise of what Paul had to say in chapter 4 of Second Corinthians. The treasures of Christ are distributed in earthen vessels. Here again we see God the virtuoso, performing skillfully on flawed instruments.

This reading brings us to the end of the Church's liturgical presentation of Second Corinthians. In it we have seen a great apostle at work, trying to deal with the tensions that had arisen between him and his people, reflecting aloud on the nature and implications of his ministry, defending himself against criticism, guiding his hearers to an awareness of the needs of the larger

Church and of the meaning of their own generosity. In the process we have gotten to know Paul better. We have greater reason to thank the Lord for his Church and his apostles.

FOR DISCUSSION AND REFLECTION

What weaknesses in my life keep me aware of my vulnerability and my dependence on the Lord?

How does God's power work through my limitations?

Fourteenth Sunday in Ordinary Time (C)

Galatians 6:14-18

As Paul reaches the end of his letter to the Galatians, he takes the pen out of the hand of his stenographer and writes the last few lines personally (see 6:11). In extra-large letters he sums up what he has been saying to them in a series of more or less disconnected final comments. It's almost as if he is raising his voice to them so that they will give appropriate attention to what he has to say.

He tells them that those who want them to sign on to Judaism by getting circumcised are really trying to avoid persecution. These Judaizers would have Christians appear as a sect of Judaism so that they could enjoy the special treatment that the Roman authorities had granted to the Jews. It may also be that the Judaizers wanted the Galatians to adopt Jewish practices so that they, the Judaizers, could boast about the converts that they had made.

We are now at the beginning of this Sunday's liturgical reading. When it comes to boasting, Paul says, all I want to boast about is the cross of Christ. As a result of the faithful self-giving that Christ expressed on the cross, my association with the world, with sinfulness and selfishness, is now over. I have nothing more to do with the world nor the world with me. Being circumcised or not being circumcised are both irrelevant. What matters is the "new creation," that is, our new life in the crucified and risen Christ.

He then calls down blessings on those who "follow this rule," that is, who give primary importance to the outcomes of the death and resurrection of Christ. They constitute God's new chosen people, "the Israel of God."

Then comes a personal observation. Just as slaves were sometimes identified by having their master's name branded on their bodies, so Paul can be identified by the marks of Christ on his body: the scars from the floggings and stonings he had suffered in the course of his apostolic ministry. People (including, one supposes, the Judaizers in Galatia) should not make any more trouble for him because, if they do, they will have to answer to his master, Christ.

At last comes a more or less bland and ordinary closing in which Paul prays for the grace of Christ for the spirit of those to whom he has written.

In this Sunday's reading we see and hear Paul repeating the basic message of this letter as emphatically as he can: *what matters is not observance of Jewish ritual law but the cross of Christ.*

The cross of Christ was the sign of Jesus' human self-gift in love and faithfulness to his heavenly Father. Its significance did not consist primarily in the pain and suffering that accompanied Jesus' death, but in the generosity and obedience that Jesus' death expressed. Herein lay the groundwork for a new relationship between God and humanity. Because God demonstrated his acceptance of Jesus' gift of himself on the cross by raising him from the dead, and because that new life of the risen Christ continues forever, there now existed the possibility of a new life in Christ for all those who would accept Jesus in faith, a new life that would not be bounded by time and space, nor by specifically Jewish religious observances.

All other religious practices have now been rendered

irrelevant or secondary by the primacy of the cross of Christ. It is the cross that matters. That's what puts us in touch with the Father. That's what gives importance to each and every one of us. That's what gives us something to rely on.

Our importance in God's sight does not depend on our being circumcised, on our being Jewish. Our importance in God's sight consists in our being remade into the image of the crucified and risen Christ, in our bearing the ownership marks of Christ. We have nothing to claim as our own, nothing to boast about. Our only claim to worth and value consists in our connection with the crucified Jesus.

It's easy to see how Paul could get so frustrated with the Galatians. He had taught them about the generosity of the Father through Jesus, about the free gift of the Spirit that came with their acceptance of and response to Christ. They seemed to think that what Paul had taught them was too good to be true. God couldn't possibly be that generous. God had to be looking for something more from them. They were ready to bind themselves to all the countless details of Jewish observance in order to persuade themselves that they had earned God's attention.

Paul practically shouts at them: "You can't earn. You can't deserve. All you can do is accept. If you want to try to earn and deserve, you will be selling yourselves back into slavery when God wants to make you free. It makes much more sense simply to receive the new creation that God offers you. That's how you become authentic members of God's people. Yours truly, Paul."

FOR DISCUSSION AND REFLECTION

What signs of belonging to Christ do I bear?

How is the death of Jesus important for me?

Fifteenth Sunday in Ordinary Time (A)

Romans 8:18-23

Paul has told the Romans that, as a result of the salvation brought to us through Jesus, we are free from the obligation to observe the Jewish law and free from any obligations to "the flesh" (see last Sunday's reading). In the verses that come between last Sunday's reading and this Sunday's, he tells them that the Spirit of God brings them into a new relationship with God, a relationship that allows us to call God "Father" (as Jesus did), provided only that we are willing to share Jesus' sufferings.

This Sunday's live letter begins with a tie-in to suffering, but directs our attention to still another new relationship that arises out of salvation.

The present may be a time of suffering, the reading says, but the suffering we bear here and now is nothing in comparison with the glory that awaits us, a glory that the whole of creation will share with us.

Creation lost its original orientation through the sin of Adam. Because of its association with humanity, when humanity sinned, creation no longer meant the same thing it had meant before. It was now "subject to futility" that is, in a state of aimlessness, without meaning and direction. Yet there was a dimension of hope still left (presumably founded on God's promise of the eventual defeat of the forces of evil that is suggested in Genesis 3:15). Creation looked forward to the fulfillment of this hope that would be found in the context of the glorious liberation and redirection that would come to humanity.

We already enjoy the beginnings of that final newness of creation and of the ultimate freedom of humanity. It comes to us through the Spirit of Christ. But there is still more to come, still a final fulfillment that is not yet here, that which Paul calls "the redemption of our bodies" at the end of time, the full status of our adoption by God. We look forward to that final state with profound anticipation. We groan for it and creation groans with us, aching to give birth to the final fruits of its original destiny.

There are two important teachings implicit in this Sunday's reading. The first is that the final destiny of material creation is connected with the final destiny of humankind. Creation was and is linked to the status of humanity.

This suggests that the world in which we live is not just a source of things for us to use. It is not just a kind of handy convenience store in which we can find what we need and then leave behind. On the contrary, the created universe in which we find ourselves is destined to share the salvation, the redemption, the sanctification that God offers to us. It is part of what we are all about. It is directed toward a final fulfillment even as we are. When we speak of the "salvation of the world" we don't mean just the human beings in the world. We mean the world itself in consort with us.

Ecology has become an important element in contemporary behavior, both individual and corporate. We recycle soft drink cans and take care to dispose of old batteries properly. There are international treaties about the ozone layer and about whale hunting. And all that is good. It means that we have learned that we have to use our world carefully or run the risk of using up its resources. But there is a further dimension to the Christian view of creation. We believe that we must treat creation carefully not just in order to preserve its usefulness for ourselves, but because creation isn't ours. It belongs to God. We have it on loan. We are allowed to enjoy its benefits, but we have to keep reminding ourselves that God has further plans for it.

The second teaching that is implicit in this Sunday's live letter is that, although we have been saved, although the Spirit of Jesus lives in us, we have not yet reached the fullness of what God has in store for us. God isn't finished with us yet just as God isn't finished with the world yet. The final, unchangeable bond between ourselves and God still lies ahead of us, and we have to wait for it.

This call to waiting involves two things. One is that we still have work to do. God expects us to cooperate with his love for us, to respond to the new life that has been given to us. We are supposed to grow and develop, not just by passive acceptance of the gifts God gives us, but by doing our part to receive and share them. The other element of our having to wait is the assurance that what happens here and now in this world is not final. The challenges and sorrows we are asked to bear, as well as the achievements we bring to conclusion, are not the last word. They are "nothing compared to with the glory that will be revealed for us."

God has given us a complex and wonderful world to enjoy and a wonderful life to live. But the best is still to come.

FOR DISCUSSION AND REFLECTION

In practice, how should Christians relate to the world around them? How is waiting part of my Christian existence?

Fifteenth Sunday in Ordinary Time (B)

Ephesians 1:3-14

This Sunday's reading begins a series of seven semi-continuous readings from the letter to the Ephesians. Paul knew the Christians at Ephesus well, and so the impersonal tone of Ephesians and its lack of particular and personalized details have led many scholars to conclude that it was written by one of Paul's disciples rather than by the apostle himself. This same impersonal tone has also given rise to the opinion that the letter was a kind of circular missive, addressed to several local churches.

In almost all the letters that have come down to us from Paul and his followers, the opening greeting is followed by a thanksgiving section in which the author offers gratitude to God for some benefit that God has conferred on the addressees. In Ephesians the specific thanksgiving for the faith and love of the Christians who are being written to is preceded by a long and eloquent "blessing" passage in which the author offers thanks and praise to God for the whole plan of salvation.

This "blessing" passage constitutes our Sunday reading. It is a rich and complex section of the letter, almost symphonic in its construction, containing a deep and complex theology of salvation that reaches from before the beginning of the world to after its ending. In the Greek text, all twelve verses are contained in a single sentence! It's not an easy passage to summarize, and the best that can be offered is a kind of road map to alert readers to the main points that they need to notice in order to appreciate what is being said and to guide them in their reflections.

The passage offers God praise and thanksgiving ("blessed be God") for six blessings that have come to us from God our Father. First, God has chosen us for holiness; second, he has made us his adopted children; third, he has redeemed us and forgiven our sins; fourth, God has shared with us the knowledge of his secret plan of salvation ("the mystery of his will"); fifth, he chose the Jews to keep the hope of the Messiah alive in the world; sixth, he has included the gentiles in his project of definitive salvation that is constituted by eternal association with God in the praise of his glory.

This song of praise and thanksgiving for the Father's plan of salvation is about Christ, too. Each of the blessings comes about in him or through him. Redemption and forgiveness are "by his blood." The plan of salvation is to bring together everything in heaven and on earth "in Christ." The Jews' claim to glory is that they "first hoped in Christ." The gentiles have been redeemed because they "have believed in him." Whatever blessings the Father has given us have been given in Christ.

All this is wrapped up and sealed, as it were, by the gift of the Holy Spirit who acts as the down payment that the Father has made on our eternal destiny as God's possession.

What we have in this passage, therefore, is a lyrical expression of how the triune God is involved in the salvation of human beings. The author will develop these insights through the rest of the letter as he explores the implications of all things being summed up in Christ and being brought together into unity in his body, which is the Church. But this highly developed theology of the Church is planted in the praise and gratitude that is expressed in this opening passage.

Praise and gratitude are good criteria with which to measure our spiritual maturity. Some people never bother to thank God at all. They take everything for granted as if it were owed to them. Others offer praise and thanks to God when they are aware that they have received from him some special favor that they have been asking for. They see God as a distant grandfather to whom it is wise to send a thank-you note for a nice birthday present because there will be more birthdays in the future.

Other people make praise and gratitude a regular part of their prayer life, but they tend to focus on their own personal world: their health, their family, their friends. There's nothing wrong with that, of course, but it seems to be addressed to a rather limited God.

The Church's liturgy gives us some direction about the kind of praise and gratitude the Lord expects from us. Every day at Mass, in the preface to the Eucharistic Prayer the priest prays in the name of the people: "We do well always and everywhere to give you thanks through Jesus Christ our Lord." Then he goes on to mention motives for thanks and praise, reasons that resonate with the sort of things we found in today's live letter.

We owe God thanks and praise for everything, but in our effort to thank him for the smaller things, the personal things, the immediate things, we shouldn't overlook the big things, the fundamental things that give meaning and direction to our whole life, indeed, to our whole universe. "Every spiritual blessing in the heavens" is ours from God. "It is right to give him thanks and praise!"

FOR DISCUSSION AND REFLECTION

For what am I most grateful to God?

How do I express my praise and thanksgiving to God?

Fifteenth Sunday in Ordinary Time (C)

Colossians 1:15-20

This reading begins a series of four consecutive selections from
Paul's letter to the Colossians. Colossae was an unimportant little
town that Paul had never even visited. Its people had been
evangelized by Paul's colleague Epaphras. Paul, now in prison
somewhere, has learned from Epaphras that there are problems in
Colossae. Some unhealthy teachings are being circulated there.
These heterodox teachings included a call to observe certain
Jewish practices such as circumcision and the celebration of
special days and seasons. But more troublesome were the pagan
elements of the heresy. The Colossians were being asked to
believe that certain angelic beings, each of them containing a
part of the fullness of divinity, had control over human affairs and
even over all creation. If you wanted to appease these super-
beings and keep them happy you had to get possession of certain
specialized kinds of "knowledge." Since these ideas undermine
the full role of Christ as Lord of the universe, Paul's corrective
letter to the Colossians concerns itself primarily with the nature
and mission of Christ.

He is barely finished with the opening formalities of the
letter when he launches into what sounds like a grand finale, one
of the most important theological statements about the person of
Christ in the whole New Testament, and one of the most beautiful.
This is our reading. Scholars think that these verses were
originally a Christian hymn. The hymn may have undergone some

editing by Paul. In any case, it constitutes the doctrinal highpoint of the letter. The whole rest of Colossians is a kind of reflection on what is said here.

The hymn is presented to us in two strophes or verses. The first has to do with Christ's role in creation. He is the Lord and master of it all. Whatever came from the creative will of the Father finds expression and visibility in Christ. In him and through him and for him everything came into being. He is its pattern and its purpose. Paul offers his readers a list of the aspects of creation to which Christ is superior: things in heaven and on earth, visible and invisible, thrones, dominions, principalities and powers. (These last are seemingly some of the super-beings that the Colossians were concerned about.) Christ is prior to all of this and gives it all unity and meaning.

In the second verse of the hymn we hear about Christ's role in redemption, in undoing the harm to creation that had been done by sin. As the first to rise from the dead, Christ was the beginning of a new kind of life. Just as he was the instrument and purpose of creation, so is he of redemption, and is thus outstanding in every sphere. The Church, the community of faith, finds its unity and direction in him alone. Because the totality of godliness is in him, everything, on earth or in heaven, comes together and finds its ultimate significance in him. His gift of himself on the cross brings everything back together again.

This passage is one of those pages of the Bible that are almost inexpressibly rich. No matter how often we have read it or reflected on it, new insights still present themselves, new depths that we had not noticed before.

Implicit in these verses is a whole theology of the Trinity: the Son as full reflection of the Father, the image of the Father in which every expression of God is already contained. Because all creation somehow includes likeness to God, all creation includes likeness to Christ, the Son of God. He is the model and therefore the master of it all.

Also contained in these verses is a theology of redemption.

We are redeemed because we are like him. That likeness to him, that sharing in his risen life is what puts us in touch with the Father, as well as with all the other redeemed who make up his body, the Church. The whole purpose of redemption was to bring sinful creation into oneness in him. He brings earth and heaven together in the unity of his person.

But this breathtaking theology is not just a matter of lofty speculation. It has its implications for each one of us, here and now. In this passage God's word is teaching us that the worth and value of everything and of everyone comes in and through Christ, and that nothing makes any sense except in him. Our world has meaning and beauty because it is a reflection of him. Other human beings are to be respected and protected because of their relationship with him. Everything from the vastness of the created universe to the limitless realms of the human spirit, "all things in heaven and on earth, the visible and the invisible" fit together, have sense and worth, only in him. This is the Christ who offers himself to us in the sacraments of the Church and its teachings, in the word of Sacred Scripture, in the quiet of personal prayer. He is Jesus of Nazareth, but his is also the cosmic Christ. He is the Lord of the universe, but he is also our brother and friend.

FOR DISCUSSION AND REFLECTION

How is Christ sovereign Lord of my life?
Where do I see Christ in the world? In the Church?

Sixteenth Sunday in Ordinary Time (A)

Romans 8:26-27

We continue to read from the long section of Romans, stretching from the end of chapter 3 through chapter 8, that is concerned with the nature and the results of salvation. Salvation consists in living the life of the risen Christ. We have access to it through faith. Once we have been introduced into the state of being saved, we are free from the obligations of the Jewish law and from the demands of self-seeking. We are in a new relationship with God that enables us to call him our Father in the same way that Jesus did and that invites us to look forward to a state of glorious and final fulfillment in the company of all creation.

In verses 24 and 25 of chapter 8, Paul says that our longing for the final fulfillment of creation finds its validation in hope. Hope enables us to wait with persistence.

In this Sunday's reading, Paul speaks of another element that is involved with our looking forward to God's final gifts to us: the Spirit who prays in our hearts.

We are weak, the text says, and we don't really know how to pray. We know we are supposed to be aching for final union with God, but we are not quite sure how to express our desires. (The text does not go into detail about why this is the case, but it would not be hard to think of reasons why we are inarticulate before God. Our human limitations, our association with sin, our orientation toward selfishness, our limited knowledge and experience of God, our natural desire to want to save ourselves without having to depend on God—any or all of these characteristics could make it difficult for us to communicate with God.)

To help us overcome these obstacles to communication, God gives us his own Spirit to speak through our hearts, to address the Father for us in ways that are too deep for human utterance. God is intensely interested in us, in our deepest desires, and is anxious to listen to the Spirit when the Spirit speaks through us and on our behalf. The Spirit can express what the Father longs to hear from all those who are saved ("the holy ones").

These two short verses teach us quite a bit about prayer. First of all, they suggest that our prayer is not supposed to be concerned only about our day-to-day needs, about the little things we think we (or those we love) have to have from God if we are going to be able to serve him properly. Appropriate as prayer for such things may be, prayer also has to be concerned with ultimates, with the deepest meaning of our existence, with the final destiny toward which God is directing us. We tend to concentrate on immediate and superficial things in our prayer, "because we do not know how to pray as we ought."

But God doesn't leave us to our own devices when it comes to prayer. God doesn't sit back and let us figure it all out for ourselves. No, God's very own Spirit prays with us and in us. Just as the risen Christ acts in us and speaks in us, so also the Spirit of Christ prays in us. We never have to count exclusively on our own spiritual resources and skills when we speak with God. We never have to address the Father alone. When we speak to God, we speak to him with his own voice. We speak God's language because God's Spirit speaks when we pray.

This doesn't mean that we don't have to exert effort in our prayer or that we can expect the Spirit to do it all for us. No, we have to practice prayer, we have to get skilled in it, we have to train ourselves in prayer just as athletes have to train themselves in their sports. But our own efforts are not our only resources. Whenever we address our heavenly Father, the Spirit prays with us and elevates our conversation with God to the level of the Father's conversation with the Son and the Spirit.

The liturgy gives us some good indications about what to pray for and how to pray. The prayers of Sunday Mass, for example, are quite general, yet quite instructive: "help us to know your will and do it with courage"; "show us the way to peace"; "help us to live in your presence"; "grant us an unfailing respect for your name." These are the things God wants us to desire. And how are we to pray for them? "Through our Lord Jesus Christ who lives and reigns with you in the unity of the Holy Spirit." God is involved in our dialogue, not only by teaching us what to pray for but also by becoming personally involved in our expression of it.

All of this suggests that we have to leave room for God to be involved in our prayer. We have to allow him to lead us in our prayer. We have to listen to what God says to us in our prayer.

Some years ago one of our priests asked to meet with me for a half-hour because he wanted to discuss his ministry with me. When he got to my office, he talked without stopping for forty-five minutes, telling me, among other things, that he was a skilled listener. I didn't get to say more than a few words. By the time he left I was more than a little annoyed because I felt that he had used me to build up his own ego. I wonder if God might not feel that way sometimes about our prayer.

FOR DISCUSSION AND REFLECTION

How do I know what to pray for or how to pray?

How do I leave room in my prayer for the Spirit to speak to and for me?

Sixteenth Sunday in Ordinary Time (B)

Ephesians 2:13-18

One of the most sensitive issues in the early Church was the relationship between Jews and gentiles. The Jews saw themselves as a people apart, chosen by God to be his special people. This choice, this specialness, was symbolized by practices such as circumcision, dietary laws, restrictions regarding marriage and other forms of social interaction. The gentiles were seen, by their very nature, as outsiders, rejects, strangers, aliens to God, rightly separated from inclusion in God's people.

Now came Jesus, a Jew yet receptive to gentiles. As his followers reflected on what he has taught them, both before and after his death and resurrection, it became clear that gentiles were dear to God, too, and that whatever Jesus came to bring to Jews was available to gentiles as well.

This still left the question of whether, in order to share the salvation that Christ offered to both gentiles and Jews, the gentiles had to take on the observance of the Jewish law. Many early Christian leaders seem to have thought so. It took a while to clarify the basic insight that, in Christ, the obligatory nature of the Jewish law had been done away with and so it was no longer necessary for people to observe the Jewish law in order to be pleasing to God. This clarification involved a long and difficult struggle which is described in some detail in the Acts of the Apostles and lies in the background of many of the Pauline letters.

The letter to the Ephesians deals with the unity of the Church and, in the reading for this Sunday, addresses the basic Jewish-gentile question.

Our passage speaks of those who were far off (gentiles, to whom the letter is addressed) and those who were near to God (the Jews). Those previously far off have now been brought near by the saving death of Christ. The divisions that had existed between Jews and gentiles have now been done away with, thanks to the abolition of the demands of the Jewish law. The two corporate entities that had existed in hostility to one another were now united into one person with Christ. (Earlier in Ephesians Paul had spoken of the Church as Christ's body.) Jews and gentiles have been brought together by Christ's death into a state of peace: peace with each other and peace with God. (Note that, in biblical language, "peace" generally signifies the fullness of all that is good. It is a synonym for "salvation.") This unity and peace that Christ effected by his death allows all of us together to approach our heavenly Father united in one Holy Spirit.

The tension between Jews and gentiles in the Church may seem like a distant and irrelevant historical question to us now. It may have been an important issue during the earliest times of the Church, but that struggle is over. However, although that particular issue may have been solved, there are still tensions and struggles in the Church. The peace that Christ established does not seem to be flourishing in its fullness.

Christianity is divided into various churches. Sometimes these church communities have expressed hostility toward one another for hundreds of years. We are now beginning to examine the reason for these hostilities and to move toward resolving them, but the reasons for the diversity and the paths to reunion are not always clear. We still have a long way to go.

But there are also tensions within our Roman Catholic Church, even within our own parishes sometimes. The location of the tabernacle, the removal of the communion rail, what kind of hymns we sing at Mass and whether we kneel during the Eucharistic Prayer, how our parish shares its financial and personnel resources with less fortunate parts of the Church, whether the parish priest is sufficiently "liberal," or sufficiently "conservative," or tries to use inclusive language: these issues and others like them can raise "dividing walls of enmity" and divide the whole parish in the "near" and the "far off."

Issues like this are not unimportant or without implications, any more than the issue of observing the Jewish law was unimportant or without implications. But we need to see these questions and deal with them in the light of Christ's redemption of us all, in the context of God's gift of salvation. We all suffer from a tendency to oversimplify the religious reality in which we live. We are inclined to impoverish the richness of the mystery of Christ.

The Son of God became a human being in Jesus. He offered his life in faithfulness to his Father, and so brought the offer of salvation and peace to the whole world. He gave us the Holy Spirit to unite us all in intimacy with God. He still acts in his sacraments and gives us his teaching in the Church. That's what our faith is all about. That's what's really important. That's what binds us together into the one body, which is the body of Christ.

Maybe we should thank God for the Church today and ask

ourselves what we can do to bring it the peace and unity that Christ intended.

FOR DISCUSSION AND REFLECTION

What can I do to foster unity among the Christian churches?
How can I foster unity in my parish?

Sixteenth Sunday in Ordinary Time (C)

Colossians 1:24-28

Paul has opened the main section of his letter to the Colossians with a symphonic proclamation of Christ's role in creation and redemption. He then reminds the Colossians that they have benefited from Christ's action by means of their faith, a faith of which he, Paul, is a minister.

In this Sunday's reading, Paul continues to present his credentials, gently persuading these new Christians to pay attention to what he has to say, even though he is not personally known to them.

This passage is quite rich in content, but rather rambling, each clause leading into the next in a way that is not conducive to clarity and easy understanding. If the same ideas were to be presented in the kind of written expression that we are used to, it would probably read something like this:

> I am a minister of the Church, and have been called by God to this service. The purpose of my calling is to bring people like yourselves to the full holiness that God offers them. This is not an easy task. My ministry costs me suffering, but my suffering extends the meritorious self-giving of Christ and strengthens the Church. I deal with God's mystery, his long-term plan that is now being made known even to the gentiles. That plan is Christ in you.

That's your source for the hope of eternal glory. Christ is the content of my ministry, a content I proclaim to everybody everywhere so that I can help everybody become everything that God wants them to be.

There are lots of things that call for reflection in this brief passage, as is so often the case in the Pauline writings, but two stand out with particular urgency.

The first is what Paul says about suffering. His ministry demands suffering, he says, but he doesn't mind because he is "filling up what is lacking in the afflictions of Christ." This does not mean that Paul thought that the redemptive suffering and death of Jesus was incomplete, as if Christ really hadn't finished the mission on which he has been sent by his Father. Nor is it meant to imply that the success of an apostle's ministry is dependent on his suffering, as if God were pleased by our pain or somehow made happy with our hurts. Paul's point about suffering here seems to be that the effort involved in preaching the gospel, the patience required in dealing with the enemies of the faith provide credibility to the preacher's mission. They are evidences of the apostle's faithfulness to Christ, even as Christ's suffering and death were evidence of his faithfulness to the mission he had received from his Father. It is the dedication that is behind the suffering that provides likeness to Christ, that extends Christ's saving mission into new places and new times, that renders the results of the suffering of Christ more accessible and more universal.

What Paul says here gives us some insight into our own sufferings. Traditionally Christians have seen suffering of whatever kind as an occasion for growth in virtue, as something to be "offered up" to God as a gift to him. This doesn't mean that our human suffering gives God some sort of gratification he wouldn't otherwise have. It means rather that our faithfulness to God in times of suffering, our acceptance of what God in his wisdom sends us constitutes an expression of our trust in him and our faithfulness to him. It makes us more like Christ whose love and faithfulness persisted to the very end of his life, in spite of the rejection and pain that resulted from that love and faithfulness.

The second major point that calls for consideration in this passage is Paul's definition of "the mystery," of God's plan for salvation. It doesn't consist in esoteric knowledge or special ritual practices or keeping heavenly powers appeased and happy, as the Colossians were being invited to believe. God's salvation "is Christ in you," he tells them. Christ in us is what constitutes justification, salvation, redemption, freedom, sanctification, transformation. Christ in us is what takes our sins away and makes us pleasing to our heavenly Father.

Sometimes people are overwhelmed with the complexity of the Catholic Christian faith. That's understandable because it has been the subject of reverent reflection and speculation for two thousand years and because it reaches into every aspect of our human reality. The basic exposition of Catholic faith and practice, the *Catechism of the Catholic Church*, runs to 688 pages! Yet it all hangs together, it's all based on a single reality: Christ in us. Everything in our Christian life is a response to Christ in us. Everything is directed toward developing Christ in us. Everything is a consequence of the implications of Christ in us. What does it mean for us to be members of the Church? It means to have Christ in us and to believe and behave accordingly. Absolutely every aspect of our faith is a preparation for or a consequence of that basic reality.

FOR DISCUSSION AND REFLECTION

What role has suffering played in my life?

How would my life be different if Christ were not in me?

Seventeenth Sunday in Ordinary Time (A)

Romans 8:28-30

As Paul approaches the end of this long main section of his letter to the Romans, he begins to summarize. The whole project of salvation is due exclusively to the goodness of God. This goodness is not erratic or unpredictable, dependent on God's momentary impulses, but a carefully planned out project of kindness and generosity. That's the theme of this Sunday's reading.

The text begins by pointing out how "all things" contribute to the well-being of those who are the beneficiaries of God's initiative and who, consequently, love him. By "all things" Paul probably means the elements of salvation that he has just been speaking about. Human sufferings, creation's destiny to glory and its groaning till that glory is fulfilled, Christian hope, the Spirit-filled prayer of the believer: it's all part of a highly articulate plan on God's part. Note that the love for God that the text mentions is a *result* of people being called according to God's purpose and not the cause of their being called.

In the rest of our reading, Paul explains and expands what he has just said. First he reminds us of God's purpose. Everything that God did as part of his saving plan had for its purpose to reconfigure human beings into the image of his Son, Jesus. Christ Jesus was to provide the likeness, the genetic material, as it were, according to which an immense family of sisters and brothers, all sharing and extending the life of Christ, was to be born.

Next he tells us how God's project is brought to fulfillment. It is a five-step plan, expressed in the passage's verbs: foreknew, predestined, called, justified, glorified. From all eternity, God knew what he wanted to do and had decided to take whatever steps were necessary to bring salvation to human beings ("Those he foreknew he also predestined"). Next came the implementation of the plan: the call to faith and baptism. Those who accepted what God offered were "justified" (that is, made holy in Christ), and were given the beginnings of what would eventually become the life of everlasting glory with Christ in heaven.

This passage from Romans is very important in the history of Christian theology because it is the basic Scripture text about predestination. "Predestination" is the term used to refer to God's foreknowledge and arrangement of events, and the theological speculations about predestination are concerned with who is chosen by God for salvation and who is not. Are some destined by God to eternal damnation while others are destined to eternal happiness? If so, is it possible to determine on what basis God makes this decision? Is it in view of God's knowledge about how the individual is going to spend his or her life, or is it a matter of God's free and arbitrary choice? These questions occupied the attention of Saint Augustine, Luther, Calvin, the fathers of the Council of Trent and centuries of post-Tridentine theologians.

Catholic teaching on this matter is that God predestines nobody to evil, but wills the salvation of all human beings. The only people who are not brought to salvation are those who deliberately refuse it. This refusal is the result of the exercise of their free will, an exercise that God permits but does not predetermine.

The thing to remember about this Sunday's reading is that its subject is not God's relationship with individual saints or sinners, but his general plan for salvation. Paul's point here is that our heavenly Father is not a capricious God who blesses or mistreats his subjects according to whim, but is rather a careful planner who brings together into one concerted undertaking a whole symphony of individual saving elements. This certainly has consequences for God's relationship with individuals, but these relationships evolve in accord with God's general scheme of salvation. God cares about me because God cares about us all.

Sometimes Christian believers are ridiculed for their constitutional optimism, for their conviction that everything will turn out all right in the end. "Pie in the sky when we die," is the way the enemies of faith put it. But our confidence in the final future is not a mindless conviction, an unrealistic fantasy to distract us from the grim reality around us. It is a deep religious conviction, based on what God's own word tells us. There is a plan at work. It is God's plan and its final outcome will be what God has planned for it to be. We may not understand how God's plan applies to each and every detail of our individual human existence, but that doesn't mean that there is no plan or that God's project has gone astray.

And how do we know that there is such a plan, that what we hold as God's word is true? We know because we have already experienced a part of the execution of the plan in our own individual lives and in our participation in the life of the community of Christ, which is the Church. The individual history of each believer includes the assimilation of Christ's teaching, participation in his sacraments, personal growth as a result of our membership in his community of faith. We know there is a plan because we have been part of it. We know that it is God's plan. And we know that it is good.

FOR DISCUSSION AND REFLECTION

In what specific ways have I experienced God's saving providence?
What would our life be if God had not made plans for our salvation?

Seventeenth Sunday in Ordinary Time (B)

Ephesians 4:1-6

Most of the Pauline letters follow a standard pattern. They are composed of a salutation to the addressees and a thanksgiving, followed by the body of the letter. Then comes the formula of conclusion. The body of the letter is generally divided into two sections, one which deals with the teaching that the writer wants to impart, the other with directions or exhortations for moral behavior. Ephesians follows this general format, and this Sunday's reading is the beginning of the section that gives behavioral directives based on what the author had taught about the Church.

In the doctrinal part of the letter, the author had emphasized the unity of Jew and gentile in the body of the one Christ. Now, calling on the memory of the imprisonment that Paul had endured in order to invoke the apostle's authority on the exhortation, he calls for behavior that will foster unity.

The basis for the directions he gives his addressees is at the end of our passage. It is oneness: one body (the Church), one Spirit, one hope, one Lord (Christ), one faith (in Christ), one baptism, one God who rules everything and pervades everything and sustains everything. Oneness is what life in Christ is all about: oneness in the faith community, oneness in the Trinity. It is understandable, therefore, that he calls for attitudes and actions that will reflect and promote unity: humility, gentleness, patience, willingness to bear with others' faults, eagerness to preserve the unity and peace that are the gift of the Spirit. All these virtues involve putting oneself in second place for the sake of promoting oneness in Christ, the Spirit, the Father. If you are going to be united, that's how you will go about it. Right at the beginning of the passage, however, the author gives a general principle that not only governs the pursuit of unity in the local church, but that also provides the basic directive of all of Christian moral life: "Live in a manner worthy of the call you have received."

Living as a Catholic Christian believer is not a matter of keeping rules. It's not a question of studying up on the particulars of moral theology so that you know how much you can get away with. ("How far can we go before it's a mortal sin?") What Christ expects of us is not that we behave in a certain determined fashion so that we will deserve salvation when we die, but rather that we act in consistency with what he has already made us to be. The question that true believers have to address in deciding what to do or what to avoid is not, "What do the regulations say?"

but "What is in accord with my existence as a sharer in the life of Christ, as a member of his one body, as one united with the Father through the action of the Holy Spirit?"

The way we govern our personal (and corporate) behavior says a lot about our deepest attitudes toward Christ and salvation and the Church and our brothers and sisters in the Lord. I suspect that there are a lot of "selfish saints" in the Church, people who do what's right and avoid what's wrong because of what they see in it for themselves. They don't commit sins because committing sins puts them on the outs with God, and they want to be able to say when judgment comes that God has no reason to be on the outs with them. There are others in the Church whose behavior may be exactly the same, but who guide themselves by what God has already done for them rather than by what they are trying to get out of God in the future. They wouldn't dream of fornicating or telling lies or being harsh with the people around them or missing Mass on Sunday not because they are afraid of what might happen to them if they do, but because they are so aware of how much they have already received, so grateful for what God has already made them to be that offending God is simply unthinkable. It doesn't make sense to be selfish (which is what all sinfulness ultimately is) if you are aware and appreciative of the generosity of God. Looking out for yourself at the expense of others is ridiculous if you really appreciate the self-giving of the Lord Jesus. Participating in parish factions is absurd if you are conscious of the many kinds of unity that lie at the roots of our faith.

Of course there are rules of behavior for believers. We are not free to do as we please on the basis of self-deluding attitudes of what Jesus would or wouldn't approve of. We have to be objective about what is right and what is wrong. But the criteria on which we are to base the decisions of our conscience are not the criteria of legal hair-splitting or spiritual self-serving. They are the criteria of consistency with the love of Christ in us, the criteria of acting in accord with the gifts that a generous God has given us.

Living in a manner worthy of the call we have received can sometimes be much more demanding than merely keeping rules. But it's much more in accord with what we are and much more harmonious with what God intends us to be when our struggles here are over.

FOR DISCUSSION AND REFLECTION

How do I decide what is appropriate behavior?

What image best matches my idea of God: judge, father, benefactor, friend, disappointed lover, enforcer, creditor?

Seventeenth Sunday in Ordinary Time (C)

Colossians 2:12-14

In this series of readings from Colossians, we have heard Paul's lyrical proclamation of the cosmic Christ, Lord of creation and redemption. We have seen him presenting his ministerial credentials to the Colossians and calling for their attention to his teaching. In this Sunday's reading from chapter 2 he is teasing out some of the implications of God's mystery of salvation, "Christ in you."

In verses 9-10, he offers a general statement: in Christ you share the fullness of divinity. Then comes a series of images, each of which casts light on an aspect of Christ's being in us. In verse 11, immediately before our reading, he says that being in Christ constitutes the equivalent of circumcision, making us members of God's people.

Our reading presents three further images. First of all, Christ's life in us is like being buried with him and rising from the dead with him. This association with Christ requires the power of God, but also our faith in that power, that is, our openness to accept what God offers us.

Secondly, Christ's being in us involves the forgiveness of our sins. Our human sinfulness constituted a state of death. When the Father made us live with and in Christ, we began a new life that included the forgiveness of our sins.

Thirdly, Christ's life in us means that we are freed of the burdens and formalities of the old Jewish ritual observance. Here Paul uses the image of "the bond against us with its legal claims." He envisions the old law as a kind of document that God destroys by nailing it to the cross, thus freeing us from its demands.

In verse 15, immediately after our reading, there is still another image: God leading away "the principalities and powers" (that is, the forces opposed to Christ) in a kind of triumphal procession.

Christian existence, life in Christ, is such a rich and complex reality that no one image can convey it all. That's why Paul uses a whole series of images when he wants to explain to the Colossians what God's mystery, "Christ in you," implies. Of course, these implications that Paul lays out for the Colossians are also applicable to us. Because of the fullness of godliness in Christ, Christ's being in us involves membership in his people, participation in his risen life, freedom from sin, liberation from useless religious observances and release from the demands of any other cosmic forces.

It's important for us to be aware of all this because, if we aren't, we run the risk of looking on our Christian faith and Christian life as something other than what it really is.

To begin with, Christian life is not a series of obligations. Sometimes people look on it that way. You have to go to Mass on Sunday. You have to get married in the Church. You can't practice birth control. You have to be against abortion. Granted, each of these statements is true. There are obligations and expectations connected with being a member of the Church. But these obligations and expectations are not the primary and basic thing.

The primary and basic thing is Christ in us. Everything else is a consequence of that, and if we just look at the consequences without knowing where they come from we are going to get a false idea about Christian faith.

Likewise, being a member of the Church is not a matter of cultural inheritance. "Of course I'm Catholic. All my family is Catholic and that's what I was brought up to be." People sometimes give similar reasons for being Democrats or Republicans. They've never really thought about it. They simply conform to the people around them. Their religious faith (or political affiliation) is a kind of protective coloring that keeps them from standing out from the crowd. Whatever one might think appropriate as a process for choosing a political position, just going with the flow is not an appropriate way of professing religious faith. Religious faith demands awareness and commitment: awareness of God's love for us and commitment to the implications of that love. It may very well be that lots of people who consider themselves Catholics have never really made an act of faith, of self-giving in response to God's generosity.

Real Catholic Christian faith involves the acceptance of Christ in us. It is a reply to God's initiative, to God's mystery of love for our salvation. It's not a burdensome series of obligations, not a semi-automatic involvement of ourselves in the cultural inheritance of our family and friends. Real Christian faith is consciously joyful about and deliberately attentive to God's gift of himself to us. It is an intentional gift of ourselves to the Lord who gives each and all of us community with himself, participation in his life, forgiveness of our sins, liberation from irrelevant religious demands and the security of knowing that Our Lord is the Lord of all. What a shame to reduce all that to burdensome rules and cultural conformity!

FOR DISCUSSION AND REFLECTION

How do I find joy in Christ's life in me?

Which of Paul's images of salvation do I find most appealing?

Eighteenth Sunday in Ordinary Time (A)

Romans 8:35, 37-39

When I was in the seminary—a long time ago—we had a flamboyant French Passionist priest as our professor for one of our courses in philosophy. Whenever we came across some principle or some idea that he found particularly interesting, he would shout out, "This ought to be set to music and sung in Gregorian chant!"

Many scholars feel that way about the passage in Romans (8:31-39) whose conclusion constitutes this Sunday's live letter. (The first part of the passage is used for the Second Sunday of Lent for Year B.) Paul has reached the end of the main section of his extended reflection on salvation. He has laid down the basic teachings that Christians need to know and profess about being saved. Then (in verse 31) he asks, "What then shall we say to this?" What's the bottom line to it all?

He begins his response to that question by using judicial imagery in verses 31-34. Who can dare to object to God's favor for us? Will anybody dare to lodge a complaint about us if God is in our favor? Is anybody going to convict us if Christ Jesus speaks for us?

This is where this Sunday's passage begins. Having established that there is no way that we could be subject to a verdict of guilty since God is on our side, he asks if there are other forces that could pry us loose from God's love. First (verse 35) he lists tribulations that might afflict us in the context of our natural, ordinary human existence, a whole series of things that people tend to be afraid of. Paul proclaims that none of these can force us away from the love that Christ has for us. Christ's care for us is stronger that any or all of them! If these are our enemies, we will certainly be the winners!

Then (verse 38 and following) he offers another list of threats, this time a series of forces that people of his time thought of as cosmic or supernatural powers that influenced life on earth:

heavenly beings, astrological forces, the personified energies of life and death, the potencies of time. Paul is absolutely sure that no incorporeal force or power in the whole universe can deprive us of the love that God has for us in and through Christ Jesus our Lord.

The bottom line to Paul's treatise is that salvation is constituted by God's love and favor toward us and that nothing in all creation—physical or spiritual—is powerful enough to strip us of that love and favor. In the face of every possible uncertainty, God's gift of salvation will prevail.

This pivotal passage of Romans is an invitation to confidence, to assurance, to trust. God's love for us is more powerful than anything we can imagine and it comes to us not as recompense for heroic spiritual efforts or superhuman dedication on our part. It comes to us as God's free gift, which we don't need to earn, and, in fact, which we cannot earn. There is no need for doubt or question on our part about the strength and vigor of God's love. Salvation is already finalized in Christ's love for us and nothing can force us loose from it.

Of course we can reject salvation if we wish. Our own human will can push it away so that we don't accept it to begin with or can repudiate it once God has given it to us. Salvation does not supersede the possibility of selfishness and sin on our part. Paul is quite conscious of all this, as we learn elsewhere in his writings. But here he's not talking about us. Here he's talking about God and about the invincible power of God's love for us, a love that he had experienced in his own personal history, a love that was the central theme of his evangelizing mission.

There are consequences of all this for individual Christian believers. One is that we are called to be optimists. There is absolutely no power that can separate us from God's gifts unless we ourselves agree to the separation through sin. True, our human life is a struggle, but it is a struggle that God himself guarantees we will win. The good guys are going to come out on top and God has seen to it that each one of us is among the good guys.

Another consequence of what Paul says here is that it is appropriate for us to be certain and secure about what lies ahead of us. We don't have to wonder if God is going to change his mind. We don't have to worry that somehow we are going to end up in the dark outside at the end. God loves us in and through the risen Christ. That's the basic truth of salvation and there's nothing that can change that. Some people are more inclined to diffidence than others. Some find it hard to determine how general principles are to be applied in concrete situations. Some find it hard to decide to decide. But all that is relative and secondary. God understands how limited we are and makes allowance for that. The basic reality is God's love for us, and there can never be any question about whether or not we should rely on that.

This is a passage that ought to be set to music. It's a hymn of praise to God's care for us. It's a hymn that all Christians are expected to know how to sing.

FOR DISCUSSION AND REFLECTION

Where do I look for stability in my life?
In what aspects of my life am I most vulnerable?

Eighteenth Sunday in Ordinary Time (B)

Ephesians 4:17, 20-24

This Sunday we continue our reading from the moral and directive section of Ephesians.

The author begins our reading by invoking his teaching authority "in the Lord." He goes on to tell his readers that, if they have really learned the truth that is contained in the teaching of Christ, they will not live like pagans. A pagan life involves not only hard-heartedness and sexual misbehavior (mentioned in verses 18 and 19) but also aimlessness of life, being guided astray by false promises that lead nowhere, corrupted by the pursuit of illusory desires. Strip yourselves of that sort of thing. Instead, dress yourselves in newness. Put on a new self that is characterized by authentic godliness. (In these references to undressing and dressing, the author may be alluding to the practice of the baptismal candidate's divesting him or herself of ordinary clothes to go down into the baptismal water and then being clothed again with the clean baptismal robe after emerging from the pool.)

In this passage, Ephesians is offering its readers—and us—two basic directives about Christian moral life, one negative, the other positive.

The first directive, the negative one, is to give up living like "gentiles," that is, like pagans, like people who don't believe in the true God but devote themselves to idols. When we think of pagan behavior, we tend to imagine Technicolor sex orgies or crowd scenes in which a beautiful maiden is being sacrificed to an ugly statue or thrown to a hungry wild animal. There were such aspects to pagan religion, but there are other facets to paganism that were more subtle, facets that are still with us today.

Whenever we set up and pursue final goals other than those that are founded in and lead to the love of God, we are engaging in idolatry. We are acting like pagans. Such goals may be success, wealth, bodily beauty, political power, sexual fulfillment or any number of other things. Each of these things has its place in human life, but when they become ultimates, when they become the basic directive forces of a human life, they become idols. Nothing but God can rightly be the basic directive force of human existence.

Pursuing such idolatrous goals can only lead us astray. As this Sunday's reading tells us, idolatry involves "futility of mind" and "deceitful desires," false truths that lead us to emptiness and yearnings which can never be fulfilled or which, if fulfilled, yield only barrenness.

These pagan, idolatrous goals are not bizarre ideas espoused only by small groups of off-beat religious eccentrics. They are part of the very fabric of the society in which we live. Newspaper ads, TV commercials, movie scenarios, the words of popular songs, the outcomes promised by stockbrokers, car salesmen and beauticians: they all offer us happiness if we are rich, successful, beautiful, popular, powerful. One of the most attractive and common goals that we are encouraged to pursue is "feeling good about ourselves." Of course, there's nothing wrong with feeling good about oneself if we do it for the right reasons, based on the right principles. But all too often, feeling good about ourselves involves putting ourselves at the center of the universe. It is a refined label for deliberate self-centeredness. Paganism is all around us. We do well to heed the warning that Ephesians give us in this passage.

The second directive that this reading gives us is positive: put on the new self, the new self of godliness. Earlier on in chapter 4 (verse 15), the author had told his addressees to "grow in every way into him who is the head, Christ." The new self, the new man that we are invited to put on is, therefore, Christ.

Christian moral life, Christian spirituality consists in assimilating and developing the life of Christ that we received in baptism, the life of Christ that constitutes our salvation. Given the richness and complexity and depth of the life of Christ, we cannot expect to respond to it fully and appropriately with a single act of acceptance or a single moment of self-dedication. As believers we are called to ongoing conversion, ongoing receptivity and response, ongoing growth. There is always more to do in our moral and spiritual development because Christ always has more to give us. His relationship with us is without limits.

Our vocation as followers of Christ is nothing less than a calling to be like God, to mirror the righteousness and holiness of Christ. That's a lifetime job, but a job that will lead us to our true destiny, to the development of the true worth that God gave us when he made us members of the body of Christ.

This Sunday's reading addresses aspects of our life that we have to deal with every day. The call to paganism and idolatry is always sounding in our ears. The call to growth in Christ is always sounding in our hearts. Over and over again we have to decide which call we will answer.

FOR DISCUSSION AND REFLECTION

What pagan attitudes and values have I come across recently?
How does God help me to grow in the likeness of Christ?

Eighteenth Sunday in Ordinary Time (C)
Colossians 3:1-5, 9-11

In this Sunday's reading (the last of our series from Colossians) Paul begins the second main part of his letter, the part concerned with moral guidance.

He begins with a general principle that links this part of the letter with what went before. He had told the Colossians that the center of salvation consisted in Christ's being in them and living in them. They were now sharers in the life of the risen Christ. Since that is so, he now says, you have to live accordingly. You have to pursue heavenly things rather than earthly concerns. Your life in Christ is not visible to everybody around you, but it is no less a new life for that reason. In fact, when Christ comes again in glory, your life in him will be manifested. (The implication is that, therefore, you have to start living now a life that is in accord with your future glory.)

Before all else, he tells them, you have to root out and destroy "the parts of you that are earthly." This doesn't mean that Christian believers don't need to be concerned about the realities of their life here on earth, but that they should do away with everything that doesn't fit with their new heavenly life in Christ. Then he gives a little list of the kind of behavior he has in mind: immorality, impurity, passion, evil desire, greed. These are all varieties of selfishness.

So is lying, playing fast and loose with the truth for our own benefit. This is not in accord with what you are, he says. You have a new self that requires still further development as you learn what it means to exist in the image of God.

Finally we have a repetition of a teaching that we have already heard from Paul in First Corinthians (12:13) and Galatians (3:27 and following): distinctions that used to divide people from one another (Jew from gentile, slaves from free persons) are no longer significant. It is not that everybody is suddenly the same, but that human differences are no longer significant in comparison with the likeness that all can share in Christ. If Christ is everything and in everybody ("all and in all"), nothing else matters much. Even Scythians, the most barbarous of the barbarians, can belong!

Christian moral behavior is a matter of consistency, of living out our daily lives in a way that fits in with who and what we are: extensions of the life of the risen Christ. All of Catholic Christian moral theology, all the do's and don'ts that we learn as we grow up and develop in our faith are simply specifications of the basic Christian vocation to live in Christ Jesus. And Christian maturity consists, to a great extent, in learning that the details of behavior that we sometimes find so burdensome are nothing other than the particulars that derive from our participation in Christ's life.

It should come as no surprise, then, to hear that all of Christian morality consists somehow in recognizing Christ and in giving ourselves to him in the unfolding of our earthly life. If these are the basic Christian virtues, the fundamental sins are idolatry and selfishness.

Idolatry consists in making something into god that is not God. We tend to think that idolatry is something that savages engage in, grass-skirted natives dancing around a statue. It's a sign of a lack of civilization. But that's not really true. Some of the most civilized societies in human history have been riddled with idolatry. When people overlook God and decide that religious faith is basically irrelevant and instead give their attention to success or comfort or looking good or being popular, that's idolatry. In our reading we hear Paul telling the Colossians that greed, unbridled acquisitiveness, is idolatry, too. All these are types of idolatry and we shouldn't be too quick to tell ourselves that that sort of thing is not a danger for us.

The other basic sin is selfishness, putting ourselves and our needs and desires first at the expense of everybody else. Most of the Ten Commandments are concerned with selfishness. Most of the sins, big or small, that people—we—commit are varieties of self-seeking. Sins of impurity and theft, sins of violence and desire, sins against family and society: they're all manifestations of putting ourselves first.

Idolatry and selfishness are the basic sins, and basic virtue consists in acknowledging God in our lives and in extending God's love to others. This brings us back to Paul's fundamental insight: salvation consists in living in Christ Jesus.

And that's what makes us all one. Greeks and Jews and Scythians all belong together because they all share (or can share) the life of the one Christ. Self-seeking distinctions between various kinds of people are not appropriate in the light of our sharing the one life of the one risen Christ.

Living a Christian life is not really very complicated. It's quite simple. It means living in Christ Jesus. Of course that doesn't always make it easy!

FOR DISCUSSION AND REFLECTION

What aspects of my life are incompatible with Christ in me?

How does Christ in me help me deal with the differences I find in the people around me?

Nineteenth Sunday in Ordinary Time (A)

Romans 9:1-5

Paul has completed two major sections of the exposition of his teaching that he is offering to the Romans. He has explained how everyone is in need of salvation (1:6-3:20). He has given an overview of the nature of the salvation that God offers us and of some of the consequences of that salvation (3:21-8:39). Now he begins a new section, chapters nine through eleven. This part of Romans is concerned with the place of the Jews in God's plan of salvation.

Most Christians of Paul's time would have been aware that, although Jesus lived and died in the context of Judaism and that, although much of his teaching is based on Jewish Scripture and Jewish religious categories, yet most of the members of the Church were not Jews but gentiles. This situation raised a whole swarm of questions. If both Jews and gentiles needed salvation, as Paul has demonstrated in the first part of his letter, why did the Jews seem to reject it? If the law and the prophets pointed toward Jesus, why did gentiles seem to recognize this more than the Jews? Did God change his mind about his plans for the Jews? If God changed his mind about the Jews and their salvation, couldn't God also change his mind about us gentiles? These are all questions that Paul will deal with in the next three chapters.

Our reading for this Sunday is a kind of prologue or overture to the long disquisition to follow. It is worth noting that there is no lead-in to the new section, no connection with what has gone before in Paul's letter. He starts off cold, without any preparation for this new theme, as if it would be obvious to his readers that the question of the Jews should come next.

With great earnestness he attests to his affection for his people and to his sorrow at their present posture. With fervent rhetorical exaggeration he says that he would even be willing to give up salvation for himself if that would be of any benefit to his "kin according to the flesh."

Next he lists seven privileges and prerogatives that give the Israelites their importance and that are the source of Paul's continuing love for them. They are God's adopted children, chosen as God's son at the time of the exodus. They have been touched by the glory of God dwelling in his temple in their midst. They have been involved in God's covenants with Abraham, Isaac, Moses, David. They have had the benefit of God's gift of the law to them and have participated in the worship God directed them to offer. God made irrevocable promises to his people through Abraham, Isaac, Jacob, Moses, David. God gave them giants of faithfulness, the patriarchs, as their ancestors. Finally, from among them, came the humanity of the Messiah. God's anointed one is their kinsman. For all this, let glory be given to God! (Because the early Greek manuscripts were without punctuation, it is not clear whether the end of verse five means, "...comes the Messiah, who is God over all, blest forever," or "...comes the Messiah. God who is over all [be] blest forever.")

After this elaborate opening, Paul will go on in chapters 9 and 10 to explain that not all those are true Israelites (that is, pleasing to God) who happen to be physically descended from Abraham. Consequently, not all qualify for God's blessings. Moreover, many Israelites mistakenly looked on God's gift of righteousness as a reward for their scrupulous observance of the law, and so disqualified themselves from salvation by faith.

What do these abstruse theological inquiries have to do with us? For one thing, they remind us that, although we may speculate about the general outlines of God's providence, we have to be very cautious about speaking of the "rejection" of salvation on the part of any individual or group. Salvation in Christ is offered to every human being of every race and nation. God wants all of us to share the holiness of Christ and God doesn't play favorites. Salvation involves the mysteries of individual human freedom and nobody but God can sort out degrees of responsibility and blame for any apparent "rejection" of salvation.

The same thing does not apply in the other direction. We cannot determine why some people do not have faith, but we can say why some do. If people have faith and so share in God's gift of justification, it is not because of their own personally acquired virtue, but because of what God has done for them.

This passage and the reflections that follow it in chapters 9 and 10 of Romans teach us that we have to be very respectful about our attitudes toward God's initiatives and the way they are addressed to other people and to ourselves. God's gifts and their intent are far beyond our capacities of comprehension and interpretation. We are not able to understand everything that God does or everything that God intends. We can try to understand, of course, as part of an effort to appreciate God's goodness in our individual regard. But final truths and final explanations belong to God alone.

FOR DISCUSSION AND REFLECTION

To what extent have I ever tried to gain salvation by my own good works?

How do the gifts and privileges granted to the Israelites contribute to my salvation?

Nineteenth Sunday in Ordinary Time (B)

Ephesians 4:30-5.2

The author continues to offer directions for Christian behavior that are based on the fundamental theme that he has been treating throughout Ephesians, that is, the unity of the body of Christ which is the Church.

In this Sunday's reading he calls on his readers not to sadden the Holy Spirit who is the bond of unity in the body (see 4:3 and following) and who had given them the godly identity they would carry into eternity. They were to give special attention to avoiding sins of speech and the sinful mind-set that underlies these sins. Instead of all that sort of divisive conduct they were to practice thoughtfulness and understanding toward one another. They were to forgive as God had forgiven them. In doing that, they will be expressing their family resemblance in Christ and will be loving as Christ loved, even though that love cost him his life in sacrifice.

Sins of speech in a church context did not go out of fashion in the first century. Our culture does not approve of big displays of irate passion, and raising our voice in public is considered bad form. Yet there are plenty of ways in which we injure one another and the community we share through what we say. Little remarks that raise questions about somebody else's sincerity, ungenerous interpretations of another's motives, a barbed comment whispered to the person next to us: all these work against the oneness that Christ meant us to share in our togetherness with him.

Sometimes not speaking can be as destructive as what we say. A word of encouragement left unsaid, a helpful question left unasked, a kind greeting left unoffered: that, too, can undermine the vigor of Christ's body.

More important than these specific actions or omissions, however, are the basic moral attitudes that we find at the end of our passage: love and forgiveness. These are fundamental characteristics of Christian life and underlie practically everything else that our faith calls for from us. It's important for us to understand them.

Loving means wanting or willing or doing good for the person that we love. Loving can involve moonlight and roses, but it can also involve kindness and care offered to somebody of whom we are not particularly fond. Love is an act of the will, deciding and wanting something good for somebody else. It doesn't necessarily involve affection. That's why Jesus can tell us to love our enemies. He's asking us to do good to them even if they want and do no good for us, even if our emotions find them repulsive.

Forgiveness is a subdivision of love. It means loving in spite of the evil that another may have done to me. Forgiving does not involve pretending that no evil has been done or that the harm we have suffered really didn't hurt us. It does not require us simply to forget what has happened as if it never was. No, forgiveness allows us to be quite explicit and quite realistic about the harm we may have suffered, but it calls us to want and do good to the person who inflicted the harm in spite of what the person has done.

Our Catholic Christian faith calls us to love and forgive, and the reason it calls us to love and forgive is because of who and what we are. We have been remade to share the life and the likeness of Christ. As a result of our faith and our baptism, Christ now lives in us and enables and invites us to express his life through our own life. Our behavior as believers is a matter of consistency, of acting in accord with the life of Christ within us. We are not called to act as if Christ were in us. We are called to act in certain ways because Christ is in us.

Christ's life in us does not guarantee that these basic Christian virtues of loving and forgiving will be easy or without unpleasant consequences. Christ, the prime lover and principal forgiver, ended up on the cross! Yet his death there was an expression of consistency, of carrying out the logical conclusions of who he was and what he had come to do. As a result the Father saw his death "as a sacrificial offering" that had "a fragrant aroma." In the same way, our struggles to live out the life of Christ in love and forgiveness can seem to push our capabilities to their limit, but the struggle to remain faithful constitutes a pleasing sacrifice to God.

Just as the whole of God's saving work can be summed up in the notion of divine filiation, in our being remade to share the life of Christ as his adopted brothers and sisters (see Ephesians 1:3-6), so the whole of Christian morality can be summed up in the concept of imitation and consistency. What does God want from us? He wants us to act in accord with what he has made us to be.

What our live letter tells us this Sunday is relatively simple: in accord with the life of Christ that you share, respect and foster the unity of Christ's body by loving and forgiving as Christ does.

FOR DISCUSSION AND REFLECTION

Have I ever harmed the Christian community by my speech (or my silence)?

Have I ever witnessed people sacrificing themselves for the good of the Christian community?

Nineteenth Sunday in Ordinary Time (C)

Hebrews 11:1-2, 8-19

This Sunday begins a short series of four readings from the last part of the Letter to the Hebrews. We had an extended selection from this book of the New Testament in Ordinary Time of Year B. Hebrews is a discourse of encouragement addressed to Jewish Christians who were seemingly wavering in their dedication to Christ and were homesick for Jewish religious observances.

In the early parts of the letter from which we read last year, the author writes of the superiority of Christ over the angels and over Moses. He describes the superiority of Jesus' priesthood, his sacrifice, his ministry in the heavenly tabernacle. In chapter 10, the author begins to draw his conclusions, inviting his readers to have trust in Jesus and not to draw back from their commitment to him. After all, he says (in 10:39), we are "among those who have faith and will possess life." The rest of the letter concerns itself with examples of faith from the past and with the implications of faith for the present and the future.

The reading for this Sunday is from chapter 11. This chapter is a long review of how faith affected the lives of men and women throughout the history of God's people of the former covenant ("the ancients"). Over and over again we hear the phrases "by faith," "in faith," "because of faith." This account reaches from Abel through the age of the patriarchs and of Moses all the way to the time of the Maccabees. The long reading assigned for this Sunday, however, includes only the statement of the theme at the beginning of the chapter and the material about Abraham.

First we have a description of faith. It includes the conviction that the future will be as God has promised and a sense of assurance that things that may not be present and visible nonetheless can be real. (Thus described, faith involves loyalty, endurance, hope, confidence and well-founded expectation. Of course faith is not a purely human achievement. It is also a gift from God.) It is their faith that makes "the ancients" worthy of our admiration.

The reading now turns to the story of Abraham and the role of faith in his relationship with God. First of all, faith gave him the courage to leave his homeland for a land that God would give him but whose identity he did not know. He lived as an outsider as he looked forward to the future dwelling that he was sure God would build for him.

God also promised to make him a father, even though both he and his wife were beyond the age for becoming parents. He trusted in God's promise and became the father of numerous descendants. All this from a man who was "as good as dead."

Neither Abraham nor his descendants lived to enjoy all that God had promised. But they continued to have faith as they looked forward to the homeland that God had invited them to await. It wasn't an earthly one. If an earthly homeland was what they wanted, they could have gone back to where they came from! No, they were really seeking a heavenly homeland. And God was proud of them for their trust in him.

Abraham's faith led him to agree to sacrifice Isaac, the son who was so wondrously born to parents beyond the age of having children and who was to be the link with Abraham's descendants. Abraham's trust in God led him to be convinced that God could bring Isaac back from the dead if that's what was necessary to fulfill the promises he had made. Isaac's escape from death served as a symbol of something more that was still to come: Christ's escape from death many centuries later.

The author of Hebrews offers his readers the example of Abraham's faith to assure them that their faith will enable them to respond to the demands of Christian life. Abraham had to face living as a stranger in foreign lands, even though he had been promised a new homeland of his own. He had to take God's word that he would father a son when such a thing was simply unthinkable, humanly speaking. Then he had to be willing to sacrifice that son as a testimony to his confidence in God's word. His faith enabled him to respond to all this. Our faith will enable us to respond to what God asks of us.

Abraham's faith is of importance to us because we, too, are a people of promises. The promises that God has made to us, the gifts he offers us are different from what he promised and offered to Abraham. But what he spoke of to Abraham was symbolic of what he offers to us in the context of our life in Christ. Instead of an earthly homeland he promises us a heavenly one. Instead of belonging to a numerous earthly people we belong to a community of saints without number for whom earthly constraints of space and time are irrelevant, saints who enter life in a way different from the ways of human generation. Instead of testing us by asking us to give up what is most dear to us, God offers us a share in the life of him who has already been sacrificed and raised from the dead. We are called to be strong in our conviction that God means what he says and that what is promised to us is for real.

FOR DISCUSSION AND REFLECTION

What sacrifices have God's promises demanded of me?
Who are models of faith for me? Why?

Twentieth Sunday in Ordinary Time (A)

Romans 11:13-15, 29-32

Paul has been trying to account for the seeming rejection of salvation on the part of most Israelites. Last Sunday we saw how, in chapters 9 and 10, he explains their persistence in rejection: many were not really Israelites at all, in the deepest and most spiritual sense, and many misused the law in a way that made it impossible for them to accept salvation.

In chapter 11, Paul is more positive. Just as not all the Jews rejected Christ, so also widespread Jewish rejection of Christ would prove to be only temporary. A better situation lay in store for them in the future.

Our Sunday reading is an abridgement of a much longer and more complex argumentation that runs throughout chapter 11. As the lectionary presents the text to us, it is an essay in contrasts.

Paul begins with the contrast between gentiles and Jews. He has been sent to bring salvation to the gentiles and is grateful for his vocation. But that ministry is also partially directed toward the Jews ("my race"). The abundance of gifts given to the gentiles may serve to make some of the Jews "jealous" (that is, may elicit a spirit of competition), and so lead them to salvation.

If reconciliation has been made available to "the world" (that is, the gentiles) because of the Jews' rejection of it, what blessings will flow from their ultimate acceptance of it? Nothing less than a restoration of true life for them!

Now comes the sentence on which the whole of Paul's argumentation rests: God has not revoked his gifts to the Jews. He still calls them to be his people.

More contrasts follow. The Jews' rejection of Christ made room for salvation to be given to the gentiles, and the gentiles' former state of disobedience to God elicited God's mercy for them. Similarly, in view of the mercy shown the gentiles, the Jews' present disobedience may elicit God's mercy for them, too. Mercy is God's response to disobedience, and since God allowed both gentiles and Jews to be disobedient, he will have mercy on them all.

This is a rather complex passage and, if it is to be understandable, we have to be very clear about the antitheses that Paul is drawing: you/they; rejection/acceptance; disobedience/ mercy. And all this has to be viewed in the light of God's mercy and God's irrevocable gifts and calling addressed to gentiles and Jews alike.

We saw Paul in last Sunday's second reading trying to explain why individual Jewish people might have missed out on salvation. In our present reading he is painting with a wider brush, not about the personal failings of individuals, but about God's plans for whole groups, Jews and gentiles alike. In the final analysis, God plans to be merciful to us all.

It is important for us to realize that none of us stands alone before God. Our relationship with the Lord obviously involves our behavior as individuals and we will be judged on the personal decisions that we have made. But that's only part of the reality. There is also the social or communitarian dimension of our vocation to salvation and grace. The life of each one of us is influenced by the lives of those around us. Our attitude toward other human beings, our expectations of life, the quality of our commitment to God: all these are affected by the people with whom we come into contact from birth to death. We learn from them, we are changed by them, we are moved by them. Likewise, the people around us are influenced by us, some in ways that we can perceive and acknowledge, some in ways that we are totally unaware of—for better or for worse. We all live in an interactive context of others.

But there is also the context of God. The presence and providence of God are as much a part of our daily existence as are the presence and action of others on us and of us on them. We are free to try to maintain an awareness of God's involvement or to try to forget about it. It makes more sense to try to be conscious of God's involvement with us because it's more realistic! But God is there, whether we choose to notice or not.

God doesn't protect us from every hurt any more than a human parent preserves children from every knee-scrape. God doesn't arrange our life so that it's an unending series of pleasant experiences, any more than human parents provide limitless ice-cream cones. Sometimes we find God's plans for us to be deficient because we and God work on different levels. We want immediate satisfaction and full comprehension of what's going on. But God's plans are plans of kindness and mercy, whether or not we understand and appreciate them.

In this part of his letter Paul reminds the Romans that God looks out for his people, individually and collectively. God offers kindness and mercy to us all, Jews and gentiles alike. God has plans for us all. And the bottom line to God's plans is salvation and grace and eternal life for all who will accept them.

FOR DISCUSSION AND REFLECTION

How has God's providence for others influenced my salvation?
How has the history of my salvation influenced others?

Twentieth Sunday in Ordinary Time (B)

Ephesians 5:12-20

In this reading the author of Ephesians continues to set forth the general principles of Christian moral life. Next Sunday we will find him writing about more specific matters.

Our reading this week begins by reminding the readers that the times in which they live are fraught with evil. For that reason they should live cautiously, take advantage of the opportunities for good that God offers them, and exert whatever effort it takes to become wise in the ways of the Lord. If they want exhilaration in their lives, it should come not from wine but from spiritual enthusiasm in the Holy Spirit expressed in words and music that come from their inmost selves. This Spirit will inspire them to be in touch with the Father through Christ offering thanks "always and for everything."

Two main points in this reading seem to call for comments. The first is that the demands of Christian moral living are not always clear and obvious. We have to work at figuring out what they are, not because God wants to play hide and seek with us, but because the world in which we live has its own agenda to put before us, an agenda that is often much more simple and plain and appealing than God's agenda. Fornication, for example, is often far more attractive than a lifetime of faithfulness in marriage. Making lots of money for ourselves seems to make a lot more sense than looking out for poor people.

If we are not attentive to what God asks of us, if we don't exert some degree of effort to know God's will and carry it out, we can easily end up following the world's agenda to our own ultimate destruction. "Watch carefully how you live," the text tells us.

One of the gifts we receive from God's Church is detailed moral direction. For centuries wise and holy people have been reflecting on the meaning of our humanity, of salvation, of human actions and the fruit of that reflection is the science of moral theology. We don't have to figure everything out for ourselves every time. We simply have to be willing to take advantage of the opportunity for direction that the Church offers us. When the Church teaches us about sin and virtue (for example, in the *Catechism of the Catholic Church*) it is not so much giving out rules for us to follow as it is teaching us the implications of our being children of God, remade in the image of Christ. It doesn't make much sense to overlook this kind of guidance. It seems much better to live "not as foolish persons but as wise.... Do not continue in ignorance."

The other main point that seems to call for emphasis in our reading is the author's encouragement to the readers to give thanks, "always and for everything."

At the very beginning of our reading of Ephesians (on the Fifteenth Sunday in Ordinary Time) we saw that thanksgiving plays a regular part in the Pauline letters, and we heard the author of this letter offering thanks and praise to God for his saving plan on our behalf. Here he tells his readers that thanksgiving has to be part of the basic fabric of their relationship with the triune God, "always and for everything."

Why give thanks for everything? Because everything, to the extent that it is God's work, has goodness in it somewhere. We may not always be able to see where the blessings lie, but God is wise and powerful enough to confer blessings in ways that are beyond our comprehension. Giving thanks for things we don't understand is simply a way of expressing our faith in the fundamental goodness and power of the God.

Of course, there are the things we do understand: the beauty of a sunset or a flower, the love of family and friends, a deeply stirring piece of music. For them, too, we owe God our thanks, because whatever is attractive or appealing in them is somehow a reflection of God's own glory and majesty. We are called to be grateful to God for all the good that surrounds us, because, in the final analysis, it's all God's doing.

The same reasons apply for giving thanks "always." There is

never a time at which God is not reaching out to us with his goodness, never a time in which we are not being blessed by him. From morning to night, "Thanks be to God" should be part of our Christian stream of consciousness. We give thanks "always" because there is "always" something to be thankful for.

This posture of continuous and universal thanksgiving is not just a nice religious practice for pious people. It is also a way to develop and express a wholesome and explicit personal relationship with the Lord, a way to assimilate ever more deeply the life of Christ that is in us. And it's also a good way to prepare for eternal life, because, when we have reached the fullness of the kingdom, our main agenda item as saints of God will be to give thanks, "always and for everything."

FOR DISCUSSION AND REFLECTION

How do I train myself to make moral decisions?
What part does gratitude play in my life?

Twentieth Sunday in Ordinary Time (C)

Hebrews 12:1-4

Chapter 11 of Hebrews was a kind of historical overview of the heroes of faith, a commendation of the men and women who shared the conviction that the future would be as God had promised and that things not present and visible were nonetheless real. At the end of the chapter, the author points out that, although these people deserve respect for their faith, they didn't personally receive what God had promised. That wouldn't come for them until the gifts provided for us Christian believers had been made available.

Now, in chapter 12, the author deals with some of the

implications of faith and Christian commitment for us. He begins with an image. He imagines this great throng of holy women and men from the past no longer as giving testimony to us of their faith, but watching us as we develop ours. They are like a crowd in a stadium watching athletes run a race. We are those athletes and the race we are in is not a sprint but a long distance run. The author encourages us to get rid of anything that might encumber us in our run ("every burden and sin that clings to us") and to commit ourselves to the course that lies ahead of us. We are not to keep our eyes on the spectators, but on Jesus, who has shown us the way of faith and who has worked out all its implications.

Now he reflects on how Jesus did this. For the sake of heavenly life, he suffered the pains of the cross, without regard for the shame that it entailed. As a result, he has now entered into eternal heavenly glory with his Father. ("Seated at the right of the throne of God" seems to be another allusion to Psalm 110, which has already been cited so often in Hebrews.) Jesus' acceptance of effort and suffering in his earthly mission should be an encouragement for us to persevere in our struggles. After all, the author says, we may be engaged in a struggle against sin, but we have not yet been asked to shed our blood as Jesus did.

This short passage gives us some important teachings about faith. Faith is not a once-and-for-all thing, like a credit card that offers us unlimited use once we have received it. On the contrary, faith is a relationship and relationships require attention if they are to persist.

In addition to that, our faith relationship with God is under constant threat. First and foremost, it is threatened by our own sinfulness, the inclination to selfishness that persists even after we have accepted faith in Christ. But our faith is also threatened by the world around us. In many ways, our world is just as pagan as was the world of the first readers of Hebrews. We are constantly bombarded with distraction, with sounds and sights that keep our attention focused away from the good things that God offers us. Our culture offers us false goals (wealth, amusement, comfort) and, through various kind of narcotics, liberation from all pain and discomfort. It encourages us to look for immediate satisfaction of every need and every want, and to discount any possible benefit that could come through suffering. In the face of all that, it's not easy to keep our eyes trained on Jesus and to keep running in a race that most of the people around us consider a waste of effort.

There is more than one way to get out of the race that faith involves us in. One is simply and deliberately to give up our faith. "I don't really think that God cares about me. There's no longer any point in continuing a struggle that I no longer believe in." Another way of getting out of the race is to ease up slowly until we are no longer running. We can spend more and more attention on the demands that our world makes of us and less and less on the demands of Jesus. We can become erratic in our participation in the community of faith. We can deliberately begin to question whether all this religious stuff in our life makes any sense. And before we know it, we're no longer running. We're sitting down on the track, or even walking away from the course entirely.

This passage of Hebrews calls us to look after our faith, to take care of it just as we take care of our bodily health, just as we take care of our personal relationships with the people we love. Looking after our faith involves a conscious personal relationship with the Lord Jesus, an awareness of his participation in our lives. It involves daily prayer, deliberately turning our attention to Jesus in praise and thanksgiving. It involves regular attendance at Sunday Mass. Sunday Mass is not just one more obligation for believers. It's the source of meaning and energy that keeps us going for the rest of the week. Taking care of our faith also involves nourishing our faith with personal reflection, with contact with sacred Scripture, with other kinds of spiritual reading. In addition to all that, looking after our faith also demands extending the love of Christ to those around us.

This live letter reading uses verb phrases like "persevere," "keep our eyes fixed," "endure," "not grow weary," "struggle," "resist." There's more to faith, of course, than all of that, but without all of that, our faith is not likely to survive.

FOR DISCUSSION AND REFLECTION

How do I cultivate my faith?

What elements of the world are most dangerous to my faith?

Twenty-first Sunday in Ordinary Time (A)

Romans 11:33-36

The verses from Romans assigned for this Sunday's readings follow immediately on last Sunday's. They constitute the conclusion not only of the chapters (9-11) in which Paul has been speaking of the future of Israel, but of the whole section of the letter that has been dealing with salvation (1:16-11:36). These verses are, if possible, even more intense and rhapsodic than those we heard three weeks ago when Paul was concluding his general teaching on salvation (8:35-39).

This highly charged passage is composed of exclamations and questions, followed by a theological declaration and a final acclamation. It is a classic of reverence, wonder and awe.

The wealth, and the understanding, and the intelligence of God are without limit, Paul says. They are deep beyond measure. There is no bottom to their amplitude. God's processes of thought and planning are beyond the examination and grasp of anyone beside himself.

To express himself still better, Paul quotes two passages from Scripture (Isaiah 40:13 and, in paraphrase, Job 41:3). Who has ever been able to give God advice? Who has ever been able to force God's generosity by being generous to him first?

Now comes a one-line theological statement that gives the basis not only for the present hymn of glory and praise, but for whatever else Paul has said so far in Romans. Everything that is (including, presumably, the universal plan of salvation), comes from God, is sustained by God, is directed toward God. God is source, agent and goal of creation, salvation and final fulfillment for everything and everyone that exists.

"To him be glory forever. And I really mean it (that is, Amen)!"

Perhaps the best way to address this glorious passage of Paul is to reflect a bit about glory and about glorifying God.

"The glory of God," or "the glory of Christ" is mentioned in every book of the New Testament (except for the letters of John and the letter to Philemon). We speak of God's glory as the goal toward which our human life is supposed to be directed: "All for the honor and glory of God."

"Glory be to God" is an important phrase in Christian spirituality and worship, a significant expression in our relationship with God. On big feast days we sing, "Glory to God in the highest." One of the most commonly used Christian prayers is the Gloria Patri: "Glory to the Father and to the Son and to the Holy Spirit," used to conclude just about every psalm and canticle in the Liturgy of the Hours. At every celebration of the Mass we conclude the Eucharistic Prayer offering through, with, and in Christ "all honor and glory" forever to the Father.

What is the relationship between God's glory and giving glory to God? The dictionary defines glory as "great beauty and splendor," and as the quality of being distinguished or resplendent. God's glory, then, is his quality of being God expressed in terms of visibility. It is divinity expressed in categories of sight, or, better, in categories beyond sight. After Moses had encountered God on the mountaintop his face was so bright that the Israelites couldn't look at him. He had been touched by the glory of God.

When we speak of giving glory to God in our worship or in

our actions, we do not mean that we are giving God something new that he doesn't already have. "Glory be to God" is rather our attempt to acknowledge the greatness and splendor of God, to recognize God's inexpressible godliness, to speak out as explicitly as we are able the greatness and majesty of God. "Glory be to God" means "I/we know you are God, that you are good and gracious and beautiful, and that everything we can say about you falls short of your reality."

Giving glory to God is closely linked to praising God. Praise is the acknowledgment of excellence. When we applaud at a concert we are expressing praise for the expertise of the musicians. In our human relationships, we are sometimes stingy with praise, in part because people who are praised are sometimes reluctant to have their excellence recognized, in part because we are not always sure that others deserve our praise or because we are afraid that praising others might diminish ourselves. Obviously, offering praise to God is always appropriate because God's worth and excellence surpass all limits and can never be adequately acknowledged by mere creatures.

Closely allied to praise is thanksgiving. If we acknowledge the goodness and generosity of God, we are necessarily acknowledging that God has been good and generous to us. There is no aspect of our being (except the sinfulness in which we may willingly engage ourselves) that is not appropriate subject matter for thanksgiving. If everything is God's gift, then we need to be thankful for everything!

Glorifying, praising and thanking God are important things for Christian believers to be engaged in, not only because they are always appropriate here and now but because they will be our principal occupation for all eternity in heaven. Glory to God forever!

FOR DISCUSSION AND REFLECTION

In what way have I experienced God's glory in my life?

What roles do glory, praise and thanksgiving play in my personal spirituality?

Twenty-first Sunday in Ordinary Time (B)

Ephesians 5:21-32

This selection brings us to the end of the semi-continuous reading of Ephesians that the Church offers us this year. It deals with themes that we have seen before in this live letter: the Church and Christian behavior. But these verses also offer us some counter-cultural material that we have to be careful to understand properly.

In this passage the author is setting up a parallel between relationships in marriage and the relationship between Christ and his Church. Since Christian marriage is supposed to mirror the way Christ relates to the Church, we'll begin our reading of the passage by pointing out what it says about the Church and its Lord.

Christ is the head of the Church. But Christ's headship is not a matter of domination over the Church, but of love. He gave up his life to make the Church holy and clean and beautiful, totally without defect. The members of the Church become members of the one Body of Christ, even as God, at the beginning, provided that man and wife should constitute "one flesh." The relationship of Christ to the Church is "a great mystery," one of those carefully planned, breathtakingly rich ways in which God expresses and carries out his love for us.

Now we can examine what our passage has to say about human relationships in the light of Christ's relationship with the Church. The first principle that the author gives is that everybody in the Church is to be subordinate to the others because of the presence of Christ in the members of the community ("out of reverence for Christ"). Then he gets more specific. Wives are to be subordinate to their husbands as the Church is subordinate to Christ and husbands are to love their wives as Christ loves the Church, because it is his own body.

There are lots of surprises in this reading, lots of things to wonder about, perhaps even some things that we find hard to accept. This may be the reason why the Church gives us a shorter (and less troubling) version for use ad libitum. I believe it's better to use the longer and more challenging version. After all, the fact that some parts of sacred Scripture are hard for us to understand or accept does not mean that they are any less inspired or any less God's word than the parts we happen to find comforting. All Scripture is addressed to us all.

First of all, then, there is the matter of subordination. We are all to be "subordinate to one another out of reverence for Christ," the text says. We twenty-first century Americans don't like to be subordinate to anybody. We are free men and women, each standing on our own feet. Subjection is not something that sits well in our culture. But the context here is not about domination or "being the boss," but about Christ's love for the members of his Church. Just as Christ gave himself up for our well-being, so, because of our relationship with him, we are called to give ourselves up for the well-being of our brothers and sisters in the Lord. We are called to love one another, and love means putting ourselves second for the sake of the good of the other. Love involves subordination, and the refusal to put ourselves second out of love for the other constitutes selfishness.

Then comes the paragraph about wives being subordinate to their husbands. This kind of talk doesn't sit well with our culture, either. Over the centuries women have suffered all kinds of oppression and abuse because of the male domination that was (and often still is) current, and they don't want any more of it. That's understandable. But we mustn't allow ourselves to forget that the author is not talking about subjection and servitude, but about love, about the gift of the wife's self in response to the husband's love just as all believers give themselves to Christ in response to his love.

Then comes what, in fact, might have constituted the most counter-cultural demand of all: "Husbands, love your wives, even as Christ loved the Church." In a time when women were looked on as property, when men were the undisputed lords of every aspect of their family's life, a directive like this must have been deeply troubling to this letter's first readers. Yet it is consistent with the parallel the author has discovered between husband and wife and Christ and the Church.

What the text has to say about the relationship of Christ and the Church has a counter-cultural dimension, too. What Old Testament believer, familiar with God's relationship with his chosen people, could have imagined God giving his life away to make sinners holy and entering into a warm, familial relationship with human beings, making himself one with them? Yet that's exactly what God did in Christ. As we become increasingly familiar with the living word of God in Scripture, we have to be careful to maintain an appropriate perspective. The important thing is not how that which God says fits with our world and our way of seeing things, but rather how our world and our culture and our experience fit with God's word and God's will.

FOR DISCUSSION AND REFLECTION

How do Christian marriages that I am familiar with mirror the relationship of Christ and his Church?

In what ways am I subordinate to others?

Twenty-first Sunday in Ordinary Time (C)

Hebrews 12:5-7, 11-13

Last Sunday's reading spoke about the need for perseverance in our faith, for continued attention to our relationship with God, for constant regard for our conviction that God is faithful and that the realities that we might not see with our earthly eyes really do exist.

This Sunday's reading deals with another aspect of our life of faith: being willing to be trained by God even though the training demands struggle, effort and even pain.

The author starts off by telling his readers that, if they are finding the demands of faith too heavy to bear, it's because they have forgotten a fundamental lesson. Then he cites the Book of Proverbs (3:11 and following), which calls those who would be wise to welcome the fatherly, though sometimes stern, intervention of God. Though painful, such interventions are important elements in the education of God's sons and daughters. These interventions are also a sign that their recipients are legitimate children of the household, officially recognized by the father. If they weren't legitimate offspring, the father wouldn't bother to try to educate them.

The author goes on to acknowledge that, while the training God offers us may be hard to take, it results in a sense of well-being in those who accept it and increases their maturity and virtue.

Finally, the author offers two more scriptural citations to make his point. The first is from a passage in Isaiah (35:3) in which the prophet is encouraging his hearers to strengthen themselves for the return trip from exile. The second is again from Proverbs (4:26), where the author is talking about walking the road to wisdom. If you walk carefully on that road, Hebrews says, your aches and pains will go away.

The word that the author of Hebrews uses to express God's educational intervention on our behalf is *discipline* (*paideia* in Greek). It occurs no less than five times in the six verses of our reading, plus another three times in verses 8-10. There's no doubt what this passage is about. *Discipline* (and its Greek equivalent) signifies learning and knowledge, education and training and instruction, but also correction and punishment. It suggests that growing up, acquiring knowledge and skill, is not an easy undertaking. It requires effort, struggle, even suffering, sometimes inherent in the matters we are concerned with, sometimes administered from outside as part of the methodology of a teacher. We may not go in much any more for the kind of corporal punishment mentioned in verse 6, but every good teacher knows that he or she has to make serious demands on students if they are going to learn what is being taught. (Which of us does not remember with gratitude somebody in our lives who helped us learn by making us exert more effort than we thought appropriate at the time?)

The author doesn't describe in detail the sufferings and annoyances his readers had to endure as part of their faith. Last week's reading told us that they hadn't yet had to face martyrdom. Maybe they were being inconvenienced by little discourtesies from their pagan neighbors, by feeling like outsiders to the culture in which they lived. Maybe internal tensions in the community of faith were causing them annoyance. It could also be that their longing for their former religious practices was a source of suffering. Perhaps they didn't see in themselves the immediate results that they expected from belonging to the Church, or feel the consolations they had experienced before. In any case, the author's lesson is clear: Christian faith is not a matter of going with the flow, of simply pursuing whatever turns you on, of engaging in a comforting spiritual hobby. Christian faith is something that has to be rooted in the innermost parts of our being. It's something that changes just about everything in our lives. Granted, it's something that we get all at once, at baptism, but it's also something whose assimilation requires attention and effort from us for the rest of our lives. Christian faith is a relationship that we have to work at. Being a believer is a skill that we have to learn, and all learning that is worth the name requires attention and effort. God never promised anybody that loving him and being in touch with him would be easy.

It's not that God sets out to make faith hard for us, by making us endure discipline for its own sake. It's rather that the lessons that God wants us to learn in the context of faith tend to be harder than we might have expected at first.

There's one more aspect to all this. All of us are always children in relationship with God. We might like to think that we have been practicing faith for a long time now, that we have reached a plateau of maturity, that there isn't much more we need to experience or learn. But no matter where we are in our faith life, God still has more to offer us, still more to teach us. We are always in need of his discipline.

In today's live letter we hear these early Christians being told: "Pay attention to the teacher! You need to learn how to shape up and walk straight." That's a message that we all need to hear once in a while.

FOR DISCUSSION AND REFLECTION

What aspects of my faith life require the most effort from me?

How have past suffering and effort strengthened my faith?

Twenty-second Sunday in Ordinary Time (A)

Romans 12:1-2

This Sunday's reading brings us to the last main section of Romans (12:1-15:13). As is so often the case in the Pauline letters, this final section of Romans is devoted to ethical exhortation, to directives for practical living. Since Paul was not personally acquainted with the members of the Church at Rome, the exhortation section in Romans is rather generic. Paul gives general directives for all moral life rather than responding to specific questions or problems (as he does, for example, in First Thessalonians).

These chapters deal with Christians' relationship with one another (12:3-13), with relationships with those outside the community of faith (12:14-13:14) and, finally, with the principles that should govern Christians' response to Jewish dietary laws (14:1-15:13), an issue that seems to have called for resolution in many of the early local churches.

The two verses that constitute this Sunday's reading serve as a general introduction to the whole section.

As the text has been edited for the lectionary, a very important word has been left out at the beginning: "Therefore." This word not only serves as the stylistic connective with what has immediately preceded, but also has a theological function. What Paul has said about salvation and faith and God's plans for Jews and gentiles has some practical consequences. These consequences are what Paul now presents to his readers.

Because of God's gift of salvation, because of the nature of faith, because of the replacement of the Jewish ritual law by new life in Christ (all of which are manifestations of God's mercy), God looks for a new kind of sacrifice and a new kind of worship from the faithful. Paul calls on the Romans to make a sacrifice of themselves, to offer God no longer the animal sacrifices of the Old Law, but the gift of their very own persons. Because of the gifts of salvation that the faithful have received, such an offering of themselves is "spiritual worship," "holy and pleasing to God."

Next come some comments on their relationship with the world around them, and with themselves. They have to be different from the world, and they have to work on making themselves ever more in accord with the life of Christ that has constituted them in a new kind of life. Through ongoing spiritual growth they will become ever more in tune with God's plans for them, that is, with that which is "good and pleasing and perfect."

There are at least two important principles for Christian living in these verses.

First of all, Christian life does not consist in the mere performance of certain actions, in the external observance of a set of rules and regulations. Clearly there are standards of behavior for Christian believers, some things that are right and some things that are wrong, and we have to follow these moral directives whether we like them or not, whether we understand them or not. But all that is only the beginning. The real heart of Christian morality, the real pragmatic response to the salvation we have received consists in a conscious and deliberate response to what God has made us to be. The basic, underlying principle of Christian behavior is to live out the life of Christ in the circumstances in which we find ourselves. That makes us pleasing to God because that constitutes consistency with the gifts God has given us.

The second important principle that is implicit in this Sunday's live letter is that living a Christian life is not a once-and-for-all thing. It is not a set of behaviors that we acquire and then use more or less automatically, as we might learn and use a language. It's not just a habit that determines the specifics of our existence. Christian life includes an ongoing relationship with the world around us and an ongoing relationship with God, and relationships involve development and growth.

People relate to the world around them in one way in childhood, in another way in adolescence, and in still another way in maturity. We relate to the world differently at different times because we ourselves are different. We grow in wisdom and experience. We acquire resources of various kinds. As our understanding of our world grows, our capacity to influence it grows and the way we relate to it changes—or should change.

Similarly, we grow in faith. As the years pass, if we are attentive enough, we learn more and more about the Lord, we experience the life of Christ in us in different ways, we become more at home with the presence of God in our lives, we begin to see the world around us more and more from the perspective of Christ. Our spirituality matures. We become different.

We are all called to transformation. We are all invited to an ongoing renewal of our spirit. It's a transformation and a renewal that requires effort and attention, but it's an essential part of the Christian vocation we have received.

FOR DISCUSSION AND REFLECTION

To what extent is the quest for transformation part of my life?
What criteria do I use to discern the will of God?

Twenty-second Sunday in Ordinary Time (B)
James 1:17f, 21b-22, 27

This Sunday's reading begins a series of five readings from the Letter of James. We don't know who the author of this book is, whether it was one of the two apostles named James, or "James, the brother of Jesus," or someone who saw himself as a disciple of one of these and wrote in his name. This short letter is addressed to "the twelve tribes in the dispersion," but we don't know whether that means that its intended readers were Jewish Christians only or all Christians scattered throughout the known world. The letter does not deal with one general theological theme, like Ephesians, nor about specific and detailed community problems like the letters to the Corinthians. It is rather a kind of general exhortation to virtuous living that deals with themes like wealth and generosity and appropriate speech and temptation.

Our series of readings begins with some verses from chapter 1 which is a list of more or less unconnected sayings that offer a foundation for Christian morality.

The author reminds us that we have been enlightened by the creator of light itself, the source of all goodness, who is totally unchangeable and completely reliable. This enlightenment from God consists in a new birth, in truth that transforms us into the "firstfruits of his creatures," that is, belonging to God in a special way. Next he points out that what God has given us (faith) brings us salvation if we receive it with humble thanksgiving and carry out its practical implications. Faith without practice is self-delusion. Finally the reading tells us what constitutes the practice God wants from us. It's not just a matter of going to church and saying prayers. It also demands looking out "for orphans and widows in their affliction" (caring for those in need), as well as a willingness to be carefully detached from the world around us.

There is some important teaching in these three disconnected pieces from the first chapter of James. First of all, they teach us about faith. Faith is a gift, a kind of new birth, a "word of truth" that comes to us from the initiative of the Creator. Faith gives stability and equilibrium to our lives because it is the gift of one who himself is stable and unchangeable. James does not go into much theological detail about the nature of faith, and we need to read other authors of the New Testament to learn that faith is a participation in the life of the risen Christ. But James does tell us that faith makes us pleasing to God ("firstfruits"), and that it involves more than what we tend to think of as "being religious." Faith involves more than the acceptance of God's gift to us. It involves carrying out in practice the implications of the gift.

There are two extremes that we have to avoid when we think about faith and good works. The first is to look on faith as something we earn or deserve. "If we are good enough and try hard enough, then God will be pleased with us and our efforts will make us pleasing in his sight. He will owe us salvation." The other extreme is to emphasize the gratuity of faith and grace, the fact that it comes to us by the free gift of God, to the point that we overlook its demands. "Once we have been gifted by God, no more effort is required. We can just sit back and wait for him to welcome us into the kingdom at the end of our lives." The truth is that, while our behavior as Christian believers is important, it's secondary to God's initiative. And while God's initiative is important, it requires our acceptance and our response, expressed in a way of life that can sometimes demand self-sacrifice and suffering.

The examples of "religion that is pure and undefiled" at the end of our reading are important teaching for us, too. James gives us two examples of what God expects from us.

The first example is caring for "widows and orphans." In the world of the New Testament (and the Old Testament, as well), widows and orphans were unimportant people *par excellence*. Being without family, they were vulnerable, without resources, without protection, without influence, without power. They were people who could easily be disregarded, but precisely for that reason they were people for whom God calls for special care from those who claimed to serve him. They may not have been important to other people, but they were important to God. We take better care of widows and orphans in our society, but there are still other "unimportant" people whose need gives them a claim to our attention.

The second example of pure and undefiled religion that our reading gives us is keeping oneself "unstained by the world." It's easy to see how a Christian would want to keep his or her distance from the world of the first century. Paganism reigned supreme. Cruelty and injustice were everywhere. Greed was the order of the day. Obviously one couldn't just opt out of the world, but one could take pains not to be besmirched by it. One is inclined to wonder how different the situation is for the Christian believer of today.

FOR DISCUSSION AND REFLECTION

Who are the "unimportant" people that demand our attention?
What steps do I take to stay "unstained by the world"?

Twenty-second Sunday in Ordinary Time (C)

Hebrews 12:18-19, 22-24a

In these recent Sunday readings from Hebrews the author has held up for his readers the example of heroes of faith from long ago. Then he spoke of the need for perseverance and for a willingness on our part to accept the efforts and suffering that faith entails. He used the image of athletes in a race and called on this group of Christian believers to be strong and to remain on the right track.

In this Sunday's reading he tells them where that track has been leading them. He contrasts the assembling place of the old covenant with that of the new.

For the reception of the old covenant, the people gathered on an earthly mountain, Mount Sinai. There God manifested himself in lightning and clouds, in tempests and the sound of heavenly trumpets. The author is alluding to the accounts of the giving of the law that are found in Exodus 19:16 and following, and in Deuteronomy 4:11 and following. The people were so awestricken by the sound of God's voice that they thought they were going to die. For that reason the people asked Moses to serve as their intermediary. He should speak to them instead of God (see Exodus 20:18 and following).

In contrast to all that is the assembly of the new covenant. Here the gathering is not on an earthly mountain, but a heavenly one, Mount Zion, the heavenly Jerusalem. This is not a stage on a journey for a wandering people, as Mount Sinai was, but a city, founded with permanence in mind. In this city, the people of faith join numberless throngs of angels in joyful celebration and praise of God. "The assembly of the firstborn" is there, too. This probably signifies those persons of faith that we heard about earlier and who have a special place in God's affection. "The spirits of the just made perfect" are those who have undergone judgment by God and who have now entered into a final stage of fulfillment. There is Jesus, too, whose ministry brought this new covenant into being, and the blood whose outpouring constituted our salvation. This blood, continuously presented to the Father in heaven for the sake of forgiveness, is more eloquent than the blood of Abel shed on earth and calling for vengeance.

This passage is a kind of summary of the whole Letter to the Hebrews. Recall that the occasion for this letter was the nostalgia for the former covenant that these converted Jews were experiencing. In our passage, the author points out that, while the old covenant was initiated on an earthly mountain, the new covenant is fulfilled in heaven. The old covenant involved dread and fear, while the new is an invitation to a festal assembly composed of angels and saints. The old covenant evoked such fear that the people begged not to have to listen to God's voice. The new covenant involves immediate contact with the God who saves us. The new is better in every way!

Notice that, in this passage, we hear again some themes that were developed in the earlier chapters of the letter: angels (no longer superiors as mediators of the law, but fellow citizens of heaven), the new covenant (definitive, redemptive), the sacrifice of Christ (once and for all, eternal).

This summary passage invites us to hope. Christian faith is not a matter of gloom and doom, of a pettifogging God anxious to catch us out in our faults. It's not a matter of rules and regulations and burdens, all bathed in perennial threats of punishment. Christian faith is a matter of being loved and welcomed by God rather than of fear and trembling.

That's not to say that our faith invites us to an ongoing state of mindless euphoria, as if there were no possibility of failure, no need for effort. In fact, immediately after this Sunday's passage, Hebrews warns its readers not to be inattentive to God, since God expects to be listened to. Yet even here the author adds that what God offers us is the possibility of unshaken assurance of final success, which calls us to serve him with gratitude.

I suspect that we all know Christian believers who seem to find great comfort in negativity. The world is in terrible shape! The Church is full of sinners! People don't believe any more!

People don't seem to know what's right and, even if they do, they don't carry out what they know is God's will! We're going to have a hard time when the day of judgment comes! There is some truth in all that, of course, but these are only secondary things. The primary reality of our faith, and of the new covenant, is that Jesus died on the cross to bring us salvation and that salvation will come to all those who are willing to receive it. Believers with a healthy faith are necessarily joyful and optimistic. Christ is already victorious over death!

Hebrews is an elegant and theologically sophisticated book of the New Testament, filled with scriptural learning, obviously the fruit of profound spiritual maturity. But the message it offers—to its first readers and to us—is quite simple: be faithful; be joyful; be grateful.

FOR DISCUSSION AND REFLECTION

How is my life oriented toward the heavenly Jerusalem?

How is my faith a source of joy for me and for others?

Twenty-third Sunday in Ordinary Time (A)

Romans 13:8-10

Prior to this section, Paul has been instructing the Roman Christians about their obligations to one another and about how they are to relate to civil authority. He has told them that they should obey civil authority because it comes from God, and that they should fulfill the obligations that are enjoined on them, not only taxes of various kinds but also appropriate respect and honor. They should stay fully paid up in all that is required of them.

At the beginning of this Sunday's reading he summarizes

what he has just said and then gives them a general principle that applies to the observance of all law.

They shouldn't owe anybody anything, Paul tells them. But, if there is to be something that is owed, that something is love. Loving constitutes the complete observance of all law. (There is an implication here that we can never be fully and finally "paid up" in loving. There is always something or someone more to love, so it's all right to "owe" in this context.)

The fundamental law, he tells them, is the law of love. Basic human concerns like familial relationships, the sanctity of life, and the security of property (and everything else besides) will be taken care of if we love our neighbor. Laws and commandments of whatever kind are merely specifications in greater detail of the command to love. (Note that in this context, "neighbor" does not mean a fellow Christian or even a fellow countryman. The term embraces all human beings. One wonders if Paul was thinking here of Jesus' parable of the "good Samaritan" [Luke 10:29-37], whose point is precisely that the claim for neighborly behavior is constituted by human need rather than by religious or political relationships.)

In the concluding verse of our reading, Paul says it once more in a slightly different way: love excludes harming the neighbor and excluding harm to the neighbor is the purpose of law. Consequently, loving our neighbor accomplishes the purpose for which laws exist, and therefore loving constitutes the fullness of all our legal obligations.

The obligation of love for our neighbor is an important element in Paul's teaching because it is an important element in the teaching of Jesus (see, for example, Matthew 22:34-40). If we are to grasp the full import of the teaching, we have to be clear about what love is. In the context of this universal moral precept, love means wanting and doing what is beneficial for the other person, willing and doing good for our neighbor (that is, for everyone). Love is not a matter of the heart, but of the will. Whether or not we feel affection for the person we love is secondary. What's important is what we want for the neighbor, not how we feel about the neighbor.

The reason why love constitutes the observance of all law is that all law is supposed to be aimed toward the common good, toward the well-being of those for whom the law is made. This is obviously true of basic law like the Ten Commandments, given to us by God in order to help us to live in accord with what God made us to be. But it is also true of all other just laws, even the most trite and ordinary ones. If you don't stop at a red light, somebody is going to get hurt. If you don't pay your taxes, certain needs of the country will not be attended to and the country's citizenry will suffer. All law has good for its purpose, and loving means wanting and bringing about good for the other.

To look on law as a specification for loving doesn't make observing the law easier. In fact, trying to respond to the purposes for which laws are provided (by God, Church or civil society) can be much more demanding than merely observing the letter of what is asked of us. Making our whole life an exercise in wanting and doing good for ourselves and for those around us necessarily excludes formalism (just going through the motions), minimalism (doing as little as possible while still complying) and legalism (careful calculation of technical demands so that we don't go beyond what the law intends and demands).

Loving also plays an important part in determining how we relate to the women and men around us. Wanting and doing good for the other is not something we owe just to those who are near and dear to us. It's something we owe to everybody: to relatives and friends, to strangers and foreigners, to political colleagues and political opponents, to the Nobel Prize laureate and the criminal on death row. We are called to love them all, to want and to do good for them all not because of what they have done for us but because of what God wants us to do for them.

We are bound by all kinds of laws from many different sources. Some are of absolutely fundamental importance, while others don't seem to amount to very much at all. Yet, if they are just laws, they call for our response. And the response owed by the Christian believer is the response of loving, of wanting and doing good for all those whom law is intended to benefit.

FOR DISCUSSION AND REFLECTION

Why/how do I observe laws?

Whom do I love and why?

Twenty-third Sunday in Ordinary Time (B)

James 2:1-5

The members of the early Church were not generally important people. They were not rich or influential members of society. They were members of the poorer classes, even slaves. And when there was contact with people of greater economic substance, the contact was not without danger. The danger consisted in dividing up the Church.

In this Sunday's reading, James warns against giving in to personal consideration of the rich, then shows one of the forms such discrimination takes and then gives reasons for the warning.

If you are committed to faith in Jesus, he says, if you are an adherent of the Messiah who died and rose from the dead, you cannot act as if some people are more important than others. Then he presents a little drama by way of example: here comes Mr. Goldring in his dazzling outfit and, at the same time, a nobody in rags. You make a fuss over the well-dressed person and find him a seat up front, but shove the poor man off to the side somewhere. What's going on here? You are dividing up the community, making judgments about the worth of people, and bad judgments at that. Why is it wrong to favor the rich? Because God favors the poor. He enriches them with faith here and now and promises them eternal happiness in the reign of God that still lies ahead.

Who is really important? What constitutes importance? Those are the issues here. Jesus made it quite clear that, in his eyes, it is the poor who are important. At the very beginning of his public ministry he proclaims, "Blessed are the poor in spirit, for theirs is the kingdom of heaven" (Matthew 5:3; see also Luke 6:20). Already in the Old Testament those without material possessions, the poor, had a special place in God's care (see Isaiah 61:1; Zephaniah 2:3). Jesus adds "in spirit" to indicate that blessedness was not simply a matter of one's bank balance. It required some religious orientation even among the materially poor. Similarly, even those of a more exalted social rank could qualify for the blessedness Jesus promised if their spirit was touched with poorness. But poorness there has to be. That's what qualifies people for blessedness. That's what makes them important.

Why are the poor blessed? Because the poor are acquainted with one of the most basic and important prerequisites of religious faith: a sense of dependence. The economically poor are those who have no resources of their own, who have to rely on somebody else's generosity in order to survive. The spiritually poor are those who recognize their complete dependence on God. The economically poor have the advantage over the economically rich, because they are already equipped with an awareness of their need. But that awareness has to be there. Otherwise the generosity of God won't mean much to us.

The trouble with being rich is that wealth brings security. We are not much threatened by the world around us if we have a nice safe home and plenty to eat and drink. We are inclined to believe that we can get along quite nicely on our own resources and that we don't need anything beyond what we have. We are comfortable, and we plan to stay that way.

But this attitude can easily lead us astray from the Lord. If we don't think we need what God offers us, if we wave off God's offer of life in Christ, or even if we make it a low priority in our lives, we are cutting ourselves off from what really matters in our lives, from what will provide us with eternal importance long after property and bank accounts have faded away.

True importance can only come from God, from sharing in his life, from expressing his generosity and faithfulness in our lives here and now. True importance means letting God be God in us and being willing to value everything as secondary to his love and attention to us. And in order to do that, we have to acknowledge our dependence, our poorness.

This is why making judgments between people, valuing some as more important than others, really doesn't make much sense. In God's sight we are all poor, all needy, all dependent. None of us has anything to rely on except the Lord. The gold ring on the finger and the expensive suit are of minuscule importance compared with God's offer of love, life and eternal glory. When it comes to being important, we are all equal. And we are all important to the extent that we are poor.

I'm not sure that the little drama that James describes in this reading is played out very often in the contemporary church. For one thing, people don't seem to dress up much to come to church on Sunday any more, so it's harder to tell who is rich and who is poor! But the issues that this reading raises are of ongoing significance for us all. It's important for us to be aware of our radical equality. It's important for us to know wherein our importance lies.

FOR DISCUSSION AND REFLECTION

Whom do I consider important? Why?

Am I poor? How? How poor?

Twenty-third Sunday in Ordinary Time (C)

Philemon 9-10, 12-17

The letter to Philemon reflects a complicated and touchy situation in Paul's life. Onesimus, a slave, had run away from his master Philemon, a Christian of Colossae. He may have stolen some money from his master in the process. Somehow Onesimus has attached himself to Paul (who is now in prison) and has become a Christian. Paul is sending him back to his master in Colossae. Onesimus had every right to be apprehensive, because a slave owner was permitted to inflict any punishment he wished on a runaway slave. The purpose of this brief letter from Paul is to get Philemon to treat Onesimus kindly. (It is probable that this letter was sent to Philemon at Colossae at the same time that the much larger Letter to the Colossians was sent.)

Just before the verses selected for this Sunday's reading, Paul had told Philemon that he (Paul) had every right as an apostle to give orders to Philemon about what to do with Onesimus. Instead of that, he says at the beginning of our reading, that he prefers to plead with him, to appeal to his kindness in view of Paul's old age and his situation in prison, and in view of the relationship that has now grown up between Paul and Onesimus. Paul looks on Onesimus as his own son in the faith. Sending Onesimus back is like sending his own heart.

Paul says that he had thought about keeping Onesimus with himself. He might have been of assistance to Paul in his imprisonment, perhaps to take care of Paul's personal needs, perhaps becoming involved in some aspect of ministry. He could have been a sort of representative of Philemon. But Paul decided not to do that because he didn't want to do anything that Philemon might not want. (There was also the fact that harboring a fugitive slave was strictly against the law.)

So now Paul invites Philemon to put the best possible face on what Onesimus had done. Maybe it was all part of God's providence to make Onesimus precious to Philemon in a new way, even as he was now dear to Paul.

At the end of our reading comes the punch line: "If I am of any significance to you," Paul says, "welcome back Onesimus as you would welcome me."

The Letter to Philemon is more than a historical curiosity, more than a personal appeal between acquaintances. It is a practical application of a fundamental and repeated teaching of Paul's: among those who share the life of Christ there is neither Greek nor Jew, neither slave nor free. Philemon would hear these words when the Letter to the Colossians was read out in the liturgical assembly. Paul had told the same thing to the Corinthians and the Galatians. What did that mean in practice? It meant that Philemon was expected to treat Onesimus, who, legally speaking, was property and a lawbreaker, as a brother. He was to receive him kindly and forgive him whatever harm he might have suffered from him. Paul doesn't go into detail about how Philemon was to do this. He didn't tell him to set Onesimus free or to send him back to Paul to help him in prison. Philemon is merely to welcome him as he would welcome Paul. The particulars are up to him.

There is one more detail that is important. This letter is not just addressed to Philemon and his wife. It's also addressed to "the church at your house." This wasn't something that Philemon was to deal with in the privacy of his office. It was to be read out to the whole liturgical assembly, just as the more official Letter to the Colossians would be. The reason for this semi-public status of Paul's letter to Philemon was not just to put a little more pressure on him to comply. It was also to teach the members of the Colossian church that the way they treated each other, treated even the least deserving, was a matter of concern for the whole community.

Each of us could probably make our own list of people who have treated us badly and people we don't particularly want to be nice to. The list might include a difficult spouse, an unfair employer, an irritating colleague. There are some people who get on our nerves just by being around. There are thoughtless people who rub us the wrong way without even realizing it. There may be people in our lives who have done us deep, long-lasting harm. There are others that we don't like because they are different, because they don't act or talk or live like we do, because they don't really "belong." And in all these contexts, there is the teaching of Paul, that, compared with our togetherness in Christ, everything else that might divide us, however understandable the division might be in human terms, is really irrelevant and doesn't deserve our attention.

In this briefest of the Pauline letters, God's word speaks to Philemon and to us. "Love your neighbor," it says. "Here is your neighbor, not particularly virtuous, not particularly attractive, not particularly loveable. How are you going to react?"

FOR DISCUSSION AND REFLECTION

What kinds of people do I find it hard to respect?

To whom do I owe forgiveness? From whom should I ask forgiveness?

Twenty-fourth Sunday in Ordinary Time (A)

Romans 14:7-9

In the last major section of Romans, Paul treats the question of the observance of the ritual Jewish law by Christians. It is not clear whether Paul had learned from somewhere that there was tension in the Roman church over this matter, or whether it was such a widespread issue that he simply presumed that the Romans could benefit from some guidance on it from him. (His decision to include something about this question may be connected with the fact that the Corinthians had big problems over the matter of Jewish observance, and Paul was in Corinth when he composed his letter to the Romans.)

In the verses that immediately precede this Sunday's reading, Paul tells the Romans that the real issue is not whether one observes the Jewish law or not, but the reason for which one does what one does. It's all supposed to be for the service of the Lord, and one servant of the Lord should not easily judge another servant of the Lord. "Who are you to pass judgment on someone else's servant?" he asks in verse 4. If you observe special feast days, it should be for the Lord. If you abstain from certain foods or make it a point not to abstain from them, that should be for the Lord, too.

As our reading begins Paul moves away from the specific question of patience and toleration over the question of Jewish observance, and offers an absolutely fundamental principle about Christian life in general, a principle that applies to every aspect of our existence as believers.

"We are the Lord's." That has to be the central reality that governs every facet of our being. We are not masters of ourselves, directors of our own destiny. Whatever we do when we are alive is for the Lord, and whatever happens to us after we die is for the Lord. By his victory over death and his ongoing risen life, Jesus has demonstrated that he has authority over every aspect of created reality. There is nothing that is not subject to him. He is "Lord of both the dead and the living."

In the general context of this reading, Paul is offering us an important teaching for some of the tensions that are still with us in the community of faith today. The question of whether or not to observe Jewish ritual has long been settled, but we still have tensions between the scrupulous and the "enlightened," between conservatives and liberals. In chapters 14 and 15, Paul tells the Romans to be careful not to make too much of these distinctions. They need to be forbearing and tolerant and patient with one another. Not everything has to be settled immediately once and for all. Differences of practice and differences of opinion have to be seen in the proper perspective.

Obviously there are non-negotiables in the Christian faith.

Not everything is up for grabs. But, by that same token, not everything is essential and it is not a betrayal of the faith to be tolerant of others whose opinions on some matters are different from our own. The essential thing is that we acknowledge that we are all subject to the Lord, and that the Lord to whom we are subject is the one Savior, Christ Jesus.

The lordship of Christ Jesus is central to our individual lives, too. It is that lordship which gives worth and significance to each of us. It is our relationship with Christ who has died and risen from the dead that gives direction to our life and meaning to our death. Without that relationship, we are in a state of separation from God and of ultimate isolation from our fellow human beings. Through faith and baptism, we are sharers in the life and history of Jesus, in his ministry, his death, his risen life. Everything worthwhile about us is relative to that. Nothing else about us is as important as that.

The lordship of Christ, then, is the central element of Christian spirituality. Our common allegiance to him is what gives cohesion to the community of faith. It is the focal point that provides the perspective from which we can best deal with one another, from which we can best come to terms with the nature of the Church. The lordship of Christ is also the center around which our personal existence has to be structured. The fact that we are the Lord's provides direction and consistency to the choices we are called to make each day. The fact that we are the Lord's in both life and death means that our personal history is not limited to a few years here on earth, but has a dimension that has the same permanent significance as the risen life of Christ.

From this point in Romans, Paul goes on the say some more about the Jewish ritual question. Then he shares his missionary plans with the Romans, including his intent to visit them on his way to Spain. He brings the letter to an end with greetings to individuals and a closing prayer of praise.

Romans is long and complicated. Its subject matter, the nature of salvation, is profound and of immense theological significance. Yet one might contend that the whole letter is summed up in the phrase we hear in this Sunday's reading: "We are the Lord's." That's what salvation is all about.

FOR DISCUSSION AND REFLECTION

What does it mean to me that other people are "the Lord's"?

What does it mean to me to be "the Lord's"?

Twenty-fourth Sunday in Ordinary Time (B)

James 2:14-18

The relationship between faith and good works has been an issue in the Church more than once. It was one of the main questions at the time of the Protestant revolt in the sixteenth century. It was the principal item of contention when Saint Augustine opposed the Pelagians in the fifth century. There are those who say that the New Testament itself gives evidence of differences of approach to faith and works in apostolic times. They cite, for example, Ephesians 2:8-9 ("By grace you have been saved through faith, and this is not from you; it is the gift of God; it is not from works, so no one may boast.") against James 2:20-24, which concludes, "a person is justified by works and not by faith alone."

This Sunday's reading is the classic exposition of one side of this question, but it also gives us the wherewithal to see how the issue is to be dealt with.

The author is quite clear about where he stands. Right from the beginning he says that faith without works is no good to anybody. It cannot save. Then we have another little drama in which the person of faith closes his heart to the person in need. What good is that kind of faith? If faith doesn't result in good works, it's lifeless and of no worth to the one who has it. Nor does it make any sense, the author says, to claim that faith and good works are divisible, and that some people have faith while others have works. The person without good works has no means to demonstrate his faith. It's as good as non-existent. The person with good works, on the other hand, shows the existence of his faith by the works it produces.

It is not clear whether the author of James is trying to correct a Pauline teaching that had been taken out of context and misrepresented, as some scholars think. It is clear that both Paul and James held that there is no such thing as self-redemption. But in dealing with redemption, they emphasize different aspects and use terms in different ways. In the final analysis they both say more or less the same thing, and in the process offer us precious teaching.

For Paul and his followers, "good works" meant works of the Jewish law, things like circumcision and the observance of dietary restrictions. For James, "good works" meant works of mercy, things like taking care of the poor man we hear about in our reading.

When James talks about faith, he means the intellectual acceptance of certain truths. Just after the conclusion of our reading, he will speak about the demons who also "believe" the truth of God's oneness, and adds that such belief, of itself, merely causes them to tremble. When Paul and his school talk about faith, they mean full commitment of one's person to the Lord, the full gift of ourselves to God. Later theological development will call the first kind of faith *fides quae* (content faith) and the second kind *fides qua* (commitment faith). Obviously both kinds of faith have to be part of our relationship with God. It doesn't make much sense just to commit ourselves to God if we don't have any clear concepts about who and what God is and what God has done, nor does it make sense to give conceptual assent to everything the Church teaches if that assent is not accompanied by real personal dedication to Father, Son and Holy Spirit.

Given these distinctions, it's easier to understand the relationship between faith and good works. First of all, works of the Jewish law have been superseded by the redemptive life and death of Christ, and so they are no longer either required or efficacious for salvation. What is required is commitment to God and the acceptance of his gratuitous offer of salvation in Christ. Works of mercy, however, are natural consequences or outcomes of our dedication to God. If we love God, we will necessarily love our neighbor. If there are no works of love for our neighbor in us, it is clear that there is also no living faith. Believing the truth of what God has revealed is important, but it is only one aspect of the faith that God offers us. "Content faith" is necessary but not sufficient. In fact, it can be a lifeless ornament in our relationship with God if it does not result in works of love for our neighbor.

Good works are not the cause of God's life in us (that is, justification/salvation). But God's life in us is the cause of good works. As James says later in chapter 2 (verse 22) when he is talking about the faith of Abraham, "Faith was active along with his works and faith was completed by the works."

All this is not just a matter of theological distinctions. It is a matter of knowing what's real and important in our relationship with God. We need to have faith (both content faith and commitment faith). That faith is not earned or caused by our good works, but, if it is real, should result in works of love and mercy. There is no such thing as real faith without good works. There are no real good works that are unconnected with faith. Faith activates the works. Works complete the faith.

FOR DISCUSSION AND REFLECTION

What kind of faith do I have?

What is the source and purpose of my good works?

Twenty-fourth Sunday in Ordinary Time (C)

I Timothy 1:12-17

The First Letter to Timothy, that we begin to read from today, together with The Second Letter to Timothy and The Letter to Titus, are known as the "pastoral letters." They are addressed to individual church leaders and are concerned with the problems and challenges faced by these leaders as the first generations of Christian believers gave way to later ones. While all three pastoral letters are attributed to the authorship of the apostle Paul, Scripture scholars tend to think that they are not Paul's work in the same way Romans and Galatians are his. Given their subject matter, which seems to reflect a more developed Church, it seems more likely that these letters were written when Paul was already dead. They are presented as his work, as addressed to his helpers, by a later author as if to say that this is what Paul would have written to his friends if he were still with us and still writing letters today. Of course, the fact that these letters might be the work of somebody other than Paul does not mean that they are any less inspired, any less the word of God.

As First Timothy begins, we find the author reminding his audience that Christian faith involves moral behavior. There are certain kinds of conduct that are simply incompatible with being a follower of Jesus. Proclaiming this is an important part of ministry.

Now, as our Sunday reading begins, the author has something to say about ministry as well as about the meaning of salvation. Ministry comes through selection and appointment by Christ. It's a gift that Christ's mercy offers to those he has chosen. The author, "Paul," points out that he is a minister because he has been "mercifully treated" by God. Previously he had been a persecutor of the Church, though out of ignorance. He was a conspicuous sinner whom Christ chose as an example of mercy for others who would come to believe. He has been gifted by Christ with divine favor, with gifts of faith and love from Christ.

Now comes the central point that the author wishes to make in this section. He highlights it with a solemn introduction. We can almost hear him raising his voice as he dictates the words: "Christ Jesus came into the world to save sinners." "I know that," he seems to say, "because I was a big time offender myself and I have been saved." This elicits from him a little hymn of thanksgiving: "Glory and honor forever to God, eternal, always alive, too great to be seen by human eyes."

I suspect that we don't give enough thought to the idea that Christ came into the world to save sinners. Most of us were "born Catholics." Faith and life in Christ and the acceptance of Christian morality have been part of our lives from the beginning. It's part of the atmosphere we breathe and we tend to take it for granted.

But faith and life in Christ and the acceptance of Christian morality are all gifts, and we need to acknowledge them as such. If we don't, if we take it all for granted, we run the risk of devaluing our salvation, of somehow thinking that that's just the way things are meant to be.

An appreciation of our salvation requires two convictions. The first is that we ourselves are sinners. We may not be blasphemers and persecutors of the Church as Paul was, but none of us can say that we are good enough to be able to demand God's favor. More basically, none of us can lay any claim whatsoever to a share in the life of God, which is what our salvation consists in. Thanks to our inherited human flaws and moral deficiencies, we are all detached from God, destined for self-destruction. In one way or another we are all sinners, and it's important for us to be aware of that.

The other reality that we have to be aware of is that God is merciful, that he cares about sinners, that he sent his own Son to be our savior, that the salvation Christ offers us is nothing less than participating in his divine life.

Sinner/salvation/Christ: those are three of the fundamental realities that constitute the basic context of our Christian existence. If we are not sinners, there's no need for salvation. If there's no need for salvation, there's no need for Christ. If there's no need for Christ, there's no need for us to be his followers, and we're OK off on our own. It all hangs together. If we're not sinners, there's no point in being saved. If we're not saved, we have no connection with Christ.

The message of Christ does not call us to a life of guilt and anxiety. It calls us to praise and thanksgiving, the kind we heard from the author of First Timothy at the end of our reading. But that praise and thanksgiving can only resound in our hearts if we are in touch with reality. The reality that we need to be conscious of is our own need for forgiveness and mercy and Christ's desire to transform us through the abundance of his love.

FOR DISCUSSION AND REFLECTION

What does "being saved" mean to me?

Is an awareness of being "mercifully treated" part of my personal spirituality?

Twenty-fifth Sunday in Ordinary Time (A)

Philippians 1:20c-24, 27a

This Sunday's reading begins a series of four selections from Paul's letter to the Philippians. This letter is a letter of joy, full of warmth and affection, reflecting the special fondness that Paul felt for the church he had founded at Philippi, the first Christian community in Europe.

Paul is writing to the Philippians from prison, perhaps during his three-year stay at Ephesus (see Acts 19:23-41). The Philippians had been consistently generous to Paul, helping out in his times of need. Now he writes them this letter to bring them up to date about what is happening to him and to encourage them to faithfulness.

Paul leads up to our Sunday reading by telling the Philippians that his imprisonment is not without its blessings. The gospel continues to be preached, both in the prison and outside it. Some of the preachers seem to announce the gospel out of a sense of rivalry with Paul, but that's not particularly important as long as the gospel is being proclaimed.

In our reading, Paul reflects on this situation. He is confident that God will be glorified by his ministry and life ("in my body") whatever happens to him ("whether by life or by death"). Either eventuality has something to be said for it, because both involve Christ. If he lives on in this world it will be a life of fruitful labor for Christ's gospel. If he leaves this world, he enters a new life with Christ. He is not sure which alternative he would choose if the choice were his. He is inclined to want to leave the present life because being with Christ would be better than life here. At the same time, he knows that remaining alive here would bring blessing to the Philippians (and, presumably, to others as well).

The last sentence of the reading encourages the Philippians to live consistently with their faith. This sentence alludes to the direction in which Paul's continued efforts would lead them, but also serves as a bridge to the instructions for the community which come next in the letter.

This reading offers us an interesting insight into Paul's personal attitudes toward his life and ministry, toward his attitudes about death, toward the people he addressed in his ministry, toward his relationship with Christ Jesus. Paul sees his existence as abounding in blessing, as a menu of options each of which is attractive for one reason or another. What we have here is the portrait of a confident and happy man, smiling in his imprisonment, cheerful even at the prospect of death, secure that his existence is directed toward happiness whatever its next elements might be.

But all this is not particular to this individual person in these unique circumstances. What Paul expresses in these verses proclaims the basic realities of every Christian life.

As believers we know that Christ lives and works in each one of us and that Christ will continue to live and work in us as long as we are willing to have him, even for all eternity. For us, as for Paul, "life is Christ." Christ is the component that makes our existence worthwhile, whether here or hereafter. And the Christ that confers worth on us is not a Christ that we have to earn or deserve, but a Christ who gives himself to us freely, on his own initiative. And it is a gift that he will never take away from us.

But that's not all. Our life here and now is not just a waiting period, a portion of time that we have to endure before the real action begins. Our life here and now is important because it is a context in which the love of God for his human creatures is extended and unfolded through the agency of women and men like us. God has chosen to operate through human instrumentality. This means that human activity has a dimension of divine providence to it. Each one of us has a part to play in Christ's project of salvation, a part that plays itself out in our relationship with our family and friends, with all those whose lives touch ours. It plays itself out in our work, in the Christian service we are able to offer the community of the faithful. Even when we are weak and suffering, even when it seems that we are really no good to anybody, the Lord is still able to exercise his loving care for the world through us. Christ is at work in every aspect of our life.

Committed Christians look toward the end of their life with confidence because they know that "death is gain." But committed Christians also know that "life is Christ," even the daily existence that we tend to undervalue because we have grown so accustomed to it.

This passage of Philippians is an invitation to us to be conscious of the value of our lives, both here and hereafter. Because of the dimension of Christ in us none of us is unimportant to the Lord. None of us is a throwaway creature. In this live letter, God calls us to appreciation and gratitude.

Where do I see Christ working in the circumstances of my life?

For what reasons might I prefer life to death or death to life?

Twenty-fifth Sunday in Ordinary Time (B)

James 3:16-4:3

The New Testament offers a mixed picture of the early Church. It seems that sometimes everything was peace and joy, as in the early days after Jesus' Ascension into heaven when the apostles and others "devoted themselves with one accord to prayer" (Acts 1:14) or, after the coming of the Holy Spirit, when the believers "devoted themselves to the teaching of the apostles and to the communal life, to the breaking of the bread and to the prayers" (Acts 2:42).

But there was also the self-serving of Ananias and Sapphira (see Acts 5:1-10). There were the factions in Corinth (see I Corinthians 17-22) and the frictions arising from false teachers (see I Timothy 6:5). Sacred Scripture teaches us that there was plenty of unrest in the early Church. Maybe God's word intends to keep us aware that the internal problems of the Church today are not unique to our times.

This Sunday's passage from James speaks of the sources of both tranquility and turmoil in a Christian community. The author has been speaking about the need for control of the tongue, especially on the part of those who exercise a teaching function in the Church. As our passage begins, he has shifted to more general considerations.

First of all he points out that upheavals in the Church have their origin in self-seeking. Then he deals with wisdom, the wisdom that cultivates peace and that results in holiness. (Note that peace in most scriptural contexts does not mean the absence of war, but the harmony that arises, through God's gift, from everything working together for the good of all.) This peace-bringing wisdom is straightforward, not tinged with duplicity. Through kindness, patience, forgiveness it contributes to the well-being and tranquility of the community. Unrest in the community has a different source, namely, the self-seeking he had mentioned before ("your passions that make war within your members"). This is a habit of mind that desires to possess at the expense of another what it does not have. It cuts down other people and begrudges them what they have. It pits members of the Church against one another and divides the community into warring factions. This self-seeking vitiates the prayer of the one afflicted by it, either because it keeps him or her from praying at all, or because it leads to the kind of self-centered prayer that God cannot answer.

This passage teaches us that sharing faith in Jesus is not enough to guarantee peace and harmony in the Christian community. That faith has to be expressed in ways that build up the body of the Church. Destructive behaviors have to be eliminated.

The contrast that James outlines between "wisdom" and "passions" is the contrast between generosity and selfishness. Generosity looks out first of all for the well being of the other. It wants and does what is good for the other (and is, thus, a synonym for loving). It encourages people to come together in thought and action without consideration for its own needs.

Selfishness, on the other hand, puts me first. It wants what it wants, even if that means taking it away from another. Self-seeking is divisive and conflictual by definition. Taking second place and letting others have the advantage is totally foreign to the selfish heart.

Of course "generosity" and "selfishness" translate into generous and selfish individuals. Generous people are the answer to a pastor's prayer. They help the community work as one. They bring a sense of cooperation to the local community. They are artisans of peace and tranquility, real agents of the love of Christ for his Church. Selfish people, on the other hand, bring division, suspicion, strife. My ideas, my needs, my preferences: that's what really matters, and that's all that really matters. These are people who always need to be right, no matter what the question; whose personal preferences become law for the others to obey; who view attempts at reconciliation and understanding as a sell-out of the faith. Enough people like that can lead a community into a state of ongoing turmoil, of unrelenting conflict, whether the community be a parish, a diocese or even a whole country.

We have all had our generous moments, when we were able to extend ourselves for the good of others, when we contributed in some significant way to the righteousness and peace of the Church. We have also had our selfish episodes, when something seemed so important to us that our care and concern for others got lost in the struggle for it. After the struggle is over, whether we have won or lost, we find ourselves wondering how we could have gotten so passionate over so little.

This Sunday's live letter does not invite us to look around and try to categorize our fellow believers, but to look into our own hearts and ask whether the Church is more peaceful or more turbulent because we are members.

FOR DISCUSSION AND REFLECTION

Have I ever experienced the wisdom that brings peace?
Where do I see selfishness in my own life of faith?

Twenty-fifth Sunday in Ordinary Time (C)

I Timothy 2:1-8

There are two main subjects in First Timothy. One is to warn the addressee about the dangers of false teaching. The Sunday lectionary does not include any readings from this letter on that subject. The other principal subject is the ordering of public worship, how the liturgical life of the community is to be structured. This Sunday's reading is the beginning of the section of the letter that deals with that.

The author starts off by saying that prayers for public officials are a matter of prime importance for the Christian community. The text offers four different terms for prayer, but they probably all mean more or less the same thing. The reason why prayer for public officials is important is so that "we may lead a quiet and tranquil life," that is, so that the prayers of the Christian community might bring God's blessing of peace on the civic community, but also so that tensions between Church and state could be avoided.

The author gives three fundamental reasons for his insistence on community prayer for civic authorities. First of all, because the one God wants everybody to be saved and to come to the knowledge of the truth. God's benevolence embraces even pagan agents of government. Second, because the redemptive work of the one and only mediator between God and humanity, Christ Jesus, is also directed toward rulers of peoples. He offered himself for everybody, as he himself proclaimed during his earthly life. Finally, the whole ministry of Paul was dedicated to bringing God's gifts to the gentiles. Because they were the objects of his work, they are worthy of Christians' prayers. (Many scholars believe that, in verses 5 and 6, the author is quoting an early Christian creed.)

The final verse of our reading is really a link to the next section of the letter in which the author is going to talk about appropriate roles for men and for women in the community's liturgy. As it is presented here to us, however, the verse seems to suggest that concord and tranquility in the Church community are a necessary component for prayer to be made appropriately.

This is a passage about the oneness of God's saving will and of the redeeming action of Christ, both of which were fundamental to the ministry of Paul. Notice how often we hear the words *everyone* and *all*. "Pray for everybody in authority because God's love is directed to all of them."

One might also find in this reading another practical application of Paul's conviction that, in the context of Christ's mission, there is no longer Jew or Greek, slave or free (see Colossians 3:11; I Corinthians 12:13; Galatians 3:27 and following). Two weeks ago we saw how this teaching applied to the situation of Onesimus and Philemon. Here we see how it affects the Church's prayer life and its relationship to the wider world.

We owe concern to everybody because God is concerned about everybody. It's no longer just Jewish people who are important to God, but everyone. All human beings are precious to God because *all* have been redeemed by the one Christ, and so all human beings must be precious to us. We can exercise this concern we owe to others in many ways. One of the primary ways is public prayer. When we pray for people, even people with whom we do not enjoy close human relationships, we are not persuading God to be good to them. We are rather opening ourselves up to be agents of God's care for them. Inclusiveness in prayer helps those who pray to reflect more clearly the inclusiveness of God. It keeps them conscious of how wide their horizons need to be.

In addition to the concern that Christian believers owe to all other men and women, there is also the fact that by praying for "outsiders" we are enriching the context for the preaching of the gospel. Christians are more likely to reach out to others if they are regularly reminded in their prayer life that those others are beloved by God just as we are.

There is another facet of this Sunday's reading that calls for a word of comment. This reading from God's word makes it clear that it is not God's will that his Church withdraw from contact with the world around it. True, there is a demonic dimension to some aspects of the world. True, a time would come when the agents of government, those for whom First Timothy calls us to pray, would inflict heavy sufferings on the Church community. But, by and large, the Church is intended to be part of what is going on in the world. The people who rule us in civil government are our brothers and sisters in the Lord. As believers we have contributions to make to the well-being of our world, contributions that go beyond the prayer that this Sunday's reading calls for. Jesus did not come to save the world by taking his followers out of that world, but by encouraging them to take part in that world's life as his representatives. Christian believers need to be involved with the world because Jesus was—and is.

FOR DISCUSSION AND REFLECTION

How and when do I pray for persons in authority?

How do I see myself as united with all of humankind?

Twenty-sixth Sunday in Ordinary Time (A)

Philippians 2:1-11

At the end of last Sunday's reading, Paul began one of the two sections of Philippians dedicated to practical instruction in Christian life. In the first exhortative passage (1:27-2:17) he calls his beloved Philippians to steadfastness in the faith, to unity of heart and mind, and to cheerful dedication to the demands of the gospel.

This Sunday's reading gives us the section on unity.

Elsewhere in his letters (for example, Romans 14 and 15), Paul calls for patience and tolerance of various approaches to spirituality and religious observance, though always in the context of our common life in Christ. Here he is emphasizing the need for oneness of mind. He offers the saving self-gift of Jesus as the context on which this union of familial love should be founded.

Our passage begins with a series of motivating forces. If Christ's love and compassion and mercy inspire you in any way, if Christ's Spirit means anything to you, then make me happy by your oneness of mind, heart, love and spiritual orientation ("thinking one thing"). Your communion should not be a matter of each one looking out primarily for him or herself, but of each looking out for the well-being of others, each putting him or herself second, each regarding the others as more important.

Next there follows the main point that Paul wants to make: think and act toward one another the same way Christ thought and acted toward us all. To illustrate what he means, Paul now offers a long poetic passage, probably an early Christian hymn, which outlines what Christ did for us and the response of the Father. Christ gave up the glory that was due to him as God and became a human being, further humbling himself by accepting an ignominious death. In response, the Father conferred a unique glory upon him that involves the adoration of all creation and universal acknowledgment of his lordship. The confession of this lordship brings new and unlimited praise to the Father.

The justification of Paul's appeal to the Philippians, that is, the quote from the early Christian hymn, is well known to us. We hear it each year on Palm Sunday as the theological explanation of the passion and death of Jesus. It's probably among the best-known passages of the New Testament. But it is to the first part of the reading that the Church wants to draw our attention on this Sunday, that is, to Paul's appeal for fraternal love and generosity. This is the original context in which the hymn of Christ's passion is situated, the original point that Paul intended the quotation to illustrate. Moreover, it is this first part of the reading that is presented by the lectionary in the optional shorter version. Even if we don't read the whole reading, we at least have to pay attention to the first part.

Paul is really asking a lot of his readers in this passage. He's asking them to love one another and to be generous to one another not to the extent that they find it convenient or appealing, but to the extent that Christ was loving and generous to each of us. Christ's attitude is to be their attitude. Christ's mind is to be their mind. They are to be Christ for one another. Paul is telling the Philippians—and us—that our common life in Christ makes demands on us. It may also be that Paul means to teach them—and us—what the life of Christ makes possible for us.

One way to follow Paul's directive is to strive to reproduce in our life the behavior of Jesus, to make him the model on which we form our earthly existence, to examine the life and ministry of Jesus and to work into our own relationships as much of him as we can. "The imitation of Christ" is a fundamental part of Christian life, something to which we are all called, something to which the Church directs us over and over again.

But there is another way to respond to what Paul recommends to the Philippians. Having "the same attitude that is also in Christ Jesus" can mean more than just looking on Jesus as an exterior pattern on which to fashion our individual lives. It can mean acknowledging the presence and the life of the risen Christ in ourselves and striving not so much to make ourselves live "like Jesus" but rather striving to let Jesus live in and through us. Rather than having John Doe, Christian believer, reproducing and interpreting the life of Christ as best he can, we can have Christ continuing his life and ministry in the tonality and particularity of John Doe. One might suggest that what Jesus had in mind in his project of redemption was not to have a whole lot of followers each reflecting a little piece of him in their lives, but to have one life—his—expressed fully in each of his followers.

In whichever way we choose to interpret Paul's exhortation to the Philippians, it is clear that the Christian way of life makes significant demands on those who would be part of it and that it necessarily involves accepting and sharing the life of Christ. Nothing less than that will do.

FOR DISCUSSION AND REFLECTION

To what extent do I put the needs of others ahead of my own?
How is my life guided by the self-gift of Jesus?

Twenty-sixth Sunday in Ordinary Time (B)
James 5:1-6

Being rich is dangerous. This is a recurrent message both in the Old Testament and in the New. The prophet Amos (6:4-7) threatens early exile for those who were leading lives of luxury. Isaiah (5:8 and following) promises woe to those who are greedy for land. Similarly Jesus says (Luke 6:24), "Woe to you rich, for you have received your consolation." In this Sunday's reading James takes up this theme. (Given what we know about the socio-economic composition of the early Church, it is likely that James's readers would be the victims of the rich rather than the rich themselves. In the verse immediately following our passage, the author addresses himself to the "brothers" who are obviously different people than the rich who have just been rebuked.)

Our passage opens with an invitation to the rich to weep and wail over the chastisements that await them. First of all, their wealth will turn out to be of no use to them. It is already rotten and useless and the clothes and precious metals that were intended to serve as adornment will become an instrument of suffering for them. Their treasure will become their torment when the day of judgment comes. What makes their wealth worthy of condemnation is the way in which they have acquired and used it. They deprived their workers of their just wages (a crime that Deuteronomy [24:14 and following] says calls to heaven for vengeance). They have spent their wealth on lavish living, which only served to fatten them up for the day of slaughter. They have oppressed righteous and unresisting poor people to the point that life was no longer possible for them.

As we read about the sins and excesses of the rich that are alluded to in our passage, it is natural for us to feel a certain degree of indignation. What a terrible way to treat other people! How sad to misuse wealth in these ways! Woe to the rich, indeed.

By most standards, most of us are rich. Almost all of us have a comfortable and safe place to live. We have enough resources to guarantee regular and healthy nourishment. Most of us are employed in work that offers guaranteed wages and at least some further benefits like retirement and health insurance. We have means of transportation to take us effortlessly wherever we want to go. We have come to expect comforts like central heating in the winter and air conditioning in the summer. Most of the people who have ever lived on this earth over the centuries have not enjoyed the standards of living that we take for granted. Most of the people who live on this earth now do not live as well as we do. We are the rich.

Does that mean that we fall under the strictures that James levies against the rich people of his time? Not necessarily. Together with the comforts and opportunities that our standard of living brings, we have also learned that we have responsibilities. Most of us try to be generous in sharing our personal resources with those who are less well off than ourselves, needy people here in our country or elsewhere. We contribute to church collections, to civic drives like United Appeal, to special efforts to help alleviate the needs of those who have experienced disaster. We do this, not just out of a sense of pity for the misery of others, but because we are aware that we owe care and concern to others, because we know that what we have is mostly the result of God's generosity to us and must therefore be used for God's purposes. Being rich does not necessarily mean being selfish or sinful.

But our state of well-being is not necessarily permanent or universal. There exists even here in our prosperous country a whole level of persons who are unable to provide a decent living for themselves. The minimum wage, established by law as the norm to enable people to support themselves, is no longer pitched at an appropriate level. Being able and willing to work no longer guarantees people a share in our nation's wealth. One wonders how the cries of these people sound in the ears of the Lord of hosts.

In addition to that, the difference between the very wealthy and the rest of us seems to be widening. It seems that middle-class people (not to mention the poor) have to run faster and faster just to stay in the same place while others have more than they really know what to do with, more even than their counterparts in other wealthy nations.

We have some responsibilities for these matters, too. Because we live in a democracy, the rules and rewards of our life together are determined by all of us. We are all responsible for the kind of life and the level of well-being that is available to each of us. Solutions to complicated social and economic problems may not always be clear, but that doesn't mean that we can stop looking for them.

This reading is the last of the lectionary's semi-continuous presentation of the Letter of James. The basic teaching of this book of the New Testament is that a living Christian faith calls for practical Christian love. One without the other is not possible.

FOR DISCUSSION AND REFLECTION

In what way am I rich?

What use do I make of my riches?

Twenty-sixth Sunday in Ordinary Time (C)

I Timothy 6:11-16

In this last Sunday reading from First Timothy, the author is offering words of challenge to his disciple.

The passage begins with a list of virtues that the church leader should pursue, all of which serve to strengthen and invigorate the life of the ecclesial community. The next verse shifts into a military metaphor: fight for the faith, attack and seize eternal life. You were called to this eternal life when you made public profession of your faith. (This seems to refer to baptism.)

Now comes the central directive of this passage, cast in the language of a solemn charge: "Keep the commandment without stain or reproach." "Keep the commandment" means remaining faithful to what Christ asks of us in the context of our faith. (One translation, in view of the military metaphor, renders these words, "Obey your orders.") This faithfulness is called for as a condition of the eternal life promised by God and in imitation of Jesus' public faithfulness as he stood before Pilate. Eventually Christ will return (by implication, to reward the faithful). In the context of Christ's second coming, our text launches into a lyrical passage about the majesty of God. The time of this second coming will be determined by God, the universal king and Lord, who lives far beyond the limits of human life, human access, human vision, the all powerful who has the right to expect our reverence and respect. (These last lines of the reading may be a quotation from a liturgical hymn on the author's part.)

"Be faithful!" That's the directive that the author gives to this leader of a local church. It is offered in the context of struggle: fight, attack, seize. Since the basis on which this faithfulness is called for seems to be the baptismal commitment, it is not inappropriate to see the directive addressed also to us.

Faithfulness involves dedication and consistency, the dedication of our life to sharing and extending the life of Jesus, the consistency that expresses the life of Jesus loyally and persistently and coherently in every aspect of our individual human existence. This faithfulness isn't always easy.

For one thing, it isn't always clear in full detail what consistency and dedication to Christ call for in the concrete circumstances of our life. Yes, we are called by Christ to love our neighbor, but what does that mean when we don't know what is really good for this person I'm dealing with or how the love I offer is going to be received?

Sometimes faithfulness is demanding just because of what God asks of us in our extension of the life of Christ. Love your enemies. Do good to those who hate you. Be patient with those who mistreat you. Learn to restrain your inclinations to lust, avarice, self-pity. None of that is easy, yet it's what God requires of his faithful people.

Sometimes faithfulness to Christ is not welcomed in the world in which we find ourselves. Lifetime dedication to the marriage partner, sexual self-restraint, absolute respect for human life, justice for even the most despised members of society: these are all called for by our faithfulness to Christ, but they are not things that necessarily win respect from the men and women around us. For that matter, even the idea of being faithful to the directives of a God we cannot see, a God who demands obedience from us human beings, is not something that finds acceptance from everybody whose lives touch ours. Religion is not guaranteed to win popularity. Faithfulness can be difficult.

This is why our passage also offers us sources of courage. Courage implies firmness of mind and will in the face of difficulty. The author recalls for us the determination and resolution of Christ standing before Pilate. It reminds us that Christ will come again at the end of time to unite us once and for all with his Father, "the King of kings and Lord of lords," who is the source of unending life and inextinguishable light. In view of what Christ suffered, in view of the glory that lies ahead of us, the demands of faith are not insupportable.

Sometimes people seem to think that God asks too much of

them. God's law and God's expectations seem unrealistic. Does God really want us to live that way? Does God really demand sacrifices like that from us? Why isn't it easier? Everything worthwhile demands struggle. Nothing valuable comes without effort. If this is true of, say, graduate education or raising a family or being successful in business, we shouldn't be surprised if it's also true in the pursuit of unending happiness with God in heaven. Our consistent dedication to God is an important element in our lives, indeed, the most important element there is. If anything is worth struggling for, it is maintaining our contact with the Lord, our consistent dedication to responding to his call.

But God wants us to succeed. The Lord who gives the challenge also gives the courage. "To him be honor and eternal power. Amen."

FOR DISCUSSION AND REFLECTION

How does my life of faith require courage?

To whom/what do I look for strength?

Twenty-seventh Sunday in Ordinary Time (A)

Philippians 4:6-9

Last Sunday's reading was from the first exhortatory section of Philippians. This Sunday's is from the second, a few chapters later. Most of the time there is only one well-defined section of pastoral instruction in a Pauline letter. Consequently, some scholars think that these two separate sets of moral directions may originally have come from two different letters, which were later brought together by an editor into what we now know as Philippians. The immediate context of this Sunday's reading as it now stands is Paul's attempt to overcome some interpersonal tensions that existed between two members of the community, Euodia and Syntyche. He expands his suggestions beyond the concerns of these two people to a more general reflection, offering all his readers a formula for godliness and peace in their lives.

The reading consists of two paragraphs. In the first, Paul tells his readers what they have to do if they want the "peace of God" to flourish in their hearts and minds and offer them its protection. They have to ask God for whatever they need, but their requests should be directed to God in a context of thanksgiving for what they already have received and with a sense of trust, without panic or worry.

The second paragraph is about peace, also. If you want the God of peace to be in you, he tells them, you have to think and behave in a certain way. Your thinking should be focused on those virtues that make for healthy relationships between people, virtues like truth and fairness and single mindedness and kindness and thoughtfulness. Look out for the positive and virtuous aspects of the people around you rather than for what you can criticize.

As regards behavior, Paul tells them to keep doing what he had taught them to do and to keep imitating what they had seen him doing. (In 3:17 Paul had already told the Philippians to be imitators of him. He offers the same direction to the Corinthians [I Corinthians 11:1] and recalls with satisfaction how the Thessalonians had become his imitators [I Thessalonians 1:6]. What we have here is not a runaway ego but an awareness that authentic Christian life consists in what Paul had dedicated himself to: the ongoing expression of the life of Christ. Paul doesn't want his followers to imitate Paul. He wants them to imitate the Christ that lives in and through Paul.)

The peace that Paul promises to the Philippians in these paragraphs is not just the absence of conflict or interpersonal tension. It is a state of deep interior harmoniousness, an imperturbable condition in which every element of our existence works productively together, in which everything in us is and performs in accord with the highest goals that God has for us. Sometimes (for example, Ephesians 2:14-17 and Romans 5:1) the Pauline tradition speaks of Christ as peace and as the instrument of God's gift of peace to us. One wonders if that's what Paul had in mind here when he speaks of "the peace of God that surpasses all understanding" protecting us "in Christ Jesus." In any case, it's easy to see how the virtues that Paul mentions will contribute to peace. They are all concerned in one way or another with working together, with promoting what is good rather than just resisting what is bad. They each have something to offer to the quiet and positive dynamic of peace. They are aspects of the Christian mind-set that none of us can afford to neglect. Ongoing negativity is hard to reconcile with peace.

Then there is the role of prayer in the pursuit of peace. Paul tells us that we shouldn't be afraid to ask for whatever we need. God doesn't mind hearing from us, even when what we ask for is not what he would most willingly give us. But our asking should not be a tactic of desperation: "When all else fails, pray!" Anxiety has an undercurrent of mistrust in it. We feel we have to worry a lot because God might not take care of us. One of my wise relatives used to say that worry is an insult to God. She was right. We are supposed to pray intensely and regularly not in order to keep God informed about our needs or in order to persuade God to keep looking after us. Intense and regular prayer is intended to keep us aware of the extent to which we are dependent on God. God will do all the worrying that is necessary.

Thanksgiving has to be part of the fabric of our prayer, too. If we need to keep asking God for things because we need to be kept aware of how deeply we need him, we have to thank God constantly to remind ourselves of how much we have already received. Ongoing gratitude is not a condition for further attention from God, but a sort of accompaniment to our prayer to keep it pleasing to God's ears. Gratitude is one of those essential components of Christian life that is always required and always appropriate.

No anxiety, pervasive gratitude, confidence in God's care, harmony within and without, exemplifying in ourselves the life of the risen Christ: all that is part of the peace God means us to enjoy even now. Not bad!

FOR DISCUSSION AND REFLECTION

How is God's peace manifested in my life?

To what extent is gratitude part of my prayer of petition?

Twenty-seventh Sunday in Ordinary Time (B)

Hebrews 2:9-11

This Sunday's live letter begins a series of excerpts from the Letter to the Hebrews. The lectionary gives us seven successive selections from Hebrews in Year B, and four more in Year C.

Although Hebrews ends like a letter, its main body is in the form of an extended sermon. It is intended to be a message of encouragement addressed to Jewish converts who seem to have been growing weary under the demands of their Christian faith. The author's approach is to demonstrate the superiority of Christ and of faith in him to everything that had gone before in Israel. He shows how Christ is superior to the angels and to Moses, then how his priesthood and his sacrifice are superior to what the Jews had. In the concluding chapters he offers examples of faith to encourage his hearers.

Hebrews has been called one of the most impressive works of the New Testament. It is sophisticated in its theology and its use of sacred Scripture and elegant in its literary style. No wonder the Church gives us so much of it for our Sunday reading!

This first Sunday passage is from the part of the letter that is concerned with demonstrating that Jesus is of greater significance than the angels. The angels were important in some Jewish traditions because they were thought to be the agents that God used to deliver the covenant. Wouldn't a covenant delivered by a human be inferior to one delivered by angels? Our author, having cited a series of texts from the Old Testament to demonstrate the superiority of Jesus to the angels, now undertakes to explain that the humanity of Jesus was essential to the work the Father had sent him to do.

Granted, Jesus was human and so was lower than the angels for a time. But that made it possible for him to experience human death. The Father, who is the source and goal of everything that exists, intended to bring his human children in great numbers to salvation. He had determined that the one who would be their leader and guide to salvation (Jesus) should share and experience the fullness of their nature, not excluding suffering and death. Moreover, since both the savior (Jesus) and we who are saved by him have a common origin in the Father, Jesus openly and gladly calls us his brothers and sisters. (Notice that the he "for whom all things exist" refers to the Father, while the other he's refer to Jesus.)

The point of this reading is twofold: to highlight the real humanity of Jesus and to explain our redemption as contingent on that humanity.

It took a while for the Church at large to accept the full humanity of Jesus. It seemed too good to be true that the Son of God should be a human being just like us. Some thought that Jesus' humanity was merely apparent, others that God relinquished Jesus' humanity at the time of his death. Some thought that Jesus could not have had a human soul or a human will. The real truth, that finally came to full expression after several centuries of theological effort is that Jesus is fully human, just like us, with body and soul and will, with human desires and emotions.

The reason why it is important for the divine Son of God to share our complete humanity is that he came to redeem us completely. Jesus lived a human life as God had intended human life to be lived from the beginning, a life of dedication and generosity and obedience. He was faithful in his human dedication to the Father even when it brought him to suffering and death. He made up for centuries of human sinfulness and self-seeking by his fully human life of generosity and submission to the Father's will. Every aspect of humanity was made holy in and through his life and death. Anything human that had not been part of our savior's life would not have been redeemed. But because our complete and full humanity was in fact shared in his life, our complete and full humanity was redeemed, saved, made holy through and in him.

As a result of Jesus' sharing in the fullness of our humanity, he became our brother and we became his brothers and sisters. Yet we relate to him not only because he is a human being like us, sharing a common Father, but also because, through faith, we are now also connected with the life of God through him. Indeed, we actually participate in the life of God through him. That's what constitutes our salvation. That's what it means to say that we have been redeemed.

The life and death of Jesus turned humanity around to face once more in the direction of the Father. That turn-around of humanity would have had a totally different meaning if our guide and leader had not himself been one of us.

In one of the offertory prayers of the Mass we pray that we may "come to share in the divinity of Christ who humbled himself to share in our humanity." That self-humiliation of Jesus consisted in his being willing "for a little while" to be "lower than the angels."

FOR DISCUSSION AND REFLECTION

How does the humanity of Jesus influence my prayer life?
What implications does Jesus' humanity have for my relationships with other people?

Twenty-seventh Sunday in Ordinary Time (C)

II Timothy 1:6-8, 13-14

This Sunday begins a series of four readings from the Second Letter to Timothy. Second Timothy, like the other two pastoral letters (First Timothy and Titus), is concerned with problems that began to face Church leaders at a time later than that of, say, the letters to the Corinthians or the Galatians. We saw a few weeks ago that scholars do not believe that the pastoral letters are the immediate work of Paul, but represent the work of unknown writers trying to extend Paul's teaching and mind-set into a new church context.

The relationship in time, authorship and content between Second Timothy and the other two pastoral epistles is not clear. Yet scholars seem to think that Second Timothy may be earlier than First Timothy and Titus, and might even have a closer link to the historical Paul than the other two. In any case, this letter offers us a warm and eloquent appeal from a senior apostle to a junior one in a time of uncertainty and change.

The first two Sundays' readings from Second Timothy are from chapters 1 and 2, in which the author is exhorting Timothy to carry forward the faithfulness in the service of God's people that has characterized the apostles' work until now.

He begins our reading by reminding Timothy of the gift that he had been given by the imposition of hands. (The imposition of hands was a gesture that was meant to express the communication of spiritual gifts and powers. It is still used in conferring the sacrament of holy orders. See Acts 6:6 and 8:17.) This spiritual gift should be a source of courage, energy and direction for him. It should strengthen him to sustain the demands of preaching the gospel without shrinking from the public dishonor that sometimes accompanied it. (The author speaks as one imprisoned for his preaching.)

The text then goes on to speak of the need for consistency and coherence with the teaching that had been presented in

Christ's name from the beginning. The faith and love that believers receive from Christ Jesus constitutes a precious deposit that we must carefully preserve with the help of the Holy Spirit.

Preserving what has been entrusted to us, that is, safeguarding the deposit of faith, is a recurrent theme in First and Second Timothy. One could almost say that this concern is one of the primary subjects of these two letters. No less than five times (I Timothy 1:18 and 6.20; II Timothy 1:12, 1:14, 2:2) we hear of what has been entrusted, or what is to be entrusted, or something precious that is to be looked after. This concern to protect and hand on what we have received is understandable at a time when the original apostles, those who had seen Jesus, were passing away and leaving their task of faithful proclamation to a succeeding generation.

Concern about safeguarding the deposit of faith is part of the Church's life today. After all, the teaching that we have received from our elders in the community is not a man-made product to be changed or modified in accord with changing contemporary needs and desires. It is the teaching of Christ himself, Christ's account of God's love for us, expressed in his words and his actions, a teaching whose acceptance on our part is what constitutes salvation.

This is why the Church is necessarily involved with a tradition, the tradition of Jesus and his first followers. In such a context, tradition does not mean customary religious practices like praying the rosary or abstaining from meat on Friday. Nor does it mean a body of abstract teachings that we are expected to sign onto and pass on to future generations, as if it were a sort of theological diskette that contains all the answers. Obviously customary religious practices can be useful in expressing our faith, but they depend for their worth on the authenticity of the faith they express. Likewise, exact doctrine is absolutely necessary for the preservation of the "deposit" of tradition, but it is a means to an end and not an end in itself. Tradition, in its fullest sense, is more than all this.

The tradition that the Church strives to preserve and defend comprises everything that contributes to our life of faith, everything that constitutes and advances the holiness of Christian life. It is expressed in the teaching, the life and the worship of the Church. It is perpetuated and handed on to all generations by what the Church is and what the Church believes. One might also say that the tradition that lies at the heart of the Church is nothing less than God's self-gift to us in the person of Jesus Christ, an offer that the Church has the responsibility both to safeguard and to extend.

Every member of the Church shares responsibility for the tradition. We are all called to reply to the invitation that is inherent in it. We are all called to defend its purity. We are all called to proclaim and propagate it. The words of today's reading are not a historical curiosity, relevant to a long gone period of Church history. They are a call to faith and dedication directed to believers of today.

FOR DISCUSSION AND REFLECTION

How do I stay in touch with the Church's tradition?

What is my role in handing on the Christian tradition?

Twenty-eighth Sunday in Ordinary Time (A)

Philippians 4:12-14, 19-20

Paul's letter to the Philippians is drawing to a close. Just before the final greetings, there is a section (4:10-20) in which Paul offers special thanks to the Philippians for their generosity toward him. Apparently they had made some financial offering to him in the context of his current imprisonment. But there had been previous gifts several times before, at the beginning of his friendship with them, when he was preaching the gospel in nearby Thessalonica. Their present generosity makes Paul remember their past gifts. (Some scholars think that these verses were originally a separate thank-you letter which was later joined to other communications to make up our present single letter.)

In verses 10 and 11, Paul alludes with gratitude to the Philippians' kindness to him in his present difficult circumstances, but hastens to add that he really didn't need anything since he has learned to be self-sufficient.

Now, as our Sunday reading begins, Paul goes on at some length about making do with what is available. He is able to enjoy abundance, but he is also able to tolerate hunger and need, no matter what the circumstances might be. It's not that he can do all this out of his own personal resources. Rather, his capacity for coping comes from the Lord who strengthens him.

Next come a few words of gratitude, almost embarrassed in tone: it was good of you to help me in my need.

The reading that the lectionary presents to us omits four verses here. These verses detail some of the past history of the Philippians' help to Paul in his Thessalonian days. But they also give Paul's evaluation of their kindness: "It is not that I am eager for the gift; rather I am eager for the profit that accrues to your account" (verse 17). That is, the benefit of your gift is not just in what it does for me, but mostly in what it does for you. He goes on to call their gift "an acceptable sacrifice, pleasing to God" (verse 18).

Our lectionary text resumes with Paul telling the Philippians that—in view of their generosity to him—God would, in turn, be generous to them, as generous as the "glorious riches" of Christ make appropriate. The reading closes with a prayer of praise, elicited seemingly by the generosity both of the Philippians and of God: glory forever to our God and Father.

Some scholars think that the selection of verses that the lectionary gives us here has not been skillfully made. Surely verses 17 and 18 should have been included. However that may be, the reading teaches about doing without and with giving.

Paul was very sensitive about accepting gifts from those to whom he ministered. He didn't want to be supported by the people to whom he was preaching the gospel, even when this unwillingness became a source of criticism (see I Corinthians 9). He took some degree of pride in preaching the gospel "free of charge" (I Corinthians 9:18; see also I Thessalonians 2:9). This was due not so much to a spirit of bullheaded independence on Paul's part as to a desire to entrust himself as fully and as publicly as possible to the care of Christ, to give God's power a chance to manifest itself in him.

Consumership is not a virtue. Using as much of the world's goods as possible, always running after the latest product, throwing things away as soon as possible so that we can get new things, constantly needing more is not part of the Christian way of life. Paul's example suggests that it makes more sense to limit our material requirements, sometimes to "do without" entirely, so that we can give attention more fully to the work of the Lord.

As regards giving, this Sunday's reading suggests that the blessing of generosity lies not so much in what it does for the recipient as for what it does for the giver. Even Paul was open to receiving in view of the spiritual benefit that would accrue to the ones who gave (see verse 17).

We are becoming more aware of this basic Christian truth as we become more experienced in the practice of stewardship. We are called to share our resources (time, talent, money), but not because of the needs out there that have to be tended to. God can find plenty of ways to tend to the needs without having to depend on our generosity. (After all, God took care of Paul well enough even when Paul refused to accept help from other people!) Rather, we are called to share our resources because sharing our resources is a blessing for us. It is one of the basic ways in which we can express our awareness of God's generosity toward us. The need that motivates Christian giving is not on the part of the receiver, but on the part of the giver. It is not so much that others need to get as it is that we need to give.

Paul loved the Philippians and they knew it. For them he made an exception to his policy of doing without and accepted their help. But he is careful to let them know that his willingness to receive their gifts was really a gift to them from him.

FOR DISCUSSION AND REFLECTION

In what ways have I experienced God's generosity in the context of my giving?

How do I practice restraint in my use of the world's goods?

Twenty-eighth Sunday in Ordinary Time (B)
Hebrews 4:12-13

The author has been talking about the superiority of Jesus and his people over Moses and the Israelites, particularly in their wilderness experience. God had promised rest to the children of Israel, but that rest never came to them because they were disobedient to God's word. The rest that God had promised to them was still to come, then, and it would come to the new people of God, to the followers of Jesus, to us as long as we strive to enter it through our obedience to God's commands.

Now begins this Sunday's reading, a two-verse jewel about the word of God. Note that here "the word of God" does not signify the Bible, nor Christ (as in the prologue to John's Gospel). In this passage, the word of God means God's commands or directives. The author's teaching about God's word arises from his teaching about the Israelites' disobedience and the need for the contemporary Christian people of God to obey God's commands.

The commanding word of God has life and power. It constitutes a means of judgment, in that our worth or value depends on our response to it, on how we measure up to it. It is subtle and keen, capable of evaluating everything about us, the spiritual, the physical, the intellectual. It can make divisions and distinctions that are impossible for human beings. There is nothing that can be hidden from God's probing word and all of us will eventually be subjected to its scrutiny. No part of us can escape examination.

The force of these verses is the same for us as it was for their original hearers. It is easy to drift away from the challenge of God's word through boredom and distraction and stagnation, as the murmuring Israelites did in the desert and as the first addressees of Hebrews seemed to be in danger of doing. These verses remind us that the gospel is not something to be trifled with and that God's directives to us are not mere suggestions to be responded to in whatever way we see fit. God's word looks into the deepest recesses of our personhood and lays bare our innermost intentions. Occasional attention and superficial conformity to his directives are not enough. He wants serious response and obedience from every component of our being, even the deepest, the most complex, most subtle elements of our hearts and minds. The power of his word is able to discern what lies in those most hidden areas of our life.

It would be possible to read these two verses and turn ourselves into scruple-ridden men and women who spend all their time and energy agonizing over the extent to which they have sinned and how God is going to punish them. While such extremes of fear are unhealthy and certainly not what God calls for from us, the fact remains that some degree of concern about our standing with God is not inappropriate. We shouldn't be too quick to tell ourselves that everything is all right between ourselves and God and that there is nothing more in thought or word or deed that he looks for from us, nothing more that we can do in response to his word. Which of us can say that the deepest recesses of our hearts and minds are pure and unsullied enough to pass muster before the all-knowing God to whose eyes "everything is naked and exposed?" God is serious about his will for us and expects us to be serious in our response.

At the same time, God is kind and merciful. It is true that we will have to render an account to him for the life that we have lived. Our faith teaches us that. But our faith also teaches us that we do not, indeed, cannot earn our salvation. Whatever we have to offer God, whatever we have to show in response to his commands and expectations is itself his gift. Salvation, redemption, grace, the life of Christ in us—it's all God's gift, it's all God's doing. We can't earn any of it. We can't achieve any of it. All that we can do is respond to God's generosity.

Maybe that's the core of Christian life, the center of our response to God's word: to acknowledge our dependence on God, to express our unworthiness, to offer as much as we can in return for God's generosity, always aware that the most that we can give is ridiculously inadequate to respond to the least that God has done for us.

The one thing that we cannot, dare not do is to come to think that God owes us something for all that we have done for him. God's gifts exceed not only our response but even our awareness of his generosity. We can't even imagine how much God has done for us!

God's word is a challenge. It challenges us to be aware of our own limitations and failures. It challenges us to extend ourselves in response to his initiatives. It challenges us to place our confidence not in our abilities, but in his mercy, generosity, and forgiveness.

God's word is like a surgeon's scalpel, able to make the most delicate and refined incisions. And God's word, like the surgeon's incisions, is directed not only to cutting out what is diseased but also to protecting and supporting what God wants to save.

FOR DISCUSSION AND REFLECTION

In what ways do I experience the word of God as a positive force in my life?

In what ways do I experience the word of God as a challenge or threat in my life?

Twenty-eighth Sunday in Ordinary Time (C)

II Timothy 2:8-13

This Sunday's reading is parallel to last week's. The senior apostle, suffering in prison for his faith, continues to call his younger colleague to courage and perseverance. In the earlier verses of chapter 2, he has invited Timothy to look on himself as a good soldier, as an athlete contending for victory, as a hardworking farmer. Now the senior offers himself as a model for the younger man to follow.

He may be suffering like a criminal, but somehow what he is being asked to bear will contribute to the salvation of those to whom his preaching is addressed. He may be chained, but the gospel is not chained, the gospel whose basic message is that Jesus Christ was a man from the family of David who was raised from the dead. Therein lies strength and encouragement for Timothy. (Note that Jesus' true humanity and his resurrection seem to be the fundamental constitutive elements of the gospel. That's what the gospel is about!)

Now the author offers further encouragement by quoting what seems to be an early Christian hymn, perhaps used in the liturgy of baptism. It consists of four couplets. The first two couplets seem to apply to the situation at hand, but the author keeps right on quoting to the end. Dying with Christ guarantees our life with him. Perseverance will bring triumph. That's what Timothy needed to hear. The rest of the hymn gives us the flip side of this, but also a surprise. If we deny Christ, he will deny us. (This couplet seems to be an allusion to Jesus' words recorded in Matthew 10:33.) But if we are unfaithful, he is not unfaithful in return. Christ cannot be unfaithful to us because his love for us is so much a part of him that he wouldn't be himself if he stopped loving us.

These verses offer us an insight into the demands of the apostolate in the early times of the Church. But they are not just of historical interest. They also speak to us about our own situation.

For one thing, we are all called to preach the gospel of Christ as Timothy was. The gospel and the faith that comes from it are not "things" that we receive and that we are then responsible for keeping safe. They constitute a relationship with God, which, if it is full and healthy in us, necessarily impels us to sharing. If we are serious about our participation in the life of the risen Christ, if we understand what it means to live God's life, we will want others to be part of it, too.

This doesn't mean that every Christian believer has to be a full-time preacher or engage in public proclamation in the center of town. But it does mean that Christian faith has a social dimension, that believers are expected to let other people see what faith means, that practicing our faith should be a public part of our ordinary life, that living in Christ is something that we are supposed to be willing to talk about and invite others to share. Faith is not something that belongs in our safe-deposit box!

Another aspect of our life to which this reading speaks is that we are imprisoned even as the author of Second Timothy was. We are not languishing in chains in a Roman jail somewhere. But our circumstances are such that our wanting to share with those around us the good news of Jesus and the offer of his life is hindered in many ways. Our chains are not physical, but they are real.

The hindrances arise not from judicial decisions that have

been imposed on us but from the social and cultural atmosphere in which we find ourselves. Religious faith is not something that we are encouraged to talk about. Baseball scores are more socially acceptable. Living in and with Christ for all eternity is not something that most people are very interested in. Our world gives a lot more attention to sexual fulfillment and economic security. In our world, a good stereo system is generally much more eagerly sought after than eternal life. We live in a pagan atmosphere, and that atmosphere impedes us in carrying out our responsibilities as agents of Christ's gospel.

That doesn't absolve us of the responsibility, however. We have to bear with the difficulties in which we find ourselves just as the author of Second Timothy had to bear with his, with the realization that our struggle to remain faithful to Christ's calling is itself a source of fruitfulness.

The shackles that our culture imposes on us can also serve as a reminder that it is not we who are the primary agents of faith. Faith comes from Christ through the working of the Holy Spirit. We are merely the instruments, and it is important for us to remember that God doesn't have to have perfect instruments in order to get the work done. Even if the instruments can't work freely, God still wants to use them. And God will use them because God is faithful and wants us to be part of his work.

FOR DISCUSSION AND REFLECTION

How do I participate in the preaching of the gospel?

What are the greatest obstacles to my giving witness to Christ?

Twenty-ninth Sunday in Ordinary Time (A)

I Thessalonians 1:1-5b

As our liturgical year draws to a close, we begin five weeks of consecutive readings from the first letter of Paul to the Thessalonians. Probably this letter was chosen for this place in the calendar because it is concerned (in chapters 4 and 5) with the second coming of Jesus and the final conclusion of God's work of redemption. We'll be hearing from these chapters in a few weeks.

This letter is important, however, not only because of what it has to say about the second coming of Christ, but also because it is the oldest part of the New Testament and so the oldest existing Christian writing. It was written about the year 50, some twenty years after the death and resurrection of Jesus and about twenty years before the earliest gospel.

Acts (17:1-9) tells us that Paul had started to preach the gospel to the Jews at Thessalonica. Some of them were converted and some gentiles as well. Other Jews thought that Paul and his companions were dangerous, so they trumped up some charges against them and the missionaries had to be smuggled out of town at night. Paul wanted to maintain his contact with his recent converts and continue to offer them his encouragement, so he wrote them this letter, thus instituting a whole new means of Christian communication.

Ordinary secular letters of the time opened with the name of the sender and of the addressee. There followed a short greeting and a brief word or so of thanksgiving. This is the pattern that Paul follows here (and in most of his other letters), except that the thanksgiving section here is disproportionately long, constituting about sixty percent of the whole letter. Maybe Paul wanted to be sure that the Thessalonians knew how fond of them he was. It may also be that he was still groping with the ins and outs of the literary form that he was creating.

Paul offers thanks to God most of all because of the

Thessalonians' perseverance. Conscious of their election by God, that is, their call to salvation, they have been persistent in their "work of faith and labor of love and endurance of hope in our Lord Jesus Christ." All this came as the result of the persuasive power of the Holy Spirit that they had perceived in Paul's preaching.

There are two things that seem worthy of special mention as we reflect on these earliest extant words of Christian documentation.

The first is that the very first words of the letter after the conventional opening are words of thanksgiving, not just conventional words that could have been found in any letter of the time, but heartfelt and earnest words of gratitude that will continue, off and on, for much of the rest of the letter. "We give thanks to God always for all of you." The first words we hear from the silence of the Christian past are words of gratitude.

This suggests to me that the very beginning of our own encounter with God and with our fellow believers ought to take place in the context of gratitude. The first things for us to present in prayer and in our relationships with one another should be the expression of thanksgiving for what we have received. It is a theme that is always relevant, a subject on which there is always more to be said. Giving thanks is never inappropriate. Being grateful is never out of season. This centrality of gratitude is expressed not only in these first words of the first writing of the New Testament, but also in every celebration of the Eucharist in which we take part. Every time the priest prays the preface of the Eucharistic Prayer in the name of Christ and the people, he says to God, "We do well always and everywhere to give you thanks...."

The other thing that seems worthy of comment is the theological richness of these few verses. From this very beginning of recorded discourse in the Church we hear about the Persons of the Trinity: the Church is "in God the Father and the Lord Jesus Christ;" the gospel came to them "in the Holy Spirit." We also hear about faith, hope and charity, the foundational virtues of Christian life that define the Christian condition and color everything we are and do. If we read the text carefully, we will see that Paul speaks of these virtues not as accomplishments of the Thessalonian Christians, but as gifts of God that the new Christians have received. "Your work of faith and labor of love" refers to the Thessalonians' response to God's initiative and God's gratuitous invitation to life and community with himself. Likewise, "endurance in hope of our Lord Jesus Christ" involves patience in trials but also the certainty of salvation that is grounded in God's faithfulness. Finally, Paul also speaks of "our gospel." This is not a set of propositions or a portfolio of information, but the proclamation of who Christ is and what Christ did and how Christ's life, death and resurrection constitute our salvation.

In this ordinary yet very special reading, God's word offers us the gentle voice of the apostle coming to us from the very beginning of the Church's mission, offering God thanks as we are called to offer thanks, and speaking about matters of faith that are still essential to us today.

FOR DISCUSSION AND REFLECTION

What part does thanksgiving play in my personal spirituality?

What elements of the Christian faith do I see as most basic?

Twenty-ninth Sunday in Ordinary Time (B)

Hebrews 4:14-16

Our author has been dealing with the superiority of Jesus over the angels and Moses. Now he begins to demonstrate that the priesthood and the sacrifice of Jesus are superior to what was granted to the Israelites. These are the themes that will occupy us for the final five readings from Hebrews for this liturgical year.

In this Sunday's passage, which is a bridge passage to the central chapters of the letter, the author touches two basic themes of his sermon: encouragement to his Jewish readers to remain faithful to their Christian faith and the full humanity of Jesus that we already heard something about two weeks ago.

He tells his hearers that they should remain faithful because the priest who represents us, Jesus the Son of God, has gone up into heaven. (He seems to have in mind the fragrance of the Old Law's burnt sacrifices, which was thought to rise up to heaven through the sky and bring pleasure to God.) Yet this priest is just like us. He has experienced all the temptations that accompany our humanity, all its limitations and failures, excepting only sin. He can represent us well there because he knows what it's like to be human. As a result, we are now able ourselves to come confidently before God, ask for whatever we need, and expect to receive it. (Note that "the throne of grace" recalls the "mercy seat" in Judaic cult, the top of the Ark of the Covenant, where God sat when he met with Moses [see Exodus 25:22].)

This passage tells us that, as a result of the humanity of Jesus, of his faithfulness to his Father in spite of trial, of his willingness to undergo even death in obedience to God's will, we human beings have a whole new relationship with God.

First of all we have a representative in the presence of the Father who can represent us adequately. Jesus is fully human like us. He has to be fully human, acquainted with every aspect of our existence, because he intended, in his life and work, to redeem every aspect of our humanity. Yet, he is sinless and so can stand in the presence of the Father without shame and sorrow.

This makes it possible for us to stand with Jesus, side by side in the presence of the Father, in hope and confidence because, just as he is like us, so also we are like him. Under the law of Israel, believers were to keep at a distance from the place of God's presence, and even their high priest could approach only once a year, in fear and trembling. After the life and ministry of Christ, it's different. We are all invited to come near to God's presence, not in fear and trembling, but with trust and assurance that we will receive there everything we need. That kind of a relationship is worth holding on to!

What does all this say to us? I think it gives us two warnings. The first is not to be afraid of God. God is indeed the creator and Lord of the universe, more powerful than we can ever fathom, more ingenious than the most imaginative of us can fantasize about. God is holy and pure beyond anything that we have ever experienced. He is all knowing and all just, aware of our innermost thoughts and desires, aware that our most virtuous intentions and our most generous actions are stained with human imperfection. We have every reason to approach God in fear and trembling. Yet God doesn't seem to want that. His word encourages us to approach him confidently with the expectation that he will grant us whatever we need.

Our passage also warns us about the opposite extreme. God is not some sort of smiling Santa Claus who overlooks the dirtiness and defects of the children sitting in his lap. He is not a rich uncle who mindlessly keeps handing out gifts to his nieces and nephews in spite of their inattention and lack of gratitude to him. God is not a father who spoils his children because of his own need to buy their love. God is God, all knowing and all just. Our salvation wasn't a matter of God jovially agreeing to wipe the slate clean and start over with us as if nothing had happened. God demanded that we human beings make up for our sins, but he gave us the wherewithal to do it in giving us the divine Son in fully human form to make amends for all the sinfulness of human history. Our heavenly Father welcomes us to his presence and invites us to approach him confidently because we are like his Son who is the full image of the Father as well as like us in all things but sin. The relationship that God offers us is founded on justice, on the repayment for human sinfulness made by Jesus. But it is also a relationship that is founded on love, on God's love for his human creatures and on the Father's love for the Son in the Holy Spirit.

The key to it all is Jesus. Our salvation is through him. Our likeness to God is through him. Our access to the Father is through him. Our hope for eternal happiness in the life of Father, Son and Spirit is through him. We can do nothing of ourselves except to sin. All that is good and worthy in us is his doing.

FOR DISCUSSION AND REFLECTION

How confidently do I approach God?

How important is my relationship with Christ in my daily existence?

Twenty-ninth Sunday in Ordinary Time (C)
II Timothy 3:14-4:2

About halfway through chapter 2, the senior apostle begins to deal with the false teachings and other dangers that are facing the Church or that will soon face it. He laments the haggling over words and the foolish debates that people are engaged in (see 2:14 and 2:23). Some people are asserting that the final resurrection has already taken place (see 2:18). It's not hard to foresee the moral decay that will arise as the end draws near (see 3:2-5). The author encourages Timothy to continue to follow his example of perseverance in times of trial.

At the beginning of our Sunday reading, the author exhorts Timothy to be faithful not only to what he has seen in the life of the senior apostle, but also to the teaching he has learned from him. What he has learned and believed is reliable both because it has come from an apostolic source and also because it is contained in sacred Scripture. Scripture offers not just information, but direction and insight that make our faith in Jesus more effective for salvation. (The author is alluding to the Hebrew Scriptures here, those books of the Bible that we refer to as the Old Testament. Since most of the members of the Church were gentiles, they would have been acquainted with this part of the Bible through the Greek translation known as the septuagint.)

The author goes on to explain why Scripture is so helpful in our life of faith. First and foremost, it is all inspired, that is (as the New Testament original puts it) "breathed by God" into the heart and mind of the human author. It has a value beyond that of the wisest of merely human words. Consequently, Scripture is useful for teaching and guiding, for reproving and calling to repentance. Scripture has to be part of the equipment of anyone who wants to be properly outfitted for doing God's work. No one who wants to be in touch with God can do without it.

Now, one more time, the senior apostle calls his young colleague to faithfulness in ministry. He reminds him of the context in which they work: God and Christ Jesus are present in our midst; the final judgment is coming; the Lord will appear to rule heaven and earth. In view of all that, keep proclaiming the word! This proclamation is to be an ongoing activity, not just something that is engaged in when all the circumstances are right. The teaching and guiding, the reproving and calling to repentance in which Scripture excels are to be the consistent task of those called to announce the gospel.

Catholics are more familiar with the Bible than they used to be. We get a richer dose of it in the liturgy through the Sunday three-year cycle of readings and the weekday two-year cycle. If we attend Mass regularly and listen attentively to the readings, we can acquire a much deeper knowledge of God's word than Catholics used to have. In addition to that, there are the Scripture reflection and prayer groups that have grown up over the years in which lay men and women open themselves to the guidance of the Holy Spirit that is offered through God's inspired word. There is also the fact that Catholic Scripture scholars, who used to be looked on as rather retrograde, are now generally acknowledged as leaders in professional Scripture studies.

The Bible is important for us. It provides the basics of belief and morality on which our Catholic faith is built. Saint Jerome says that to be ignorant of Scripture is to be ignorant of Christ.

This is not to say that the Bible is our only source of knowledge about God's will for us, or that the meaning of the Bible is immediately or effortlessly clear. It is not to say that the Bible provides detailed directions for every contemporary human need or that knowing the Bible by heart will insure an immediate answer to every question.

The Bible is the inspired word of God, but it is also the result of human effort. It has to be read and studied with both its divine and its human authors in mind. It offers us the story of God's care for his human creatures from the creation to the end of time, and so we have to be clear about how each individual part fits into the whole. Like every product of human words, it has to be carefully read both in the context in which it was written and in the context in which it now finds itself. Our use of the Bible requires guidance from the tradition of the Church (that we spoke about a few weeks ago) to insure that we use it correctly. But the fact remains that sacred Scripture is an essential component of the Christian's life of faith. It has been so from the very beginning, as this Sunday's reading reminds us.

There is another lesson that is implicit in this Sunday's reading. Although the author is addressing himself to a "professional" church leader, it does not follow that all proclamation of the gospel is to be done by Church leaders. In our reflections on earlier portions of Second Timothy we have seen that we all share responsibility for making Christ known. The "non-professionals" in the Church are not passive recipients of what Christ offers. We are all called to make Christ known. We are all fellow workers of the apostles.

FOR DISCUSSION AND REFLECTION

How is sacred Scripture helpful to my personal spiritual life?

How does sacred Scripture influence my witnessing to the gospel?

Thirtieth Sunday in Ordinary Time (A)

I Thessalonians 1:5c-10

In this Sunday's reading we continue to hear from the extended thanksgiving section that opens Paul's letter to his beloved Thessalonians. Paul speaks in this section of a kind of chain reaction that reaches from his preaching to them to the rest of the world.

He begins by reminding them how he had preached the gospel to them and how, in spite of the turmoil that the gospel brought into their midst, they received it joyfully and so became imitators of himself. (Elsewhere, for example, I Corinthians 4:16 and 11:1, Paul does not hesitate to encourage his readers to become his imitators. The point is not that they copy the personal characteristics of Paul, but that they be touched by Christ and become participants in Christ's life as Paul was.)

The Thessalonians' imitation of Paul caused them in turn to become a model for other believers, not only in the Roman provinces of Achaia and Macedonia (modern Greece, Albania and Macedonia) but all over the world! The example of their faith and commitment has become so appealing that preachers of the gospel need only mention it without having to say anything else.

The last verses of the passage detail what it was that was so attractive in the example of the Thessalonians. First of all, they welcomed Paul and his message with great warmth. Then they abandoned the worship of false gods to commit themselves fully to the service of the one true God. Finally, they had accepted the deliverance brought by the risen Christ and were now looking forward to his final coming in glory.

Paul's grateful memories of the Christians of Thessalonica and his great affection for them may have led him into a bit of overstatement here. It seems a bit much to say that the example of their faith has assumed so energetic a life of its own that now preachers of the gospel all over the world don't need to do any more than hold them up for imitation. Yet what Paul says here does teach us something about the nature of faith and the effects that faith is supposed to bring with it.

The commitment of ourselves to God through faith is not just a private relationship between the individual and God. It does involve God and the individual, of course, but it also involves a present relationship with everybody else that shares our faith and a potential relationship with all those who do not. We are all linked together by the one life of the risen Christ either in fact or in possibility.

This profession of faith on our part should have a public, visible dimension. We are called to encourage the faith of others by allowing them to perceive the effects of our faith. One dimension of evangelization, of the proclamation of the gospel in which we are all called to partake, is an invitation to imitate and that which is to be imitated must be perceptible. You can't follow what you don't see.

This doesn't mean that we have to go around making a spectacle of our faith, posturing in the spotlight so that everybody will be impressed with us. The issue is not promoting ourselves, but promoting God. We have to be willing to let others see what it means to have our heavenly Father as the center of our lives, to live in the Lord Jesus, to be energized by the Holy Spirit. We have to broadcast with our lives the contentment that comes from being in touch with God. We have to demonstrate the sense of direction and meaning that comes from responding to God's love for us. We have to appreciate and treasure our faith in such a way that it becomes appealing to others. Our faith should be so attractive that the people around us want to be part of it. Our faith should call for imitation, not because it is ours, but because it is faith, that is, because of the inherent attractiveness of the salvation that God has given us.

It is in this context that we can see the value of living in the community of other Christians. Being surrounded by other believers keeps reminding us of the importance of our commitment to God. Seeing how others practice faith, hope and love in their lives encourages us to continuous efforts in our own life. We get clearer ideas of the multitudinous ways in which our Christian profession can be lived out if we have before us the examples of large numbers of other believers. How many ways are there to express and respond to the grace of Christ? As many ways as there are believers, and each way can teach us something about our own relationship with God. Without the ongoing example of large numbers of other believers, our own faith runs the risk of becoming thin and self-centered. Similarly, without the rich and varied example of lots of believers, those in our midst who do not believe will get only a limited exposure to the implications of faith.

We owe each other the example of our faith. Sincerely following out the implications of our dedication to God and of God's dedication to us is not just a blessing for ourselves. It is a gift to those around us, believers and non-believers alike.

FOR DISCUSSION AND REFLECTION

What examples of faith have influenced me?

How and to whom am I an example of faith?

Thirtieth Sunday in Ordinary Time (B)

Hebrews 5:1-6

This Sunday's reading follows immediately upon last Sunday's. There our author spoke of Jesus as a high priest. Now he begins a long and involved discussion of the implications of the priesthood and sacrifice of Christ by explaining the notion of priesthood and showing how the notion applies to Christ.

There are three elements to being a high priest, he says. The first is that he shares the humanity of those he is to represent, for whom he is to make sacrificial offerings. The second is that he is sympathetic with human weakness since he himself is weak and vulnerable. This is why priests have to make offerings to purify themselves of their own sins before they can offer sacrifices for their people. (We saw last Sunday, however, that sinfulness is not part of Jesus' humanity.) Finally, the priest is called to priesthood by God. It's not an office he takes by his own choice. Now our text goes on to show how Christ meets these qualifications, beginning with the last one. (The other two qualifications are not dealt with in our reading.) Christ did not make himself a priest. He was called to that office by his Father. The author demonstrates the Father's call by citing two psalms. (These two psalms were originally addressed to a king, perhaps at his coronation, but they were frequently understood to refer also to the Messiah God would send.) The author of Hebrews imagines them being spoken by the Father and addressed to Christ. "You are my Son.... You are a priest forever." Jesus' priesthood derives from his relationship to God the Father and from God's own determination that the Son be a priest.

But what about Melchizedek? What does he have to do with all this? Melchizedek appears briefly in Genesis (14:18-20). There we see him as both king of Salem and priest who made an offering of bread and wine and pronounced God's blessing on Abraham. He appears again in Psalm 110 (cited in this Sunday's passage) where the king (and, by implication the Messiah) is called a "priest forever according to the order of Melchizedek." There seem to be four areas of correspondence between Melchizedek and Christ. Both are kings as well as priests; both are characterized by sacrifices of bread and wine; both have a priesthood directly from God and therefore different from the priesthood of Aaron that came through family descent. Finally, as the author of Hebrews will explain at great length in chapter 7, it is an eternal priesthood. Since Scripture records neither the birth nor the death of Melchizedek, he is seen as an anticipation of Christ whose priesthood is eternally valid.

Jesus, therefore, fulfills the requirements for priesthood, but it is a priesthood different from (and better than) the priesthood of the Old Law.

What does this rather arcane and involved argumentation teach us? For one thing, it assures us one more time that we have a friend at the heavenly court, Jesus the priest, the Father's Son.

But it also gives us some indication of how we ought to look at the priests who serve us today and how we ought to understand their vocation.

First and foremost, priests are human beings like the rest of us. They are not ethereal and unapproachable semi-divinities who live in some sort of detached world, separated from the rest of humankind, out of touch with reality.

The center of their calling is to minister the mercy and the compassion of God. They are called "to deal patiently with the ignorant and erring." Sometimes people seem to have the impression that priests will be scandalized or turned off if they find out how "ignorant and erring" the members of their flock really are, or that they won't understand. Priests are well acquainted with sinfulness, because each one of them has his own share of it to deal with. When the priest prays in the name of the people in Eucharistic Prayer I, "Though we are sinners, we trust in our mercy and love," he is praying for himself first of all.

Like Aaron and Christ, the Church's priests do not take priesthood on themselves. They are called. That is, they have a "vocation." There are several aspects to being called to priesthood. One is the individual psychological aspect. Those who become priests experience, at some point in their lives, some degree of affinity for priestly work. They also discern that they have the human equipment of intelligence and emotional balance required to train for priesthood and do priestly work. But this is not yet an authentic "vocation." The real vocation comes when the candidate, who has discerned his willingness and capacity to be a priest, is formally called to the reception of sacred orders by the bishop. Without that call, there is no vocation. Without the conferral of sacred orders by Christ through the hands of the bishop there is no priesthood. No one takes it upon himself.

What the author of Hebrews described in our reading still constitutes the norms for priesthood today.

FOR DISCUSSION AND REFLECTION

How do I look on the priests who serve me?

What can I do to encourage vocations to priesthood?

Thirtieth Sunday in Ordinary Time (C)

II Timothy 4:6-8, 16-18

This reading brings us to the last part of Second Timothy. The author, a senior apostle, is encouraging his younger colleague by offering him the image of Paul in the last phase of his life. The author uses bits of information gathered from an older tradition to put together the portrait of Paul facing the conclusion of his ministry and reflecting on the meaning of what was happening to him.

The reading is in two parts. In the first part, we have general reflections from the missionary on the final stage of life in which he now finds himself. His life has proven to be a sacrifice, a liquid poured out to honor God. It has been like an athletic contest, a race in which he has contended well and whose finish line he is now crossing. He can rightly expect the laurel crown that athletes received as a trophy. The crown would not be awarded by a human judge, but by the Lord. The same crown will be given to all those who have looked for the action of the Lord in their lives and their world. The main claim to victory that Paul expresses is that he has kept the faith. He has been tenacious and resolute in maintaining his relationship with the Lord. That's what constitutes the worth of his life.

The second part of the reading deals with some of the details of the situation that Paul found himself in. There had been a court hearing and nobody was there to help him. Yet the Lord had helped him to conduct himself in a way that was beneficial to the gospel. He was saved from the immediate threat ("the lion's mouth," a quote from Psalm 22). These details (abandonment by friends, prayer for the forgiveness of those who have done harm, the allusion to the psalm that Jesus prayed on the cross) seem to suggest that Paul saw his situation as a parallel with the sacrifice of Jesus. These reflections are followed by an expression of final confidence, of conviction that he would be brought at last to the glory of God's heavenly kingdom.

The verses that constitute this reading are important not only because of what they might tell us about the last events of Paul's life, nor because of the motives for encouragement that they might offer to a young church leader. They also offer challenge and enrichment to every Christian believer.

They remind us, first of all, that our Christian existence involves struggle. The author speaks of competing in a race, of striving for a prize, of being emptied out like a sacrificial offering.

Sometimes believers seem to think that their religious faith demands too much of them. Mass each and every Sunday, sexual restraint, lifetime faithfulness to a marriage commitment, love and concern offered to people who don't deserve it: these are heavy demands. Did God really mean for it to be this hard?

The struggles of Christian life are not a matter of God's setting up obstacles for us to overcome, but of our having to make choices from several conflicting itineraries. The Lord offers us options that lead to one goal. The world around us offers different choices that take us in a different direction. Often the world's choices are more attractive because they yield immediate and comfortable results, while God's choices seem to require still further expenditure of energy, still further postponement of satisfaction. God's road seems to run uphill a lot. The reason it seems that way is not because God wants to make things hard for us, but because our views and values are skewed. We don't fully understand what God has in mind for us and so following his directions seems difficult. We end up competing with ourselves.

These verses also challenge us to give some thought to what constitutes the value of our life. Our reading shows us Paul finding reassurance in the fact that he has "kept the faith," that is, that he has remained consistently in relationship with Christ Jesus, that he has persisted in carrying out the mission that had been entrusted to him.

All of us need to keep asking ourselves where our values lie. What is important to me? What is significant in my human existence? What criteria do I use to make the choices I make? We need to ask ourselves these questions for several reasons. One is because it is so easy to deceive ourselves, to think we are acting out of generous and godly motives when, in reality, we're really being selfish. Another is because the world around us has a significant agenda of its own that is constantly being marketed to us and that we can buy into almost without realizing it. Still another is because we are skilled in minimalism, crafty about settling for the smallest expenditure of effort that will allow us to maintain our relationship with the Lord. As a result, our life can easily degenerate into an ongoing bargaining session with God instead of a generous sacrificial outpouring of ourselves.

When we hear Paul saying, "I have kept the faith," it's almost as if he is suggesting an epitaph for himself. It might be interesting to ask ourselves to what extent that same epitaph would be appropriate for us.

FOR DISCUSSION AND REFLECTION

In what way does my life involve struggle?

When the end of my life comes, what will I be most proud of? Most grateful for?

Thirty-first Sunday in Ordinary Time (A)

I Thessalonians 2:7b-9, 13

Paul continues his long ballad of gratitude. At the beginning of chapter 2 he reminds the Thessalonians how he and his colleagues had come to them after having been mistreated in Philippi and urged to leave town. They came to Thessalonica and announced the gospel there in an honest and straightforward manner, without rhetorical frills. They could have made demands on the Thessalonians, but they didn't.

As our passage begins, Paul recalls the gentleness and affection that had characterized his relationship with them. He treated them like a mother treats her child. The missionaries offered their converts not only the gospel but their very own selves.

They even worked at a trade, earning their own keep so that they would not constitute a burden to the new Christians. (We shouldn't underestimate the importance of this gesture on the part of Paul and his companions. For one thing, in Paul's time itinerant preachers expected to be paid. For another, the day and night toil that Paul mentions would have been more characteristic of a slave than of a free person. He and his companions were giving up benefits that they would have had a right to in order to share their very lives, everything they had, with the Thessalonians.)

Paul is grateful not only for this affectionate relationship with the Thessalonians, but also for the depth and sincerity with which they accepted what these preachers had to say. They received it not as a human word but as God's word, which was now at work in them because of their faith.

Some years ago I met with all the priests of our local church in small groups to talk about their ministry and to listen to what they wanted to tell me about their service to God's people. Among other things, I asked them to tell me what they found most invigorating, most positive about the work they did. I still remember vividly one priest's answer to that question. "I am always astounded how the people keep coming, week after week," he said. "I am not always at my best. Our parish's music is not all that great. Many of our parishioners have sizeable families, and it takes a lot of effort to get the kids ready to come to church. It would be so easy for them just to stay home. But they come, and I get to celebrate the Eucharist for them and talk to them about God. It never ceases to amaze me. I can't tell you how grateful I am."

Priests (and other Church ministers) will resonate to that reaction, even as they resonate to Paul's congenial memory of his work among the Thessalonians. What's at issue here is not just gratitude to the flock we serve for their attention to us. It's also gratitude to the Lord for having given us the gift of being able to help look after his people.

It's not always easy to be a minister of God's word. Those who speak for the Lord are often victims of misunderstanding and unrealistic expectations. Sometimes there are personality clashes between shepherd and flock. Sometimes we get tired and discouraged. Not every priest is gifted with limitless energy and talent, and not every parishioner is particularly receptive. There's a lot of humanity in the Church!

Yet most of us wouldn't dream of spending our lives in any other way than in ministry. We are grateful for the opportunity to express the love of the Lord Jesus for his people, to act as his representatives in the celebration of the Church's sacraments. We take pleasure in speaking God's word to his people, in offering them hope and meaning for their lives. We get to set before our "customers" the most important and the most beneficial "wares" that anybody would ever want to offer: participation in the life of God and in unending happiness. Everything we do in our ministry is directed toward bringing about the coming of the kingdom of God. Every aspect of our work has dimensions of eternity.

Those of us who are called to spend our lives in service to salvation like what we do. We are thankful for our vocation. We love the people we have been sent to serve and we are grateful for the respect and response that our people give to us. We are happy to spend ourselves in their service. Pastors' love affairs with their congregations have not been limited to first-century Thessalonica.

Yet it isn't just full-time "professional" ministers who have been called to preach the gospel and reach out to God's people. Every Christian believer shares some measure of responsibility for bringing about the fullness of the kingdom. No Church member is called to passivity. We are all called to share the blessings that have been entrusted to us, even if all we can do is let others see how much we appreciate what we have received from the Lord. We may not all be called to working night and day in the Lord's vineyard, but we all have at least a part-time job there.

FOR DISCUSSION AND REFLECTION

In what ways do I perceive the dedication of the Church's ministers addressed to me?

How hard do I myself work at spreading the gospel?

Thirty-first Sunday in Ordinary Time (B)

Hebrews 7:23-28

The author of Hebrews has shown us a sinless Christ present to the Father in heaven, appointed high priest by the Father. This Sunday's reading speaks of the ongoing nature of the sacrifice of Christ the priest.

The author is continuing his teaching about the superiority of Christ and his sacrifice to the Levitical priesthood and the sacrifices of the Old Law. He begins this week's passage by pointing out that the Aaronic priesthood required many priests because each of them was subject to death and so could only exercise an impermanent priestly ministry. The risen Christ, on the other hand, will never die and so exercises a priesthood that lasts forever. For that reason he is fully, totally and without interruption interceding with God for those whom he represents, that is, for all of humankind. In Christ, the author says, we have the kind of priest we need, holy and sinless, distinct from sinners (though not without concern for them), established in the presence of God. His sacrifice is not a repeated offering for his own needs and then for the needs of his people. It is the ongoing presentation to the Father of his once for all offering of himself (an offering he made throughout his life and which reached its peak in his death on the cross). Moreover, the priesthood of Christ is not the result of the provisions of the law that established the priesthood of Aaron. Christ's priesthood was established subsequent to the law, to replace it, by a special oath on the part of God. (The allusion here is to Psalm 110, which we have already heard, and in which the messiah-king is addressed: "The Lord has sworn and he will not repent: 'You are a priest forever according to the order of Melchizedek.'") It is God's Son who is our priest and who makes an offering that is eternally pleasing to God.

("Once for all" Christ offers his unique, unchanging sacrifice. This phrase could almost be a summary of the whole teaching of the Letter to the Hebrews. The Greek words it translates occur no less than eleven times in this book of the New Testament.)

This Sunday's live letter is important for our understanding of the unique sacrifice of the Church, the holy Eucharist. There are two facets of the eucharistic sacrifice that we need to be aware of if we are to understand it correctly.

First of all, the Eucharist is the re-presentation of the sacrifice of Jesus. When the bread and wine are transformed into the body and blood of Christ, Jesus' sacrifice of himself—offered throughout his life, culminating in his death on the cross—is once more made present in our midst. It is not a new sacrifice, as if Jesus were dying on the cross another time. It is one and the

same sacrifice that Jesus made "once for all" and that continues
to be offered by the risen Christ, our priest in the presence of the
Father. It's as if somehow we are granted access to the heavenly
court and enabled to join ourselves to the one, ongoing self-
offering of Christ. Through the Eucharist we are associated with
the offering of the "priest forever according to the order of
Melchizedek," the offering of the Son "made perfect forever."

At the same time, however, the eucharistic sacrifice is also
the offering of the Church, of the entire Church of every place
and every time, as well as of this particular portion of the Church
that is present at this particular offering of the Mass. When we
participate in the Eucharist, we become associated with the self-
offering of Christ in heaven, but we also make our own offering of
ourselves. We pray for forgiveness. We ask God's help with our
problems and our burdens. We intercede for our loved ones. We
pray for our enemies. It is Christ's sacrifice, to be sure, but it is
ours as well.

The ordained priest who offers the Mass represents Christ
crucified, glorified, standing in the presence of the Father. But he
is also the representative of this group of believers, here, today.

Each celebration of the Eucharist is the same, because each
celebration of the Eucharist represents the "once for all" sacrifice
of Christ. Yet each celebration of the Eucharist is different,
because each is a different combination of priest and people, of
needs and wants, of past history and present circumstances. We
need to participate in the offering of the Eucharist regularly—
over and over again—because we have an ongoing need to unite
ourselves with the sacrifice of Christ. One might say the repeated
offering of the Mass is the Church's most important task. Yet,
while each Eucharist represents a different moment in our
relationship with God and with our brothers and sisters in faith,
each Eucharist is also one and the same sacrifice of Christ.

There is a fine point of English vocabulary that is relevant
here. It's the difference between *continual* and *continuous*.
Continual means frequently repeated with short interruptions.

Continuous means absolutely without interruptions. The Church offers the Eucharist continually. Christ's offering is continuous.

FOR DISCUSSION AND REFLECTION

How frequently do I participate in the Eucharist? Why?
What do I pray for at Mass?

Thirty-first Sunday in Ordinary Time (C)

II Thessalonians 1:11-2:2

Like the first letter to the Thessalonians, the second is also a letter of consolation and encouragement. The Thessalonians seem to have been fascinated with the Church's teaching about the second coming of Christ at the end of time (which theologians call the Parousia), and seemed to need reassurance about certain aspects of it. Second Thessalonians treats the Parousia at greater length than does First Thessalonians, but it is prominent enough in both letters to make them appropriate for reading as the Church's year draws to an end. We have a series of semi-continuous readings from First Thessalonians at the end of Year A and from Second Thessalonians on Sundays thirty-one to thirty-three in Year C.

Scholars are not clear about whether Second Thessalonians is the immediate and personal work of Paul. Some think the letter was written later than Paul's time. Others that it was written in Paul's name by one or more of his collaborators. Whoever the author, this short letter is nonetheless the inspired word of God.

The reading for this Sunday is composed of the ending of the blessing that begins the letter and the beginning of the main body of the letter in which the author sets forth his teaching about the Parousia.

The author assures the Thessalonians that they are in his

prayers. He prays that God will continue to help them mature in their discipleship, and assist them in the pursuit of goodness and the deepening of their faith that has already begun. At the same time, he also prays that they themselves may respond appropriately to the gifts they have been given so as to become agents of God's glory.

Next the author begins to deal with the Thessalonians' concerns about the Parousia. Apparently somebody had been telling them that the definitive gathering of God's holy ones that would constitute the context for the final coming of Christ had already begun. Christ would appear any day now! The author appeals to them not to allow themselves to be upset by such ideas, whether the ideas' source be some supposedly spirit-inspired utterance, or a philosophical teaching, or even a letter claiming to be from Paul. The author (in verses that follow our Sunday reading) then goes on to remind them that they had been taught that great tribulations had to come before the end and that these tribulations had not yet appeared.

Although what the author has to say to the Thessalonians in these verses is immediately addressed to issues that no longer seem urgent to us, his teaching still has something to say to us.

In the blessing section of this Sunday's reading, we are reminded of several basic realities in our relationship with God. First of all, in speaking of our being made worthy of God's calling and of the fulfillment that lies ahead for our efforts, the author is teaching us that faith and discipleship are not once and for all matters, like objects that we are to hang on to. No, faith and discipleship constitute a relationship that admits of growth and development. We are not true disciples unless we are deepening our personal connection with the Lord.

This growth requires the ongoing action of God. It is God who makes us worthy of his calling and who brings our good purposes to fulfillment. All growth, all gift comes from him. Yet we have a part to play, too. We are not just passive recipients of God's grace. Just as God is to be glorified by the generosity that is manifest in us, so also we are to be glorified by the degree to which we assimilate and respond to what God offers us. Holiness is God's doing, but it won't happen unless we do our part.

The fascination of the Thessalonians at the prospect of the immediate coming of Christ and the response that Second Thessalonians offers to them have something to teach us, too. They suggest that we need to be cautious about buying into what might be called "shortcut spirituality." It is not unusual for believers to run across self-appointed prophets who claim to offer quick and simple access to final fulfillment. All you have to do is say this prayer a certain number of times! All you have to do is go on pilgrimage to a certain place! All you have to do is get more involved in the liturgy! All you have to do is put social justice into a more prominent place in your life! Everything is simple, everything is speedy if you just find the one universal key. No further struggle will be required, no uncertainty, no perseverance. "All you have to do is..."

Of course it's not that simple, whether the "all you have to do" is sit down and wait for the Lord to come or dedicate yourself to more up-to-date spiritual fashions. Christian life is an ongoing effort that is contextualized in time and complexity. You have to work at it and it's not easy. That's the message that we begin to hear in this reading and that we will hear more of in the next couple of Sundays' live letters. It's a message that will help us keep our spiritual balance.

FOR DISCUSSION AND REFLECTION

How is my spirituality a matter of collaboration between God and me?

Have I ever been tempted to get involved in "shortcut spirituality"?

Thirty-second Sunday in Ordinary Time (A)

I Thessalonians 4:13-14

Jesus had taught his followers that, although the kingdom of God had already begun in him, there was a final stage of it that was still to come. He himself would return from heaven triumphantly to judge the living and the dead and to unite all of creation with the life of the Trinity. Jesus' teaching would not be set down in writing in the gospel accounts for more than twenty years after the composition of First Thessalonians, but the teaching would have been presented orally to the Thessalonians by Paul and his colleagues.

Jesus' promise that he would return again in glory (a return that theologians refer to as the Parousia, or final presence of the Lord) was the source of some questions in the early Church. Most Christians of the first generation or so (including Paul, at least during the early years of his ministry) seem to have looked for the coming of Christ in their own lifetime. What they wanted to know was how they could know that it was drawing near. What signs would indicate its coming? Another question that arose, especially as the years went by and some of the earliest believers died without experiencing the Parousia, was whether those who had died would somehow be deprived of their participation in the Lord's glorious return.

Paul deals with the first of these questions in chapter 5 of First Thessalonians. We will hear his answer next Sunday. The second question is the subject of the end of chapter 4 that we read from on this Sunday.

Paul begins by assuring the Thessalonians that their attitude toward their loved ones who had died should be different from the attitudes of non-believers, that is, those "who have no hope." Believers who have died ("fallen asleep") will be united with Christ who not only died but also rose from the dead.

He goes on to assure them, with full apostolic authority, that being alive at the time of the Parousia will not bring with it any particular benefit that those who have died will not enjoy. When the Lord returns in glory in the midst of angelic voices and the sounds of the celestial symphony, those who are already dead will rise from their graves. Those who are living will be joined with them to be united with the Lord. All will be with the Lord forever. This prospect should be a source of confidence and comfort for them all.

We Christian believers of the twenty-first century do not seem to make as much of the prospect of the Lord's second coming as did the Christians of the first generations. True, in the Creed we still profess our belief that Christ "will come again in glory to judge the living and the dead and his kingdom will have no end." But one suspects that not many of us spend much time worrying about whether that coming will occur today, or in the near future.

Yet this article of our faith is not without meaning even for us. We may not be much concerned about what is going to happen to whom when the end comes, but we still need to acknowledge that there will be an end, that our present world only expresses God's interim plan, that there is something much more complete, much more final, much more perfect that is still to come. We also need to be aware that Jesus promises us final justice, that, when he comes again in glory, every human being and every human situation will be subject to and finally evaluated by the judgment of God. We also need to remember that our final happiness will be constituted by our being together with and in the Lord and that, by implication, those who have rejected the Lord will find that they have placed themselves beyond the pale of ultimate fulfillment.

What Paul tells the Thessalonians in this reading also offers us reassurance in our concern for our loved ones who have died. We Catholics tend to be careful about our dead. We not only see to the celebration of appropriate rituals of death and burial. We also pray for our dead and have Masses offered for them and look forward to being with them in the final kingdom. It's as if we instinctively know that they are somehow already with the Lord and that that contact with the Lord offers some kind of contact with us who are still here and still in touch with the Lord in a transitory and earthly way. The final state, in which all of us "shall always be with the Lord," has somehow already begun for them and we somehow maintain contact with them through the Lord.

The Church's teaching about the second coming and about our ongoing relationship with those who have preceded us in death is important because it keeps us aware of the relativity of our present existence. We are indeed called to proclaim Christ's salvation to the world around us. We are expected to extend the life and ministry of Christ here and now. But the world around us and the here and now are only the prelude to the final state that God has in mind for us. Earthly effort and suffering, success and failure in the course of our life, separation from our loved ones in death are only momentary episodes in the drama that God has written for the world. Jesus' teaching about the Parousia invites us to look forward to something more, when "the voice of an archangel" has spoken and "the trumpet of God" has sounded.

FOR DISCUSSION AND REFLECTION

What part does the second coming of Christ play in my spirituality?
What closeness do I feel to my loved ones who have died?

Thirty-second Sunday in Ordinary Time (B)

Hebrews 9:24-28

The author of Hebrews continues to encourage his listeners to perseverance in their faith by showing them the superiority of Christ and of his sacrifice to the Jewish laws and rites.

This Sunday's reading opens with a look at the Holy of Holies in the Jerusalem temple. This most sacred part of the temple was intended as a representation of heaven, so holy that the high priest could enter it only once a year. Jesus did not make his sacrifice in a sanctuary like this, which only represented heaven. His offering of himself takes place in heaven itself, in the real and immediate presence of God. Moreover, the sacrifice of Jesus wasn't something that had to be done each year, over and over again, a repeated offering of sacrificial blood. It was a one-time sacrifice that never needs to be repeated, a sacrifice that takes away sin once for all forever. This sacrifice constituted the beginning of the definitive age of creation. No further sacrifice, no further covenant would ever be needed. The final chapter of God's relationship with us has now begun.

Toward the end of our passage the author draws a parallel between the death and judgment of ordinary people and the final coming of Christ. Just as judgment follows our death, so also is there a judgment that will follow Christ's giving of himself. The difference, however, is that, after our death we are the judged. The consequence of Christ's sacrificial death "offered once to take away the sins of many" (that is, of all), is that he will come at the end of time not to be judged but to judge. He will bring final fulfillment and unending happiness to all those who have been faithful in looking for his arrival.

Our reading teaches us that Christ offered his life to the Father once. His sacrificial offering has conducted the world into its final age, "once for all." There is nothing more to look for because we have already received all that God can give us. No further sacrifices are needed because the self-offering of Jesus has won forgiveness for the sins of all those who will accept what he offers them. All that is left is to await the final fulfillment of creation when Jesus appears a second time "to bring salvation to those who eagerly await him."

Again we hear "once for all," the recurrent refrain of Hebrews. We don't have to worry about what will happen next, because the most important thing that can occur has already taken place, "once for all."

"Once for all" is a good watchword for Christian spirituality. There is always a dimension of change in our lives. We grow from childhood to adolescence, from adulthood to old age. As we look back along the path that we have already traveled in our journey we see that we are not the same as we were. The adult is not the same as the child, the older person is different from the adolescent. As we review our lives, we all sometimes wonder how we could have been so childish back then, so adolescent, so immature. In addition to such ordinary changes there are the specific details of our individual human existence, the events and sorrows and achievements, the joys and the pains that make us the particular person that we are. We sometimes wonder how it all happened, how we managed to do and endure everything that has gone into our personal life story. We are always in a state of change.

But the Lord is always there for us, unchanging and faithful. In the presence of his Father, Jesus intercedes for all his human brothers and sisters, unerringly, unswervingly, continuously, "once for all." His love is the fundamental constant in our human existence, the unchanging background on which our individual human drama is played out. We don't have to wait for him to decide whether he's going to love us and care for us. That has already been determined, "once for all." We don't have to be concerned about whether forgiveness will be available for us when we have sinned. Jesus has already made up for the sins of all the world "once for all." Our task is not to change God's mind so he will look on us with favor, but to open ourselves to the favor that God already offers us through Jesus.

This "once for all" spirituality is expressed in the devotion that Catholic Christians have for the celebration of the holy Eucharist. Week after week, year after year, in times of pain and in times of prosperity, in days of doubt and days of determination, whatever our age or level of maturity, we all know that we have to hang on to the Mass, that it is there that we find the center and the directing energy of our lives. Our faith leads us to the awareness that it is the Lord Jesus, "once for all" representing us in the presence of his Father, who gives unity and significance to all the stages of our human existence as we move through them and offer them on the altar in conjunction with his ongoing offering of himself. Our life gets its meaning from the "once for all" risen life of Christ, the risen life we encounter in the Eucharist.

FOR DISCUSSION AND REFLECTION

How would my life be different if I never went to Mass?

In what ways have I experienced Christ as an element of continuity in my life?

Thirty-second Sunday in Ordinary Time (C)

II Thessalonians 2:16-3:5

Last Sunday's reading consisted of the end of the beginning and the beginning of the middle of Second Thessalonians. This Sunday's reading is composed of the ending of the central portion of the letter (in which the author set out his teaching about the signs of the coming of the Parousia) and the beginning of its conclusion (in which the author presents practical exhortations).

He has been describing the trials that are to come before the final return of Christ and reassuring the Thessalonians of their calling to glory.

As this Sunday's reading begins, Paul is summing up his reassurance of the Thessalonians. He prays that the Lord who has already given them his love and encouragement and hope will continue to give them ongoing fortitude and stamina in doing good. (This call for persistence and stability in living out their Christian life is one of the recurrent themes of Second Thessalonians.)

Next our reading offers us the opening of the concluding

section of the letter in which the author deals with practical applications of the teaching he has offered them. This Sunday's reading offers us two of these exhortations. A third one will constitute next Sunday's live letter.

The author asks his hearers first of all to pray for him. He reminds them how productive God's work had been in their midst and invites them to ask God to make it equally productive elsewhere. He also asks them to pray for God's protection for him from evil and faithless people.

The mention of people without faith triggers the next item the author wants to talk about: the faithfulness of God. "Not all people have faith, but God is faithful." He invites them to be reassured of God's protection of them. Then he has still more to say about perseverance. He is confident that they are already carrying out his instructions, and that they will continue to do so. He hopes that their hearts will be directed toward the love of God and toward the steadfast faithfulness of Christ.

Encouragement, hope, strength, continuing in faithfulness, endurance in responding to the demands of faith: these are the things to which Second Thessalonians calls its addressees. This is a letter about perseverance and steadfastness, and therein lies its significance for us.

These readings serve to remind us that having faith is not a matter of a one-time burst of enthusiasm, but of ongoing dedication.

Of course it is true that God's relationship with us rests on what we might call "surprise interventions," on one-time, non-repeatable events that change the whole direction of reality. Such "surprise interventions" include creation, the Incarnation of the divine Son of God in human nature, Jesus' Resurrection from the dead, and (still to occur) the final coming of Christ to judge the living and the dead at the end of time. These are all unique events that depend entirely on God's initiative. They are unpredictable and we can't make them happen. They take place in ways and times that God has chosen. They constitute the foundations of our faith and hope, the rationale for our love of God and neighbor.

Most of our life of faith, however, is spent in responding to and assimilating these cosmic surprises. God calls us not just to waiting for the next surprise to occur but to be active in carrying out the implications of what God has already done, in digesting the gifts that have already been given us. To be sure, nothing can happen without the breathtaking energy and creativity of God. But God's undertakings will not reach their fulfillment unless we do our part in making them our own. The Thessalonians' mistake did not consist in their looking forward to the second coming of Christ, but in their putting everything else on hold while they waited.

In this interim time between the basic acts of salvation that took place in the context of Jesus' life and the final completion of redemption in Christ's Parousia we are called to be Church. We are called to ongoing and patient incorporation of ourselves in the life of the risen Christ that we began to live in baptism. We are also called to making this life of Christ appealing and accessible to others. All this takes place not in intermittent and random spurts of fervor, but in days and years of steady responsiveness, in days and years of ongoing encouragement of others to share what we ourselves have been given. Of course waiting for the end is part of our Christian faith, but we are called to be busy while we wait.

It's all God's doing. It's all God's initiative. It all happens on God's schedule, and it's not over yet. The Thessalonians thought they had God's schedule all figured out and that they could just sit back and wait. They were wrong. We don't have God's schedule figured out any more than they did, but at least we know that, while everything isn't over yet, there is plenty for us to do in the meantime.

What part does waiting for the Parousia play in my spirituality?

What contributions do I make to the Church's ongoing mission?

Thirty-third Sunday in Ordinary Time (A)

I Thessalonians 5:1-6

Having dealt with the Thessalonians' worries about how those who had died would participate in Christ's second coming, Paul turns his attention to their other question: when would it happen and how could they tell it was coming? (The Thessalonians seem to have been much preoccupied with the Parousia. In Second Thessalonians we learn that some of them had given up working because they thought that the Parousia had already occurred. It could be that the seeds of errors like this were already present when Paul addressed this first letter to them.)

At the beginning of this Sunday's passage Paul tells them that they don't need to have access to God's timetable because they have already been taught everything they need to know about the second coming. He then reminds them of the teaching they had received.

First of all, the people who live without any awareness of what lies ahead of them, who think that everything will forever stay exactly as it is now are in for some shocks. The Parousia will come upon them as an unpleasant surprise, like the surprise the householder experiences when he finds a thief in the house in the middle of the night. It will be inescapably painful, like the pains that a woman experiences in childbirth.

But it doesn't have to be that way for believers. They are not vulnerable to thieves in the night because they live in the daylight, the daylight that is constituted by their faith. This means that they have to live in consistency with that faith life, attentive and self-controlled, not complacent and careless like the sleepy people of the night.

In effect, Paul sidesteps the Thessalonians' question about the timing of the Parousia. Its scheduling is not important, he tells them. What's important is the way the prospect of the Parousia impacts our life now. That's the message for us, too.

One might say that the apostolic teaching about Jesus' return in glory to judge the living and the dead is a call for planning, for long-range planning and for short-range planning.

Our faith tells us that God's loving justice will triumph in the end. At some point, a point that is known only to God, all the uncertainty and equivocation and ambiguity that go into our human existence, corporate and individual, will be wiped away. All the evil that seemed to flourish without check will be punished. All the good that never seems to receive adequate recognition will be manifested and rewarded. Everything will at last be what our deepest and purest aspirations have always wished. God will be fully and finally in charge of everything. All creation will share in God's own life.

This is what we have to look forward to. But our place in the final kingdom, our position in God's final ordering of things will depend on what we have made of ourselves here and now. Every choice, every moral decision we make now helps form and prepare us for what we will be then. The values that shape our life here will also shape our life there. Our present priorities will determine our eternal aptitudes. God will not judge us capriciously. He will rather verify and validate what we have made of ourselves throughout the course of our lifetime, how we have collaborated with or frustrated his gifts and plans.

This means that our day-to-day existence has an eternal and final dimension to it. We will not be permitted to make our fundamental decisions in the final seconds of creation, just before Christ returns. We make our fundamental decisions each and every day, and those decisions determine what we will be for all eternity. It all contributes to our long-range planning for our future.

But Christ is not absent from us as we work and plan for our participation in the kingdom. Christ is not waiting offstage for his cue to return to the world in glory. Christ is in our midst now, in the heart and soul of each believer, in the worth and dignity of each human being. In fact, he teaches us that the relationship that we can expect to have with him in the future is determined by the way we treat him now in his brothers and sisters who are also our brothers and sisters (see Matthew 25:31-46). Every human encounter that we experience is an opportunity to encounter Christ.

In addition to Christ's presence in other human beings, Christ also offers himself to us in his sacred Scripture, in his sacraments, in the teachings of his Church. He is with us in our prayer. Christ is all over the place and wants us to recognize him and respond to him everywhere. Our day-to-day existence has to be attentive and watchful. While we are planning for our ultimate future, we also have to be making and carrying out plans about our relationship with Christ now.

It really doesn't matter when God has scheduled the Parousia. It may come tomorrow afternoon or in a million years. What does matter is whether I am awake and ready for it today.

FOR DISCUSSION AND REFLECTION

How am I attentive to the final coming of the Lord?

How do I stay attentive to the Lord's presence in my life now?

Thirty-third Sunday in Ordinary Time (B)

Hebrews 10:11-14, 18

The readings we have heard from Hebrews have taught us that Jesus is a true priest "according to the order of Melchizedek," that he belongs to a priesthood superior to that of the descendants of Aaron, that he offers a superior sacrifice and a more effective forgiveness. This Sunday's reading reiterates these teachings and recasts them in a slightly new framework.

Our text begins by contrasting once more the priesthood of the Old Law and that of Jesus. The Jewish priests had to stand at the altar offering their animal sacrifices over and over again because what they had to offer was never able to take away sins definitively. Jesus, on the other hand, sits at the right hand of God, his sacrificial task now concluded. The only thing still to come is the final fulfillment when everything comes under Jesus' ultimate dominion. (The text alludes to the messianic psalm [110] that we have heard from so often: "Sit at my right hand till I make your enemies your footstool.") The one sacrifice of Jesus is complete and those for whom it was offered are forever forgiven.

At this point in the full text of Hebrews the author cites a passage of Jeremiah (31:33 and following) that is omitted in the lectionary text. Jeremiah speaks of the establishment of a new covenant between God and his people. The citation's last words promise that God will remember "their sins and evildoing" no more. Our lectionary picks up the full text here and concludes with the assurance that, because "these" offenses have now been forgiven, there is no need for further sin offerings.

In this passage, the word "forever" serves as a catchword, just as "once for all" did in other passages we have heard. Jesus is seated "forever" at God's right hand. This signifies not that Jesus no longer intercedes for us, but that his basic sacrificial task is now completed and that no further exertion is needed from him. There is no more that needs to be done. Those for whom his sacrifice was offered no longer need anything else. They are made perfect "forever," liberated from all future requirements. In the context of the Jewish sacrifices, there is no "forever," but rather "never." Their sacrifices will not ever be fully effective.

God's word is not telling us here that no effort is required on our part to attain salvation or that we need not struggle against sin. But it is assuring us that everything that is necessary for our salvation has been accomplished, once for all and forever, through the sacrificial self-giving of Jesus. Any deficiency, any detachment from God, any vacillation in our attachment to the Lord is on our part, not on God's part. We may walk away from Christ and the salvation he offers us, but Christ will never not be enough for us. His sacrifice has achieved full forgiveness for everybody. There's no need to repeat it. There's no need to look for anything else. It's all been taken care of, forever.

These passages that we have heard from the Letter to the Hebrews are rich with Scriptural allusions and seemingly arcane interpretations. They offer us a theology of salvation that is sometimes hard to understand. In the final analysis, though, they offer to us the same thing they were meant to offer their first hearers: hope and encouragement. If we have read Hebrews carefully, we will never need to wonder whether we are really saved. We will never need to fear that maybe we have missed out on something, that there's still more to come that we may not be part of. We will be assured that our day-to-day efforts to remain faithful and our rejection of the attractive come-ons that the world offers us resonate with the ongoing self-gift of Jesus who, although his sacrifice is now complete, still offers himself on our behalf.

The teaching of Hebrews also enables us to approach the Eucharist and the other sacraments with appropriate understanding. Jesus doesn't die again each time the Mass is celebrated. Jesus doesn't have to decide again whether to forgive us when we go to confession or whether to strengthen us when we receive the anointing of the sick. We don't have to persuade him to make us like himself in baptism or to watch over us in matrimony or holy orders. All that is already taken care of. Our celebration of the sacraments constitutes the application to these particular people of the salvation that Jesus has already achieved for us all. Our task is to accept, to respond to what Jesus has done for us once for all and forever.

Next Sunday will mark the end of the Church's liturgical year. It seems appropriate to spend the last weeks of our year assimilating the assurance and encouragement that Hebrews offers us, so that we are able to look forward with confidence to the final fulfillment at the end of time that Christ the King promises us.

FOR DISCUSSION AND REFLECTION

What elements of my life can I expect to last forever?

What have been the most constant elements of my life so far?

Thirty-third Sunday in Ordinary Time (C)

II Thessalonians 3:7-12

In this last reading from Second Thessalonians, the author sets forth one more time the theme that he has presented more than once already: the need for steady perseverance in carrying out the demands of our Christian faith. Shortcuts lead nowhere!

Some members of the young church of Thessalonica had decided that work need no longer be part of their lives. This decision may have been based on the expectation of an immediate Parousia, so that any involvement with things of the world would be useless. It may also have been rooted in the pagan Greek attitude that work was for slaves. It may have resulted from a kind of condescending mind-set on the part of some that, since they were more spiritual than the rest, they could not be expected to share in mundane responsibilities like earning a living. Whatever the justification for their aversion to work, by their espousal of off-beat ideas they were undermining the good order of the community.

In our live letter reading for this Sunday, Paul (or the disciple of Paul who is writing in his person) is calling them back to order.

First of all, he tells them that they should follow his (Paul's) example of working to pay his own way when he was with them. He seems to take a saintly pride in the fact that he didn't just move in and expect to be taken care of. On the contrary, he supported himself by hard work "night and day."

Of course he had the right to be taken care of! This came with his being a preacher of the good news to them. But he chose not to exercise that right in order to give them an example of how they themselves should behave. (Paul's insistence on supporting himself in the course of his apostolic work seems to have been a personal characteristic of his and of his immediate associates. He speaks of it in First Thessalonians 2:9 and in both letters to the Corinthians [I Corinthians 9:3-18 and II Corinthians 11:7 and 12:13]. It seems that in Corinth Paul's insistence on self-support was seen by some as an indication that he wasn't as important as other preachers of the gospel who, presumably, allowed themselves to be taken care of by the local community. Paul's references to his work in the Corinth letters have a defensive ring to them. He certainly has no hesitancy about calling the Christian faithful to imitate him.)

Next our author moves from inviting the Thessalonians to imitate Paul to giving them explicit directions. He reminds them of the directions that Paul gave them when he was with them, namely that refusal to work constituted a forfeiture of the right to be cared for. Then comes the former direction in a new format: "Don't be so busy about getting other people to agree with your point of view that you can't do productive work," he says in effect. He instructs them "in the Lord Jesus" to stay busy with productive work and to maintain responsibility for caring for their own needs.

Catholic Christian thought has given lots of attention to the idea of work since the time of the Thessalonian letters. The basic Pauline insight into the importance, indeed, the virtue, of being willing to look after ourselves as best we can has developed into a whole Christian theology of work.

Work is not just something we engage in to keep ourselves away from the troubles that come with idleness. Nor is it just a task that we have to perform in order to earn a living. Paul's directions to the Thessalonians have led Christian thinkers to the conclusion that work has a central—and positive—part to play in our lives in the Lord.

Work is the contribution that each of us makes to the development and unfolding of creation. God left much of the task of bringing the world to fulfillment to us human creatures. We engage in that task by the words and actions of our work life, by the way we bring together and modify the elements of creation that God has given us. Each day the world is a little different because of all the work that human beings have done. That difference is our human contribution to the created reality that God has entrusted to us.

Catholic social teaching has also come to see that people have a right to work. Simply because they are human beings, they are qualified and expected to participate in the development of creation. To deprive people of the possibility of engaging in this developmental project is to deprive them of an important element of their human existence. This means that society has a responsibility to help men and women become skilled and educated enough so that they can make their personal contributions to the ongoing creative process.

The example that Paul gave the Thessalonians to imitate and the directions that today's live letter provides are only the initial components of Christian awareness about the implications of work. Certainly we work to stay out of trouble. We work to make a living for ourselves. We work to keep our community peaceful and productive. But we also work to help God bring creation to its fulfillment.

FOR DISCUSSION AND REFLECTION

Is there anyone I find it helpful to imitate? Who? Why?

How does the work I do contribute to the development of creation?

PART SIX

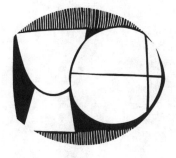

solemnities

Our Lord Jesus Christ the King (A)

I Corinthians 15:20-26, 28

The sovereign lordship of Christ is celebrated often during the course of the Church's liturgical year. It is implicit in the feasts of Epiphany, of Easter, of Ascension. We also recall the ultimate triumph of Christ in every celebration of the Eucharist: "Lord Jesus, come in glory;" "Through him, with him, in him...all glory and honor is yours, almighty Father."

In addition to all that, however, there is the solemnity of Christ the King, which we celebrate on the thirty-fourth Sunday in Ordinary Time. Pope Pius XI established the feast of Christ the King in 1925 to be celebrated on the last Sunday of October. He intended it to be an antidote to the increasing atheism and secularism of his time. In the liturgical reforms of Vatican II, the tonality of the feast became more cosmic and eschatological (that is, concerned with the end of the world and the ultimate destiny of humankind), and its observance was moved to the last Sunday of the Church's year. In its theme and in its place in the calendar, the feast of Christ the King has to do with finality—but also with futurity.

The live letter that the Church gives us for this feast is a heavy passage from chapter fifteen of First Corinthians. Some members of the young church of Corinth seem to have thought that the resurrection of the dead had already occurred, perhaps at the coming of the Holy Spirit, and that nothing more should be expected. Paul answers that, if they deny the resurrection of the dead, they must deny the Resurrection of Jesus, too. But Jesus' death and resurrection and ongoing life constitute the cornerstone of their faith, and, if there is no such thing as resurrection (for Christ and for us), our faith is meaningless.

This is where our passage begins. The fact of the matter is that Christ has risen from the dead and that his Resurrection is just the beginning of what all the faithful will share. There is a parallel between Christ and Adam. Adam brought death for everybody and Christ brings life for everybody. It doesn't all happen at once, of course. Christ's Resurrection constitutes the beginning. When he returns in glory at the end of time, all those who belong to him will arise, too.

After that will come cosmic completion. Christ will have achieved dominion over all the hostile powers of sin. Finally (in the general resurrection) he will have triumphed over death itself, that most basic consequence of sin. Then Christ will offer "the kingdom" (that is, a redeemed humanity, a redeemed creation) to his heavenly Father. At that point ("when everything is subjected to him"), the humanity of Christ will be definitively subjected to the Father, so that all reality is now once more in obedient union with God.

Our passage is filled with references to Christ as King: "those who *belong* to him;" "he hands over the *kingdom* to his God and Father;" "he must *reign*;" "everything is *subjected to him.*" In all these different ways Paul is teaching the Corinthians that Christ is still alive, that he is in charge of things now, and that the ultimate conclusion of everything will be the dominion of Christ which will be offered to the Father.

Most of us find the Corinthians' difficulties with resurrection rather quaint. Theirs are not the concerns that we are busy with. Yet what Paul has to say to them is not without relevance to us. Paul's teaching in this passage reminds us that we have a corporate future, that our human existence is not just a matter of living without reproach until our allotted days have run out and then gratefully taking the place that has been individually assigned to us in heaven. Paul invites all of us who are in Christ to look forward together to a final, universal, symphonic society in which the significance of the contributions of each of us will be manifested, in which each of us will be aware of how the lives of all of us had a part to play in the all-embracing love of Christ for his human brothers and sisters. We will all arise in new life, but that life will be one life, the life of Christ the King.

Our present task is not just to stay out of trouble until we are liberated from this world of sin. Our present task is to contribute to the formation of the kingdom, to extend the presence and action of Christ to the world around us so that every aspect of that world will fit into the final harmony that is constituted by the universal dominion of Christ.

Reflection on the kingship of Christ invites us to awareness that our present life is not a waiting room, a gathering place where we pass the time until we are called to go elsewhere. On the contrary, our present life is a workroom where all of us together are invited to collaborate on a final future that will consist in the completion of redemption and the handing over of all creation to God.

As one year ends, we look forward to the beginning of another. But we also look forward to a time when there will be no more endings or beginnings because Christ the King will have brought everything to a final, unending present.

FOR DISCUSSION AND REFLECTION

How do I experience the dominion of Christ in my life now?

How do I participate in the building up of Christ's kingdom?

Our Lord Jesus Christ the King (B)

Revelation 1:5-8

This Sunday is the thirty-fourth and last Sunday in Ordinary Time. It is the end of the Church's liturgical year, and on this day the Church celebrates the feast of Christ the King. Jesus is the Lord and ruler of creation already, thanks to his faithfulness and generosity to his Father in his earthly life. But Jesus is also still to come in glory at the end of time. He is king of the future as well as of the present.

Our second reading for this Sunday is from the Book of Revelation. Revelation is a difficult book of the New Testament for most people. We will be seeing more of it during the Sundays after Easter in Year C. For now, it is enough to say that it was written to give reassurance to the troubled and persecuted Christians of the early Church. Our reading for today is from the beginning of Revelation where the author is introducing the main characters of his book: the glorified Christ and his heavenly Father.

This reading could be described as a series of fanfares, jubilant blasts from the brass section of the heavenly orchestra, each of which identifies some aspect of Christ or his Father.

In the first fanfare we hear about who Christ is: he is the one who was faithful to God till death, the first to return to life from death, and therefore the one exalted above the loftiest of the earth.

The second fanfare offers glory to Christ for what he has done. He has loved us and redeemed us and brought us all together as his kingdom to offer adoration in the presence of his Father.

Now comes some thematic material about Christ from the Old Testament. He will return on the clouds of heaven (as Daniel saw in the first reading). Everybody will lament the price that the Messiah had to pay for their sinfulness (as Zechariah had proclaimed [see 12:10]).

Now another fanfare to introduce the Father: "I am the beginning and the end. Past, present, and future are mine. I am supreme over everything."

These rich and sonorous verses teach us that there is a final moment in our salvation, a moment yet to come in which the glory of Christ and his oneness with the Father will be fully and finally manifested when they come to take final possession of the world for which they have done so much. This teaching also implies that it is important for us to appreciate the significance of our present situation in the world. Yes, we are still on the way to the

Father. Yes, we are still afflicted with our own sinfulness. Yes, an important final resolution is still to come. But the main things have been taken care of. The final triumph of Christ and the Father are assured. At the end it is not human sinfulness or the power of evil that will triumph and reign, but Jesus, the faithful witness, and God the Father, the almighty.

This feast of Christ the King helps each of us to maintain a healthy personal perspective as we come to the end of another Church year. It may well be that we don't seem much closer to God than we were on the First Sunday of Advent of last calendar year. We may have had crosses to bear this year and not be sure how successfully we have carried them. Maybe our life has been bland and ordinary and we have just plodded along from Sunday to Sunday. Have these weeks of my life been of any usefulness to the Lord? Maybe we find ourselves wondering about the direction our life has taken. Where are we really headed? What meaning is there in our daily efforts? These are all appropriate questions, all fitting things to reflect upon. But the feast of Christ the King tells us that there are responses to them all and that the responses rest in him. Our salvation does not depend just on us. Our own life is not determined exclusively or even principally by our own achievements or failures. There is no need to wonder how things are going to turn out. "Behold, he is coming amid the clouds and every eye will see him, the firstborn of the dead, the ruler of the kings of the earth." We know how the story is going to end. We know that the ending will be a happy ending, and we know that we will be part of the happy ending if we choose.

Apart from questions about personal salvation, there are also reasons for Christian believers to wonder about the state of the Church. Christ is rejected by many in the world, unknown by most. Even those who profess belief in him are often lukewarm. We seem to spend a lot of time fighting with one another in the community of worshipers that Christ established. As we look around among our fellow believers, we don't see many who seem to reflect the full splendor of the Lord we serve. Yet as each year of our service to the Lord draws to an end, the Church reminds us that there is still something more to come, still an ending that will be proclaimed by the coming in glory of the Christ who died for us and who will take us forever, as his kingdom, his Church, into the company of his Father.

Whether the context be our individual salvation or the future of the Church at large, true believers are necessarily optimists.

FOR DISCUSSION AND REFLECTION

For what am I most grateful in this liturgical year that is now ending?

What do I most look forward to from the final coming of Christ?

Our Lord Jesus Christ the King (C)

Colossians 1:12-20

It's always helpful to know where you're going. When we start on a long journey, we need to know where we are going so that we will know what roads to take. As we come to the end of various stages on the journey, we keep reminding ourselves of our final goal. That way we reassure ourselves that we have been headed in the right direction and reorient ourselves, to the extent necessary, toward the goal we have been pursuing.

The kingdom of Christ is the goal toward which our life of faith is directed: the fullness of redemption, the final embrace of all believers into the life of the Holy Trinity, the conclusive validation of all the crosses and blessings that have made up our communal and individual life on this earth.

The Church's liturgy calls us to orient ourselves toward the kingdom of Christ at two different yet overlapping points in the year. At the beginning of the Church's year, on the First Sunday of Advent, the liturgy's theme is the second coming of Christ. It's important to know where we are going as we begin a new chapter in our life of faith. The end of the Church's year—the Thirty-fourth and last Sunday in Ordinary Time—calls us to renewed awareness of our goal with the solemnity of Our Lord Jesus Christ, the King. From beginning to end, from end to new beginning, Christian life is concerned with the Lordship of Christ. That's what gives sense and meaning and direction to everything.

Our live letter for this Sunday is from the beginning of the letter to the Colossians. (We already saw most of this reading earlier in the year as we began our semi-continuous reading of Colossians.) This is a passage of praise for the lordship of Christ.

Paul begins by reminding us why we should be grateful to the Father: because he has made us inheritors of heaven and, in forgiving our sins, has delivered us from submission to evil. God has done this by making us participants in the kingdom of his Son. The passage goes on to explain the kingship of the Son (Christ Jesus).

Christ is the master of creation because, as full image of the Father, he is the pattern according to which everything of every sort has been created. He precedes everything and keeps everything in being.

Christ is the master of re-creation, too, the source of a new kind of life that reflects him and that brings everything that had been fragmented by sin into oneness in himself. Through his offering of himself on the cross, Christ brought everything in heaven and everything on earth into a final and permanent unity with himself.

In this profound and radiant passage Paul tells us that Christ is the beginning and the end of everything. Everything good that has ever been has its origin in him. Everything good that is still to come will be a participation in his life. From beginning to end, the Son is in charge. Christ is king. Christ is the kingdom.

This passage teaches us about time, an appropriate lesson for the ending of the year. Christ is the source of our present worth.

Everything good in us is somehow derived from him. Talents, achievements, associations with other people, spiritual gifts that come to us through Scripture and the sacraments: they are all gifts of Christ. We are now, at this present time, creatures of value and dignity, sharing the very worth of God's Son. Christ makes our present precious.

But we are not yet complete. We are still able to sin, still capable of undoing what Christ has done. We are still capable of growth, too, capable of deepening our life in the Lord, of intensifying our relationship with him, of strengthening our participation in the life of others who share his life. Still to come is final reconciliation, final fullness, final peace. We have a future as well as a present, and that future is Christ.

Present and future, already but not yet: those are the contexts in which our Christian life unfolds, the settings in which the kingdom of God develops. It's already here, but it's still to come. But both in present and in future, the kingdom is nothing other than Christ himself. The kingdom is not a project that Christ works on, as if it were something distinct from himself. He is the kingdom and we participate in the kingdom to the extent that we are in him.

Today's year-end celebration reminds us that all creation images Christ now, and that all creation, flawed and damaged by sin as it is, is nonetheless directed toward future fullness in Christ. Every value that is, every goodness that will ever be is rooted in the life of Christ.

Years end and years begin. We have all come a long way on our journey. We still have a long way to go. Today's feast reminds us that, wherever we may be on our journey, both our present and our future find their worth and meaning only in Christ the King.

FOR DISCUSSION AND REFLECTION

How is Christ the center of my life?

Is my life more present or more future oriented?

Most Holy Trinity (A)

II Corinthians 13:11-13

The liturgical celebration of the Holy Trinity, unlike Easter or even Christmas, is not an ancient observance in the Church. In fact, it was made a mandatory part of the Church's liturgical calendar only in 1334. Before that, it was thought that there didn't need to be a special day for honoring the Holy Trinity since the Trinity is sufficiently honored daily in the ongoing, ordinary prayer life of the Church.

Most of the liturgical year is concerned with reflecting on the life and ministry of Jesus. Special celebrations of a single mystery (like the Trinity which we celebrate on this Sunday or the Eucharist which we commemorate next Sunday) are outside the general pattern. Nonetheless, these "special" celebrations do have a place in the Church's community life. They call to our attention the fundamental realities that underlie our whole Christian existence and that energize it as it moves forward to the kingdom's final fulfillment.

This feast's second reading for Year A comes from the very end of Paul's second letter to the Corinthians. It is a short reading in two parts.

First of all, Paul calls on the Corinthians to live together in unity and peace, to take joy in their life in the Lord, to be forgiving, agreeable and encouraging toward one another. They were to reach out to one another and be aware that the whole church was embracing them. All this would guarantee the presence in their midst of the love and peace of God. (What Paul calls for here is particularly significant when we recall that the Corinthian church was beset with factionalism and interpersonal tensions.)

Next comes a final blessing, cast in Trinitarian form. He prays for grace from Christ, love from the Father and fellowship from the Holy Spirit for all his readers. (Scholars point out that this is one of the clearest Trinitarian passages in the New Testament. That would seem to account for its selection for this

Sunday's feast.)

It took several centuries of reflection and discourse for the Church to be able to enunciate its belief about the Trinity in a clear and unequivocal way. While the New Testament authors do seem to have some instinctive grasp of the ideas of person and nature that would be more precisely defined in future centuries, they speak of the Trinity more often in experiential terms.

We, too, relate to the Trinity in the context of prayer rather than in the terms of dogmatic definition. In fact, directing ourselves toward the Trinity constitutes the basic fabric of our corporate prayer life. We generally begin our prayer with the Sign of the Cross. The action is indeed a cross, but the words are a commitment to the Trinity of what we are about to begin. Two of the three greetings that are provided for the beginning of the celebration of Mass are Trinitarian, one of them being a direct quote from our reading. The priest's presidential prayers in the Eucharist are generally addressed to the Father and conclude with an allusion to the mediation of the Son and the Holy Spirit. Most Catholics know the little "Glory be to the Father..." prayer. This may be the most frequently used prayer of the Church's liturgy, since it comes at the end of every psalm and canticle and a couple of other times besides in the liturgy of the hours, so that those who recite the breviary pray it some fifteen times a day.

The Church guides us to keep in touch with the Trinity in our prayer because the Trinity constitutes the basic reality with which our salvation is concerned. It is the source of our being and our redemption. It is the context in which our Christian life unfolds. It is the goal toward which our human destiny is directed.

We find it hard to think and speak with full theological correctness about the Trinity. Even professional theologians choose their words carefully when they deal with the relationships between the Persons and with the predication of qualities to the Persons and to the divine nature, not to mention more esoteric aspects of the Trinity like perichoresis and the communication of idioms.

Yet we also feel an instinctive comfort in dealing with the Trinity. We are at home with the three divine Persons and the one divine nature. We know that through the Trinity we are involved with generosity and love and fellowship. We know that the Trinity is involved with us in creation and salvation and the final life in the Lord that we look forward to at the end of our earthly journey. Our experience in prayer with the Trinity teaches us that God is not solitary, inert, detached, self-centered, but rather that God involves community, communication, self-sharing, unity in love, that God is all-powerful, all-expressive, all-embracing. We are grateful that God has struggled to explain himself to us through the life and teaching of Jesus, but we also know that we only understand enough to be able to say that God is infinitely more than we can grasp.

FOR DISCUSSION AND REFLECTION

What part does the Trinity play in my prayer life?

How does the Church's teaching about the Trinity enable me to relate to God more closely?

Most Holy Trinity (B)

Romans 8:14-17

Before the lectionary brings us back to its semi-continuous readings of the New Testament's live letters in the readings for the Sundays in Ordinary Time, we have two "special interest" Sundays: the feast of the Holy Trinity and (next Sunday) the feast of the Body and Blood of Christ (Corpus Christi). These are liturgical observances of two matters of fundamental doctrinal importance that would never be highlighted if the reading cycle confined itself exclusively to events in the life of Christ or the Church.

The Trinity is the center of everything in our Catholic Christian faith. It is the source of creation and redemption, the goal toward which our existence is directed. It gives sense and meaning to all that is and constitutes the final happiness toward which we struggle.

Yet the Trinity as such was not a major item in the teaching of Jesus. Although he spoke often of the Father and of the Spirit (the Paraclete), he never sat his followers down and said, "Now I'm going to tell you about the triune God, one divine nature in three Persons." He preferred to have them experience the Persons of the Trinity through their relationship with him.

It was the same with the Church. From the very beginning, the Church's teachers spoke quite familiarly about Father, Son and Spirit, but it took three or four hundred years of hard intellectual struggle for the Church to be able to set down in clear propositional form the theological truths that Jesus and his first followers proclaimed and that are found implicitly in the writings of the New Testament. God's providence seems to have called for us to know the Trinity before being able to know about it.

The second reading for Trinity Sunday in Year B is from Paul's letter to the Romans. He has been talking about the tensions between flesh and spirit in our human existence. Then he tells the Romans that they live in the spirit if the Spirit of God dwells in them. The indwelling of God's Spirit gives them a new life.

This is where our reading begins. It's not just a new kind of life that we receive from the Spirit, Paul says, but a whole new relationship with God, a relationship of filiation, of being sons and daughters of God. This new life is not a matter of different rules to follow in order to please God, but of being related to God in such a way that we can call God "Abba, Father, Dad." (Jesus seems to have used the word Abba as his own special term for addressing his Father, a term that now becomes appropriate for us to use thanks to our life in Christ.) But there's more. If we are children of God, as the Spirit assures us, then we are also heirs just as Christ is God's heir. (Note that heir in this context does not signify somebody who comes into property when somebody else dies, but somebody who belongs to the household and has a right to share in the family's life even now. Being heirs with Christ means that we belong to the life of God just as Christ does.) This relationship may call for our suffering as Christ suffered, not in order for us to earn our participation in God's life but to demonstrate that we really belong.

This reading from Romans teaches us about the Holy Trinity by teaching us how God relates to us. The Spirit that unites Father and Son also unites us with Christ, the Son (by making us co-heirs with him), and so makes us children of the Father, family members of God, as it were. We are participants in the community that is constituted by Father, Son and Holy Spirit.

There are lots of questions that arise as Paul teaches the Romans about the meaning of their experience as Christian believers. Is the Son as truly God as the Father is? Is the Holy Spirit God, too? Is the relationship between Son and Father the same as the relationship between Holy Spirit and Father? How do Son and Holy Spirit relate to each other? What words can we appropriately use to signify what Father, Son and Holy Spirit share in common? How can we express their differences from each other? What is the nature of these differences? Are undertakings outside of God (like creation and redemption) particular to Father, Son or Spirit or are they the work of all three together? There are lots of aspects of the Trinity to offer employment to those who engage in theological speculation. Saint Augustine was one such, and his book on the Trinity (which came before many of the final words on the Trinity were said by the Church) runs to 471 pages!

Precise theological terminology and clear teaching about the Trinity are important. But more important is the awareness on the part of God's people that God is community, energy, love, knowledge, gift, power, self-expression, completeness—and that we have been called and enabled to share the life of God.

FOR DISCUSSION AND REFLECTION

Is the Holy Trinity at the center of my faith life or on the periphery?
To which Person of the Trinity do I relate most familiarly? Why?

Most Holy Trinity (C)

Romans 5:1-5

We have come to the end of the Easter season in which we
recalled the events of Christ's suffering, death and resurrection.
Last Sunday we celebrated the events of the first Christian
Pentecost: the manifestation of the Holy Spirit and the Spirit's
sending the apostles forth to preach the gospel to the world. Now
the Church's calendar returns to Ordinary Time, a long series of
weeks that serve to celebrate the ongoing unfolding of God's plan
of salvation. But before we enter fully into Ordinary Time, the
Church gives us two special Sundays, Sundays on which we
reflect on and celebrate not events but two central realities that
lie at the heart of Christian life: the Holy Trinity (this Sunday)
and the Holy Eucharist (next Sunday).

Most Catholics know that in God there is one nature, but
three distinct divine Persons. We know that the Trinity is a
mystery, something we can't really understand but that is
somehow involved with our salvation. We are aware that the Holy
Trinity is an important doctrine of our faith, but we don't really
pay all that much attention to it. That may be one reason why the
Church gives us a special liturgical celebration in honor of the
Trinity each year!

Scripture tells us about the Holy Trinity, but in an indirect
and allusive fashion, not in a set of technically exact propositions
but in contexts of God's reaching out to care for us. Today's live
letter is an example of Scripture teaching us about the Trinity at

the same time that it explains to us some of the elements of God's saving action in our lives.

Paul has been telling the Romans about how they are saved or redeemed by faith in Christ rather than by the exact observance of Jewish law. In our passage he begins to draw some conclusions.

Because we are "justified by faith," we are at peace with God. This relationship comes to us through Christ (the Son of God). God's generosity comes to us through him, and puts us in a position in which we take joy in the fact that we can look forward with confidence to sharing in nothing less than the glory of God.

But there's more. We relate to the Father through Christ, but the Holy Spirit is involved as well. The Spirit has poured out the love of God in our hearts. This love enables us to face up to and even take joy in our afflictions. Our confident confrontation of our trials leads to a firmness of character that brings us to unshakeable hope.

In this passage, Paul tells us that, thanks to the intervention of Son and Holy Spirit, faith leads to hope through the love of the Father for us and through our relationship with the Father. Christ's saving action of the past brings us into a present from which we can look forward courageously to a glorious future. The Spirit gives us the strength to move forward to that future. Our salvation is a complex affair. It involves past, present and future; faith, hope and love; Father, Son and Spirit.

Paul does not speak this way to his readers in order to give them technical theological information about the nature of God, about the Persons of the Trinity, about the Persons' relationships with one another. Later Church teachers would concern themselves with questions like that. Paul's teaching is rooted in his desire to make his readers aware of the depth and complexity of God's involvement in their lives, of the many-sidedness of the care that God expends on them. His purpose is not to communicate knowledge of the Trinity but to elicit appreciation of the love for us expressed by Father, Son and Holy Spirit.

One of the things that we Catholic Christian believers have to remind ourselves of with some regularity is that our relationship with God is deeper and richer and more intricate than we tend to think. We want simple answers to simple questions. Am I going to go to heaven or not? Does God love me and care for me?

Of course there are simple answers to questions like that. God does love me and care for me and I will get to heaven if I stay close to him. But there is more to what God is and does than simple answers—more depth, more richness, more complexity. It is not that God enjoys making things difficult for us to understand, but that God's giving reflects his being in ways that exceed our human expectations, our human ways of understanding.

Faith, hope, love; past, present, future; Father, Son, Holy Spirit; our participation in the interpersonal reality of God; our sharing in the happiness and glory of the timeless Trinity: all of that is part of the answer to the questions we ask about ourselves and about our future. What God offers us is nothing less than the communication of himself and if we are not aware of the infinite mystery and richness and glory of God, we will necessarily undervalue that gift. We need to encounter the Holy Trinity in order to maintain some degree of awareness of how deeply and how elaborately God loves us.

FOR DISCUSSION AND REFLECTION

Do I find God's relationship with me simple or complex?
How do I experience the Trinity in my life?

Most Holy Body and Blood of Christ (A)

I Corinthians 10:16-17

Like the feast of the Holy Trinity, the feast of the Body and Blood of Christ is not an ancient feast in the Church. It only goes back to the time of Urban IV who established this liturgical observance for the universal Church in 1264. (Thus this feast of Corpus Christi is about seventy years older than the feast of the Holy Trinity.) Urban IV was responding to some visions and miracles connected with the Eucharist that seemed to call for greater attention from the Church to the sacrament of the altar.

Our live letter for this feast comes from First Corinthians. In the section of First Corinthians from which our reading is taken, Paul is dealing with the question of idol meats. Was it appropriate for Christian believers to take part in banquets in which the meat came from animals that had been sacrificed in pagan temples? The answer is yes and no. On the one hand, the pagan gods do not really exist, so what has been offered to them is no different than if it had not been offered to them. On the other hand, less sophisticated believers could be confused to see their brother or sister apparently partaking in pagan celebrations. They might be led to think that it was acceptable to worship these pagan gods. In addition to that, pagan gods are often stand-ins for demons and getting involved even remotely with pagan cults could open the door to the powers of evil in the lives of Christians.

In our reading, Paul uses the Christians' experience of the Eucharist to make a point about their need to be cautious about involvement with pagan religious practices.

He reminds them that, when they share in the Eucharist, they become participants in the body and blood of Christ. They are given a share in the life of Christ. Likewise, because the Eucharistic bread is one, all those who partake of it share in one body. They are made one in the one body of Christ.

Paul's main point here is that there is a parallel between the Eucharist and other sacrifices. Sacrifices establish a communion.

If you take part even in the marginal formalities of a pagan sacrifice, you run the risk of establishing communion with the demonic pagan gods, as well as with the believers who form the pagan community.

Paul is talking about a particular pastoral problem of his time, but what he says is still of significance to us today. He reminds us that the Eucharist is about unity. The unity it expresses and brings about is both vertical and horizontal. Sharing in the Eucharist makes us one with Christ, but also one with all those with whom we share Christ's life.

It's important for us to be aware of the unity that is called for and provided by the Eucharist, because the temptations we face are not all that different from those the Corinthians faced.

First of all there are the demonic pagan gods. We may not worry much about Jupiter and Venus, but we are nonetheless threatened by demonic forces hostile to our Christian beliefs and priorities. In many different ways our world tries to teach us that self-fulfillment is what's really important, that sex is an entertainment, that every desire should find immediate attainment, that the value of human life is determined by its convenience, that our worth depends on our possessions and our individual accomplishments. These are all pagan ideas. We need to stay in constant touch with the Lord Jesus in order to keep these anti-Christian energies from getting into our souls.

We also face temptations to horizontal disunity. There are the temptations to undermine the Church by buying into the values of the pagan community around us, but there are also temptations to disunity within the context of the Church itself. The issue here is not matters of taste and opinion and personal judgment. There will always be differences over whether the church thermostat is set too high or too low, over whether the school principal's contract should be renewed or not. These are matters that mature people can disagree on and still remain friends. What is dangerous to the Church is the kind of difference that involves personal judgment and rejection. "How can those people love

Christ if they are not deeply involved with the latest social protest movement?" "Those people can't possibly believe in the real presence if they want to move the tabernacle." "Nobody can really be a good Catholic unless he or she thinks exactly as I do."

Shortly before his death, Cardinal Bernardin established the Catholic Common Ground Initiative. This organization is dedicated to helping people speak and listen respectfully to one another in the context of the Church community, to bringing those of different viewpoints together in the context of their common Catholic faith. The criticism and, indeed, hostility that was addressed to the cardinal's undertaking was disappointing in a community that claims to express unity in Christ.

We need the Eucharist to maintain our identity as individuals and as community. We need the Eucharist to foster and nourish our unity with Christ and our unity with one another.

FOR DISCUSSION AND REFLECTION

What contemporary "demons" are most appealing to me?

How does my participation in the Eucharist strengthen the unity of the Church?

Most Holy Body and Blood of Christ (B)

Hebrews 9:11-15

The feast of Corpus Christi is not an ancient feast in the Church's calendar. It grew up gradually in the Middle Ages, in part because of increased devotion to the Real Presence of Christ in the reserved eucharistic species, in part because of a concern that the liturgy of Holy Thursday could not give adequate attention to the holy Eucharist because of the other demands for attention made by Holy Week.

In the universal calendar of the Church, the feast of Corpus Christi is a holy day of obligation and is observed on the Thursday after Trinity Sunday. Here in the United States it has never been a day of obligation. Yet Church authorities thought it deserved more attention than it received as a mere weekday observance. So in 1969 the Holy See determined that, in places where the feast was not a holy day of obligation, it was to be observed on the Sunday after Trinity Sunday. The result is that now more American Catholics know and celebrate the feast of Corpus Christi. Of course its observance on Sunday also postpones for one more week the return to the Sundays in Ordinary Time and the continuation of our reading of Second Corinthians.

The holy Eucharist is both sacrament and sacrifice. Like all the sacraments, it is an encounter with the risen Christ in which he strengthens and directs us. But it is also the re-enactment, the re-presentation of the sacrifice of Christ, of Christ's gift of himself to the Father at the culmination of his life, a once-and-for-all act of submission and generosity that brought salvation to all of humankind.

Our second reading speaks of the sacrificial aspect of the Eucharist. It is from the Letter to the Hebrews. This book of the New Testament is addressed to Jewish converts to Christianity who were experiencing difficulty and doubt in their faith and who were nostalgic for the Jewish rituals they had grown up with. In order to offer them encouragement, the author of Hebrews writes of the superiority of Christ and his priesthood to what they had known before. In this Sunday's passage the author deals with the superiority of Jesus' sacrifice to the sacrifices of the Jerusalem temple.

He portrays Christ as the new high priest, replacing the Jewish high priest. He points out that Jesus presented his sacrifice not in a man-made sanctuary but in the inner chambers of heaven itself. His sacrifice of himself is so effective that it does not need to be repeated as did the sacrifices of the Old Law. His sacrifice did not consist in the blood of animals, which merely symbolized human self-gift and could only bring about ritual purification. Jesus' sacrifice consisted in his own blood, his own life freely offered as part of his mission. This offering reversed the history of human self-centeredness and sinfulness and brought humanity into a new posture of interior cleanness. Human beings were now fit to offer appropriate worship to God. This sacrifice of Jesus made up for all the sins of the past and oriented the future humankind to a sharing in the intimate life of God.

The celebration of the Eucharist in our churches is a re-enactment of the self-sacrifice of Jesus on the cross. It does not constitute a new sacrifice. Jesus doesn't suffer again. But the once-and-for-all gift of himself that Jesus made through the offering of his physical body and blood on Calvary is offered again under the appearances of bread and wine. The purpose of this offering is not to make up for any deficiency in the original sacrifice, as if Christ's death has to be repeated over and over in order to keep the Father satisfied. The purpose of the weekly—and daily—offering of Christ in the eucharistic sacrifice is to provide us with an opportunity to be part of his self-giving, to direct his self-sacrifice to the needs of our own particular human context. We are thus enabled to join with Christ in offering honor and glory to the Father through his gift of himself. His offering becomes our offering.

This is why active participation in the eucharistic sacrifice is so important. When we go to Mass, it isn't merely to have a chance to receive Holy Communion. It isn't to be a spectator as Christ offers himself to his heavenly Father. Our presence at Mass is an opportunity for us to be part of Jesus' sacrifice, to give ourselves in union with him in reparation for our sins and the sins of all humankind. When we sing and pray and respond together in the various parts of the Mass, we join in offering praise and thanksgiving to God, and the praise and thanksgiving we offer is not just ours but Christ's as well.

At the end of the Eucharistic Prayer at every Mass the Christian community gives its solemn "Amen" to the priest's proclamation that, in the unity of the Holy Spirit, all honor and glory is given to the Father "through him, with him, in him." As participants in the eucharistic celebration we are part of the gift. We are part of the giving.

FOR DISCUSSION AND REFLECTION

What aspects of the holy Eucharist do I find most beneficial?

What does it mean to me to unite myself with the self-sacrifice of Christ?

Most Holy Body and Blood of Christ (C)

I Corinthians 11:23-26

Last Sunday we celebrated not an event but a reality, the central fact of the Holy Trinity, a foundational truth that underlies the whole of the story of salvation. This Sunday we celebrate another reality, another fact, another truth: the holy Eucharist. We celebrate the Body and Blood of Christ given to us, given for us sacramentally. Just as the Holy Trinity underlies everything that happens in salvation history, so the Eucharist underlies and expresses Jesus' ongoing, saving communication of himself to his believers throughout that portion of human history that stretches from the cross to the second coming.

In this third year of the lectionary's cycle of readings we are given an account of the institution of the Eucharist from Paul's first letter to the Corinthians. This letter is one of the earliest books of the New Testament, written some fifteen or twenty years before the Gospels, and so this account of what Jesus did at the last supper is the oldest narrative of it that we have.

Paul has been dealing with problems of church order among the Corinthians. Apparently they celebrated the Eucharist in the context of a dinner party. The more affluent members of the community seem to have provided themselves with elaborate foods and lots to drink while the poorer members went hungry. Paul found this kind of selfishness hard to reconcile with the fundamental significance of the Eucharist.

Our passage begins with Paul reminding the Corinthians about what he had taught them about the institution of the Eucharist, a teaching that has its roots not in Paul's imagination but in Jesus himself. Jesus was about to be "handed over," that is, given up to his enemies. With that in mind, he had taken bread and given it to them telling them that this was his body, the body that would be offered for them. Similarly, at the end of the meal, Jesus had had them drink out of a cup. This sharing constituted a new sacrificial covenant, a new agreement between God and humanity that replaced the covenant that had been in force until then. In both contexts, Jesus told them to continue doing this—sharing food and drink—"in remembrance" of him. Paul says that to "eat this bread and drink the cup" would "proclaim," that is, announce and make present the death of the Lord until the end of time.

The selfishness and the pursuit of comfort that the Corinthians expressed in their manner of celebrating the Eucharist were simply not in accord with the generosity and self-giving that Jesus intended the Eucharist to declare. Here was an anticipation (and then a re-presentation) of his own gift of himself on the cross, an event to which the only appropriate response is generosity and self-giving on our part.

When we participate in the celebration of the Eucharist, we, here and now, are taking part in a re-presentation of the gift of himself that lasted throughout Christ's whole earthly life, but which reached its climax in his death on the cross. Christ's saving life and death were not to be one time events that took place a long time ago and that we would be invited to remember from a great distance of time. No, Christ's gift of salvation would continue to be made present and active in the Eucharist.

In the Eucharist the body and blood of Christ, ritually separated in the separate consecrations of bread and wine, are offered once more to the heavenly Father as they were offered the first time on Calvary. That offering expressed in definitive form the faithfulness and obedience of Christ. Christ continues to make that same offering to his Father in heaven now, but it is also made present for present-day Christian believers on earth through the eucharistic offering.

But this sacrificial offering is not just a renewal of the action of Christ. It also involves the Christian community at large as well as the individual members who are present at a particular eucharistic celebration. The Church, through the priest who represents the people as well as Christ, unites itself with the offering of Christ, so that the sacrifice is no longer merely the self-gift of Christ, but of his people as well.

When we participate in the celebration of the Eucharist, we offer Christ to the Father, but we also offer ourselves, our needs, our gifts, our problems. We "plug into" the sacrifice of Christ, as it were, so that it is ours as well as his. The celebration of the Eucharist links our life with the peak point of the life of Jesus.

This peak point of salvation, in which we associate ourselves with Christ's gift of himself to the heavenly Father, is what we will continue to celebrate and to savor in heaven. Being definitively in touch with the generosity of Christ will constitute our eternal happiness.

The Eucharist connects us with the past and the future and gives meaning to our present. It constitutes the spiritual fabric of our lives, the reality that is so close to us that we could take it for granted if we are not careful. That's why it's good to have the feast of Corpus Christi each year!

FOR DISCUSSION AND REFLECTION

How would my life be different without the Eucharist?

How do the following elements contribute to my concept of the Eucharist: event, presence, thanksgiving, promise, challenge, sacrifice, remembrance?

Assumption of the Blessed Virgin Mary (ABC)

I Corinthians 15:20-27

The most important aspect of our Christian existence is our likeness to Christ. This likeness, in which our final worth consists, is not a matter of pretending to be like Christ or acting like Christ, but actually being like Christ. This likeness, which we call grace, constitutes our salvation. It is given to us in baptism, is developed throughout the years of our earthly existence, and receives its final, full expression in our participation in the Resurrection of Jesus at the end of time.

Mary, the mother of Jesus, was the most perfect of all those whom Jesus saved. She was the great success story of redemption. Thanks to a special provision of love on God's part, she was never without grace, never separated from the life of God. She lived her life in closeness and dedication to Jesus. Then, when the course of her earthly life was finished, she began to share in a unique way in Jesus' Resurrection. She was taken up body and soul into heavenly glory so that she might be the more fully conformed to her Son. That final, loving acceptance of Mary, both body and soul, into the realm of Christ's glory is what we call the Assumption. It is the event that we venerate on this feast day.

In order to help us better understand the implications of Mary's Assumption, the Church offers us a reading from the First Letter to the Corinthians that is concerned with the significance of the resurrection of the body in Christian doctrine.

The Corinthians had problems with the resurrection of the dead. They seem to have been willing to accept that Christ had risen from the dead, but not that there would be a general resurrection. "There is no resurrection from the dead," they said. Paul's answer is that, if there is no resurrection from the dead, then Jesus didn't rise from the dead either. This is where our reading begins.

In fact, Paul says, Christ has risen from the dead and that fact is full of implications. Christ's Resurrection is only the beginning of a vast harvest that will include us all. Just as death came to us all through one man, Adam, so resurrection will come to us all through one man, Christ. Obviously this hasn't happened yet. Christ's Resurrection is the beginning of something that will come to fulfillment at the end of time when all opposition to God's kingdom will be swept away. Even death will disappear. To confirm this teaching, Paul cites Psalm 8, referring it to Christ and the Father: "he subjected everything under his feet."

The resurrection of the dead is not some quaint superstition that got the early Christians excited but which doesn't have much connection with contemporary Christians who are more sophisticated than the Corinthians. The resurrection of the dead is the final act of the redemption, the full acceptance of humanity into the life of the Trinity.

Moreover, the resurrection of the dead, body and soul, teaches us that every aspect of our humanity is precious to God, that our corporeality is not a temporary embarrassment that we are well rid of when we die. Just as the salvation that Christ brought about for us was accomplished through his human body, so also our eternal happiness will be expressed in our bodies as well as in our souls. Nothing that God created in us is useless or irrelevant. Somehow or other it will all be taken into the life of Christ when the kingdom reaches fulfillment.

The assumption into heaven of Mary, the mother of Jesus, body and soul is not just a nice thing that Jesus did for his mother, a special favor granted because of her closeness to him. The Assumption of Mary constitutes her participation in the Resurrection of Jesus, but also an anticipation of the resurrection of all other Christians. The resurrection of the dead that Paul wrote about is not just confined to Jesus. It has already been extended to the humanity of Mary. She, therefore, serves as a kind of model or prototype for the universal resurrection in which we will all share.

But Mary also serves as a model of the Church. The sinlessness that was hers from the beginning, her glorification of body and soul are images of what the Church will be when the present period of struggle has come to a conclusion. She is a prototype who is already gifted with what the Church will eventually share.

The Assumption of Mary has a special importance in a world in which the human body and human life are disregarded and degraded in so many ways. We kill unborn children, use human sexuality for amusement, experiment with ways to produce human bodies for spare parts. Some human beings are considered to be too worthless to notice, while others are prized for mere physical beauty apart from any dimension of virtue or morality. It is good for us to be reminded that God treasures the humanity which he shares, that God has plans for the humanity of each of us that includes the same glory that he has conferred on his mother.

FOR DISCUSSION AND REFLECTION

How do I look forward to the resurrection of the body?

How has the example of Mary been important to my faith?

All Saints (ABC)

I John 3:1-3

The word "saint" has more than one meaning. We use it in
ordinary talk to signify someone who is conspicuous for goodness
or generosity. "She took care of her invalid husband for years.
She's a saint." In a Catholic Christian context we use "saint" to
mean somebody who has been officially proposed to the faithful
as a model and intercessor. These are people whose virtue
exceeded ordinary human virtue and whose lives have been
carefully examined in the process of canonization. Saint John
Neumann and Saint Elizabeth Seton are saints in this sense. The
New Testament uses the word "saint" to signify women and men
who are believers in Christ, who are members of the Church.
Paul, for example, addresses Second Corinthians to "the saints [or
holy ones] throughout Achaia." There are almost sixty
occurrences of the word's being used this way in the New
Testament.

Catholics have venerated the saints for a long time. At the
beginning, they offered special attention only to those who had
given their lives to the faith in martyrdom. Then they began to
include men and women who had suffered for the faith, even
though they had not been killed for it. Later the veneration of the
saints included hermits and saintly bishops, as well as religious
and priests and laypersons.

The history of a liturgical celebration in honor of All Saints
is not fully clear, but it is clear that on this one day we are
invited to offer our thanks and praise to God for all saints of all
kinds, known and unknown, canonized or not.

The second reading for All Saints Day is from First John and
offers us a reminder of what is involved in being a saint.

The author invites his readers to be attentive to the fact that
they are really and truly children of God. If the world does not
recognize them as such, it's because the world doesn't recognize
God, either. Moreover, our present relationship with God is only

the beginning. There are still deeper degrees of association and likeness in store for us that we are not yet aware of or acquainted with. Being children of God is a source of hope, but it also demands a response from us, and that response is being pure as God is pure, that is, living a godly life in accord with the godliness that has been given us.

One of the most important truths of our faith is that holiness, that is, being a child of God, or being a saint, is not something that we are called to achieve or acquire, but something that we are invited to accept. None of us can make him or herself holy. None of us can earn or deserve to become a member of the trinitarian family of God. We can only respond to the holiness that we receive when we begin to live the life of Christ through baptism. Holiness or saintliness is a gift, not a recompense for our spiritual accomplishments.

This is not to say that our holiness does not involve effort and that Christian life is just a matter of sitting back and enjoying what God has given us. On the contrary, God expects us to work hard at living up to what we have been made to be in Christ. God's grace and holiness in us demand a posture of continued purification, of ongoing work to allow God's gifts to be ever more effective in our lives. After all, thanks to original sin, we are constitutionally inclined to selfishness, to wanting to snatch control of our lives away from God. If we allow ourselves just to drift along, we will drift into alienation from God. We won't be saints any more, not because God has changed his mind and taken holiness away from us, but because we have rejected it by our indifference and self-centeredness.

The "official" saints, the kinds of people the Church canonizes, are those who are most aware of their own vulnerability, most conscious of their own need for God's action in their lives, most alert to the role of God's generosity in their human existence. Consequently, their response to the life of Christ in them is more generous and more consistent than that of the rest of us, to the point of reaching even heroic proportions.

But their holiness is the same as ours, because there is only one kind of holiness, and that holiness is constituted by sharing in the life of the risen Christ. That's what made the Blessed Mother a saint. That's what lay at the foundation of the holiness of the martyrs. That's what gave inspiration and energy to the Church's great preachers and teachers and ascetics and apostles. That's what constitutes the holiness of each and every one of us.

This annual celebration of all saints reminds us that the saints are not all alike. There are many different kinds of saints. It also reminds us that the saints are not just those whose names are on some official list somewhere. Many saints-perhaps most saints-are not known to us by name. Finally, this feast reminds us that, to the extent that the life of Christ is still in us, we are all saints. The only question is the extent to which we respond to the gift of sainthood we have received.

FOR DISCUSSION AND REFLECTION

Who are the saints who have played a part in my life?

In what ways does my sainthood manifest itself?

The Immaculate Conception of the Blessed Virgin Mary (ABC)

Ephesians 1:3-6, 11-12

Many people mistakenly think that the Immaculate Conception of the Blessed Virgin Mary has to do with the virgin birth of Jesus. Actually the "Immaculate Conception" has to do with the conception of Mary herself. The phrase refers to the fact that, from the first moment of her conception, through a special intervention of God and in view of the merits of Jesus, Mary was preserved immune from all stain of original sin. That is, unlike all the rest of us, Mary was never separated from God, never without the life of God that we call grace.

The second reading for this feast is part of the great thanksgiving section at the beginning of the letter to the Ephesians. The author is talking about the nature of the salvation that has been offered to all of us. In assigning this reading for this feast, the Church suggests that the special gift that was offered to Mary is somehow the same salvation that we have received, yet with differences.

The text offers thanks to God because God has conferred heavenly blessings on us. God has chosen us to be holy and without blemish, to be like Christ. This is not something we have earned or have deserved. It comes exclusively from God's generosity. We have received a destiny from God, a calling to faith and hope in Christ that will bring us to a new existence whose purpose will be the praise and glorification of God.

Chosen, destined, blessed, holy, without blemish, for the praise of God's glory: these are all gifts that belong to us who have accepted Christ. In part we enjoy them now, in part their fulfillment is still to come. These same qualities also apply to Mary, the mother of Jesus, but differently than to us. We are like her and she is like us, yet we are different.

We are like her because we are all recipients of God's generosity. We haven't earned and cannot deserve a share in his life, any more than Mary did. Yet grace is always there, at least as God's offer. Grace is a consistent component of our lives, to the extent that we are willing to accept it. And like Mary, each of us is called to express Christ to the world "for the praise of his glory." God's gratuitous consistency is part of our make-up as it was of hers.

But there are differences. God's grace, God's life has not always been present in our lives as it was in hers. We had to receive it at a certain point in time through baptism. Even after that, God's grace has not been a constant part of our life as it was in hers. We have all sinned to a greater or less extent. And our lives have not been totally and fully oriented to bringing Christ to the world as hers was. We are not totally and always like our Blessed Mother.

But there is more. Mary is similar to and different from the individual believer, but she is also similar to and different from the Church. The Church and Mary are alike, but different.

The Church is like Mary because the Church is the recipient of God's generosity. Its teachings, its sacraments, its structure are not the result of human ingenuity or human achievement, but of God's gift. They are all grace. And these gifts of grace are not on-again off-again elements of the Church's life, but continuous elements of its being. There never was a time when the Church has not been gifted and graced by God. And this state of ongoing giftedness is for the purpose of expressing Christ to the world. Gratuity, continuity and mission are constituent elements in the Church's being, just as they were in Mary's.

The Church is different from Mary because the Church is not just a graced instrument of Christ's salvation but also an ingathering of imperfect and sinful people. It is a mixture of bad and good. At some times the Church is more effective in its mission than at others because at some times its members are more in tune with God's gifts. While the basic mission of the Church and God's commitment to his people persist always, the response and cooperation of its members to God's call and God's gifts can and do vary. In Mary there is no mixture of bad and good, no variance in her response to God's call, no deviation in her faithfulness to the destiny to which she was called. Mary and the Church are different.

Mary, the individual believer, the Church: we are all similar, but we are all different.

We do not celebrate the feast of the Immaculate Conception of the Blessed Virgin just to remind ourselves of a wonderful thing that happened to one person a long time ago. We celebrate the feast of the Immaculate Conception to renew our awareness of God's loving call to all of us and of the destiny of holiness for